A Practical Guide to Acceptance and Commitment Therapy

A Practical Guide to Acceptance and Commitment Therapy

Edited by

Steven C. Hayes

University of Nevada, Reno
Reno, Nevada

and

Kirk D. Strosahl

Mountainview Consulting Group
Moxee, Washington

 Springer

Library of Congress Cataloging-in-Publication data

A C.I.P. Catalogue record for this book is available
from the Library of Congress.

ISBN 0-387-23367-9   Printed on acid-free paper.
eISBN -0387-23369-5

Printed in the United States of America.

9 8 7 6 5 4 3 2

springeronline.com

To my doctoral graduates, all 24 of them, whose hard work helped establish ACT and RFT as viable approaches

S. C. H.

To my wife Patti for her undying loyalty and partnership in my "journey." To all of my clients over the years, with problems big and small, who have taught me more than I can ever repay.

K. D. S.

Contributors

Patricia Bach, Department of Psychology, Illinois Institute of Technology, Chicago, Illinois, 60616

Jennifer Block-Lerner, Department of Psychology, Skidmore College, Saratoga Springs, New York 12866

Frank W. Bond, Department of Psychology, Goldsmiths College, University of London, New Cross London SE14 6NW United Kingdom

Kara Bunting, Department of Psychology, University of Nevada, Reno, Nevada 89557

Michelle R. Byrd, Department of Psychology, Eastern Michigan University, Ypsilanti, Michigan 48197

Lisa W. Coyne, Department of Psychology, University of Mississippi, University, Mississippi 38677

JoAnne Dahl, Department of Psychology, University of Uppsala, Uppsala, Sweden

Victoria M. Follette, Department of Psychology, University of Nevada, Reno, Reno, Nevada 89557

Elizabeth V. Gifford, Center for Health Care Evaluation, Veterans Administration Palo Alto Health Care System, and Stanford University Medical Centers, Menlo Park, California 94025

Jennifer Gregg, Palo VA Health Care System, Palo Alto, California 94025

Steven C. Hayes, Department of Psychology, University of Nevada, Reno, Reno, Nevada 89557

James D. Herbert, Department of Clinical and Health Psychology Drexel University, Philadelphia, Pennsylvania 19102

Chad LeJeune, Psychologist in private practice, San Mateo County Psychiatry Residency Program, San Mateo, California; Adjunct Professor, University of San Francisco, San Francisco, California 94143

Tobias Lundgren, Department of Psychology, Uppsala University, Uppsala, Sweden

Jayson Luoma, Department of Psychology, University of Nevada, Reno, Reno, Nevada 89557

Amy R. Murrell, Department of Psychology, University of Mississippi, University, Mississippi 38677

Gunnar L. Olsson, Karolinska Institute, Stockholm, Sweden

Susan M. Orsillo, Department of Psychology, Suffolk University, Boston, Massachusetts 02108

Jacqueline Pistorello, University of Nevada, Reno Counseling Services, Reno, Nevada 89557

Patricia Robinson, Mountainview Consulting Group, Moxee, Washington 98936, and Yakima Valley Farmworkers Clinic, Toppenish, Washington 98948

Lizabeth Roemer, Department of Psychology, University of Massachusetts at Boston, Boston, Massachusetts 02105

Alethea A. Varra, Department of Psychology, University of Nevada, Reno, Reno, Nevada 89557

Kirk D. Strosahl, Mountainview Consulting Group, Moxee, Washington 98936

Michael Twohig, Department of Psychology, University of Nevada, Reno, Reno, Nevada 89557

Robyn D. Walser, National Center for PTSD, Palo Alto, California 94025

Rikard K. Wicksell, Astrid Lindgren Children's Hospital, Karolinska University Hospital, Uppsala University, Uppsala, Sweden

Kelly G. Wilson, Department of Psychology, University of Mississippi, University, Mississippi 38677

Robert D. Zettle, Department of Psychology, Wichita State University, Wichita, Kansas 67208

Preface

This book is the most practical clinical guide on Acceptance and Commitment Therapy (ACT said as one word, not as initials) yet available. It is designed to show how the ACT model and techniques apply to various disorders, settings, and delivery options. The authors of these chapters are experts in applying ACT in these various areas, and it is intriguing how the same core principles of ACT are given a nip here and a tuck there to fit it to so many issues. The purpose of this book, in part, is to emboldened researchers and clinicians to begin to apply ACT wherever it seems to fit.

The chapters in the book demonstrate that ACT may be a useful treatment approach for a very wide range of clinical problems. Already there are controlled data in many of these areas, and soon that database will be much larger. The theory underlying ACT (Relational Frame Theory or "RFT"—and yes, here you say the initials) makes a powerful claim: psychopathology is, to a significant degree, built into human language. Further, it suggests ways to diminish destructive language-based functions and ways of augmenting helpful ones. To the extent that this model is correct, ACT *should* apply to a very wide variety of behavioral issues because of the centrality of language and cognition in human functioning. Only time and research will determine the degree to which that is true, but so far the ACT model is working even in areas (e.g., psychosis) that some would not expect to be responsive to these methods. Importantly, ACT is "working" both in terms of the emerging research on treatment outcomes and in terms of predicted processes of change.

This book is organized into three parts. The first describes the theory underlying ACT as a treatment approach and the core intervention processes that encompass ACT. We show you how to conceptualize cases using an ACT framework, and how to link technologies to that conceptualization. This book is not meant to be a stand alone volume, however. You should plan to read the "ACT book" (Hayes, Strosahl, & Wilson, 1999) in addition to this book before trying to apply (or even fully understand) the model. The second section presents ACT as it is applied to some typical behavioral disorders encountered by mental health and substance abuse practitioners. The last section examines ACT as it applied with a variety of other populations, problems, settings, and modes of delivery.

No book such as this one can cover the incredible range of behavioral health issues that are encountered in human service settings. There are clinical problems not covered in this book that have at least preliminary empirical support for ACT as a treatment modality. These include eating disorders (e.g., Heffner, Sperry, Eifert, & Detweiler, 2002), sexual deviation (e.g., Paul, Marx, & Orsillo, 1999), sexual dysfunction (e.g., Montesinos, 2003), bereavement (Luciano & Cabello, 2001), working with retarded clients, couples and family interventions (Biglan, 1989), aging populations, and prevention, just to name a few. As the research and clinical base grows, we expect these clinical problems will have to be revisited in subsequent works.

We would like to thank our families and students for their patience while this book was being completed, and to each of the contributing authors for giving so much of themselves and their expertise. We would also like to acknowledge the authors for their tolerance of the heavy-handed editing needed to give this book a common voice.

To you the clinician, we sincerely hope this book provides you with the kind of "how to" guidance that will truly make this an every day resource in your practice. Some of the interventions described in this book may seem difficult to understand or even counter-intuitive. If you experience this response at any point while consuming the information in each chapter, we ask only that you remain open to trying, and that you listen to what your clients are telling you (verbally and behaviorally) about what truly works.

STEVEN C. HAYES
KIRK D. STROSAHL

Contents

II. ACT with Behavior Problems

A Practical Guide to
Acceptance and
Commitment Therapy

Part I

An ACT Approach

Chapter **1**

What Is Acceptance and Commitment Therapy?

STEVEN C. HAYES, KIRK D. STROSAHL, KARA
BUNTING, MICHAEL TWOHIG, AND KELLY G. WILSON

Human beings use language to shape their world: to structure it and give it meaning. Language builds our skyscrapers, imparts the strength to our steel, creates the elegance of our mathematics, and forms our art's depiction of beauty. Language has been the source of so much human achievement that it is only natural that we look to it first to identify a problem and craft a solution. But it is precisely because language can be so useful that it can also be problematic. Language not only enables human achievements, but also our ability to project fearsome futures, to compare ourselves to unrealistic ideals and find ourselves wanting, or to torment our souls with the finitude of life itself. Language is at the core of the remarkable human tendency to suffer in the midst of plenty.

The internalized experience of language presents itself not as sounds or symbols, nor as responding of any kind, but as a form of immediate experience. This feature of language is part of its utility, but also is a reason that language and thinking can be dangerous. The skyscraper imagined seemingly "exists" in our mind's eye, as does the grim vision of a future without a lost loved one. Drawn into a symbolic world *about* human experience, an illusion is created that this world *is* human experience.

Various religions since the dawn of time have warned us of this inherent danger in language. The story of Adam and Eve provides an example. Once humans eat from the "tree of knowledge," we "know the difference between good and evil"—that is, we begin to make evaluations. We

3

can differentiate between being naked and clothed; we can evaluate being naked as "bad"; and we can experience "shame." We can construct causal analyses, and be right "right" or "wrong" in our ideas. In the biblical story Adam has an explanation for his sin: Eve lured him into eating the apple. And Eve has an explanation: the snake tempted her into doing so. These basic language abilities—such as naming and distinguishing, evaluating, and constructing causes for problems—are at the core of the evolutionary brilliance of human language. Without them, human progress would be impossible. They have, however, a dark side and once you eat from the apple there is no going back to non-verbal innocence.

Acceptance and Commitment Therapy (shortened to the word "ACT," said as a word, not initials; Hayes, Strosahl, & Wilson, 1999) is based on the view that language is at the core of many psychological disorders specifically, and human suffering in general. ACT is an intervention approach designed to bring language to heel, so that it can become a tool to be used when it is useful, rather than an unseen process that consumes the humans that host it. This approach is based on a growing line of basic behavioral research on human language and cognition called Relational Frame Theory (RFT: Hayes, Barnes-Holmes, & Roche, 2001). Both ACT and RFT come from a pragmatic philosophical tradition called functional contextualism.

ACT and, by scientific linkage, RFT, are not merely technologies. Together, they form an integrated approach, based on a theory and set of principles that vary in focus and level of analysis, from the most basic to the most applied. ACT is not a disorder specific treatment; rather, it is a general approach that can spur the development of many protocols, focused on particular problems, patient populations, or settings. ACT integrates scientific knowledge about contingency shaped behavior and verbal relations into a more effective therapeutic whole.

In this book, we will show how ACT can be applied to a broad range of human psychological problems, in a range of settings, with a variety of populations. The chief goal of this book is to orient clinicians in the field toward recent innovations in the application of ACT principles and interventions. Leaders in these various areas have been asked to speak to you the clinician and explain how these innovative treatments are conceptualized and delivered in practice. Our hope is that, after making contact with this information, you will come away with a much better sense of how to deliver ACT with the various clinical problems you encounter in your practice, whether it is in a mental health clinic, a substance abuse treatment program, a family services agency, a school based program, a chronic pain program, a primary care clinic or a medical hospital. We encourage you to try these new applications with your patients, to assess their effectiveness and to integrate them into your practice if you and your patients are seeing good results.

In the first three chapters of the book we describe the ACT approach and put it into context. We will describe the core skills and competencies that comprise ACT technology and show how these principles can be used to formulate cases. In the eleven chapters that follow, we will then show how the ACT model can be applied to some major specific problems, populations, and settings.

Although the chapters will include some citations of the research literature, the scholarly arguments are deliberately simplified since the purpose is to consider the ACT model from a clinical perspective, and citations will be limited to the minimum. The book is also not meant to substitute for the original ACT book (Hayes et al., 1999). Specific citations will be given for specific metaphors or exercises drawn from that volume, but the text will not be reproduced.

In this beginning chapter we will answer a simple question: what is ACT? We will tell this story in a kind of reverse order, describing core ACT processes in order to give a concrete sense of the approach and providing a simple definition of it. Because the value of ACT is so much dependent on its underlying theory and philosophy, we will then back up and show how ACT is part of a broader shift within behavioral and cognitive therapy, and how its philosophy and theory drive the ACT model. This will also enable us to give a more technical definition of ACT.

THE ACT THEORY OF CHANGE: ACQUISITION OF PSYCHOLOGICAL FLEXIBILITY

Although many of our psychological problems originate in thought and language, it is not possible or healthy for us to live without language. Language can function as either a servant or a master. Unlike most forms of therapy, which seek to change the content of problematic thinking, ACT seeks to help the client bring language and thought under appropriate contextual control, using logical, linear language when it helps to do so and letting direct experience be more of a guide when that is more effective. The goal is "psychological flexibility:" the ability to contact the present moment more fully as a conscious human being, and to either change or persist when doing so serves valued ends (Wilson & Murrell, in press). From a behavioral point of view, life itself should help shape more effective behavior over time, if the dead ends and cul-de-sacs can be avoided. ACT theory (which we will review later) suggests that it is excessive verbal regulation targeted toward the wrong ends that creates these cul-de-sacs.

All ACT interventions are aimed at greater flexibility in responding and greater sensitivity to the workability of action. Because all ACT components have the same ultimate target they can be introduced in a variety of orders. ACT is a general clinical approach, not just a specific technology because the issue of psychological flexibility and rigidity is manifested is almost every human problem.

ACT assumes that significant, rapid changes in client behavior are possible. In addition to being a pragmatic assumption, rapid change is assumed to be possible because of the route through which ACT targets language. In general, ACT seeks to alter the function, not the form, of relational networks, and consequently there is no need to remove these historically conditioned responses before progress is possible. Speaking metaphorically, rather than attempting to learn how to win a game one has been chronically losing, ACT changes the game to one that is much more readily won.

ACT tends to use a relatively non-linear form of language. ACT therapists rely heavily on paradox, metaphors, stories, exercises, behavioral tasks, and experiential processes. Direct instruction and logical analysis has a relatively limited role, although it does occur. Even ACT-related concepts are treated in a deliberately flexible manner: the point is not to establish a new belief system but rather to establish a more effective approach to language itself.

The therapeutic relationship is a primary means to establish these new behaviors. The relationship itself is accepting and values focused; the therapist seeks to practice, model, and reinforce what is being taught. Therapy is a social/verbal community in which the normal contingencies supporting fusion and avoidance are removed in favor of contingencies supporting acceptance, defusion, focus on the present moment, and other ACT-relevant behaviors. In an ACT therapeutic relationship, persistence and change linked to valued ends is at the very core of the relationship itself.

The Six Core Processes of ACT

As is shown in Figure 1.1, psychological flexibility is established in ACT with a focus on six core processes: Acceptance, defusion, self as context, contact with the present moment, values, and committed action. Each of these processes helps establish change or persistence linked to chosen values. In the next chapter we will examine specific exercises and clinical steps that might promote these processes. In this chapter our focus is the model itself.

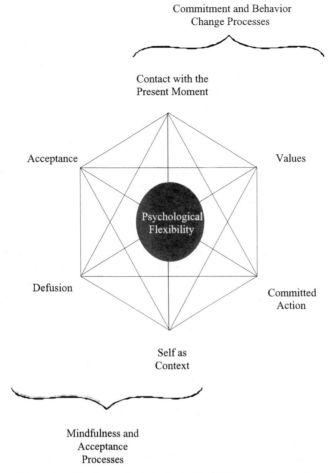

Figure 1.1. The facets of psychological flexibility according to the model of change underlying ACT.

Acceptance. Etymologically, acceptance means, "to take what is offered." Acceptance should not be confused with tolerance or resignation, both of which are passive and fatalistic. Acceptance involves taking a stance of non-judgmental awareness and actively embracing the experience of thoughts, feelings, and bodily sensations as they occur.

ACT promotes acceptance first by contacting the costs of control when control is inappropriately applied to private events. A major theme of many ACT interventions is, "Control is the problem, not the solution." Clients are exposed in an immediate and experiential way to the paradoxical effects of control in the area of thoughts and feelings, and clear contrasts are drawn between the unworkable results of control in this area versus the enormous usefulness of this same repertoire in other areas of life. The pain of not being able to solve this conundrum is linked to an accepting message: this is not the client's fault—it is a rigged game that we all play and we can walk away from it. These issues are examined in a deliberately non-literal way—verbal persuasion and intellectual insight is avoided in favor of more experiential and evocative interventions.

As acceptance itself becomes a focus, clients learn—through numerous small steps, metaphors, and exercises—the distinction between acceptance and tolerance, and acceptance skills are practiced in the context of various difficult private events, usually in a roughly graded fashion. Techniques from experiential therapies, mindfulness traditions, gestalt therapy, and other areas are used to acquire acceptance skills. Clients learn through graded exercises that it is possible to feel intense feelings or notice intense bodily sensations without harm. Concrete behavioral targets that normally would not be pursued because of the private events they evoke are pursued in the context of acceptance of those events.

Cognitive Defusion

ACT aims to alter the context in which thoughts occur so as to decrease the impact and importance of difficult private events. Cognitive defusion works by changing the contexts that support detrimental functions that occur through relational learning so that the *process* of relating dominates over the *results* of that process. Cognitive defusion interventions include exercises that break down literal meaning through experiential means, inherent paradox, mindfulness techniques and similar procedures. As defusion skills are established, literal language itself is brought under better contextual control. Clinically, we want to teach clients to see thoughts as thoughts, feelings as feelings, memories as memories, and physical sensations as physical sensations. None of these private events are inherently toxic to human welfare when experienced for what they are. Their toxicity derives from seeing them as harmful, unhealthy, bad experiences that are what they claim to be, and thus need to be controlled and eliminated.

These techniques are also used to undermine the client's fusion with the conceptualized self. Difficult thoughts and feelings often present themselves as threatening to one's sense of self. For example, depressive thoughts may threaten the idea of the thinker as a normal person. The "self" that is threatened in this example, however, is the conceptualized self, a collection of self-referential relations that generally are both descriptive (I am a male) and evaluative (I am a sick person that has problems with depression). The evaluative component of the conceptualized self is a particular threat to psychological flexibility. In ACT, networks of thoughts about the self rise up to the level of a "story" that contains within it both historical details (I was sexually abused as a child), cause and effect relationships (that event has caused me never to trust men) and explanations about contemporary behavior (because I don't trust men, I am not interested in pursuing relationships). There are an infinite number of relational networks that can be constructed around any set of events. Literally, there are thousands of potential stories that could be constructed based upon the same set of historical facts. Trying to form an "accurate" self-description that integrates one's entire learning history in a thorough manner is comparable to succeeding at a "connect the dots picture" of a Kandinsky painting where none of the dots are numbered. ACT defusion interventions not only try to reveal the hidden properties of language, but also the somewhat arbitrary way that humans try to make sense of inner events and build coherence among those events.

Self as Context: A Transcendent Sense of Self

While ACT sees excessive fusion with the conceptualized self as a threat to psychological flexibility, we consciously try to elevate contact with alternative types of self experience. One is the sense of self as the context in which private events such as thoughts, feelings, memories, and sensations occur. According to RFT, the theory that underlies ACT, deictic relational frames such as I-you; here-there; and now-then produce a perspective of "here-now" from which events can be reliably reported to the verbal community (Hayes, 1984; Hayes et al., 2001). Unlike all other events, however, "here now" is not thing-like. "Here now" is always the perspective from which events are directly experienced ("everywhere I go, there I am") and thus its limits cannot be consciously contacted for the person experiencing this process, because to contact events from the point of view of "here now" *is* consciousness. The ACT perspective is that a transcendent sense of self is built into verbal human beings and that it can be accessed through defusion and mindfulness processes. The great advantage of this sense of self is that it is a context in which the content of consciousness is not threatening. In other words, self-as-context supports acceptance. A number of core ACT interventions are aimed at helping clients directly experience the qualitative aspects of self as context. These include mindfulness/meditation, experiential exercises and metaphors.

Being Present

ACT promotes effective, open, and undefended contact with the present moment. There are two features to this process. First, clients are trained to observe and notice what is present in the environment and in private experience. Second, clients are taught to label and describe what is present, without excessive judgment or evaluation. Together these help establish a sense of "self as a process of ongoing awareness" of events and experiences (e.g., now I am feeling this; now I am thinking that).

A wide variety of techniques are used to orient clients toward the present, having removed the two primary sources of interference with being present: fusion and emotional avoidance. Mindfulness practices are often used in ACT to orient clients to the world as they experience it directly, rather than the world as structured by the products of thought. The connection with mindfulness is not merely technical. Mindfulness has been defined as contacting events non-judgmentally in the here and now (Kabat-Zinn, 1994, p. 4). In that sense, mindfulness (like acceptance itself, broadly defined) can be thought of as a combination of acceptance, defusion, self as context, and contact with the present moment. All four of these processes are in ACT, and thus ACT can be thought of as a mindfulness-based therapy at the level of process, in addition to using mindfulness techniques. At the same time, ACT is not based in a religious or spiritual doctrine or traditions and the accoutrements of religious or spiritual practice are not part of ACT work per se. Many ACT therapists introduce mindfulness and meditation practices in their own lives, however, in part as a method of gaining an experiential understanding of the "space" within which ACT is done.

Contact with the present moment can also include the behavioral and cognitive exposure techniques that are so central to many behavior therapies. The purpose of these exercises in ACT is different, however. If experiencing is done in the service of getting a feeling like anxiety to diminish, it is tangled in a cognitively fused process in which anxiety is evaluated as undesirable. Instead, ACT emphasizes the value of contacting the present moment willingly, in the service of greater vitality and psychological flexibility.

Values

ACT defines values as chosen qualities of purposive action, which can only be instantiated rather than processed as an object. ACT teaches clients to distinguish between choices and reasoned judgments, and to select values as a matter of choice. Clients are challenged to consider what they want their life to stand for in different life domains such as career, family, intimate relationships, friendships, personal growth, health, and spirituality. In order for the client to face feared psychological obstacles, there needs to be a purpose for doing so. Just knowing how to accept, defuse, and make contact with the present is important, but ACT is a behavior therapy and, as such, we seek to help the client "get in motion" and build a more vital, purposeful life. Values function as the compass headings in building an effective set of life patterns.

A variety of exercises are used to help clients clarify their fundamental values. For example, the ACT therapist may ask the client to write out what he or she would most like to see on his or her tombstone. Journaling and brainstorming are used. Contacting directly how it feels to move in one direction or another is examined.

From the direction determined by the person's values, concrete goals and specific behaviors along a valued path are then defined. Obstacles that are likely to be encountered along the valued path are also identified. Usually these barriers are psychological ones which acceptance, defusion, and being present can aid the client in navigating.

Committed Action

Once the psychological barriers of avoidance and fusion are more recognizable and a general direction for travel is defined, making and keeping specific (and often public) commitments becomes useful. Commitments in ACT involve defining goals in specific areas along one's valued path, then acting on these goals while anticipating and making room for psychological barriers. By gradually increasing the size and breadth of the areas addressed, larger and larger patterns of committed action are constructed. The client is encouraged to be responsible for the patterns of actions that result. For example, if a commitment is kept and then abandoned, the larger pattern that is being built is to keep and then abandon commitments. The moment this is seen, the client has the choice to move back onto a valued path (strengthening this larger pattern) or to indulge in self blame and helplessness (strengthening this larger pattern). The goal is to construct behavioral patters that begin to work for clients, not against them. The processes of defusion, acceptance, values, and committed action help the client accept responsibility for behavioral changes, adapting and persisting when necessary. Thus ACT balances strategies, in which readily changeable areas are the focus for change (e.g., overt behavior), and acceptance/mindfulness is the focus in areas where change is not possible or helpful.

In the behavioral domain, the intervention tactics of ACT vary greatly depending on the individual client and individual problem. They can include psychoeducation, problem-solving, behavioral homework, skills building, exposure and any number of other interventions developed in first and second-wave behavior therapies. The core ACT processes of contacting the present moment, self as context, values, and building patterns of committed action are often employed in the service of first order behavior change strategies, and ACT protocols in these areas will use existing behavior change technologies as part of the overall approach.

Psychological Flexibility

Figure 1.1 is organized to reflect other aspects of the ACT model of psychological flexibility beyond its six core processes. Each process relates to and interacts with the other processes (a total of 15 relations), as is represented by the lines connecting all points in Figure 1.1. Some of these relations involve shared functional properties: the three vertical lines are all of that kind. Acceptance and defusion both undermine destructive language processes; self as context and contact with the present moment both involve increasing effective contact with the here and now; values and committed action both involve building out the positive aspects of language into patterns of behavior change. The relations among acceptance and defusion on the one hand, and values and committed action on the other (the horizontal "X" in the middle), are dialectical relations involving the dismantling and construction of language functions in the service of acceptance and change. All of the other 10 relations among these six processes are mutually facilitative. For example, defusion helps the client make contact with the present moment. Contacting the present moment supports defusion and provides access to material that requires it. Though we do not have time to do it here, it is worthwhile to think through each of these relations as a means of understanding the breadth of the ACT model.

The center of the diagram is the psychological space we seek: psychological flexibility. In essence, psychological flexibility is an answer to this question, which involves all six ACT processes:

- given a distinction between you as a conscious human being and the psychological content that is being struggled with (self as context) ...
- are you willing to experience that content fully and without defense (acceptance) ...
- as it is and not as what it says it is (defusion), AND ....
- do what takes you in the direction (committed action) ...

- of your chosen values (values) . . . .
- at this time and in this situation (contact with the present moment)?

In essence, life asks this question of us all, over and over again, moment by moment. If the answer to this question is "yes" in a given moment, psychological flexibility is increased. If it is "no," it is decreased.

What Is ACT?

We are now ready to begin to answer the question that is the topic of this chapter: "what is ACT?" We have already intimated that the six key processes in ACT can be chunked into two larger groups. Acceptance and mindfulness processes involve the four processes to the left of Figure 1.1 while commitment and behavior change processes involve the four to the right. Combining the two provides a working definition of ACT: Said simply, *ACT is a therapy approach that uses acceptance and mindfulness processes, and commitment and behavior change processes, to produce greater psychological flexibility.* The name "ACT" itself reminds us of these two collections of multiple processes that are central to this approach.

ACT is not a specific protocol or finite collection of therapeutic strategies. Even within a specific problem area, multiple ACT protocols can readily be generated. An ACT consistent intervention package includes a wide variety of techniques in the general domains of acceptance, defusion, establishment of a transcendent sense of self, being present and mindful, chosen values, and building larger and larger patterns of committed action linked to those values. Which of these are used in addressing a given problem in a given client is based on an ACT case formulation, either with the individual or the class of patients or both. ACT draws techniques from traditional behavior therapy, cognitive behavior therapy, experiential therapy, and gestalt therapy, as well as from traditions outside of the mental health paradigm (i.e., mindfulness, Zen Buddhism, human potential movement). But what unifies these in ACT is the philosophical and scientific framework that gives it life. We turn now to that topic, and to the history that gave rise to the ACT model.

ACT and the Third Wave of Behavior Therapy

ACT is part of the behavior therapy tradition, and it will help in an understanding of ACT to back up and look at that tradition in broad terms. Behavior therapy began as an alternative approach to less empirical and research-oriented therapeutic traditions. Traditional behavior therapy was committed to the development of clearly defined empirical treatments that were based on well-established basic learning principles. Instead of vague clinical concepts, behavior therapists focused directly on overt problem behaviors, and manipulated direct contingencies (both operant and classical) in an attempt to reduce the severity of or eliminate behavioral problems. In other words, behavior therapy was rooted in the philosophy of promoting "first order change." If an individual avoided social situations, increasing time in social situations or decreasing anxiety about social situations was the target and it was approached directly. If behavioral deficits were apparent, straightforward attempts were made to detect the nature of skill deficits and remediate them through direct training. Psychoanalytic theorists were afraid that such direct behavioral interventions would not get at the root of the patient's problem, but "symptom substitution" turned out to be a far smaller issue than they imagined. Compared to the techniques available at the time, the use of behavioral principles to create first order change worked very well and the first wave of behavior therapy established itself as a well accepted empirically oriented clinical approach.

But something was missing. Both behavior analytic (operant) and neobehavioral (S-R) theories had difficulties handling the problem of thinking, and lacked interventions that could remediate the negative influence of private experiences on human behavior. About thirty years ago, cognitive methods burst onto the scene to address these shortcomings. Some early behavior therapists argued that cognition had been dealt with all along, but the objection fell on deaf ears because clinicians felt that thinking should have a more *central* role in the analysis and treatment of many psychological programs.

The theory of cognition that prompted this evolution was not very sophisticated, however. Treatment innovations were usually based on a common sense approach to human thinking. Clients with particular problems thought particular and unhelpful things. These would be documented and targeted directly, much in the same way overt behavioral problems had been targeted in the previous generation. For example, clients would learn to detect irrational cognitions and dispute them; to notice cognitive errors and logically correct them; to extract core beliefs and conduct behavioral experiments to evaluate their validity. Information processing research models were sometimes linked to the treatment rational, but usually this was an add-on and few of the techniques really required the link.

Because the underling model was more common sense than basic, this "second wave" of behavior therapy undermined the original idea that interventions would emerge from basic scientific principles. In its place came an almost obsessive focus on the outcomes of randomized controlled trials. If a manualized treatment worked in randomized clinical studies, there was only limited interest in determining *why* the treatment worked, and even less in linking these components back to basic science principles. Furthermore, while more emphasis was placed on cognitive processes, the "first order change" emphasis of traditional behavior therapy was not modified. If an individual avoided social situations, the original targets of increasing time in social situations or decreasing anxiety about social situations were simply expanded to include changing irrational thoughts about what might occur in those situations. Cognitive methods were just added to the list of interventions available, under the rubric of "cognitive behavior therapy" (CBT).

The second wave of behavior therapy is now more than 30 years old. It has had unprecedented success, as is exemplified by the number of CBT procedures on the lists of empirically supported treatments (Chambless et al., 1996). However, there are nagging empirical and theoretical issues that have created a need to move forward in the development of empirically based clinical interventions.

First, the theoretical models that explain cognitive behavioral interventions have not held up well in scientific tests. There are multiple lines of evidence that reveal the problem. Clinical improvement in CBT often occurs well before procedures thought to be central to its success have been implemented (Ilardi & Craighead, 1999). Measures of cognitive change often fail to explain the impact of CBT (e.g., Burns & Spangler, 2001), particularly in predictive studies of treatment outcome (e.g., Bieling & Kuyken, 2003). Component analyses of CBT (e.g., Jacobson, Dobson, Truax, Addis, Koerner, Gollan, Gortner, & Prince, 1996; Zettle & Hayes, 1987) have led to the disturbing conclusion by highly respected cognitive behavioral researchers that there may be "no additive benefit to providing cognitive interventions in cognitive therapy" (Dobson & Khatri, 2000, p. 913). Improvements in the general clinical effectiveness of well established CBT interventions have been hard to come by, especially with clinical problems that have been well researched.

Problems like this set the stage for change, but it requires more to actually produce it. It requires innovation. Over the past decade, new treatment models have appeared that place more emphasis on the *function* of problematic cognitions, emotions, memories, or sensations rather than their content, form or frequency. These "second order" change methods attempt to alter the function of these human experiences by focusing on contextual and repertoire building interventions such as contacting the present moment, and meditation/mindfulness. The positive empirical effects of treatments such as ACT (Zettle & Hayes, 1987), Mindfulness-Based Cognitive Therapy (MBCT: Segal, Williams, & Teasdale, 2001) and Dialectical

Behavior Therapy (DBT: Linehan, 1993; see Hayes, Masuda, Bissett, Luoma, Guerrero, in press, for a recent outcome review of both DBT and ACT) have provided support for these changes and there has been an explosion in interest in treatments of this kind (see Hayes, Follette, & Linehan, in press, for a book length review of most of these new treatments). A third wave of behavior therapy has been launched (Hayes, in press).

The Intellectual History of ACT

Acceptance and Commitment Therapy (Hayes et al., 1999) and Relational Frame Theory (Hayes et al., 2001) have played a central role in stimulating the third wave of behavior therapy. The visibility of ACT/RFT is only now becoming significant because of the development strategy we employed, but we think that our development strategy is now bearing fruit. It is worth a brief review, primarily so that readers can understand why there is much more to ACT than a mere description of its technology, and why is it only now becoming well-known and well-researched even though it claims to be an empirical behavioral therapy and is already 20 years old (a fact that has drawn strong criticism—e.g., Corrigan, 2001).

In outline form ACT and RFT were developed in the early 1980's. The first publication that began to out the ACT/RFT model was published in 1984 (Hayes, 1984) in an article that argued that a monist approach to spirituality was both theoretically important and practically useful. The first controlled study of ACT (Zettle & Hayes, 1986) and the first description of the clinical intervention package (Hayes, 1987) were published a few years later. Then ACT outcome research deliberately stopped. Why?

The first reason was philosophical. Both the first and second wave of behavior therapy were committed to first order change methods, but ACT is a contextual treatment and focuses as well on second order change methods. ACT is interested in the *function* of clinically problematic behaviors (e.g., What is this thought, emotion, impulse, behavior in the service of? Under what conditions does it function that way?), not *form* alone (e.g., is this thought logical? How often does it occur?). This is a significant philosophical departure from the implicit philosophies underlying much of both the first and second waves of behavior therapy. It seemed to us that when interest in these new forms of therapy really hit, we would need to have our philosophical ducks in row or their potential to advance the field could be frittered away in a chaotic embrace of eastern thought, or more experiential techniques, without the construction of a coherent approach. Hence, a multi-year detour was taken to get clear about the philosophical assumptions that support the radically functional change methods that characterize ACT (e.g., Biglan & Hayes, 1996; Hayes, Hayes, & Reese,

1988; Hayes, 1993). We will give a brief introduction to this philosophy shortly.

The second reason was similar but more theoretical. CBT weakened its link to basic science for a good reason: no principles of human language and cognition were available that provided a good framework for CBT packages. Information processing accounts largely failed to specify the contextual variables that clinicians might directly manipulate to improve treatment outcomes. They were used because little else was available, but the lack of clarity about contextual variables meant that the linkage to clinical practice was necessarily weak since what clinicians do is always (by definition) part of the context of client action. Basic behavioral principles were very successful with direct contingency control, but by themselves were not adequate to understand human cognition.

Sensing the need to provide a basic science underpinning human cognition that would have clinical utility, we turned to building a contextual theory of language and cognition. We wanted a concrete, experimental approach that could be useful to *all* contextual approaches, not just ACT. Relational Frame Theory (Hayes et al., 2001) was the result.

There are now scores of RFT studies comprising an extended program of research at multiple sites around the world. In our opinion, the result is a theoretically consistent set of principles of cognition that augment the available science on contingency shaped learning and classical conditioning principles, and that provide a foundation for a new wave of applied analyses and technological development. We will give a brief introduction to this theory shortly.

With those two problems addressed, we began to develop a model of psychopathology that flowed from these foundations (Hayes, Wilson, Gifford, Follette, & Strosahl, 1996). We will describe that model below.

Finally, we began to do clinical outcome research again. When we relaunched our outcome program we first wanted to see if this model was as broadly applicable as the theory said it should be, so we started with an effectiveness study that showed that training in ACT produced clinicians who were generally better at producing good outcomes across the range of clients clinicians face (Strosahl, Hayes, Bergan, & Romano, 1998). The ACT manual was published a year later (Hayes et al., 1999). And then, like a dam breaking, the outcome research began to flow. By the end of 2004 more than 35 case studies or controlled trials will have appeared on ACT, covering almost every area of applied work (see Hayes, Masuda, et al., in press). This research program is occurring world-wide. It is producing good outcomes, sometimes startlingly so (e.g., Bach & Hayes, 2002; Dahl, Nillson, & Wilson, in press). Just as important, the ACT/RFT model of change seems to be holding up in these studies (e.g., Bach & Hayes, 2002; Bond & Bunce,

2000). Several studies have shown an independent impact for various ACT components such as acceptance (Hayes Bissett, Korn, Zettle, Rosenfarb, Cooper, & Grundt, 1999; Levitt, Brown, Orsillo, & Barlow, in press) and defusion (Masuda, Hayes, Sackett, & Twohig, in press).

ACT is not a traditional behavior therapy, nor is it a classic cognitive behavior therapy. It is a behavior therapy that is based upon a philosophy of science, a basic theory of the functions of language and cognition, a theory of psychopathology and behavior change, and a core set of processes within which treatment protocols can be developed. ACT is part of a broader approach that seeks nothing short of the development of a more unified and useful discipline. Even though this book is a clinical guide, we think a short review of those features of ACT is worthwhile and will help make the rest of the book understandable. Because we are being very brief, however, this material will feel a bit dense. If it is not fully understood, we would suggest moving on and returning later. More familiarity with ACT itself will help its underlying theory and philosophy be understood, not just vice versa.

PHILOSOPHY AND BASIC SCIENCE FOUNDATION

Philosophy: Functional Contextualism

ACT is rooted in radical behaviorism, but we have rarely talked about it that way. Radical behaviorism is almost universally misunderstood, and includes conflicting perspectives under its broad umbrella. Rather than struggle under this dual burden indefinitely, we have defined the philosophical base of our approach and worked out its applied implications, using terms that allow a fresh look. Some of the unique features of ACT make a lot more sense if its underlying philosophy is understood. We will spend only a couple of pages on it here—just enough to get the flavor of the work—but readers with a more philosophical bent can pursue the matter in the works cited.

You need assumptions to develop a logical or empirical system, but they can't really be justified, only owned. If two people start with different assumptions they may end up in different places achieved by different means, but that does not mean that one is right and one is wrong. Metaphorically it is like the difference between starting from New York and heading as far west as possible on foot, versus starting from New Orleans and heading as far north as possible by boat. Neither journey is "correct" or "better" in any absolute sense. It would be silly for our two travelers to criticize each other because they are each heading in different directions, or are using different means of transportation. After all, those differences are built into the very purpose of the chosen journeys. But both journeys imply certain consistencies when considered on their own terms. For example, if the person starting from New York unknowingly starts heading east, the "as far west as possible on foot" journey will not be successful. If the New Orleans traveler takes a bus and not a boat it will be difficult to know how far north the rivers and streams go. In these cases, criticism is warranted and may be useful.

In the same way, philosophy does not prove anything: it simply specifies assumptions (e.g., where are you starting from; where are you going), and makes sure they aren't in conflict (e.g., are your methods and measures in harmony with your goals). This is a good idea clinically. If disagreements about a system of therapy occur, they might be based on disagreements about assumptions and therefore more a matter of understanding differences than of legitimate and useful criticism. Conversely, if systems of therapy bog down it might be because assumptions are in conflict or they are not being adhered to, and in that case criticism might be both warranted and helpful.

ACT is based on a variety of pragmatism known as functional contextualism (Hayes et al., 1988; Pepper, 1942). Common sense actions (we will use the example of "going to the store") are a kind of abstract model for contextualistic interpretations. These kinds of events imply an interaction between a person and a setting, and they are whole events, with a history and a purpose, no matter how expansively or minutely they are viewed. For example, "going to the store" implies a reason for going, a place to go, a means to get there, and so on, all mixed together. If the whole is lost, the features lose their meaning. Small actions, like gripping the steering wheel, and larger sets of actions, like following a map route, can all be features of "going to the store," but they make no sense if they are seen in isolation. If we brought people into the lab and repeatedly made them grip a steering wheel we would no longer be studying "going to the store," because the context of that action would have been lost.

Functional contextualism thus views psychological events as an interaction between whole organisms and a context that is defined both historically (e.g., prior learning histories) and situationally (current antecedents and consequences, verbal rules). Analyzing it (e.g., by the scientist or clinician) is itself a whole event, also with a history and purpose. Just as going to the store is defined by its purpose and is finished as an event when one gets to the store, so too from a contextualistic viewpoint the actions of a client are considered useful only to the extent that they foster valued ends, *and* scientific or clinical analyses are considered "true" only in so far as they accomplish their specified purposes. This is an unusual and pragmatic sense of truth, that differs from more typical approaches to "truth" that consider it to be a matter of correspondence, not workability. To understand this approach to truth, imagine having a picture of a house, a map to it, and a blueprint of its construction. If we ask "which is the right view of the house?" we would have to know the purpose. If the goal is getting to the house, the map would work well but the blueprint would not. If the goal is strengthening the foundation, the blueprint picture would work well but the picture would not.

Functional contextualism is precise about its purpose: it seeks the prediction-and-influence of psychological events, with precision, scope, and depth (Hayes & Brownstein, 1986). Other forms of contextualism (e.g., feminist psychology, social constructionism, narrative psychology) seek other ends (Hayes, 1993) so their analyses look different even though they share the same basic philosophy. "Prediction-and-influence" is hyphenated to indicate that this is one goal, not two. Analyses of variables that lead only to prediction, and not to influence, are relatively uninteresting from a functional contextual viewpoint. Analyses are sought that have precision (only certain terms and concepts apply to a given phenomenon), scope (principles apply to a wide range of phenomena), and depth (principles cohere across scientific levels of analysis, such as biology, psychology, and cultural anthropology).

Many features of the ACT/RFT tradition make sense given these various assumptions and goals. First, ACT is linked to an ongoing basic research program while most psychotherapies are not, because there is a commitment to analyses with precision, scope and depth, and that requires a basic account. Second, ACT tends *not* to view thoughts or feelings as causal in a mechanical sense. In order to achieve the goal of prediction-and-influence, directly manipulable events are essential (by definition, "influence" requires change or manipulation), and in a situated action it is only contextual variables that can be manipulated directly by therapists or others (Hayes & Brownstein, 1986). This helps explain why in ACT thoughts and feelings are viewed as important and related to overt behavior but it is always context (e.g., the social supports for emotional avoidance), not thoughts and feelings in isolation, that are its therapeutic targets. Third, values and goals are always critical in ACT because they provide the measure of success and thus pragmatic truth. ACT clients are often encouraged to abandon interest in the literal truth of their own thoughts or evaluations and instead embrace a passionate and ongoing interest in how to carry all of these reactions forward into a the process of living according to their values. If a client tells a story of past difficulties the issue will not be "is the analysis correct?" or even "does this story comport with the evidence?" but "what is this way of speaking in the service of?" or "does such talk move my life in a vital direction" or "can I just have that thought and move forward in the world of behavior?" Similarly, ACT and RFT researchers have no interest in the *ontological* truth of their own theories and instead embrace a passionate and ongoing commitment to developing analyses that make a difference in the lives of human beings. Fourth, there is considerable flexibility in the use of language both in the clinic and the RFT laboratory, when different ways of speaking are found to be useful. ACT and RFT are focused on discovering what is useful, not what is "objectively" true. Concepts tend not to be reified, and there is an intensely pragmatic quality both inside ACT sessions and in the research program that surrounds it. The clinical contexts justify the use of some ways of speaking (e.g., free choice) that would be anathema in the laboratory and vice versa, yet no inconsistency is implied. This quality helps explain why from the beginning of ACT and RFT rigorous behavioral theory has been intermingled with discussion of topics like spirituality or meaning (e.g., Hayes, 1984).

Basic Theory: Relational Frame Theory

Relational Frame Theory (Hayes et al., 2001) is a comprehensive functional contextual program of basic behavioral research on human language and cognition. The research on RFT is growing very quickly and there are few areas of the theory that have not been tested in some form or another. ACT theory and associated treatment strategies are thoroughly integrated with RFT at the level of basic science. ACT targets language processes that have been shown to directly control human behavior in the RFT laboratory.

At the core of RFT is the premise that humans learn to relate events under arbitrary contextual control. All complex organisms respond to stimulus relations that are defined by formal properties of related events (what are called "non-arbitrary relations"). For example, a non-human can readily learn to choose the larger of two objects, regardless of which particular objects are compared. Humans are able to bring relational responding under contextual control and apply it to events that are *not* necessarily related formally in that way. These kinds of relational responses are "arbitrarily applicable" meaning that the particular relation can be specified by social whim or convention. For example, having learned that "x" is "smaller than" "X," humans may later be able to apply this same relation to events under the control of certain arbitrary cues (such as the words "smaller than"). A very young child will know that a nickel is bigger than a dime, but a slightly older child will have learned that a nickel is "smaller than" a dime by social attribution, even though in a formal sense it is not.

For behavior to be considered verbal in RFT, it must demonstrate three main properties: mutual entailment, combinatorial entailment, and transformation of stimulus function. Mutual entailment means that if a person learns that A relates in a particular way to B in a context (the context is termed "C_{rel}" for "relational context," then this must entail some kind of relation between B and A in that context. For example, if a person is taught that moist is the opposite of dry, that person will derive that dry is the opposite of moist. Combinatorial entailment means that mutual relations can combine. For example, if a person is taught in a given context that Mike is stronger than Steve and Kara is stronger than Mike, the person will derive that Kara is stronger than Steve. Finally, the functions of events in relational networks of this kind can be transformed in terms of the underlying relations. Suppose you need help moving a heavy appliance and you know Mike is good at this. In this context (the context is termed "C_{func}" for "functional context"), it will be derived that Steve will be less useful and Kara will be more useful as a helper, without necessarily having used either Steve or Kara to move items before.

When all three features are established with a given type of relational responding, we call it a "relational frame." Frames of coordination (i.e., sameness), distinction, opposition, comparison, time, and hierarchy are examples. From an RFT perspective, relational framing is considered to be the core process in all human language and cognition (Hayes & Hayes, 1989).

What makes relational framing clinically relevant is that the functions of one member of a relational network can alter the functions of other members. Suppose a child is playing with friends and gets trapped inside a wooden box. The child gets very frightened and cries. Some of that fear and anxiety could years later transform the functions of other events where one could be "trapped," such as in a difficult class or in a relationship. There are few formal similarities between a relationship and a wooden box; what links these responses is not their formal properties but the derived relations among them in a verbal network.

As children develop, the number of relational frames and range of contextual features that govern them expands. Beginning with the simple frames of coordination, difference, and opposition, more complex frames of time, cause, hierarchy, and comparison are added. Deictic frames such as here-there or I-you establish a sense of self or perspective. These relational networks are constructed and brought to bear on new situations through analogies, stories, metaphors, and rules. Problem solving tasks make use of frames of coordination, hierarchy, time or contingency, and comparison ("because x has y features, if I do x then a beneficial q will happen"). Verbal formulae are used to control other people: first for concrete benefits from the rule giver (pliance), then to orient the listener toward contingencies in the environment (tracking), and finally to create abstract consequences and values (augmenting).

What we are saying in a just few paragraphs is supported by scores of studies and detailed analyses (see Hayes et al., 2001 for a book length summary). It is not our purpose to summarize the research on RFT here—it is far too vast. As it applies to the foundation of ACT theory, however, we can summarize a few core conclusions from the RFT research program:

- Relational frames are learned behavior processes that are a central organizing principle of human experience. Psychotherapy necessarily involves engaging with and, when necessary, altering the functions of various relational frames.
- Some of the more common skill deficits noted in our clients (weak problem solving; lack of tolerance for emotional distress, impulsivity) are due to poorly controlled or improperly developed relational repertoires.
- Relational frames tend to dominate over other sources of behavioral regulation such as contingency shaped learning because of their general utility in so many areas of human endeavor, their tendency to broaden their impact through the transformation of stimulus functions, the arbitrariness of the cues that control them, and the ubiquitous cultural drive to use language to control the behaviors of individual members of the social unit.
- As a verbal repertoire develops, humans tend to treat transformed functions (the functions of events based on their participation in relational frames) as if they are direct (based solely on the formal features of events). People have difficulty making a distinction between direct functions and verbally established functions, and thus fail to notice how much they live in a verbally transformed world. For example, the "disgusting" qualities of drinking a fresh glass of one's own saliva will be thought to be in the properties of the saliva itself and not in our thinking about it—a view that is obviously false since we all daily drink quarts of our own saliva simply by swallowing without any such disgust reaction.
- The symbolic, temporal, and evaluative nature of relational frames makes it difficult for humans to stay in direct contact with the present moment. The domination of verbal processes over other sources of behavioral regulation ("cognitive fusion") can make the person less sensitive to real life outcomes and can be a major contributor to psychopathology.
- The same properties of relational frames that permit effective human problem solving (e.g., that allow us to define a problem, detect

and alter the cause) also allow us to be in pain regardless of the current formal features of our environment (e.g., by remembering past loses or hurts), and to exacerbate our pain needlessly (e.g., by continuously comparing our situation to the ideal; by fearing the future). This negative effect cannot be controlled by eliminating the verbal relations that produce it because these relations are necessary in positive human functioning.

- Because humans are unable to control pain simply by controlling the situation they often focus on negative experience itself. The attempt to regulate distressing private events in the same way as one alters external problems (i.e., through direct, rule-governed attempts to control) often increases the intensity, frequency, or behavioral impact of these private events. This process is a root cause of human suffering in general and psychopathology in particular.
- Relational networks work by addition, not by subtraction, and thus it is difficult to alter the content of historically conditioned verbal relations via clinical interventions. For that reason, a content focused change process is often unlikely to succeed in the case of undesirable private events.
- While the presence of relational frames and their content is difficult to control, the negative function of relational framing can be contextually controlled to a large degree, even when negative relational networks remain intact. It is not necessary to control, eliminate or avoid negatively framed events in order to change their behavioral functions. Said another way, it is often more clinically important to focus on the functional context (C_{func}) as compared to the specific relational context (C_{rel}) in designing effective clinical interventions.

THE ACT THEORY OF PSYCHOPATHOLOGY: PSYCHOLOGICAL RIGIDITY

Language is repertoire broadening, when considered from the overall point of view of non-verbal behavior. Temporal relational frames allow "the future" to be considered in a different way, so verbal organisms can plan and problem-solve in a way that non-verbal organisms cannot. Comparative frames allow consequences to be considered verbally, and thus relative and probabilistic events can have more influence ("eating food x may reduce the probability of disease more so than eating food y"—a comparative process impossible without language). The combination of time and comparison allows rules about future events to induce more self-control and sensitivity to the delayed consequences of action. The repertoire broadening effect of human language is part of why such a slow and weak creature as human beings have been able to compete with other animals who are far stronger, faster, and better defended.

There is a large and important domain where language *narrows* behavioral repertoires, however. This occurs particularly in situations where the problems are produced by the excesses of language and thought. ACT is not so much interested in training minds as in liberating humans from their excesses; not so much interested in building relational repertoires, as bringing them under appropriate contextual control. We want to teach clients to use relational repertories (rule following) when they work and to use other sources of behavioral regulation when they do not.

From an ACT perspective, ubiquitous human suffering and psychopathology are dominantly the result of the repertoire narrowing effects of language in two key areas: cognitive fusion and experiential avoidance. These two processes result in psychological inflexibility, which is the inability to modulate behavior in response to how useful it is—changing behavior when change is needed and persisting when persistence is needed—so as to accomplish desired ends.

Cognitive Fusion

Cognitive fusion refers to the human tendency to interact with events on the basis of their verbally ascribed functions rather than their direct functions, while being oblivious to the ongoing relational framing that establishes these functions. The event and ones thinking about it become so fused as to be inseparable and that creates the impression that verbal construal is not present at all. A bad cup is seemingly bad in the same way that a soft chair is soft. A worry about the future is seemingly about the actual future, not merely an immediate process of construing the future. The thought "Life is not worth living" is seemingly a conclusion about life and its quality, not a verbal evaluative process going on now. The effect is repertoire narrowing because verbal relations in essence restructure our contact with events in such a way as to maintain the verbal network itself. For example, acting on the basis of "life is not worth living" will tend to produce a life that is less vital, intimate, meaningful, or supportive—a set of events that will tend to confirm the thought itself.

Part of the resistance to change that seems to occur with human language may have evolved culturally. Language is a primary means by which cultural practices are propagated. When members of a language community learn culturally supported rules, these often protect the interests of society more so that the individual. Our most basic beliefs about what goes into a "good" life plan (i.e., get a good job, get married and have a family, be a good provider at home) can often be turned into life suppressing rule following (e.g., don't stop this job no matter how unsatisfying it is because you have to provide for your family; healthy people don't get divorced, so stay in this entirely unrewarding relationship). If, however, these culturally supported rules could be easily noted, challenged, and changed, cultural practices themselves would be far more difficult to pass from generation to generation.

Behavior controlled by the rules contained in relational frames tends to be relatively sensitive to consequences surrounding rule following but relatively insensitive to direct, programmed consequences of other kinds (see Hayes, 1989 for a book length review). What this means clinically is that people can continue to engage in rule governed behavior even if aspects of the results produced are consistently bad. Cognitive fusion will hide the true source of the problem, which contributes to its persistence.

Cognitive behavior therapists are well aware of this. Classic CBT interventions often are designed to teach people to notice, test, and evaluate their thoughts and then to change the content of those that are irrational, over-generalized, excessive, untestable, and so on. This model is based on the assumption that it is the presence of dysfunctional thoughts that produces poor outcomes and thus they need to be modified: "cognitive therapy is best viewed as the application of the cognitive model of a particular disorder with the use of a variety of techniques designed to modify the dysfunctional beliefs" (Beck, 1993, p. 194). For reasons that we will explain later, there are substantial problems in that solution, which can itself be repertoire narrowing.

The problem with language-based problems, as we noted in the RFT section above, is that the ubiquitous nature of language and language-based solutions hides their nature and existence. Verbal processes are so fruitful in some areas that humans tend to apply them to all areas. The transformation of stimulus functions enabled by language allows humans to interact with verbally construed events (e.g., what is imagined or feared) as if these events were concrete non-verbal events (e.g., something that is "real"). Humans interact more with the products of thinking than with the processes that underlie thinking. The contextual cues supporting relational responses are arbitrary and ubiquitous—thus there is literally nothing that cannot evoke verbal responses and verbal responses, once formed, can be tied to almost any other verbal response. Language amplifies the impact of arbitrary social consequences which is one of the main consequences produced by language—it may be more important to be "right" than to be effective. Language helps us make sense of the "world," which can make it difficult when excessive attempts to understand is itself part of the problem. For these reasons and several more, language-based problems tend to have a life of their own, producing a notable inability to engage in forms of behavior that are not based in logical, linear language processes. Despite its utility in other ways, language contains within it repertoire narrowing tendencies.

Experiential Avoidance

Experiential avoidance is the attempt to escape or avoid the form, frequency, or situational sensitivity of private events, even when the attempt to do so causes psychological harm (Hayes et al., 1996). There are two main forms of experiential avoidance: suppression and situational escape/avoidance. Suppression is the active attempt to control and/or eliminate the immediate experience of a negative private event such as an unwanted thought, feeling, memory or physical sensation. For example, the alcoholic may increase consumption in response to the unpleasant outcome of a marital conflict in an attempt to "numb" guilt, shame, or depression. The patient with schizophrenia is filled with sadness inwardly but maintains a flat and expressionless façade. The borderline patient, in response to perceived criticism and the fear of abandonment, uses an angry outburst to quell the criticism.

Situational escape/avoidance is the attempt to alter the antecedent contextual features likely to be associated with the appearance of an unwanted private experience. The patient with agoraphobia stays at home to avoid the anxiety attack that is sure to come if the grocery store is visited. The depressed person avoids a family reunion in response to the idea that he/she will be boring and unlikable. These experiential avoidance strategies have been found to result in poorer outcomes in a broad range of disorders (see Hayes et al. 1996 for a review).

Humans construct rules of the form "If I do x, I will feel y, and that will have effect z." For example, the panic disordered person says "if I don't go to the restaurant I will not be anxious, and that is good" or the person with OCD says "If I forget to wash my hands then I will contaminate my family and they will get sick and die, and that is bad." Unfortunately, rules of this kind have self-amplifying properties. Trying not to think of something evokes thinking of it. Trying not to feel something bad to avoid a bad outcome also relates the present moment to that bad outcome and thus the present moment evokes or elicits bad feelings. There is extensive research showing that deliberate attempts to suppress private events increases their occurrence and behavioral impact (e.g., Cioffi & Holloway, 1993; Wegner, Schneider, Carter, & White, 1987) and decreases the effectiveness of exposure based strategies (Feldner, Zvolensky, Eifert, & Spira, 2003). Both suppression and avoidance based strategies will come to cue the feared or unwanted private event since they are based on (and thus strengthen) the underlying relational frames ("don't think of x" will serve as a contextual cue for "x" and for some of the functions of the actual event "x" refers to). Relational networks do not change readily and even direct, contradictory training may not break them up (Wilson & Hayes, 1996).

The process of experiential avoidance is also heavily reinforced by our "feel good" culture. The culture promotes the idea that healthy humans do not have psychological pain (stress, depression, memories of trauma, and so forth), and that the absence of negative private events is a state to be desired. Avoidant solutions (alcohol, drugs, mindless sex) are modeled in television shows, commercials, and other media.

Indeed, feeling good is often at the very heart of much of the mental health model. The very names of our disorders and treatments reveal this connection. We diagnose "disorders" based upon the presence of particular configurations of private events and experiences (self critical thoughts, suicidal thoughts, feelings of fatigue are part of "depression") and we construct treatments that are designed to eliminate these symptoms, ostensibly with the goal of returning the person to "good health".

In some areas, we have learned not to buy into this misguided culturally promoted view of health. For example, it was once considered ethical to try to remove or change homosexual thoughts, urges, and arousal. Our homosexual clients were obviously suffering; they said they were suffering because of these private events; and we as a field went along and tried to remove these events. Many therapists now consider this approach unethical. Instead, therapists work with homosexual clients to help them make room for their own feelings and thoughts and to function positively. One of the basic messages in ACT is that we ought to be looking at this issue in all of our clients. Is it the symptom itself that is harmful, or is it the culturally supported rules about what to do with such symptoms?

The result of cognitive fusion and experiential avoidance is psychological rigidity. Humans persist when they need to desist, and desist when they need to persist. They desist and persist for the wrong reasons and using the wrong means. For example, when persons experience a profound loss they tend to persist at avoidance, suppression, problem solving, and understanding in an attempt to avoid feeling the loss when the situation may call for simple contact with the loss, while engaging in effective and needed actions in the context of that loss. When faced with a self-control challenge, humans tend to focus either on the undesirable feelings that self-control initially induces (thus undermining persistence and fostering emotional indulgence) or they attempt to suppress or avoid those feelings in order to persist (but also producing second level responses such as emotional numbing or stress). Emotional indulgence on the one hand and suppressive persistence on the other form a poisonous choice that modern society and its culture of "feel goodism" seems to be forcing on us all. The impact of this culturally sanctioned model on the ability of individuals to live effective lives has been horrific. ACT presents a middle path that is neither indulgent nor suppressive.

What Is ACT?

So we return now to the central topic of this chapter. We are ready for a more elaborate definition of ACT. *ACT is a functional contextual intervention approach based on Relational Frame Theory, which views human suffering as originating in psychological inflexibility fostered by cognitive fusion and experiential avoidance. In the context of a therapeutic relationship, ACT brings direct contingencies and indirect verbal processes to bear on the experiential establishment of greater psychological flexibility through acceptance, defusion, establishment of a transcendent sense of self, being present, values, and building expanding patterns of committed action linked to those values.* It is to ACT technology that we now turn.

Chapter 2

An ACT Primer
Core Therapy Processes, Intervention Strategies, and Therapist Competencies

KIRK D. STROSAHL, STEVEN C. HAYES,
KELLY G. WILSON AND ELIZABETH V. GIFFORD

The purpose of this chapter is to present a consolidated overview of ACT treatment interventions and therapy processes. In Chapter 1 we described the philosophy, basic theory, applied theory and the theoretical processes that collectively define ACT as a clinical system. In this chapter we will examine the concrete clinical steps used in implementing this model.

Since the ACT treatment model was first published in book form in 1999, there have been many innovative developments in the model, particularly as it has been applied to a variety of clinical problems and special populations. This type of innovation is exactly what is needed to grow the approach, and is a key reason for the publication of the present volume. At the same time, ACT is a relatively focused clinical model with a limited set of core processes. The components of psychological flexibility resurface in ACT protocols. One goal of this chapter is link the core processes to intervention techniques that ACT therapists (and their clients) have invented and put them into a user friendly system. Finally we will address a question that is being asked more and more: "What are the hallmarks of a good ACT therapist?" We will present a set of core competencies that any mental health professional wishing to learn ACT can strive for. The end result of reading this chapter is that you will better understand what is at the heart of ACT treatment, how the various ACT intervention target specific aspects of psychological inflexibility and the competencies you can develop to improve your clinical effectiveness.

Moving from FEAR to ACT

The simplest way to think about the essence of ACT is to remember the processes that eventually trap the client in an unworkable way of living. The ACT shorthand for these processes is the FEAR algorithm:

- *Fusion*: Excessive attachment to the literal content of thought that makes healthy psychological flexibility difficult or impossible, particularly in the way that it makes direct, undefended contact with unwanted private events (thoughts, feelings, memories, sensations) seemingly toxic and unacceptable, and in the way that it draws the focus of living away from the present moment into the past and the future.
- *Evaluation*: Provocative and evocative evaluations of self, others, the world in general and important components of human experiences such as personal history or contemporary private experiences, when evaluations are neither needed nor helpful
- *Avoidance*: A style of dealing with unwanted private events (thoughts, feelings, memories, sensations) and distressing external events that involves emotional avoidance, numbing or other methods of experiential control even when it has significant behavioral costs
- *Reason Giving*: The over use of seeming logical and culturally sanctioned justifications that "explain" and "rationalize" the use of unworkable coping strategies and make the individual less responsive to real contingencies in the environment

ACT involves attacking the processes that support FEAR and the goal of therapy is to replace FEAR based functioning with an alternative: ACT.

- *Accept*: Accept unwanted private experiences such as thoughts, feelings, memories, and sensations as well as external events that are not amenable to direct control for what they are, not what they appear to be.
- *Choose*: Choose a set of valued life directions that would enlarge one's sense of vitality, purpose and meaning.
- *Take Action:* Build larger and larger patterns of committed action that are consistent with these valued ends

The Six Core Clinical Processes of ACT

In Chapter 1 we described six processes that are central to the ability to persist or change in the service of valued action. Collectively, these processes define the ACT intervention model. These processes are not unique to ACT—they appear in different forms in other treatment models. What is unique is that ACT treatment draws them together based in a consistent theory of the functional properties of human language and cognition. ACT treatment seeks to help the client:

- Foster acceptance and willingness while undermining the dominance of emotional control & avoidance in the client's response hierarchy (Acceptance)
- Undermine the language-based processes that promote fusion, needless reason-giving, and unhelpful evaluation and thus cause private experiences to function as psychological barriers to life promoting activities (Defusion)
- Live more in the present moment, contacting more fully the ongoing flow of experience as it occurs (Getting in Contact With The Present Moment)
- Make experiential contact with the distinction between self-as-context versus the conceptualized self to provide a position from which acceptance of private events is less threatening (Self-as-context)
- Identify valued outcomes in living that will legitimize confronting previously avoided psychological barriers (Values)
- Build larger and larger patterns of committed action that are consistent with valued life ends (Committed Action)

There are several important principles that go along with these six core clinical intervention processes. First, these processes are in practice highly interdependent and entering into the chain at any point is likely to stimulate the emergence of other processes. Practically speaking, this means that there is no "correct" order for addressing these core objectives. If you start by clarifying values and beginning to build patterns of committed action, it will likely stimulate issues like excessive reliance on emotional control, fusion with events that block behavior, or difficulties separating the spiritual or transcendent sense of self from the conceptualized content of consciousness. If you start by undermining excessive experiential avoidance, you will probably stimulate issues around fusion and loss of contact with self-as-context, and you will eventually have to put acceptance and defusion in the service of valued, committed action.

Second, your clients will exhibit unique profiles along these clinical dimensions—a topic we will address in the next chapter. Not all clients need work in all of these domains. Your client may be relatively functional in one or more areas but severely blocked in another area. This means that good ACT treatment involves considering the client's status in each of these dimensions and then targeting the area(s) that need to be bolstered. As your client exhibits more psychological dysfunction, you can anticipate that more core processes are going to have to be targeted.

Third, a good ACT therapist needs to be highly proficient at providing interventions within any of these core processes. All therapists tend to have their favorite interventions and sequencing methods, but you should avoid the trap of a "one size fits all" approach. This principle has important implications for defining the core competencies of the competent ACT therapist and, consequently, training and supervising ACT therapists.

Fourth, many ACT interventions can be used to promote progress in one or more of these core process areas. Because ACT is a contextualistic treatment, the meaning of an intervention is entirely dependent upon the client's unique learning history and life situation. Understanding that the same metaphor, for example, can have many different meanings will help you be more flexible in the application of these strategies.

Acceptance and Willingness: Undermining the Dominance of Experiential Control

From an ACT perspective, experiential control is thought to be pervasive in the human condition. However, individual clients may be more or less invested in control strategies. Some clients may, as a result of their learning history, be more open to testing out the effects of acceptance in their own experience. Others may be so entirely fused with the catastrophic outcomes of feeling depressed or anxious that acceptance is not even in the realm of imaginable experience. For the latter clients in particular, we begin by undermining the control agenda. When the dominance of the control agenda has been weakened sufficiently, we use interventions that foster acceptance and willingness.

Undermining Control

The language community largely defines "psychological health" as the absence of distressing or unwanted private content. The dark side of this message is that negative private content is toxic and dangerous, and must be controlled in the name of psychological health. Inherent in this belief is the idea that healthy people can control and eliminate negative private content and thereby gain psychological health. This is what ACT describes as the "unworkable change agenda." Basically, this agenda means you first detect the cause of the negative content and then, by eliminating the cause, you eliminate the content. This verbally established problem solving strategy works well in the external world, but often backfires when applied to events inside the skin. We are historical organisms and cannot simply eliminate our history and the experiences it contains. The more we try to squeeze out unwanted private content, the more dominant it becomes. Those suffering from clinical problems will often resort to destructive experiential avoidance strategies (i.e., alcohol, drugs, suicidal behavior, panic, depression) to try to make the change agenda work. This situation is further compounded as control focused reasons are put forward as causes of life restricting behavior (i.e., I didn't go to work because I was depressed; I can't trust men because I was sexually abused as a child). The change agenda says the cause must be controlled or eliminated before psychological health can appear, but since the cause specified in the relationship cannot be removed, the client is in a trap.

The basic goal of ACT in this core domain is to help the client see experiential control and avoidance for what it is, to get the client into experiential contact with the costs of using this strategy, and to open up to the possibility that this change agenda can never work. It is only out of that pain that the client is likely to be open to experimenting with the alternative, willingness. Some of the more basic ACT messages in this domain are:

- You are not broken, only trapped.
- You are not hopeless, but your change agenda is hopeless.
- Control is the problem, not the solution.
- The rule of mental events: The less you want of them the more you get.
- What have you tried? How has it worked? What has it cost you?
- Try to gain control of your feelings, lose control of your life.
- What would happen if you stopped the struggle?

There are various ACT experiential exercises, metaphors and self monitoring assignments that can be used to support your efforts in this domain. Some of the more commonly used tactics are presented in Table 2.1. Most of these interventions are described in some detail in the first ACT book (Hayes, Strosahl, & Wilson, 1999). Once the control agenda has been sufficiently eroded, an opening has been made for an alternative.

Developing Acceptance and Willingness

Acceptance is a kind of leap of faith—an active embrace of the present moment, fully and without defense. No one is willing all the time in all areas, thus, no matter how willing you are to be present in a given moment there is always more to do. What ACT attempts to do is to open a door to a process—life itself will show clients the value of the process as they engage

Table 2.1. ACT Interventions for Undermining the Dominance
of Emotional Control

Intervention	Clinical commentary
Creative hopelessness	Is the client willing to consider that there might be another way, but it requires not knowing?
What brought you into treatment?	Bring into session client's sense of being stuck, life being off track, etc.
Person in the Hole exercise	Illustrate that the client is doing something and it is not working, but nothing else can work until the client stops digging
Chinese handcuffs Metaphor	No matter how hard the client pulls to get out of them, pushing in is what it takes
Noticing the struggle	Tug of war with a monster; the goal is to drop the rope, not win the war
Feed the Tiger Metaphor	Teaches client that the more emotional control strategies are used, the more they are needed in a ratcheting upward cycle
Driving with the Rearview Mirror	Even though control strategies are taught, doesn't mean they work
Clear out old to make room for new	Field full of dead trees that need to be burned down for new trees to grow; let go of things that don't work
Break down reliance on old agenda	"Isn't that like you? Isn't that familiar? Does something about that one feel old?"
Paradox	Telling client confusion is a good outcome highlights the fact that the old familiar logic may not work here
Feedback screech metaphor	Its not the noise that is the problem, it's the amplification caused by control strategies
Control is a problem	How the client struggles against unwanted experience = control strategies
The paradox of control: Rule of mental events	"If you aren't willing to have it, you've got it."
Illusion of control metaphors	Fall in love, jelly doughnut: Shows that even positive emotions or thoughts can't be controlled
Consequences of control	Polygraph metaphor: Shows that the higher the "stakes" for establishing control, the more uncontrollable the result

in it. In this portion of ACT treatment, you will teach your client about willingness as a choice to make undefended contact with psychological barriers in the serve of chosen values. Typical ACT interventions for developing acceptance and willingness are presented in Table 2.2. (Parenthetically, the techniques listed in all of these tables often have applicability to more than one core processes, but for the sake of clarity we have not listed the same techniques in multiple areas).

Table 2.2. ACT Interventions for Promoting Willingness and Acceptance

Intervention	Clinical commentary
Unhooking	Thoughts/feelings don't always lead to action
Identify the problem as useless struggle	When we battle with our inner experience, it distracts and derails us. Use examples.
Defining the impact of avoidance	Avoided experiences are allowed to function as barriers to heading in the direction of valued goals.
Experiential awareness	Learn to pay attention to internal experiences, and to how we respond to them
Skiing down the hill metaphor	Change orientation from rejection to embracing feared experience
Amplifying responses	Bring experience into awareness, into the room; "Can you make that feeling a little bigger?" You can approach and play with private experiences; experience often decreases in intensity in paradoxical fashion
Empathy	Participate with client in emotional responding; "What just showed up for you? Can you just sit with it without struggle?" Teaches client to hold still and notice, rather than avoid
The Serenity Prayer	Change what we can, accept what we can't.
Practice doing the unfamiliar	Pay attention to what happens when you don't do the automatic response
Acceptance homework	Go out and find what you fear and let yourself just be there without struggle
Mind-reading exercise:	Helps client just notice a variety of thoughts that are "pulled" when asked to think about a feared or unwanted experience
Journaling	Write about painful events
Tin Can Monster Exercise	Systematically explore response dimensions of a difficult overall event; teaches client to let go of struggle and instead just accept a difficult private experience
Distinguishing between clean and dirty emotions	Trauma = pain + unwillingness to have pain; pain is natural and non-toxic but the struggle to eliminate pain creates trauma
Distinguishing willingness from wanting	Bum at the door metaphor—you can welcome a guest without being happy he's there
How to recognize trauma	Are you less willing to experience the event or more? Teach client that experiences are not inherently traumatic, unless avoided or struggled with in some way
Distinguishing willingness the activity from willingness the feeling	Opening up is more important than feeling like it. You can do an act of willingness even though you don't like what you are exposed to

(*continued*)

Table 2.2. (*Continued*)

Intervention	Clinical commentary
Choosing Willingness: The Willingness Question	Given the distinction between you and the stuff you struggle with, are you willing to have that stuff, as it is and not as what it says it is, and do what works in this situation?
Two scales metaphor	Shows client that willingness level can be deliberately set, whereas private experience is automatic and uncontrollable
Tantruming kid metaphor	Teaches client that putting qualitative limits on willingness creates a paradoxical surge of unwanted experience
Distinguish willing from wallowing	Moving through a swamp metaphor: the only reason to go in is because it stands between you and where you intend to go
Sitting face to face, eye contact exercise	Shows how even little acts of willingness can elicit huge emotional barriers

While the quality of willingness is more all or none, the context in which it occurs can vary greatly. It is possible to be willing to feel one feeling, but not another; to be open in one situation and not another; for one time frame and not another. The ACT therapist finds a way to begin the process and walks with the client step by step until the action is well known, and the client is able to continue this process of growth in normal living. After that, the contingencies themselves take hold, which is probably why continued improvement in follow-up has been regularly found in ACT outcome studies.

The key therapeutic messages include:

- Willingness/acceptance is an alternative to emotional control and struggle
- What would you have to accept to move your life toward what you value?
- Focus on what you can control and change (your behavior) and accept what you can't
- Willingness is a choice, not a decision
- Willingness is not wanting; you don't have to want something to be willing to have it
- Willingness is an action, not a thought or feeling

Generally, the exercises, metaphors and behavioral tasks that help promote willingness/acceptance as an alternative to experiential control can be tailored to fit the struggles the client has been facing. For example, one frequent ACT strategy is to elicit feared material in the therapy session and then to use various exercises (i.e., tin can monster, monsters on the bus) to help the client address that material directly with the assistance of the therapist. It is also important to emphasize that the qualitative attributes of willingness are present in the smallest act. Being willing for seconds can put the client in the same "space" as being willing for hours. This awareness helps you avoid over-reaching the clients tolerance level in the name of making some heroic change. This is not only likely to fail, but it may reactivate the client's avoidance strategies because of the perceived threat.

Some clients rapidly discover that willingness works and some don't. Generally, those who don't have significant problems with cognitive fusion.

Undermining Cognitive Fusion

The concept of cognitive fusion is central to the ACT model of human suffering. Fusion is the tendency of human beings to live in a world excessively structured by literal language. Language-based and direct functions become so fused, that humans often cannot distinguish a verbally-conceptualized and evaluated world from one that is being directly experienced. This is undesirable because it means that anything imported into human experience by language (e.g., conventional patterns of evaluation, the conceptualized past or future, emotional avoidance rules) will have its effects as if the effects are the product of nature itself.

Speaking technically, fusion is the dominance of particular verbal functions over other directly and indirectly available psychological functions. So for example, for the client who has the evaluation that anxiety is bad, anxiety, bad, and the "I" who has anxiety are inextricably fused. They are, psychologically, one thing in that moment. And, importantly, any other psychological functions that "I," bad, and anxiety might have will be obscured.

From a clinical perspective, when the client fuses with verbal content, that content can exercise almost complete dominance over the client's behavior. When fusion is combined with culturally supported messages that negative private events are toxic and the opposite of what a human being should expect, there is a very dangerous cycle that is set in motion. As the client tries harder and harder to eliminate and control private events that "must" be controlled, the more fused he or she becomes and a paradoxical ratcheting up of negative content occurs. From the client's point of view, this struggle for psychological health is life and death. While we have never treated a client who died from experiencing negative thoughts, feelings, memories or sensations openly and without defense, we know of many a client who would choose to die rather than have them.

The general goal of this core ACT process is to help the client detect the hidden properties of language that produce fusion, to shake the client's confidence in implicitly trusting the "reality" of private experiences and to recreate the "space" that exists between thought and thinker, feeling and feeler. You will try to teach the client to catch language in flight, and by doing so see private events for what they really are, not what they advertise themselves to be. This will ultimately help the client use willingness and acceptance strategies on a more consistent basis because defusing from thoughts and evaluations reduces their capacity to function as psychological barriers.

There are three particularly pernicious forms of fusion that you will attack in this component of treatment: 1) Fusion between evaluations and events they are tied to; 2) Fusion with the imagined toxicity of painful events; 3) Fusion with arbitrary causal relationships that, collectively, form the clients "story"; and 4) Fusion with a conceptualized past or future. Key therapeutic messages during this core process are:

- Your mind is not your friend, nor is it your enemy
- Who is responsible here? The mind or the human?
- Your thoughts and feelings don't cause behavior
- The most dangerous thing about your past is that your mind will make it into your future
- Which are you going to trust, your mind or your experience?
- Is it more important to be right, or to be effective?

Some of the more commonly employed ACT interventions used to pursue these clinical objectives are presented in Table 2.3. Note that there are at least four distinct levels of discourse within these interventions. One level works with the basic properties of language and thought in a direct way so as to reveal its highly automatic and programmable nature (i.e., milk, milk, milk; remember the numbers). The second level of interventions are designed to show how easily arbitrary relationships are formed at the conceptual level (why, why, why; autobiographical rewrite). These two levels are designed to help your client develop a healthy skepticism about the usefulness of the mind when it comes to "explaining" such things as personal history and/or contemporary states of mind. The third level of discourse is to attack the fusion of evaluations as human activities as opposed to evaluations as inherent properties of events (good cup, bad

Table 2.3. ACT Interventions for Promoting Defusion

Intervention	Clinical commentary
"The Mind"	Treat "the mind" as an external event; almost as a separate person
Mental appreciation: Thank your mind for that thought	Teach client how to separate self from minding and show aesthetic appreciation for the mind's products
Cubbyholing	Therapist labels private events as to kind or function in a back channel communication
"I'm having the thought that . . . "	Change language practice in session to include category labels in descriptions of private events
"Buying" thoughts	Use active language to distinguish thoughts and beliefs; makes evaluation a conscious choice, not automatic
Titchener's repetition (milk, milk milk)	Client repeats a difficult thought (I am damaged) over and over again until it ceases to sound like a thought
Physicalizing	Label; the physical dimensions of thoughts helps slow down attachment, recontextualizes experience of thinking
Put them out there	Sit next to the client and put each thought and experience out in object form; creates "distance" between event and perceiver
Sound it out	Say difficult thoughts very, very slowly
Sing it out	Sing your thoughts
Silly voices	Say your thoughts in other voices—a Donald Duck voice for example
Polarities: You are perfect, you are scum experiential exercise	Strengthen the evaluative component of a thought and watch it pull its opposite; helps highlight dialectical nature of language, self evaluations
Teach me how to walk	Try to instruct nonverbal behavior; shows limitations of language in understanding whole acts
Your mind is not your friend	Suppose your mind is mindless; who do you trust, your experience or your mind
Who would be made wrong by that?	If a miracle happened and this cleared up without any change in (list reasons), who would be made wrong by that?
Strange loops	Point out a literal paradox inherent in normal thinking
Thoughts are not causes	"Is it possible to think that thought, as a thought, AND do x?"
Choose being right or choose being alive	If you have to pay with one to play for the other, which do you choose?
There are four people in here: you, me, your mind and my mind	Opens therapy discussion on how to connect as humans when minds are listening

(continued)

Table 2.3. (*Continued*)

Intervention	Clinical commentary
Who is in charge here? You? Or your mind?	Treat thoughts as bullies; use colorful language to show that you distinguish between the client and the client's mind
Take your mind for a walk	Walk behind the client chattering mind talk while they choose where to walk; teaches client to have mental chatter and choose
How old is this? Is this just like you?	Step out of content and ask these questions
And what is that in the service of?	Step out of content and ask this question
OK, you are right. Now what?	Take "right" as a given and focus on action
Mary had a little	Say a common phrase and leave out the last word; link to automatic nature of thoughts the client is struggling with
Get off your buts	Replace virtually all self-referential uses of "but" with "and"; teaches client the dialectic of "both and"
What are the numbers?	Teach a simple sequence of numbers and then point out the arbitrariness and yet permanence of this mental event
Why, why, why?	Show the shallowness of causal explanations by repeatedly asking "why"
Create a new story	Write down the normal story, then repeatedly integrate those facts into other stories
Find a free thought	Ask client to find a free thought, unconnected to anything else shows the inherent paradox of language. To succeed requires linking to other thoughts
Do not think "x"	Specify a thought not to think and notice that you do
Find something that can't be evaluated	Look around the room and notice that every single thing can be evaluated negatively
Flip cards	Write difficult thoughts on 3 x 5 cards; flip them on the client's lap vs. keep them off
Carry cards	Write difficult thoughts on 3 x 5 cards and carry them with you
Carry your keys	Assign difficult thoughts and experiences to the clients keys. Ask the client to think the thought as a thought each time the keys are handled, and then carry them from there

cup; get off our buts). This set of interventions basically attacks the client's "attachment" to the evaluative functions of reason giving. The fourth level of interventions shifts attention toward the process of thinking, rather than the products of thinking (e.g., thank your mind for that thought; making the mind an "it"; leaves on a stream).

Getting in Contact with the Present Moment: Self as Process

Acceptance and defusion are in the service of "showing up" to the present moment, connecting with one's values, and living. Being present is revealed in qualities of vitality, spontaneity, connection, and creativity. When the therapy drifts into conceptualized content, often heavily evaluative and laden with verbal temporal relations of the past or future, the ACT therapist brings the process back into the present. This tends to undermine avoidance and fusion and grounds the clients experience in a continuing process of awareness of what is occurring now, and now, and now (what RFT has called self-as-process; Barnes-Holmes, Hayes, & Dymond, 2001).

The benefits of this focus are also felt in the therapeutic relationship and in the flexibility of the therapist. Attending to now requires a sensitivity to multiple levels of analysis when dealing with any bit of client behavior: the content of what the client is saying or doing; this as a particular kind of behavior occurring in the moment (e.g., thinking, feeling, remembering, sensing); this as a functional process occurring in the moment (e.g., emotional avoidance); this as an example of behavior outside of session; this as move in the therapeutic relationship occurring in the moment; and this as a general sample of social behavior. It is not possible to avoid content altogether, but by far the more important levels are often those that are outside of the literal story being told. The key therapeutic messages include:

- Life is not something that will be lived when you get rid of your problems—life is going on *now*
- There is as much living in a moment of pain as in a moment of joy
- Would you be willing to notice what is going on within you and between us now
- Thoughts and feelings often present themselves as about the past or future, but they are experienced now and from the point of view of now

Some of the more common behavioral tasks, metaphors and exercises are presented in Table 2.4. Amplifying the ability to notice what is present is a feature of mindfulness, and these exercises can be useful here. Interoceptive exposure, inventorying, and communications of feelings in a relationship are all examples of present focused interventions. There is overlap between self-as-context and self as process, because exercises that involve noticing that which is experienced in the present moment (self-as-process) will also be opportunities to point to the "you" that is noticing (self-as-context).

Table 2.4. ACT Interventions for Increasing Contact with the Present Moment

Intervention	Clinical commentary
Showing up for what is there	What is showing up for you right now? Brings client into the present; often used when affective shifts occur or when no affect is present
How are you feeling about this right now?	Therapy relationship interaction that brings the client into the immediate interaction with therapist relative to some provocative or evocative content
Just noticing exercise	Asks client to simply be aware of any thoughts, feelings, memories or sensations that are present
Mindfulness exercises	Controlled breathing, visualization exercises designed to get the client present; often useful to start sessions
Identifying when getting present is needed	Ask client to identify situations where being absolutely present is needed (i.e., applying first aid)
Tin Can Monster	Bring a feeling into the session and then help client see it in a new context
Experiential seeking	Getting present exercise that asks client to focus on sights, smells, sounds and other sensations in the room
Journaling continuous reactions	Asks client to journal in narrative fashion reactions to daily events, focusing on evocation of thoughts, feelings, memories and sensations
Leaves on a stream exercise	Client asked to notice each private event in an eyes closed exercise and place each event on a leaf floating down a stream; useful for creating simple awareness
Future-Past-Now	Client is asked to pull awareness into the exact moment when dialogue shifts to the past or the future
Practice being human	Try to get present with another person as a human, not an object; notice what you see and experience

Distinguishing the Conceptualized Self from Self-as-Context

Another core process in ACT is to help your client experience the distinction between the content of human private experiences and the context in which those experiences occur. Most clients have difficulty with detachment because they have insufficient skills for contacting an immutable sense of self that is available to us all. This is what ACT describes as "self-as-context." This is the context of simple psychological awareness and it has no boundaries. Self-as-context is the way we speak of the "I" that was and has always been there, has seen everything I have seen, and has been everywhere I have been. If a person cannot reliably make contact with this psychological space, then the products of daily human experience can be very threatening. If there is no distinction between the thought and thinker, feeling and feeler, then the content of these events will invite struggle. Seen for what they are, just the products of a human history, there is no particular need to struggle. In targeting this process, you will use various metaphors, exercises and behavioral tasks to help the client develop this simple, but elusive awareness. The core therapeutic messages are as follows:

- You are not your thoughts, emotions, memories, roles
- There is a you that is not "thing like" that has been present your whole life
- When something is fearsome, notice who is noticing it
- You are perfectly made to experience your own experience
- The contents of your awareness are not bigger than you; you contain them
- You are a safe place from which you can have experiences for what they are

The various ACT interventions that have been developed to promote self-as-context are listed in Table 2.5. As you will notice, this is where some of the mindfulness and meditation components of ACT appear. Your client needs to make direct experiential contact with this space, so as to appreciate its unique non-verbalizable qualities. When the client is able to discriminate between conceptualized versions of self (the client's life story, self-evaluations, etc.) and the context in which these events occur (I am the person having these thoughts, feelings, evaluations, etc), a major step in building long term psychological flexibility has been achieved.

Values

Of all the attributes that separate humans from other members of the animal kingdom, perhaps none is as important as our ability to conceive a purpose and then behave with regard to that purpose. Clients that are stuck in the trap of emotional control and avoidance slowly lose the "guidance mechanism" that leads to purposeful, enriching patterns of behavior. Their behavior becomes more and more "in the service of" controlling and eliminating unwanted private events or distressing external outcomes. The cost of this agenda over time is embodied in the ACT saying, "Work to control your feelings and lose control of your life." The ultimate goal of ACT is to help the client regain a sense of life direction that is consistent with his or her values and then begin acting in a way that is consistent with those values. In ACT, we are relatively uninterested in helping the client "get in touch with feelings, for feelings sake." There is nothing intrinsically

Table 2.5. ACT Interventions for Promoting Self as Context

Intervention	Clinical commentary
Observer exercise	Notice who is noticing in various domains of experience; brings attention back to self as source of experience
Therapeutic relationship	Model unconditional acceptance of client's experience.
Chessboard metaphor	Shows client that "good" and "bad" private events are just components of consciousness
Furniture in the house metaphor	Pretty and ugly furniture is all contained by and measured against the qualities of the house; shows client that unpleasant or negative content is not "bigger than" the human that has it
Confidence the feeling vs. confidence the action	Take actions that reflect inherent fidelity to self; teaches client that it is not the outcome of an act but the quality of self fidelity that is important
Riding a bicycle	You are always falling off balance, yet you move forward; metaphor for continuous experience of losing and regaining contact with self as context
Experiential centering exercise: Sequential expansion of perspective	Make contact with self-perspective in chair, on ceiling, from roof, from 100 miles up; shows that the same self awareness is present despite shifts in perspective
Practicing unconditional acceptance	Permission to be—accept self as is, as perfectly made and exactly as it should be
The you that you call you	Separates out what changes and what does not in human experience; thoughts, emotions, physical maturity change but consciousness never does
Two computers exercise	Teaches client that sitting back is the only way to contact self as context; up close the content is too threatening to let go
Programming process	Content is always being generated—generate some in session together; notice that there is someone observing this content
Self evaluations are different than the experience of self	Thoughts/feelings about self (even "good" ones) don't substitute for the direct experience of consciousness
Self as object of analysis	Describe the conceptualized self, both "good" and "bad"; shows client how evaluations shift and there is always an evaluator present
Getting back on the horse	Connecting to the fact that they will always move in and out of perspective of self-as-context, in session and out
Contrast observer self with conceptualized self	Pick an identity exercise

life enhancing about wallowing in one's own emotional soup. The reason for teaching clients to detach from "hot" events, to experience such events from the self-as-context, to let go of the struggle for emotional control is that private experiences function as barriers to valued actions. To pursue valued ends in life, the client has to be willing to have all of the negative content that goes along with being human. In this portion of ACT treatment, you will help the client begin to clarify valued life directions that will dignify making undefended contact with psychological barriers. The key therapeutic messages include:

- What do you want your life to stand for? And are you doing that now?
- In a world where you could choose a direction in your life, what would you chose?
- Are you willing to do what needs to be done to move toward valued ends?

Some of the more common behavioral tasks, metaphors and exercises are presented in Table 2.6. Note that in this part of ACT, whenever it occurs, there will normally be a formal attempt at values clarification. The original ACT book presents a values assessment protocol that has stimulated significant development of methods for assessing values and setting specific goals, actions and strategies. One such device is presented in the chapter on ACT in Medical Populations. There are several other values assessment questionnaires under development at the time of this writing, such as the Valued Living Questionnaire (see the Resource Appendix for more information on how to access these tools).

Building Patterns of Committed Action

What makes ACT a quintessentially behavioral treatment is that creative hopelessness, defusion, connecting with self, acceptance, contact with the present moment, and valuing must lead to actual concrete differences in the client's behavior that service those valued ends. The trap the client is in consists of highly elaborate patterns of action that lead nowhere except toward greater and greater emotional and behavioral avoidance. The goal of ACT is to help the client discover the nature of this trap, and to develop methods of dissolving it in the service of living. Eventually, the client has to "vote with his or her feet" or that time has been wasted.

At the same time, engaging in valued actions almost invariably triggers psychological barriers. No one effortlessly glides through life without hitting barriers. The key question asked by life at this point is, "Will you

Table 2.6. ACT Interventions for Values Clarification and Seeking Valued Ends

Intervention	Clinical commentary
Your values are perfect	Point out that values cannot be evaluated, thus your values are not the problem
Tombstone	Have the client write what he/she stands for on his/her tombstone
Eulogy	Have the client hear the eulogies he or she would most like to hear
What do you want your life to stand for?	Values intervention for a specific life dilemma that requires some type of response from the client
Values clarification	List values in all major life domains
Goal clarification	List concrete goals that would instantiate these values
Action specification	List concrete actions that would lead toward these goals
Barrier clarification	List barriers to taking these actions
Taking a stand	Ask client to stand up and declare a value without avoidance; helps promote intention to act
Is what you're doing in life now consistent with what you value?	Highlights discrepancy between current behaviors and valued life ends; can have a motivational impact
Traumatic deflection	What pain would you have to contact to do what you value
Pick a game to play	Define a game as "pretending that where you are not yet is more important than where you are"—define values as choosing the game
Point on the horizon	Picking a point on the horizon is like a value; heading toward the tree is like a goal
What if no one could know?	Imagine no one could know of your achievements: then what would you value?

experience the barrier and keep going, or will you stop?" It isn't so much whether this basic question will surface, but rather in what form, when, and how frequently. This core process often is the culmination of ACT because once patterns of committed action develop, life takes over and the therapist's role is done.

Committed action patterns start small, but part of the goal of this phase of ACT is to show the client how to build larger and larger patterns, so that habits of action serve the clients interests rather than compete with them. Maintaining a commitment for a moment is a start; doing so for a day is an improvement; and for a week is even better. It is not a problem that sometimes slips occur: it is precisely the moment in which barriers to building even larger patterns of committed action can be dissolved. Taking responsibility for the slip, and doing something different with it, allows a pattern of "commit and slip" (or, far worse, "commit, slip, and quit") to turn into a pattern of committed actions that are broader, longer, deeper, and more elaborated.

So far as we know, there is no finish line to this process. No matter how "big" one gets, there is more "big" to get. Making commitments does not mean a commitment to never fail. Commitment involves living the value in the extended moment. This does not mean that we will not fail: it means that we are not leaving ourselves an out, and when we failed, we take responsibility for it and rejoin the commitment.

In this core process, the major goal is to help the client develop sustainable, value driven behavior patterns that involve approach toward successive moments of now. The key therapeutic messages during this phase are as follows.

- Goals are just a process by which the process can become the goal
- Behaving confidently is different than feeling confident
- You are response-able
- Focus on building larger and larger patterns of effective action
- If you slip, notice the pattern and return to your commitment
- Can you keep moving toward what you value, even when the obstacles surface?

During this phase, ACT makes significant use of a variety of "journey" messages, where the goal is not so much reaching an outcome as it is participating in the process of seeking an outcome. Some of the more common behavioral tasks, metaphors and exercises are presented in Table 2.7. Committed action can start with limited goals and just begin to enlarge upon the client's willingness to act. We are not so much concerned with the magnitude of these acts, as we are with the extent to which they help the client make experiential contact with value driven, approach oriented behavior. In fact, it is safe to predict that, for some clients, taking even a small step in the direction of vitality will immediately produce the same psychological barriers that have stalled the client in bigger venues. For example, the chronically stuck client may struggle with the very possibility of becoming a functional, contributing member of society, because this means the client's "story" will no longer be right. Another client may get frustrated and begin withdrawing when failure occurs with a seemingly straightforward value driven goal. Whatever the blockage, you must keep encouraging the client to "play" and to learn from the process, instead of being obsessed with the outcome. Whatever the client learns from contacting the process is exactly what the client needs to learn to grow as a human being.

Table 2.7. ACT Interventions for Promoting Patterns of Committed Action

Intervention	Clinical commentary
Relationship of goals and process	Committed action starts a process in which the process becomes the goal
Skiing down the mountain metaphor	Down must be more important than up, or you cannot ski; if a helicopter flew you down it would not be skiing; works against tendency of client's to be focused on outcomes of actions
Switchback metaphor	To reach the top of a mountain requires going in directions that seem wrong but in fact are the only way to the top; helps client anticipate barriers to committed action, avoiding misleading evaluations of "progress" toward life goals
Hikers on a path metaphor	On the path up the mountain, you might be convinced you are never going to get there; a person across the valley with binoculars can see you are going in precisely the right direction; teaches client to decrease emphasis on outcome and stick with commitments
Coke vs. 7 Up	Have client choose which one is favorite drink and then ask why, repeatedly to each reason given. Highlights that choosing is an act made with reasons, but not for reasons
Choosing not to choose	You cannot avoid choice because no choice is a choice; helps client appreciate that choosing actions is ever present
Responsibility and blame	You are response-able. That is different from being to blame. Teaches client that self blame has no relationship to being able to behave
Jump from a book or piece of paper	Teaches client that it is not the magnitude of a committed act that matters; it is the quality of committed action that matters; helps avoid setting heroic commitments with a high failure rate
Sticking a pen through your hand	Suppose getting well required this—would you do it; creates expectation that some painful content will have to be accepted to move toward desired life goals
Who would be made right if you got your life back?	Addresses right and wrong issues that some clients have that may lead to self defeating results with committed action
Fishhook Metaphor	Addresses need to release another person the client blames for life difficulties
Foregiveness: To give oneself the grace that came before	Specifies that the act of forgiveness is an act of grace toward self, not a denial of wrong doing
Confronting the little kid	Bring back the client at an earlier age to ask the adult for something

Table 2.7. (*Continued*)

Intervention	Clinical commentary
First you win; then you play	Choose to be worthy (because it cannot be "earned" or logically derived) then start with committed action
Taking responsibility for each act (e.g., I am the person that chose to stop drinking, drank on Thursday, then thought "What's the point in stopping, I can't do it" and gave up my commitment")	Linearly compile the client's successes and failures with a commitment in narrative self-description; helps keep client from giving up on a commitment because of a failure or sequence of failures

Even as committed action generates barriers that will require acceptance and defusion it will also generate vitality. One of the stories we create is that there is some accomplishment that will make us feel alive, virtuous and vital. However, it is in our movement, in the present moment, that we find vitality. What this means in practice is that any movement, however small, that is values-consistent will add vitality to our clients. Of course, the client who moves a tiny bit, may stop and reflect on the fact that they could have moved years before or could have moved more. Stalling out in such a reflection is a lapse out of the here and now and into the conceptualized world of "if only." There is no vitality in that world. The only solution is to notice the lack of vitality in that moment of morbid reflection, to rejoin our commitment, and then to notice the vitality in that moment of rejoining.

COMPETENCIES OF THE ACT THERAPIST

It is difficult to describe the core competencies of the ACT therapist. Why? Because the very space from which ACT originates leads to the development of new behavioral tasks, experiential exercises and metaphors in flight, session by session, moment by moment. This is why describing ACT simply as a finite set of tasks, exercises, metaphors and homework assignments does a disservice to those who are practicing it. If the goal of ACT is to help generate psychological flexibility in the client, then surely it has to involve the modeling of psychological flexibility by the therapist. ACT is more a set of functions or processes than techniques. Nevertheless, with such a rich set of treatment strategies to draw from, it is silly to insist that technique is unimportant in producing good results. Too many qualified therapists have done too much work already within the set of processes defining ACT for this content to be irrelevant as a set of procedures focused on these processes, particularly by beginning ACT therapists.

In the end, we believe there are ways to differentiate "good" ACT treatment from "bad" ACT treatment. The distinction between good and bad is partly determined by how well the core processes just described are integrated into treatment. That involves knowledge of the core messages contained within each process as well as associated experiential exercises, tasks, metaphors, and out of session tasks. In addition, our experience in training suggests that the posture of the ACT therapist is quite distinctive and is easy to identify in the therapy room. The analogy we would draw is what it takes to be a good skier. There is a certain basic "skiing position" that all good skiers have. Without this position in place, it is impossible to make all of the specific maneuvers that will later be needed on the slope. At the same time, each specific maneuver has its own physical requirements and those must be made as well. Otherwise, the skier will fall at the time that specific maneuver is required. To go one step further, there are an endless number of ways good skiers "individualize" these specific maneuvers to fit their style of skiing. Similarly, the ACT therapist has to have a good basic ACT position, must be able to make specific ACT maneuvers based upon a thorough understanding of the core processes and must be able to individualize these maneuvers to fit the reality of each individual client. In this section, we will describe two sets of interrelated core competencies. One has to do with the general attitude, stance and demeanor of the therapist. The other has to do with understanding the core processes and delivering interventions that support those processes.

Core Competencies Involved in the Basic ACT Therapeutic Stance

The basic psychological stance of the ACT therapist is an especially important factor in providing good treatment. This involves being able to make contact with the "space" from which ACT naturally flows, as well as modeling certain facets of psychological flexibility that we seek to impart to the client. Like many treatment traditions, ACT emphasizes the importance of therapist warmth and genuineness. This stance emerges quite naturally from the core understanding of human suffering from an ACT perspective. When we see our clients trapped by language, we see ourselves and the traps which generate our own pain. An "I and thou" perspective is the natural precipitant of this recognition. Collectively, the following attributes define that basic therapeutic stance of ACT.

- The therapist speaks to the client from an equal, vulnerable, genuine, and sharing point of view and respects the client's inherent ability to move from unworkable to effective responses
- The therapist actively models both acceptance of challenging content (e.g., what emerges during treatment) and a willingness to hold contradictory or difficult ideas, feelings or memories
- The therapist helps the client get into contact with direct experience and does not attempt to rescue the client from painful psychological content
- The therapist does not argue with, lecture, coerce or attempt to convince the client of anything.
- The therapist introduces experiential exercises, paradoxes and/or metaphors as appropriate and de-emphasizes literal "sense making" when debriefing them
- The therapist is willing to self disclose about personal issues when it makes a therapeutic point
- The therapist avoids the use of "canned" ACT interventions, instead fitting interventions to the particular needs of particular clients. The therapist is ready to change course to fit those needs at any moment.
- The therapist tailors interventions and develops new metaphors, experiential exercises and behavioral tasks to fit the client's experience, language practices, and the social, ethnic, and cultural context
- The therapist can use the physical space of the therapy environment to model the ACT posture (e.g., sitting side by side, using objects in the room to physically embody an ACT concept)
- ACT relevant processes are recognized in the moment and where appropriate are directly supported in the context of the therapeutic relationship

Core Competencies for ACT Core Processes and Therapeutic Interventions

Once in the correct therapeutic posture, the ACT therapist must demonstrate competency in understanding the core processes and be technically facile in selecting and implementing interventions such as experiential exercises, metaphors, paradox, behavioral tasks and selecting home based practice. The key thing to remember in conducting ACT is that simply applying these techniques in a vacuum is not consistent with good ACT practice. The techniques must "fit" with the contextual properties of the therapeutic interaction. For various areas of core competency, we will cite some typical ACT intervention strategies. At the same time, we encourage you to generate your own innovative exercises, metaphors, and tasks, particularly if they originate from the language system and experiential context of your client.

Developing Acceptance and Willingness/Undermining Experiential Control

- Therapist communicates that client is not broken, but is using unworkable strategies
- Therapist helps client notice and explore direct experience and identify emotional control strategies
- Therapist helps client make direct contact with the paradoxical effect of emotional control strategies
- Therapist actively uses concept of "workability" in clinical interactions
- Therapist actively encourages client to experiment with stopping the struggle for emotional control and suggests willingness as an alternative
- Therapist highlights the contrast in the workability of control and willingness strategies (e.g., differences in vitality, values, or meaning).
- Therapist helps client investigate the relationship between levels of willingness and suffering (willingness suffering diary; clean and dirty suffering)
- Therapist helps client make experiential contact with the cost of being unwilling relative to valued life ends (e.g., short term/long term costs and benefits)
- Therapist helps client experience the qualities of willingness (a choice; a behavior; not wanting; same act regardless of how big the stakes)
- Therapist can use exercises and metaphors to demonstrate willingness-the-action in the presence of difficult material (e.g., jumping, cards in lap, box full of stuff, Joe the bum)
- Therapist can use a graded and structured approach to willingness assignments
- Therapist models willingness in the therapeutic relationship and helps client generalize this skill to events outside the therapy context

(e.g., uses appropriate self-disclosure; brings difficult reactions to in session content into the room)

Undermining Cognitive Fusion

- Therapist can help client contact emotional, cognitive, behavioral or physical barriers and the impact attachment to these barriers have on willingness
- Therapist actively contrasts what the client's "mind" says will work versus what the client's experience says is working
- Therapist uses language conventions, metaphors and experiential exercises to create a separation between the client's direct experience and the client's conceptualization of that experience (e.g., get of our butts, bubble on the head, tin can monster)
- Therapist uses various interventions to both reveal that unwanted private experiences are not toxic and can accepted without judgment
- Therapist uses various exercises, metaphors and behavioral tasks to reveal the conditioned and literal properties of language and thought (e.g., milk, milk, milk; what are the numbers?)
- Therapist helps client elucidate the client's "story" while highlighting the potentially unworkable results of literal attachment to the story (e.g., evaluation vs. description, autobiography rewrite, good cup/bad cup)
- Therapist detects "mindiness" (fusion) in session and teaches the client to detect it as well

Getting in Contact with the Present Moment

- Therapist can defuse from client content and direct attention to the moment
- Therapist models contacting and expressing feelings, thoughts, or sensations in the moment within the therapeutic relationship
- Therapist uses exercises to expand the clients awareness of experience as an ongoing process
- Therapists tracks session content at multiple levels (e.g., verbal behavior, physical posture, affective shifts) and emphasizes being present when it is useful
- Therapist models getting out of the "mind" and coming back to the present moment
- Therapist can detect when the client is drifting into the past or future and teaches the client how to come back to now

Distinguishing the Conceptualized Self from Self-as-Context

- Therapist helps the client differentiate self-evaluations from the self that evaluates (e.g., thank your mind for that thought; calling a thought a thought; naming the event; pick an identity)
- Therapist employs mindfulness exercises (the you that you call you; soldiers in parade/leaves on the stream) to help client make contact with self-as-context
- Therapist uses metaphors to highlight distinction between products and contents of consciousness versus consciousness itself (e.g., furniture in house; chessboard; are you big enough to have you)
- The therapist employs behavioral tasks (take your mind for a walk) to help client practice distinguishing private events from the context of self awareness
- Therapist helps client make direct contact with the three aspects of self (i.e., conceptualized; ongoing process; context)

Defining Valued Directions

- Therapist can help clients clarify valued life directions (values questionnaire, value clarification exercise, what do you want your life to stand for, funeral exercise)
- Therapist helps client "go on record" as standing for valued life ends
- Therapist states his or her own values that are relevant to therapy and models their importance
- Therapist teaches client to distinguish between values and goals
- Therapist helps client distinguish between deciding and choosing and applies this to values
- Therapist distinguishes between outcomes achieved and involvement in the process of living
- Therapist accepts the client's values and, if unwilling to work with them, refers the client on to another provider or community resource

Building Patterns of Committed Action

- Therapist helps client identify value-based goals and build a concrete action plan
- Therapist encourages client to make and keep commitments in the presence of perceived barriers (e.g., fear of failure; traumatic memories; sadness; being right) and to expect additional ones as as a consequence of engaging in committed actions

- Therapist helps client appreciate the qualities of committed action (e.g., vitality, sense of growth)
- Therapist helps client develop larger and larger patterns of effective action
- Therapist non-judgmentally helps client integrate slips or relapses into the process of keeping commitments and building larger patterns of effective action

IMPROVING YOUR SKILLS AS AN ACT THERAPIST

There are many potential ways a therapist can improve skillfulness in integrating the basic ACT posture and improving technical skill in the application of the core processes. We have found that the following training strategies help cement "fluency" with core ACT concepts. Fluency is the ability to apply ACT concepts "on the fly," adapting strategies to the reality of the client, the language style of the client, and so forth. Any of these training experiences is better than no training experience and, similarly, the more of these training experiences you participate in, the more likely it is you will improve your skills as an ACT therapist. For ways of accomplishing the experiences listed below, consult the Resource Appendix at the end of the volume.

- Read both the original ACT treatment manual and this clinical handbook thoroughly (this will help you learn the basic tenets of the ACT model and its applications, less helpful with contacting the ACT space).
- Attend one or more ACT training workshops led by competent trainers (Basic exposure to the ACT space and ACT techniques).
- Attend an ACT intensive retreat (More intensive experiential contact with ACT space; will help you learn specific ACT techniques).
- Attend a mindfulness/meditation retreat or workshop (good for contacting the ACT "space," less useful with ACT techniques).
- Read ACT research literature.
- Attend conventions where ACT and RFT studies will be presented, and discuss them with presenters (common conventions in the United States are the Association for Advancement of Behavior Therapy and the Association for Behavior Analysis; for other conventions see the ACT website).
- Look at as many protocols as possible—even when the particular application is not one you work with. Looking at many applications will give you new ideas for your own applications and will help you

to see the principles at work independent of the particular presenting complaint.

- Read ACT transcripts, out loud, trying to get a feel for the normal flow of ACT interventions (to access these transcripts, go to the ACT website, mentioned last chapter. See also the list of other resources in the Resource Appendix).
- Join the ACT (and perhaps also the RFT) list serve (see ACT and RFT websites) and discuss questions you have there.
- Submit video tapes to an ACT center of excellence (good for getting feedback on your therapeutic posture and application of techniques; see appendix for the addresses of such centers and contact persons).
- Arrange clinical consultations with an experienced ACT therapist (Good for periodic feedback about both interventions; some help in the integration of the ACT posture).
- Arrange for extended supervision of your practice by an experienced ACT therapist (Best way to really learn both the ACT posture and become "fluent" in the application of techniques).
- Learn more about Relational Frame Theory, functional contextualism, and behavioral principles.
- Organize a discussion group/reading group/peer supervision group of professionals in your area interested in ACT.
- Talk about the group activities on the ACT online discussion group to find out things other groups have done.
- Use the list above of *Core Competencies for ACT Core Processes* and self-evaluate the degree to which you can engage in each skill. Self-identified areas of weakness can then become a focus in seeking additional training (for an instrument to use for this purpose see the ACT website).

CONCLUSION

These general ACT processes are not implemented in the abstract: they are implemented with real people struggling with real problems. In the chapters that follow we consider some of the kinds of problems people come into therapy wanting help for and will show the applicability of ACT to these problems. In so doing we are not buying into syndromal thinking: these groups of problems are simply guides to the general issues that emerge in real clinical practice with ACT.

Chapter 3

ACT Case Formulation

Steven C. Hayes, Kirk D. Strosahl, Jayson Luoma,
Alethea A. Smith, and Kelly G. Wilson

Because ACT is a contextual treatment, your attempts to conceptualize a presenting problem might be different from traditional case conceptualization models. The most important principle in contextual analysis is that you are not just assessing a particular symptom with a particular topography; you are also attempting to understand the functional impact of the presenting complaint. The same clinical complaint can function in dramatically different ways for clients. Thus, your case conceptualization and associated treatment plan may differ for clients with seemingly similar problems. For example, many patients are diagnosed with major depression, single episode (a categorical formulation) based on the number and severity of symptoms described by the patient (a topographical assessment). In clinical practice however, it is fair to say that no two depressed patients are alike. Each is unique in how their life space is organized, how depression affects their functioning (and vice versa) and how depressive beliefs and behaviors define the individual's sense of self and external world.

Understanding function in this way requires a focus on the learning history of the client as well as the current context in which events happen. An ACT therapist might be interested in a client's history of early childhood trauma, but in a way that differs slightly from more traditional approaches. The traditional conceptualization might use the trauma directly to explain current dysfunction. An ACT formulation would consider how this history might alter specific functional processes within the ACT model. For example, trauma might lead to a higher likelihood of emotional avoidance, since intensely negative experiences would set the stage for the use of avoidance-based coping. If the trauma is sufficiently intense and occurs before deictic frames fully establish a sense of self-as-context through the "I-here-now" fames, this sense of self might itself be undermined as a method of emotional avoidance (as might be seen in, for example, dissociative disorders). The trauma might lead to fusion with crucial thoughts, such as "the world is unsafe" or "I deserved to be abused." The contextual viewpoint emphasizes the dynamic and interactive nature of all of these processes, considered at any single point in time. The client will bring a multitudinous learning history into the present that includes trauma but includes many other specific helpful and hurtful processes as well. How this history is functionally organized will alter how the client interacts with situational variables in a way that either promotes or defeats the client's best interests.

The ACT case conceptualization framework is unique in that it is specified how various processes may relate to psychological flexibility. Psychological flexibility involves the ability to defuse from provocative or evocative private content, accept private experience for what it is, stay in touch with the present moment, differentiate a transcendent self from the contents of consciousness, make contact with valued life ends and build patterns of committed action in pursuit of those ends. When psychological flexibility is present, the contingencies tend to shape behavioral effectiveness and individuals tend to move through life in a way that promotes vitality, purpose and meaning. In a contrasting sense, individuals tend to present for professional help when they are struggling in one or more of the six basic areas that define flexibility. This very simple principle has an important implication: you should assess for factors that promote psychological flexibility and factors that detract from it and consider the unique configuration of these promoting and detracting factors. Naming the form that suffering takes (depression, anxiety, addiction) is not as important in ACT as understanding how deficits in the various domains of psychological flexibility are contributing to the client's suffering. Similarly, the interventions you select will typically be designed to help promote more effective functioning in one or more of these domains, while being less focused on the elimination of pain per se.

While each client presents with a unique learning history, contemporary context and presenting problem, conducting an ACT case conceptualization generally involves five distinct activities:

1. Analyze the scope and nature of the presenting problem
2. Assess factors affecting the client's level of motivation for change
3. Analyze the factors that detract from the client's psychological flexibility

4. Assess factors that are promoting psychological flexibility
5. Develop a treatment goal and associated set of interventions

Table 3.1 presents a simple case formulation matrix that you might use to guide this process.

ANALYZE THE SCOPE AND NATURE OF THE PROBLEM

Your assessment should begin with an analysis of the presenting problem as formulated by the client, often leading to a reformulation in ACT consistent terms. In Table 3.1, we have identified a simple, core set of questions that will help you conduct an ACT consistent analysis of the presenting problem. A full functional analysis of client problems may go beyond these ACT-related factors, so we do not mean for the assessment and formulation of ACT-relevant processes to substitute for general clinical assessment, assessment of physical health, neurological assessment, assessment of family functioning, and similar factors. There are also cases in which ACT-relevant factors are not central. For example, a pure skills acquisition issue, if it entails no issues of experiential avoidance, cognitive fusion, or values, will not be usefully addressed by ACT formulations. As is being shown in ACT clinical trials, however, it is surprising how frequently ACT-specified factors are central to clinical difficulties.

Normally, your client will nominate a set of negative private events (negative feelings, thoughts, memories, sensations, physical symptoms, and so on) as the "problem." In the current nosology, clinical disorders are generally defined by the content of such complaints (depression, anxiety, hallucinations, and so on). While the form of the complaint will define the disorder in the usual taxonomy, it is the functions that the presenting problems reflect that will define the true disorder from an ACT perspective.

Generally clients will have this goal for therapy: If we can eliminate one or more of these private events, then my life would change in a positive direction. A client with an "anxiety disorder," for example, will usually come into therapy wanting to reduce or eliminate anxiety. If the clinician asks more about what would change if this were to happen, positive life goals tend to be stated such as: "Well, I would be able to travel" (or "I would be able to keep a job," or "I would be able to have relationships"). Answers such as this have rich meaning in an ACT model. They indicate that negative private content (e.g., symptoms of anxiety) is functioning as a barrier. They suggest that experiential avoidance (e.g., the attempts to get rid of the anxiety) and cognitive fusion (e.g., fusion with verbal formulations about how to live more positively, such as, "first feel better,

Table 3.1. A Simple ACT Case Formulation Matrix

Sources of Psychological Flexibility	Presenting Problem Analysis (Core Questions)	Analysis of Motivational Factors	Factors Contributing to Psychological Inflexibility	Factors Contributing to Psychological Flexibility	Treatment Implications
Acceptance	What private experiences (thoughts, feelings, memories, sensations) is the client unwilling to have? What patterns of avoidance are in place? Can the client "make room" for experience in an undefended, non-judgmental way?				
Defusion	Is the client overly attached to beliefs, expectations, right-wrong, good-bad evaluations of experience? Does the client confuse evaluations and experience?				
Contact with the Present Moment	Does the client exhibit ongoing, fluid tracking of immediate experience? Does the client find ways to "check out" or get off into their head? Does client seem pre-occupied with past or future or engage in lifeless story telling?				
Self as Context	Can client see a distinction between provocative and evocative content and self? Is client's identity defined in simplistic, judgmental terms (even if positive), by problematic content or a particular life story?				
Contact with Values	Can client describe personal values across a range of domains? Does client see a discrepancy between current behaviors and values? Does client describe tightly held but unexamined goals (e.g., making money) as if they are values?				
Patterns of Committed Action	Is client engaged in actions that promote successful working? Does patient exhibit specific, step by step pattern of action? Can client change course when actions are not working? Are there chronic self control problems such as impulsivity, and self defeating actions?				

then live better") may have a role in the rigid focus on unworkable solutions that chronic difficulties usually entail. They also suggest certain possible values (wanting to participate in the world, to have relationships, to make a contribution). These might both be a source of healthy pain (the pain of not living a life is often much greater than the pain of unwanted private events) and an ally in clinical change.

Superficially, ACT treatment targets are different than the client's presenting problem. Instead of "eliminating anxiety so that I can start to live" (the client's view of the presenting problem) you may eventually reformulate "the problem" in other ways (e.g., "warring with anxiety" or more specifically "not getting on about the business of living while needlessly warring with anxiety"). At a deeper level such reformulations must be consistent with the client's true goals. The therapeutic contract and consent to a treatment plan is no mere formality that for reason. We will address this issue later in this chapter.

From a contextual perspective, your interest as the therapist is to look beneath the presenting problem considered formally and to detect the functional processes that are interfering with living a more satisfying life. From an ACT perspective usually the two most important initial questions are 1) What private experiences is the client attempting to avoid? 2) What avoidance behaviors are being used and how pervasive are they? This perspective is perhaps obvious with problems like anxiety or depression, but it is important to look beneath even those complaints that look like straightforward values or even skills development issues. For example, suppose a client says his problem is "I have not been able to build meaningful intimate relationships in my life." You might ask: "If a miracle happened and this problem was totally solved, how would your life be different?" The client might answer: "Well, I would have a committed relationship. I might eventually get married and have a family." This answer would indicate that the client is speaking of a legitimate life goal that is not heavily encrusted with emotional avoidance. Contrast this with a different answer to the same question: "Well, I would feel a lot better about myself and this horrible loneliness would go away." In this case the client may have been using "relationships" to help avoid making contact with negative self-evaluations or a sense of loneliness or alienation. Further exploration might reveal that this very agenda has been part of why past relationships have not worked well. The client's view of the problem is that building relationships needs to be the focus, but they are being used as a process, not as a legitimate outcome in their own right. The ACT therapist may see emotional avoidance as the issue.

Another common occurrence is one in which a "presenting problem" functions to promote experiential avoidance of a more basic and even more threatening problem. For example, a person may present with "anxiety" but the target may eventually be avoidance of anger, or a person may present with "depression" but the target may eventually be a failure to contact and act on core relationship and self-care values (e.g., as reflected in a failure to leave an irretrievably abusive and violent relationship).

For these reasons, you should avoid buying into or challenging the initial formulation presented by the client. Take an open, data gathering stance in which you assess the client's learning history, current situational triggers, the domains of avoided private events and specific behavior avoidance patterns.

MOTIVATION

Initially, it is not only important to understand the scope and nature of the presenting problem, but also the extent to which the client is in touch with the costs of unworkable patterns of behavior. In the ACT assessment sequence, motivation is contingent upon whether the client is sufficiently open to the view that current behavior patterns are not working to consider suspending them and trying out alternatives.

There are a variety of factors that can negatively impact the client's motivation, even in the presence of significant psychological suffering. In the case formulation matrix presented in 3.1, we would encourage you to form an assessment of factors that might promote or decrease the client's motivation to change. Note that many motivational barriers may be present in more than one domain of psychological flexibility. So, for example, a suicidal patient might insist that thinking about suicide "works" to relieve pent up emotional distress, as does avoidance of situations involving the potential for interpersonal rejection. The patient also presents a "rationale" based on personal history for why changing this pattern of behavior will never work. In terms of motivational barriers, there is the pay off for not accepting unwanted private experiences (the Acceptance Domain) and a set of closely held reasons for why this pattern cannot change (the Defusion Domain). As we have stressed repeatedly in the first two chapters, the domains of psychological flexibility exist in a reciprocal, interactive relationship. If you start an intervention in one area, it will ordinarily "pull" content from other areas. Hence, you are not necessarily in a situation where you have to pick the "right" intervention for the "right" domain. The assessment of motivational factors just gives you a "snapshot" of the important treatment factor and, usually, you will pick one or more ACT interventions to counter-act these negative forces.

Some of the more common motivational barriers are listed below, along with a brief suggestion for how to address them clinically.

- *Client's history of rule following and being right.* If this is an issue, consider confronting reason giving through defusion strategies; pit being right versus cost to vitality; consider need for self-as-context and mindfulness work to reduce attachment to the conceptualized self.
- *High level of conviction or behavioral entanglement with unworkable strategies.* This is usually seen as an insistence on doing the same thing even though the client admits it doesn't seem to work. If this is an issue, consider the need to undermine the improperly targeted change agenda, using creative hopelessness interventions.
- *Belief that change is not possible combined with a strong attachment to a story that promotes this conclusion.* This is often seen in chronically distressed clients or clients with history of repeated trauma. If this is an issue, consider using defusion strategies, especially attacking the attachment to the story; revisit the cost of not trying in terms of valued life goals; arrange behavioral experiments to test whether even small changes can occur.
- *Fear of the consequences of change.* This is often seen in clients that are hiding in unsatisfying relationships or jobs for fear of the unknown. If this is an issue, consider working on values clarification and teaching qualities of committed action, choice and decision; work on acceptance of feared experiences under conditions of change.
- *Domination of a rigid, content-focused self-identity in which changing would pose a threat to a dearly held set of self beliefs.* This is often seen in "therapy wise" clients or clients with a history of treatment failure. If this is an issue, consider undermining the story using various defusion strategies such as the autobiography rewrite; consider values work to get the client to make contact with the "cost" of holding to the story.
- *Domination of the conceptualized past or future.* This is often seen in clients complaining of excessive worry, regret, or anticipatory fear that functions to block effective behavior. If this is an issue, consider self-as-process and self-as-context work, including "just noticing" interventions, and experiential exercises to help make contact with the moment. Link this to defusion work so that temporal thoughts can be caught and observed without belief or disagreement.
- *Short term effect of ultimately unworkable change strategies is evaluated as positive.* This is often seen in addictive behaviors, chronic suicidality, or chronic pain. If this is an issue, consider values clarification and creative hopelessness work tied to what have you tried, asking how has it worked, what has it cost you?

- *Social support for avoidance and fusion.* This is often seen in trauma victims, "disabled" clients of all kinds and may involve relationships, family, and financial or institutional reinforcement. If this is an issue, early values clarification work can be used to highlight the cost of not changing.

FACTORS CONTRIBUTING TO PSYCHOLOGICAL INFLEXIBILITY

The next step in ACT case formulation is to assess the factors that are contributing to psychological inflexibility. You will probably already be developing hypotheses about this area just based upon your assessment of motivational determinants. These same determinants will often "cross over" to other columns in the case conceptualization matrix (indeed, one reason we did not try to fill out many of the columns in Table 3.1 is that the same questions and issues can appear in many cells). Generally, you will want to assess the nature, strength, and contextual control over of various forms of psychological inflexibility and establish any important interrelationships. Assessment areas may include:

- General level of experiential avoidance (e.g., core unacceptable emotions, thoughts, memories, bodily sensations; low levels of intimacy)
- Level of overt behavioral avoidance displayed (e.g., what parts of life has the client dropped out of, what activities/pursuits are not occurring that would occur if the problem were solved)
- General levels of poor persistence and self-control problems that might be behavioral indicators of avoidance (e.g., procrastination, under performing, poor health behaviors, impulsive behavior)
- Level of internally based emotional control strategies (e.g., negative distraction, negative self instruction, excessive self monitoring, dissociation)
- Level of behaviorally focused emotional control strategies (e.g., drinking, drug taking, smoking, self-mutilation, suicide attempting, over eating)
- Weak life direction (e.g., general lack of values; lack of effective involvement in work, intimate relationships, family, friends, exercise/nutrition, hobbies, recreation and leisure, spiritual practice; important goals that the patient has "checked out" of due to emotional avoidance or fusion)
- Fusion with evaluating thoughts and conceptual categories (e.g., domination of "right and wrong" even when that is harmful; high levels of reason-giving; overuse of "insight" and "understanding," self-loathing, comparisons with or critical attitudes towards others)

As you conduct your assessments over time, we would encourage you to profile findings within the rows of the case conceptualization matrix presented in Table 3.1. This will make it easier for you to select target areas that might result in greater clinical impact. In addition, changes in the case conceptualization matrix over time can give you a good read on how the various sources of inflexibility are interacting.

Since ACT emphasizes that these sources of psychological inflexibility are common for clients, it is easy to stop once you have detected one or two good examples. It is worthwhile to take the time to address each area with as much detail as time permits, because you are trying to understand the person in context. Creating this "snapshot" will provide you with valuable clinical information both about the pervasiveness of ACT-relevant processes and how the client conceptualizes these problems. For example, the client may have frequent conflicts at work. Suppose you see readily that part of this is due to the client's avoidant coping styles. The client may be afraid of addressing and resolving work related problems in an open and healthy way because of the emotional reactions that process will produce. Seeing this clearly, you may forget to ask whether there is also a connection between this problem and the domination of "right and wrong" thinking. That could be a big mistake since successfully targeting acceptance of the emotional reactions to openly resolving work related problems could then open up work relationships to attempts by the client to make others see the wrongness of their views—perhaps causing more severe work conflicts. The early stages of therapy may not be the time to address these difficulties with an intervention, but if you know the lay of the land you can formulate your ideas about what might lead to what and design intervention accordingly.

FACTORS CONTRIBUTING TO PSYCHOLOGICAL FLEXIBILITY

Nearly all clients bring into therapy an array of strengths that will help promote greater psychological flexibility. Most clients have had some level of contact (however briefly and infrequently) with acceptance, letting go of disturbing private experiences, moments of being in the present, standing up for a value, or engaging in a committed act. It is important to be aware of these factors and their potential for offsetting factors that detract from psychological flexibility. For example, some clients have exposure to both mindfulness and acceptance concepts based upon previous spiritual practice or participation in one of the many human potential programs. If these experiences have been positive for your client, this might be a strength you want to build upon. The client already knows something of the concept and it may be easier to select interventions that capitalize upon this. Conversely, if previous experience is problematic—such as confusing spirituality with dogma, or using mindfulness meditation as a means of experiential avoidance—you will need to be especially cautious or your interventions will be harnessed to unhelpful processes. For example, when you address self-as-context and mindfulness skills, you will have to find ways to distinguish what you are saying from what the client has used these tactics for in previous life situations.

It is also important to assess the skills your client possesses that can promote effective working in the external world. Does your client articulate a set of values that you can mobilize to help drive a behavior change plan? Does your client possess special educational, social or vocational skills that you can activate in the pursuit of making life work better? Consider whether your client possesses the skills to build an effective plan of value-based committed action. If these skills need to be developed further, you might target skills training directly in such areas as interpersonal effectiveness, time and stress management, personal problem solving, relaxation and recreation, or conflict resolution.

In general, we tend to look for certain types of psychological assets that, if mobilized properly, can "jump start" the patient toward more effective living. These might include:

- Prior positive experience with mindfulness, spiritual practice or human potential concepts
- Episodes in life where "letting go" of urges, self defeating thoughts, uncontrollable feelings led to greater personal efficacy (i.e., Alcoholics Anonymous, smoking cessation, getting through a death)
- Moments in life when the client felt intensely present and in contact with life, even if the experience involved negative affect
- Prior experiences where laughing at oneself, seeing the irony or humor in a situation seemed to decrease the gravity associated with it
- Times in the past when the client took a course of action that was painful but was consistent with their values
- Prior experiences with setting personal goals, taking step by step concrete steps to achieve them
- Prior experiences with starting in one life direction and ending up going in another more positive direction

SELECT A SET OF TREATMENT GOALS AND ASSOCIATED INTERVENTIONS

The two main outputs of the case conceptualization process are: 1) A set of treatment goals mutually agreed to by you and your client, and

2) A set of interventions that you intend to use to achieve those goals. This requires you to eventually discuss your impression of the "presenting problem" with the client and to get the client's informed consent to proceed with a course of treatment designed to achieve those goals. Some ways to talk about ACT as treatment model in the pursuit of achieving informed consent are presented in the first ACT book (Hayes, Strosahl & Wilson, 1999).

The process of establishing mutually agreed upon treatment goals is complicated by the fact that an ACT conceptualization of the "problem" can and often is very different from the client's conception of the problem. For example, a therapist attending an ACT workshop recently asked, "how can I do ACT in an anxiety disorders clinic? People come to us to get rid of anxiety. It is not my place to challenge that goal."

It is helpful to distinguish outcome goals (the ultimate ends therapy should produce) and process goals (the means that will produce those ultimate ends). In our clinical nosology and in our culture more generally we have deeply confused the two, so it is not surprising that clients do likewise. The ultimate outcome goals are up to the client (though of course clinicians are free to decline to work for goals that they view as unethical). As noted earlier, if a client does not justify a goal by an appeal to yet another goal, it is probably an outcome goal. Process goals, however, are in large part a scientific and professional matter. Knowing *how* to produce ends is part of what the clinician must do for the client. Clients do not usually know, for example, that emotional avoidance is horrifically ineffective, and thus that it might be relatively unhelpful to ask clinicians to enter into a therapeutic agreement to "get rid of anxiety."

Clients have both outcome goals (the lives they want to live) and process goals (how they might get there). Almost always clients have been unsuccessfully seeking specific process goals before coming into therapy. Despite that failure, they will generally ask you to help them do more of the same in therapy (itself a reflection of a kind of psychological rigidity). It is not required that clinicians agree to this plan, and generally ACT treatment goals do not.

The following analogy highlights the distinction between process complaints masquerading as treatment goals and true outcome goals. Suppose a person calls a plumber because there is water on the floor. When the plumber arrives the homeowner insists that in order to stop the water leak the plumber needs to work on a natural gas pipe located behind a cabinet. In this case, both the plumber and the person calling for help hold the same outcome goal (stopping the water leak). Despite that commonality of purpose a responsible plumber will decline to do what the consumer asks precisely because working on a gas line will not stop the leak and it would be both dangerous and a waste of time and money to open up a natural gas line. It should not be assumed that the consumer has the skills to diagnose the problem or to understand how to correct it: that is probably part of why a plumber was called in the first place. The plumber might explain that this pipe does not hold water (perhaps because it is black, not galvanized; or it goes to the stove, not the sink), and may provide an alternative process account (e.g., the leak is coming from a hole in the hot water heater). If the consumer insists on the plumber opening up a live gas line anyway, the plumber should probably decline to assist in this risky and useless course of action.

Clinicians are in this exact situation all the time. Quite often, the client is interested in achieving a process goal that is shaped by cultural forces (e.g., "feel goodism") but may not serve the client's long term interests. In this case, you may need to initiate a discussion about this type of psychological "plumbing problem" and how it can be fixed. In our experience, in the vast majority of cases what clients *really* want is to live a satisfying and effective human life, and they are encouraged to hear that there may be a more direct path to that goal that can begin now.

A feature of ACT is the huge variety of clinical interventions that are available to you the therapist and the relatively tight link between these interventions and the functional model that is at the core of this work. We have covered some of these interventions in the preceding chapter and we placed it in an unusual position (before the assessment chapter) because we thought it would help to have these in mind as you consider the case formulation processes that lead to their selection. When you have identified legitimate treatment goals in partnership with the client, we would encourage you to select interventions for the domains of psychological flexibility that you will target and record in the case conceptualization matrix. Just for the sake of demonstration, we have listed a variety of typical intervention goals below and a characteristic reason or two that they might be selected:

1. Generate creative hopelessness (client has not faced the unworkable nature of the current agenda)
2. Understand that emotional control is the problem (client does not understand experientially the paradoxical effects of control)
3. Experiential exposure to the non-toxic nature of private events through acceptance and defusion (client is afraid to change behavior because of beliefs about the consequences of facing feared events)
4. Generate experiences of self-as-context to facilitate experiencing of feared events in the present moment (client is unable to separate

self from reactions, memories, unpleasant thoughts; client needs safe place from which to engage in exposure)
5. Make contact with the present moment/mindfulness (client lives in conceptualized future, e.g., worry; client is not contacting reinforcements already present in the environment)
6. Values exploration (client does not have a substantial set of stated values or is out of contact with their values)
7. Engage in committed action based on chosen values (client needs help to rediscover a value based way of living; client's behavior is not generally productive or well-directed and client could use help in maintaining consistency of life direction; client has little motivation to engage in exposure)

ACT Specific Measurement Tools

Multiple methods of assessment may be useful to help with the case formulation as well as to determine response to treatment in a standardized way. It is important that you define the mutually agreed upon "outcomes" of treatment, then select a reliable, quantifiable way to measure achievement of these goals. In addition to your case conceptualization interview, the administration of standardized assessment tools may be useful. This could involve generic outcome and/or process measures or more specific ACT-relevant measures. One caution in using generic outcome measures such as symptom inventories is that they usually measure symptom form (number; severity) but not symptoms function (believability; psychological impact). Furthermore, often these symptoms are private events that are thought to be related to outcomes (which may be true in a typical context, but not necessarily in the kind of extraordinary contexts ACT helps establish). Very commonly, there is no measure of actual overt outcomes. For example, anxiety presence will be measured while neither the function of anxiety nor the overall level of life functioning will be addressed. In essence, this is the professional version of the "plumbing problem" above, in which the field itself insists on measuring gas lines instead of water leaks. This can create a misleading impression about treatment response. For example, in one study of ACT with hospitalized psychotic patients, the ACT intervention produced a *smaller* reduction in the number of patients admitting to hallucinations and delusions among psychotic patients than usual hospital treatment (Bach & Hayes, 2002). However, ACT patients were 50% less likely to be re-hospitalized than patients treated as usual, they reported their symptoms as being significantly less believable than patients treated with usual care, and rehospitalization was particularly low for those admitting to symptoms in the ACT condition but not in the treatment as usual condition. In essence, symptoms functioned completely differently in ACT (presence and believability in essence were measures of acceptance and defusion and were both positively related to overt behavioral outcomes), but if believability of symptoms and rehospitalization measures were unavailable it would have looked as though ACT was less effective and treatment as usual based purely on symptom occurrence.

In general, the best ACT process measures seem to focus on measuring client perceptions of the literal believability (that is, are they what they say they are) of clinical symptoms, and the degree of willingness to experience them while continuing to behave effectively. These kinds of cognitive fusion and acceptance measures have regularly been empirically linked to positive clinical outcomes in ACT. Measures of this kind are not difficult to construct. For example, patient diaries for those suffering with particular disorders can be used to gather lists of thoughts, feelings, bodily sensations, and the like that are linked to ineffective actions in particular domains. The ACT approach asks second order questions about these events. Instead of rating their frequency, clients will rate their believability when they do occur, or the willingness to experience these events and still behave effectively. There will soon be many measures of this kind.

There are also generic ACT measures. The Acceptance and Action Questionnaire (AAQ; Hayes, Strosahl, Wilson, Bissett et al., in press) seems to measure factors related to acceptance and committed action. The initial validation study yielded both a 9 and 16 item version of the instrument. A second validation study (Bond & Bunce, 2003) led to a slightly different 16 item version.

In population-based studies, the AAQ seems to work well as a measure of acceptance, and several studies have used the instrument successfully to show the role of experiential avoidance in stress, trauma, anxiety, depression and the like (e.g., Marx & Sloan, in press). In general, either of the AAQ-16 versions work better as a process measure than the 9-item version. An AAQ-2 is currently under development that is designed to tap into the broader concept of psychological flexibility.

Values assessments are also under development (Wilson & Murrell, in press). It is not yet clear if this will also function as a mediator of clinical response. No specific measures of self-as-context or contact with the present moment are available, but a number of mindfulness measures now exist that seem to tap into these domains.

Developing measures of second order change processes is a very rapidly developing area of ACT work, and the best way to keep up on current developments is through the world wide community of ACT practitioners and researchers. They can be accessed through several means listed in the resource appendix, but they especially include the ACT and RFT websites (www.acceptanceandcommitmenttherapy.com and www.relationalframetheory.com) which provide materials of this kind. Sections in these websites are devoted to assessment, intervention innovation, protocols, training, email list serves, and other issues of relevance to any practitioner interested in ACT and its underlying theory.

Part **II**

ACT with Behavior Problems

Chapter 4

ACT with Affective Disorders

ROBERT D. ZETTLE

The human, social, and financial costs associated with affective disorders in general, and major depression in particular, are well-documented. Lifetime prevalence rates for major depression in the United States range up to 17.1% (Welshman et al., 1996), while those for bipolar disorder are significantly lower at approximately 1% (Myers et al., 1984). Major depression is expected to become the second leading cause of disability worldwide by 2020 and, by itself, is estimated to cost businesses in this country $70 billion annually in health care, lost productivity, and other expenses (Tanouye, 2001). Tragically, such "other costs" can include the permanent loss of employees. About 15% of individuals who have been diagnosed with major depression will commit suicide at some point during the life span (Maris, Berman, Maltsberger, & Yufit, 1992).

The major goal of this chapter is to describe an ACT approach to conceptualizing and treating both major depression and dysthymia (there are reasons to believe this model of care might be helpful for patients who are diagnosed as bipolar, see Chapter 8, but that will not be the focus of this chapter).

Two small randomized clinical trials have been conducted comparing ACT versus cognitive therapy of depression (Beck, Shaw, Rush, & Emery, 1979). Cognitive therapy was deliberately selected as a comparison treatment because it provides a fairly stringent "benchmark" against which to evaluate the efficacy of ACT and because is has a clearly distinct model of change. In the first study (Zettle & Hayes, 1986), 18 depressed women received 12 weekly individual sessions of either cognitive therapy or ACT. The cognitive therapy condition was delivered by a person (RZ) trained by Aaron Beck. Participants in both conditions improved significantly from pretreatment through the end of a 2-month follow-up. Participants receiving ACT, however, were rated by a blind, independent evaluator as significantly less depressed at follow-up than those treated with cognitive therapy. The Automatic Thoughts Questionnaire (ATQ; Hollon & Kendall, 1980) and a Reasons Questionnaire, specifically developed to assess reason-giving for dysfunctional behavior, were analyzed as process measures. Participants in both therapy conditions reported significant and equivalent reductions in the frequency of depressive automatic thoughts as assessed by the ATQ. At posttreatment, patients treated with ACT reported significantly greater reductions in their belief in such thoughts than those receiving cognitive therapy. In effect, changes in believability of depressive thoughts occurred independently of reductions in their frequency for participants receiving ACT, consistent with its emphasis on undermining experiential avoidance. Further support that ACT and cognitive therapy operate through different mechanisms was suggested by findings from the Reasons Questionnaire. Specifically, participants treated with ACT showed a significant reduction from pretreatment to follow-up in the validity they attached to private events as reasons for engaging in dysfunctional behavior. Those receiving cognitive therapy showed only a slight and nonsignificant reduction in the degree to which they viewed private events as "good reasons" for dysfunctional behavior such as being suicidal.

In a second comparative outcome study (Zettle & Rains, 1989), ACT and cognitive therapy were delivered in a group format for 12 weekly sessions. A total of 31 depressed women were assigned randomly to ACT or to one of two variants of cognitive therapy. All three groups showed significant and equivalent, reductions in depression at posttreatment and at 2-month follow-up. An analysis of scores from the Dysfunctional Attitude Scale (DAS; Weissman & Beck, 1978) again suggested that ACT and cognitive therapy mediate change through discrepant processes. Participants treated with cognitive therapy reported significant reductions in DAS scores from pretreatment through follow-up, while those receiving ACT showed only slight non-significant reductions in depressive beliefs. As predicted, ACT patients did not seem as concerned about whether their dysfunctional beliefs were "true" or "false", since the content of thinking is not a particularly important target in ACT.

A third randomized trial compared ACT to treatment as usual (TAU) with people on sick leave due to depression (Folke & Parling, 2004). After treatment, the ACT group showed a significantly lower level of depression and higher level of quality of life, general health, and perceived level of functioning compared to the TAU group.

Collectively, these findings show positive effects for ACT on depression, equaling or bettering the outcomes from cognitive therapy. ACT appears to operate through a process different from that of cognitive therapy, but consistent with the model upon which ACT is based.

FORMULATION

Before discussing some of the more specific considerations involved in conceptualizing individual cases of affective disorders from an ACT perspective, more general comments about the approach seem in order. At a most basic and general level, ACT views affective disorders as the consequence of unsuccessfully attempting to *escape* from negative private events that individuals are unwilling to experience. While the generic concept of experiential avoidance encompasses both avoidance of and escape from unwanted psychological experiences (Hayes, Strosahl, & Wilson, 1999), the latter appears to play a relatively greater role in the case of affective disorders. Often, depressed patients will talk about their feeling state as being "numb" and "uninterested", communications that suggest depression and anhedonia function to provide a sort of emotional escape. The behavior patterns that are classically associated with depression (social withdrawal, loss of interest, low energy, self-focused negative attention) all seem consistent with the goals of experiential escape. As has been shown in the research on GAD, cognitive and behavioral symptoms often function to distract attention away from even more basic unwanted private events (see Chapter 5). This is probably a core functional feature of depression as well. The more depressed a person is, the harder it is to focus on problems that cause real emotional distress, and the less is expected behaviorally.

The specific negative private events that your patient is unwilling to have and the historical contexts under which they originally occurred must be determined on a case by case basis. Commonly, your patient will be trying to escape contact with self-deprecating thoughts related to perceived personal shortcomings, unwanted emotions such as guilt and sadness following a loss, painful memories of missed opportunities to pursue valued life goals or mistreatment by significant others that the individual already has been in psychological contact with for some time. In general, patients with depression are reacting to negative events that they have already experienced and continue to endure, even if only through remembering, rather than those that they anticipate and attempt to avoid. Cognitive fusion is a dominant component of this escape behavior: thoughts are not seen as thoughts but as literally true events. The process of thinking itself is largely missed: only the products are evident.

Just as the specific negative thoughts, feelings, memories, and other associated private events that trigger experiential escape will vary from patient to patient, so does the form of escape behavior. In my experience, conducting a complicated process of differential diagnosis that attempts to distinguish one form of affective disorder from another (e.g., major depressive disorder vs. bipolar I disorder vs. bipolar II disorder) is unlikely to be of much utility in developing an ACT case formulation. Similarly, efforts to classify subtypes of depression based upon predominant symptom patterns, such as endogenous versus reactive or retarded versus agitated (Grove & Andreasen, 1992) does not typically pay large dividends in treatment planning or outcome. This more traditional approach to describing depressive states incorporates a host of assumptions about depression (it is a biomedical syndrome, symptom elimination is the goal, symptoms have meaning outside the context in which they occur) that are less compatible with an ACT formulation. Such information is likely to be of limited utility as it fails to identify the particular private events from which the individual is seeking relief, any additional functions beyond escape that the affective disorder is possibly serving, and the multiple contexts that support and maintain the dysfunctional behavior. According to ACT, actions that serve the same function may differ topographically but receive support from somewhat different sources, and psychopathological behavioral patterns that are similar in their form may serve discrepant functions (Hayes, Wilson, Gifford, Follette, & Strosahl, 1996). Put simply, a contextualistic model like ACT might predict that a manic and major depressive episode are simply different ways of attempting to escape from the same unacceptable array of psychological experiences. The appropriate focus is not so much upon the symptoms of mania or depression per se (a first order change model), but rather upon functions these symptom behaviors serve in the patient's response to problems in living (a contextualistic model).

I believe there are four critical, contextual issues that warrant assessment as you develop your case formulation. Although these issues will be discussed in a fairly logical sequence, the reader should realize that this is often not the case in actual clinical practice. The areas must be addressed on a case by case basis and the process of doing so may take unexpected twists and turns depending upon individual client reactions and responses. The ultimate goal in all instances, despite the varied pathways to reach it, is to arrive at a formulation for each client that helps you formulate an appropriate treatment plan.

The first key issue or area to be addressed is how the presenting problem is construed from the client's perspective (e.g., "What brings you here today?"). Clients usually will provide some historical information about the circumstances under which "the problem" originated. If they fail to do so, I ask them (e.g., "Tell me about the circumstances under which you first became depressed."). Such information is very useful even if it is not necessarily historically accurate or factual in nature. The patient's construction of the problem will help you identify the events that the client is struggling to deal with, the types of experiential escape that are being used and the factors that have kept clients "stuck" in their depression. For example, clients may cite some unwanted tear in the fabric of their interpersonal relationships as a "cause" for their depression (e.g., being abandoned, a divorce, discovering a spouse's infidelity, etc.). They will often combine reason-giving ("I'm depressed because of the way my husband mistreated me.") and "being right" ("And I didn't do anything to deserve it.") to set themselves up for "playing the martyr" ("Anyone who has had to put up with what I've had to would be depressed."). My sense is that more functional depressed patients are not heavily invested in this role, but it is so insidious and seemingly intractable when it does occur—clients are left having to choose between continuing to be "right" and stay depressed or risk the prospect of being "wrong," "losing face," and moving on in life—that I like to be on the look-out for it early on. My clinical experience is that patients who fall prey to this trap are more likely to experience chronic problems with depression and may be better targeted using some of the strategies described in the chapter on ACT treatment of personality disorders (see Chapter 9). For present purposes, starting the assessment and formulation by getting the patient's construction of the problem (not just symptoms, but the historical and contemporary context of symptoms) will give you lots of clinical leverage.

Another common process that I assess is the degree to which patients are fused with depressogenic thoughts, emotions, memories, etc. The tendency to meld such private responses with the events that give rise to them is very similar to what cognitive therapists (Burns, 1980) have referred to as "emotional reasoning" and can assume varying forms. For example, Beck's (1967, 1987) classic cognitive triad includes fusion with beliefs about the self ("I'm worthless."), the world ("No one gives a damn about me!"), and the future ("Things can only get worse."). Regardless of the form cognitive fusion takes, depressed clients relate to their own depressive thoughts as if they are static factual evaluations rather than transient descriptive reactions. This failure to differentiate an evaluation from a factual attribute will later become a central target in therapy, so as the therapist, you will want to know how pervasive this problem is for your patient. If necessary, clients may be asked why, for example, they feel worthless. It should be pointed out this is not done, as occurs in cognitive therapy, to initiate a process of cognitive restructuring in which evidence both for and against the target thought is systematically evaluated nor to encourage introspection to better "understand" why the client may be depressed. Rather, the purpose is to evaluate the degree to which cognitive fusion contributes to the client's presenting problem. An indication of this would be a client saying something like, "I must be worthless because I feel worthless." In ACT this kind of fusion will be targeted largely through cognitive defusion techniques, not through cognitive change.

A second key target for assessment is how clients have attempted to cope with the presenting problem. I might ask something like, "Tell me about what you have already tried on your own or through the help of other people to deal with your depression and how that has worked for you." The client's response can help identify patterns of experiential avoidance/escape behavior that will need to be undermined. Knowing what has been tried and how it has worked (or not worked) helps me to avoid reinforcing coping responses that might work for another patient, but function in the service of experiential escape for this patient. In particular, I assess both internal and external emotional control strategies that clients have tried and the extent to which they are still being used. A common example of an internal control strategy is ruminative attempts to understand or "figure out" why the client may be depressed (e.g., "If could only understand why I'm so depressed, I'd be able to figure out a way to overcome it."). External emotional control strategies may include efforts such as taking prescription, over-the-counter, or recreational drugs, drinking, maintaining a rigid regimen of activities, and in the most extreme instances, manic binges of shopping, sexual activities, and substance abuse. The numbing action of depression as an experiential avoidance strategy generally affects motivation to perform positive behaviors. That is one likely reason that behavioral activation treatments are so successful in combating depression. I typically ask, "Since you've been depressed, are there things that you used to do that you've stopped doing altogether or do much less often?" For example, clients may have stopped engaging in certain previously pleasurable activities (e.g., going to the movies, exercising, etc.) or may avoid certain settings and locations (e.g., parks, restaurants, etc.) because they are reminded of a deceased partner. This type of information is useful in determining whether some form of behavioral activation intervention might be an appropriate treatment option (Jacobson et al., 1996) in ACT. Some time ago I showed that behavioral activation and distancing were the two effective components of cognitive therapy (Zettle & Hayes, 1987) and it is not by accident that these are the two components of cognitive therapy that overlap most with ACT since the earliest ACT protocols were being developed and tested at that same time.

Because clients may be socially supported in efforts to avoid or escape from unpleasant emotional experiences, it also is pertinent to assess what input others may have had into how clients view and have reacted to their presenting problem. Forms of social support can range from sympathetic statements that reinforce client reason-giving and or reinforce evaluation based responses such as "playing the martyr" ("The way you were treated wasn't right and I'd be depressed too if that happened to me").

A common experiential escape strategy that should be evaluated in all cases of affective disorders is suicidal behavior (Hayes, 1992). From an ACT perspective, suicidal behavior is basically just a more extreme form of experiential escape. For many depressed patients, the mere thought that they can always commit suicide is in itself an emotional control strategy. Normally, suicidal behavior is a way for the patient to get out from under what is perceived as being intolerable, inescapable and unending emotional pain (a more detailed discussion of suicidal behavior from an ACT perspective is presented in Chapter 9). I will generally ask clients to describe any historical instances of suicidal ideation or suicide attempts as well as their current suicidality. As the therapist, you should try to do this in a matter of fact, non-alarming fashion. The best way to do that is to link suicidal behavior to the other forms of experiential escape that the patient has tried. Often, clients do not understand how they came to think about suicide and therefore are very intimidated by these experiences. They see suicidal thoughts and impulses as originating outside of their control and tend to try to exert conscious control over whether these thoughts occur. As is the case with experiential avoidance generally, this strategy often fails and fans the flames of more intense suicidal ideation. Reframing suicidal ideation and even suicide attempts as efforts at emotional control gives your patient a credible way to think about moments of suicidality and may even offer a measure of reassurance. When discussing previous instances of suicidal behavior, it is important to understand the function(s) that were being served ("What were you hoping to accomplish by trying to kill yourself?"). In doing so, it is also useful to know the particular psychological conditions (e.g., guilt, hopelessness, shame, worthlessness, etc.) from which clients are seeking relief by attempting to kill themselves so other ways of responding to them can be addressed in therapy. Finally, it is important to periodically reassess patients as treatment proceeds. Since suicidality is often episodic, it is wise to assess clients at each contact. This can be done very briefly and informally as you initiate the session. If suicidality is present, it is legitimate to treat it clinically as you would any other experiential escape behavior that you are targeting in treatment.

The third key issue to assess in your case formulation is why clients see their presenting problems as "problematic." Doing so may help identify multiple relational frames and larger verbal-social networks, for instance, that "being depressed" participates in. Asking clients about this (e.g., "What does it mean to be depressed? What message is it telling you?") can be tricky because of the risk of providing them reinforcement for ruminating, trying to "figure things out," and related efforts that are in the service of emotional control. I might ask, "What is so bad about being depressed?" This is a back door way of identifying the function that depression might be serving for clients. Clients commonly see depression as "being bad" because it reflects the quality of their life (e.g., "I must be doing something wrong.") or worth as human beings (e.g., "Normal people don't feel depressed, so there must be something wrong with me."), and it is held as a cause for other behaviors (e.g., "I tend to drink more when I'm feeling down.") or their absence (e.g., "When I feel this bad I can't even get out of bed to go to work.").

The last set of issues I assess in my case formulation are client values and related goals. For a number of reasons, I prefer having an initial discussion with clients about their values and associated goals at the beginning of treatment. For one, feeling dispirited and uninspired may actually be the natural and appropriate consequence of pursuing and even attaining goals that are inconsistent with closely held values. Clients unsuccessfully attempt to eliminate these unwanted emotions and as a result become depressed about being depressed, rather then reevaluating their goals and clarifying their values. Inconsistencies between client goals and values that are detected (e.g., a client indicates she wants to return to college to finish her degree but can't do so because she can make such good money by continuing to accept overtime at her work) can be addressed early on. My clinical experience is that this focus on values often (but not always) speeds up the treatment process for more functional depressed patients.

Other instances of goal-value conflicts may be more subtle and not become apparent until later in therapy when this issue is typically addressed more extensively. For example, depressed clients who ostensibly are "living the American dream" with an attractive spouse, healthy children, a house in the suburbs, and a high-salaried position at a Fortune 500 company may complain that they can't understand why they are unhappy. Such clients may have successfully, but rather blindly, followed a rule about what it supposedly takes to be happy (e.g., have a beautiful wife, high-paying job, etc.) but in doing so, have pursued and attained goals that fundamentally are in conflict with their core values.

Another reason for clarifying core values fairly early on is that they can then function as "anchors" against which to evaluate the workability of both behavioral excesses (e.g., "Does getting drunk move you closer to getting to where you want to be?") and deficits (e.g., "How useful is it for you to stay in bed and not go to work?"). Additionally, core values can be used to guide subsequent behavioral activation interventions. For example, a client who values higher education, but has avoided pursuing a college degree because of fear of failing might enroll in an initial class.

It is certainly possible for clients to experience and become mired in depression even when they actively pursue goals consistent with their values. For example, the pursuit of value-directed goals is not always a smooth one. Unpleasant psychological experiences (e.g., feeling discouraged at times, feeling incompetent, etc.) may activate relational frames, rules, and other verbal constructions (e.g., "If I have to struggle to achieve a goal, it must either be because there's something wrong with me or I'm not supposed to be going there.") that help support depression. Focusing on values is helpful in distinguishing between cases where depression primarily is related to the pursuit of goals that are inconsistent with personal values as opposed to situations where clients are unwilling to experience some of the frustration and self-doubts they may encounter in reaction to obstacles and setbacks along the way.

CLINICAL INTERVENTIONS

Some of the more common clinical issues encountered in conducting ACT with clients experiencing affective disorders are listed in Table 4.1. Interventions within ACT that may be used to address each issue are also included in the table. Space limitations prohibit an exhaustive listing and coverage of clinical issues and associated interventions. Accordingly, the discussion of clinical issues that follows emphasizes those that are most central and/or have already been alluded to in the previous section on case formulation from an ACT perspective.

Getting clients to understand and accept the unworkability of experiential escape behaviors is a core process of ACT. One method for making this happen in therapy is to use various creative hopelessness interventions (Hayes et al., 1999). My attempts to induce creative hopelessness with depressed clients typically are undertaken in a more subtle and prescriptive manner, in large part depending upon their current suicidality. I usually present a fairly modest "dose" of these techniques early on to depressed clients who have a previous history of suicide attempts that have served an apparent experiential escape function, particularly so if a sense of hopelessness was the primary emotion from which they were seeking relief. The same applies to clients who may be imminently suicidal where the intent is to run away from unwanted psychological experiences. Rather than simply addressing current suicidality from a traditional crisis intervention platform, it works better to address the experiential escape functions that are served by suicidality. For example, you as the therapist could ask, "In

Table 4.1. Clinical Issues and Treatment Implications of ACT
with Affective Disorders

Clinical issues	Treatment implications
Client indicates that they are suicidal.	Determine functions(s) of suicidal behavior (e.g., "What would you accomplish by killing yourself?"). Consider titrating level of induced creative hopelessness; distinguish it from unacceptable hopelessness. Consider involvement of martyr role.
Client remains entrenched in emotional reasoning.	Defuse client from the thought (e.g., "I really am no good") by saying it aloud repeatedly. Refer back to Chessboard Metaphor; use physical metaphors for the thought.
Client claims they need to understand why they are depressed.	Question usefulness of understanding by relating it back to Person in the Hole Metaphor (e.g., "Does understanding how you ended up in the hole, help you get out?").
Client cites past undeserved mistreatment by others as cause of depression (i.e., playing the martyr role).	Consider other possible reactions; offering forgiveness. Weaken "being right" (e.g., "Who would be made wrong by you moving on with your life?"). Consider undermining "losing face" and "looking bad."

other instances where you've engaged in suicidal thinking or behavior, what has been the impact on the way you feel about yourself or how your life is working? Do you think being suicidal has helped improve your lot in life? What have been the costs of engaging in suicidal behavior?" This is not done in a moralistic, lecturing tone, but rather is presented as an open question about the workability of suicidal behavior as the client has experienced it. At the most conservative level, the array of techniques with such clients may be limited to reflecting their sense of being stuck, while addressing the universal question of what brought them into treatment and the futility of previous efforts in coping with depression. I might say something like, "It sounds like you feel stuck and that none of the things you've tried to help yourself feel better have really worked for you or I guess you wouldn't be here. What I'd like you to consider is the possibility that anything that you try to simply get rid of your depression won't work and so a different approach is called for."

By contrast, a more full array of techniques to increase creative hopelessness, including the *Person in the Hole Metaphor* (Hayes et al., 1999, pp. 101–102) are used in working with depressed clients with no history of suicide attempts nor current suicidal intent. The same strategy is also used with clients who have been or are currently suicidal if their attempts to harm themselves do not serve an apparent experiential escape function.

In presenting the Person in the Hole metaphor, the futility of deliberate attempts at emotional control and an associated sense of hopelessness are specifically emphasized and underscored (e.g., "You can't dig your way out of the hole no matter how hard you try and as long as you hang on to the agenda of digging there is no way out for you. This is no kidding—as long as you respond to your depression from that perspective, things are hopeless.").

It should be acknowledged that there is currently no empirical support for the strategy that has just been described of titrating the level of creative hopelessness that is induced with depressed clients. It is thus possible that the level of caution I have recommended in dealing with clients at risk of suicide is unwarranted. The natural concern about using creative hopelessness interventions with depressed clients is that they may have difficulty distinguishing creative hopelessness from the type of unacceptable hopelessness that has been shown to be predictive of increased suicidal potential (Beck, Brown, Berchick, Stewart, & Steer, 1990; Beck, Steer, Kovacs, & Garrison, 1985). Creative hopelessness is not a feeling: it is the liberating action of letting go of an agenda that has not worked so that more productive and innovative actions can take place. Nevertheless, this requires really looking at what hasn't worked. My solution is to examine this failure to get what they want enough for clients to be motivated to abandon their unproductive change agenda, but not so much that it potentially justifies falling back on suicidal behavior. If it becomes clear that clients are still engaged in experiential escape strategies, additional "doses" of creative hopelessness can be provided throughout treatment. After clients have been introduced to the concepts of fusion and can better differentiate thoughts and evaluations from static facts, there is generally much less concern about applying additional creative hopelessness interventions.

In contrast to the more guarded approach just described in inducing creative hopelessness, I typically go after "emotional reasoning," reasongiving, and other forms of cognitive fusion quite aggressively in working with depressed clients. A fairly extensive array of techniques and strategies are available within ACT to enable clients to see thoughts and emotions for what they are, not what they advertise themselves to be. The techniques discussed here are the ones that I prefer and use most often; other therapists may have different personal favorites.

The *Chessboard Metaphor* (Hayes et al., 1999, pp. 190–192) is a central ACT intervention that is more commonly thought of as increasing the self as context, but one which I use to highlight the problem of fusion. Because clients often describe their depressed thoughts and feelings as dark-colored (more on this in a bit), I like to make the black pieces on the chessboard representative of unwanted psychological experiences (e.g., "Imagine that the black pieces on the board are all of the depressing thoughts, feelings of guilt, and unpleasant memories that you've been trying so hard to get rid of."). Specific white pieces are cast in direct opposition to their black counterparts by saying something like:

> Notice that the board also holds an unlimited number of white pieces that hang out together—so thoughts that you really are competent and worthwhile and that things really will work out for you in the end may team up with feelings of self-confidence and memories you have of past successes in your life. But there are black pieces on the board that are just the opposite of the white ones. So over here you may have a white piece that says, "I'm OK and things are going to work out for me." But over there is a black one that says, "Who are you kidding? You're not OK—all you've done is make a big mess of your life." It may seem like both sets of pieces can't coexist and so the back ones have to be gotten rid of. But if the pieces are merely your thoughts and feelings, can't they both be present? Can you have the thought that you're OK *and* the thought that you're not OK at the same time?

It is not uncommon for clients at this point to display emotional reasoning by saying something like, "They both may be just thoughts, but it's really true that I'm not OK." In response, I point out that the thought "but it's really true" is merely another piece on the board that is associated with another thought ("I'm not OK") and question the client about the usefulness of "true" thoughts by saying something like:

> Does having the thought that another thought is true make it so? Isn't this just another thought? Have you ever thought that something is true only to find out that it isn't? How about the opposite? Have you ever had the thought that something is not true only to find out that it is? Responding to thoughts based upon whether you have the thought that they're true or not is just one approach. I'd like you to consider the possibility that there may be another way of responding to your thoughts and feelings—that is, based upon how useful you find them to be.

Some clients at this point may protest that it is critical for them to know what is true and what isn't (e.g., "But I've got to know what's true and what isn't. How else am I ever going to be able to figure my way out of this? It would be stupid not to pay attention to something that's true."). Other clients believe that truthfulness is synonymous with usefulness (e.g., "Of what use is something that's false?"). As will be seen, "knowing the truth" usually turns out to be but one of the outer layers of the verbally constructed onion that has as its core being right, whether or not being right is useful.

Another move that can be made to weaken fusion with private events is to introduce a distinction between verbal descriptions and evaluations. This is particularly critical as the negative thoughts and feelings experienced by depressed clients that participate in emotional reasoning are typically self-focused. A variation on the *Bad Cup Metaphor* that incorporates a physical object present in the therapeutic setting and is specific to depression can be presented:

> (*Select for discussion, an object, such as a chair in the therapy room, that can be described in a manner with which clients would concur.*) See this chair here. Let's talk about how we would describe it's color (for example). How would you describe its color? I'd agree—I'd also say the chair is (name of color). Now suppose you say that that chair is a "good chair." But I say no it's not—it's a "bad chair." Which is it? We agreed on the color of the chair, but we disagree on whether it's a good chair or a bad chair. How can it be both? Where does the color of the chair reside? Do you see that it's in the chair? When we say the chair is (name of color) we are describing it's color. How does this differ from the chair being a good or bad one. Where does the goodness or the badness of the chair reside? Is it in the chair itself? If so, how could that be—how could a chair be both good and bad? Or is the goodness and badness of the chair not to be found in the chair at all but in our evaluations of it? Our evaluations of the chair can differ because we are not describing the chair but really saying something about our reaction to it. When I say the chair is a bad one, aren't I really saying in effect, "There is a chair and my evaluation of it is that it is a bad one."? Now let's apply this to some of the pieces on your board—some of the negative thoughts and feelings you have about yourself that you've been wrestling with. Let's take your thought that "I'm no good." Is that a description or an evaluation? Isn't what you're really saying something like, "I'm a human being and, at least at this point in time, I'm having an evaluation called, I'm no good"? Note that as an evaluation your "no goodness" does not reside in you—it's not an inevitable part of your being—but within your reaction to yourself. And our evaluations of things can change without whatever it is we are evaluating changing.

At about this juncture, I typically begin to have clients "take inventory" and begin exposing them to physical metaphors that help create a space between the private experience and the person that is having that experience. "Taking inventory" refers to the practice within ACT of encouraging clients to use explicit category labels in describing their private events (e.g., "I have the thought that...," "I have the feeling that . . ."). I like to link these category labels to the *Chessboard Metaphor* (e.g., "When you think about your husband cheating on you what pieces loom large for you? Can you take inventory of them?"). I've found that it is often helpful to model this behavior (e.g., "Right now I'm having the thought that maybe you think that the questions I just asked you are weird.") and, if necessary, even assign related activities as part of homework. Such assignments can consist of compiling written lists of prominent depressive thoughts and feelings that are explicitly recognized as such (e.g., "The thought that— I'm incompetent, I'll never be happy, no one likes me, etc.;" "The feeling that—everything is my fault, I'm exhausted, I want to give up, etc."). A checklist can be constructed of recurrent unwanted thoughts and feelings that clients can be asked to monitor in risk situations (e.g., "When you find yourself getting all caught up in your depressing thoughts and feelings, take out your checklist and take inventory. Just notice what is showing up that is pushing you around"). Taking inventory may help break the automatic chain of clients responding to their own thoughts and feelings as if they are literally true.

Readers may note some similarities between compiling written lists of unwanted thoughts and the use the Daily Record of Dysfunctional Thoughts that is a core strategy in cognitive therapy of depression (Beck et al., 1979). Similarly, self-monitoring of private events is a common practice in various forms of behavioral assessment and behavior therapy (Bornstein, Hamilton, & Bornstein, 1986). Where ACT differs from these other traditions is that the goal of self-monitoring is not to struggle with, control or reduce the frequency of any particular private event. The purpose is to alter the function of private events without necessarily changing their form. This leads to assignments where the only goal is to "just notice" the occurrence of events, without judging or trying to change their form. The act of just noticing itself is a deliteralization strategy that prevents the patient from participating in the rule-governed responses that are generated through fusion with relational frames. By contrast, in cognitive therapy and behavior therapy explicit efforts are made to alter the form or content of depressive automatic thoughts that are identified in self-monitoring assignments. The implicit assumption is that there are some thoughts that are "healthy" and will lead to normal mood states. Thoughts that are "unhealthy" lead to depression and need to have their content corrected. Self-monitoring of depressive thoughts within behavioral assessment is designed to serve an informative rather than therapeutic function, although the mere act of recording behavior is often reactive. For this reason, self-monitoring of private events may also be undertaken as a behavior therapy technique with a goal of reducing their frequency of occurrence or level of intensity (e.g., Harmon, Nelson, & Hayes, 1980; Williams, 1976).

I also use physical metaphors to help clients defuse from thoughts, emotions, memories, and other private events. For example, as alluded to earlier, depressed clients usually will describe their thoughts and feelings as dark colored when asked to do so:

> Sometimes we may have to back up from things that are right in our face to get a clearer picture of them. (*To illustrate this the therapist can pick up an object—a pen, newspaper, etc.—and place it so close to the clients' eyes that it becomes an indistinguishable blur.*) What color is the pen? Read the first paragraph of the newspaper article. (*After clients acknowledge that they can't describe the pen or read the newspaper, move them further in front of the clients' faces so they can.*) Now, what is the color of the pen? What does the first paragraph of the newspaper article

say? The same thing can occur with our own thoughts and feelings. When you're all caught up and entangled in them—when they're right in your face—they may be hard to see. Imagine setting down the thought that you can't do anything right some distance away from you so we can size it up and maybe get a different view of it. If this thought had a color, what color would it be?

Additional questions, in this example, might ask about the thought's size, shape, weight, density, texture, temperature, or other physical dimensions. If the "object" (in this case, the thought that the client can't do anything right) has not changed in any of its initial physical dimensions by the end of the process, the client may be asked to identify a reaction to the thought (e.g., "I feel weighed down by it.") which in turn is also put into the form of a physical metaphor. Often, clients react to physical metaphors in ways that serve to diminish the depressogenic potential of the event/experience in question. In my experience, the response of clients to this technique tends to be all or nothing, but can be quite dramatic if and when they "get it." For example, one depressed client first described her depression as a dark black, dense, impenetrable mountainous structure, with jagged spikes protruding from it that made it impossible to either move or scale. Within a few sessions, her depression was transformed into a gray-colored, misty fog that dissipated as the client imagined herself walking through it. Generally, I try to take note of any depressing thoughts or feelings that clients describe in physical terms because they often can be represented by common objects that might be available in the therapy room, or can be introduced by design with minimal inconvenience.

A core part of my treatment approach is to undermine reason giving, which I believe is a central ingredient of depression. Individuals who give more reasons for their depression also ruminate more in response to depressed mood (Addis & Carpenter, 1999). In addition, among depressed clients, those who can offer "good reasons" for their depressed behavior tend to be more depressed and more difficult to treat successfully (Addis & Jacobson, 1996). In targeting reason giving, it useful to make a distinction between reason giving that is based in historical analysis and reason giving that explains current behavior. In ACT, the client's historically based reason giving is called the "story." This is an account that clients produce to explain why they are depressed in the first place (e.g., "My depression started two years ago when I was fired without warning from the best job I had ever had."). Contemporary reason giving usually involves presenting depressed thoughts and feelings as justification for the client's inactivity and avoidance of valued activities (e.g., "I knew I should get up and go to work, but I was too depressed."). Of the two sets of reasons, those of an historical nature generally are both more difficult to undermine and instrumental in keeping clients stuck in their depression. For these reasons,

I typically address the patient's story first. Taking on the story is especially important with depressed clients who have become invested in the martyr role. A number of elements seem to combine in initiating and maintaining this role, all of which may have to be addressed to successfully undermine it.

One key element to attack in the story is the client's contention that mistreatment by significant others is the cause of current depression (e.g., "I didn't know what depression was until my husband started lying and cheating on me."). To help undermine this, I might say something like, "You have the thought that you were mistreated by your husband. You also have the thought that this mistreatment is what caused you to become depressed in the first place." Note that a deliberate separation is made between the alleged mistreatment itself in this case and the client's reaction to it. Many clients at this point may insist that the mistreatment was not a mere perception or matter of opinion on their part, but did indeed occur, which is responded to by saying something like:

> OK, suppose we both agree that you were in fact mistreated by your husband. It's a fact. Your reaction to it is to become depressed. Are there any other reactions you could have had to at the time it occurred? Are there any other reactions you could have to it right now? (Should the client fail to cite any other possible reactions, some possibilities can be suggested. Could you have become angry, felt disappointed, concluded that this was not someone you wanted in your life, cut your losses, and chose to move on, etc?) What we're really talking about is the relationship between two things here—your feeling of being mistreated by your husband and your reaction to it by becoming depressed. If it's a fact that you were mistreated by him, can that be changed? If it can't be changed and the only way you know how to respond to it is by becoming and staying depressed, you're stuck. I'd like you to consider the possibility that you are now able to respond differently to what happened. You may not have realized this and there may have been some barriers that have stood in your way in being able to respond differently.

Evaluation is part of the FEAR algorithm in ACT and it often interacts with reason giving in a way that supports the martyr role. A common element in the story is that the mistreatment in question was undeserved and unjustified. Many clients will even spontaneously mention it (e.g., "It wasn't so much that I was mistreated that bothers me so much, but the fact that I didn't do anything to deserve it. If I had done something to deserve it, maybe I could understand why I was treated the way I was."). In response, I would usually say something like the following:

> So, another piece on the chessboard about this is the thought that you didn't deserve to be mistreated. Suppose you had the thought that you *did* deserve it. What difference would that make? You say that maybe you could understand all of this better, but is understanding it going to make you any less depressed.

> Suppose I were able to convince you that you did deserve to be mistreated, how would that be useful to you? It doesn't change the fact that we've already agreed upon that you were mistreated. Suppose someone shot and killed you. Would it make any difference to you whether you deserved to be shot and killed? Wouldn't you be just as dead either way?

About this point in the process, it may be useful to raise the option of the client forgiving the person who has treated them badly. Often, clients will either express an unwillingness (e.g., "He doesn't deserve my forgiveness.") or a perceived inability to do so (e.g., "I could never forgive someone who mistreated me as badly as he did, even if I wanted to."). I gently challenge these reasons for not granting forgiveness as just another form of reason giving:

> For whom is the act of forgiveness? Who benefits from it? Who deserves the forgiveness—you or your husband? So you have the thought that your husband doesn't deserve forgiveness—does that mean you can't grant it? Notice that I'm not talking about you contacting him and telling him face-to-face or in writing that you forgive him, although you could do that as well if you'd like. What's more important is what you do for yourself. After all, what if he were dead or you didn't know where he was and had no way of contacting him? Could you still choose to forgive him? You may not want to forgive him and have the thought that you can't. Is it possible that you can choose to forgive him *and* have the feeling that you don't want to *and* the thought that you can't *and* the feeling that he doesn't deserve it? Notice that I'm not asking you to try to forgive your husband—it's something you don't try to do, but do all-or-nothing, sort of like parachuting out of an airplane. I'm merely asking you to consider this as another way of responding to your thoughts and feelings that you didn't deserved to be treated the way you were. Also, notice that I can't guarantee you that your life will be work better if you do, and even if I did say that it would, I hope that you wouldn't believe me anyway. But is there any good reason to think that it would harm you in anyway and how could you find out?

Another treatment option I have used to address this issue is a variation of the Empty Chair Exercise from Gestalt therapy (see Hayes et al., 1999, pp. 257–258).

The story often includes another evaluative aspect that thrusts clients into the martyr role—namely, "being right." Clients who see themselves as having been unjustifiably mistreated by others feel they have been deeply "wronged." This issue can be addressed in the following manner:

> So, another piece on your chessboard about this is the thought that your husband was wrong to treat you the way he did. Remember we said that black pieces like this one often have related white pieces that are their opposites. What would be an opposing, but related white piece in this case? (If clients don't respond by indicating that the counterpart to "he was/is wrong" is "I was/am right," the possibility can be suggested to them—"Is another piece that may be present the thought that 'I was right'?".) Is it necessary for you to stay depressed in

order to continue to be "in the right" about this? Who would be made wrong by you moving on with your life? (Staying depressed may function to validate the reasons why clients see themselves as depressed in the first place—because they were undeservedly mistreated and unjustifiably wronged.) Would moving on with your life in anyway minimize what happened to you? Do you have to stay depressed in order for you to be right about your husband being wrong? Do you have to remove certain pieces from the board—the thought that you didn't deserve to be mistreated and the thought that you were wronged—in order for you as the board to move on? Does your life work well when you get all caught up in trying to get rid of them? To get rid of them with the way it's all set up, don't you somehow have to trick yourself into believing that you weren't mistreated in the first place? Is it possible to move on with your life and take the thought that you didn't deserve to be treated the way that you were along for the ride? (If clients have had exposure to a physical metaphor for this thought, they can be asked to imagine picking up and transporting it—"Imagine picking up that thought, putting it in a sack, slinging it over your shoulder, and heading out.".) In the bigger picture, what's more important to you—that your life work for you or that you hold on to "being right" about the way you were treated? Which do you choose—to abandon the agenda of "being right" and move forward in life or to hang on to it and stay righteously stuck in your depression?

A few final key barriers that may have to be overcome for clients to abandon the martyr role are "looking good," "saving face," and related social reinforcement for remaining stuck. This is particularly likely when clients have been depressed for several years and have widely shared their "stories" with other family members and friends. In doing so, they may have in effect set themselves up for "looking bad" and "losing face" in the eyes of others if they somehow recovered from their depression and began living healthy functional lives. In such situations, I usually say something like:

How many people other than myself have you told your story about why you became and continue to be depressed? What would they think of you or say to you if you were no longer depressed? Suppose they said something like: "I thought you said you were depressed because of the way you were treated by your husband several years ago. You've not seen him lately to have him treat you any differently, so why aren't you still depressed? If the way he treated you hasn't changed, shouldn't you still be depressed? If you're no longer depressed, I guess what you said about how badly you were mistreated by him couldn't really have been that bad after all—otherwise, you'd still be depressed." What would you say or do in response? How would you feel and what would you think? (At this point, clients might be asked to "take inventory" of their reactions.) So you might have a feeling of embarrassment and you might have the thought that your friends think you must be even more screwed up than they thought if you've been depressed for all these years, but didn't have to be. If it's necessary for you to experience these thoughts and feelings to get unstuck, are you willing to do so? What's more important—to save face in the eyes of your friends and family by continuing to be depressed or to move on with your life and risk looking foolish in the process? Which do you choose? What if everyone you've told your history to about how you were mistreated or who otherwise knew about it, including me, were to vanish from the face of the earth tomorrow?

Some mention should be made of how playing the martyr role to an extreme degree can contribute to suicidal risk. Thus far, the focus in conceptualizing and responding to suicidal behavior from an ACT perspective has emphasized its experiential avoidance function. Another function of suicidal behavior for clients who are heavily invested in the martyr role is that it is a way of simultaneously "being right," "looking good," and seeking revenge (e.g., "I'll show them; they'll be sorry when I'm gone."). My clinical experience is that the number of depressed clients who engage in various forms of suicidal behavior with the intent to both escape from psychological suffering and to affirm "being right" is quite limited. Normally, the pre-eminent function of suicidal behavior is experiential escape and emotional control. When being right is added into this equation, you as the therapist will have engaged in a two pronged attack on the patient's suicidal potential.

Usually, I will slowly transition the treatment focus from undermining confidence in the story to attacking reason giving in the service of justifying current avoidance behaviors and/or behavioral excesses. One technique that I invariably use is the verbal convention of substituting the word "but" with that of "and" in therapy transactions (e.g., "I could have gone out with some friends this weekend, *and*—rather than but—I didn't feel like it."). Once it has been introduced, the technique can have continued application. In particular, I make a deliberate effort to use it in my own speech in talking with clients and insist that they follow it as well.

Another preferred technique to undermine contemporary reason giving is to create a distinction between choices and decisions. One of my favorite interventions is ask clients to justify their choice between two imaginary dishes of ice cream:

> Imagine that before you are two dishes of ice cream—one vanilla and the other chocolate. Which would you choose? (Once the client announces the choice, ask "why?". Continue to do so repeatedly in response to whatever answers the client provides. At some point, clients, often in frustration, will proclaim, "OK, I don't know why I choose chocolate, I just do!" At that point, say:) Exactly! Isn't it the case that when it comes right down to it that you don't know why you choose chocolate over vanilla? Oh sure, you can tell me a plausible story about it and maybe even to yourself, but isn't it the case that you choose it simply because you choose it and all the other stuff that you say about it—because you like the way it tastes and so on—is just a story to support your choice? What I'd like you to consider is that you, me—all of us—often do the same thing even if the only person we're trying to convince or explain to why we do what we do

is ourselves. And what I'd also like you to consider is that we do this not only when it comes to seemingly minor matters in life like choosing one flavor of ice cream over another, but for much more important things—like who we might marry, how many children to have, what career to pursue, and so on—in life.

To further underscore the distinction between choice and decision, I typically use a variation of *Passengers on the Bus Metaphor*. This metaphor serves multiple purposes. It helps bring into focus the concept of committed action that is generated from choice and it also introduces the role willingness will play in carrying out valued behaviors. I modify the metaphor to place clients in movement towards a valued goal and to make the "passengers" more specific to depression:

> Suppose you commit yourself to drive a small busload of children to an outing at the state fair. You were planning on going to the fair anyway and thought you'd help out. Imagine, though, that after you commit yourself to the trip, its organizer informs you that little Johnny Boogernose; the meanest, nastiest kid in the bunch; and his buddies will be riding with you. Still, you yourself want to go to the fair and, after all, you did say you'd transport a load of children. So you head off in the direction of the fair, several miles away. Imagine though, that after just a few minutes into the journey, little Johnny Boogernose and his buddies swing into action. Suppose they all start criticizing, berating, belittling, and making fun of you—saying things like: "You're going the wrong way!," "You don't know what the hell you're doing! What are you, stupid?," "Can't you do anything right!," and so on. So you pull off to the side of the road and inform them that you won't go any further until they all shut up and behave themselves. Suppose they don't. In fact, maybe they become even more abusive—"We don't wanna shut up! And who the hell are you to try and make us!." Notice what happened when you pulled over to the side of the road. Who is now in control of whether or not you make it to the fair? Is it you or the rowdy kids? What if they never shut up? You're stuck. Are you prepared to spend the rest of your life pulled over to the side of the road trying to beg, plead, or bargain with them to behave themselves? Do you see that your choice to go to the fair has now been transformed by you into a decision that it is out of your hands? Imagine further that all the rowdy kids, even little Johnny Boogernose himself, are all the black pieces on your chessboard—all the negative and depressing thoughts, feelings, and memories that you wish you could shut up. And notice that you're not just on a trip to the fair, but on life's journey. Are you going to choose the direction you take in life or are you going to let your thoughts and feelings decide for you?

Making choices is psychologically more readily done from a perspective where clients have made contact with a sense of self that is not psychologically threatened by whatever experiences are encountered. The *Observer Exercise* within ACT is used to increase this transcendent sense of self. Although the exercise is being discussed here in conjunction with clients choosing and making a commitment to valued courses of action, it can also be introduced earlier within therapy in the service of cognitive defusion. My experience is that most depressed clients benefit from this exercise. The reactions by the majority that do can be quite emotionally powerful, with clients often crying afterwards. The Observer Exercise is quite lengthy (Hayes et al., 1999, pp. 193–195), and will not be repeated here. During it, clients are asked to imagine occurrences that happened at various points in their lives; for example, when they were teenagers as well as young children. In conducting the exercise, I make sure clients are asked to remember a time in their past when they were not depressed, in order to put them in contact with a sense of self that exists apart from whether they have been depressed or not. If necessary, I will take clients all the way back to childhood, if that is the only time they can recall when depression wasn't present. While many clients will indicate also being depressed as adolescents, it is less common for them to report depression as children. If, however, I know from client histories that they were depressed as children, I will deliberately ask them to remember a time when they were not depressed.

The latter stages of therapy can be devoted to helping clients build larger and larger patterns of committed action. This is also a core process target in ACT because functionality in life is determined by action, not words. At this point in therapy, I will spend some time clarifying client goals and values to make sure that the behavioral goals we set are consistent with the client's values. If necessary, I will use a formal values clarification assessment procedure, such as is detailed by Hayes et al. (1999, pp. 222–228) or any of the other values clarification methods presented in this book. Typically, I want to clarify client values, goals, related courses of action, and barriers to taking such actions. Courses of action to be encouraged and strengthened should be considered within the context of any remaining forms of overt behavioral avoidance and/or emotional control. With depressed patients, moving in the direction of valued life ends almost invariably will turn up more basic emotional barriers. I emphasize that this tension is probably a core element of the client's difficulties with depression. For example, continuing to decline social invitations (e.g., "Some friends asked me to go to the movies with them, but I didn't feel like it.') is incompatible with a value of "being a better friend." Similarly, continuing to get drunk (e.g., "Drinking helps numb things out for me.") and missing work as a consequence does not move clients closer to the goal of "becoming a more responsible employee." I will often target goals that will elicit such instances of behavioral avoidance and emotional control. These barriers will have to be "inhaled" as clients move toward valued life ends. Under these circumstances, I would be apt to say something like:

> It sounds like whether or not to accept the invitation of your friends to go to the movies with them was a decision that was made by a feeling you had about it. Could you have chosen to go to the movies *and* have the feeling that you didn't

feel like it? Could you have taken that feeling along with you to the movies? You said you want to be a better friend. Does declining their invitation move you closer or further away from that? Can you think of anything you could actively do that would get you closer to being a better friend? (If the client has no ideas, some suggestions—such as inviting friends to participate in some activity can be offered and discussed.) You also mentioned that you continue to drink to the point of getting drunk. What does that do for you? (Look for private events from which the client is seeking escape/avoidance and discuss alternative ways of responding to them, emphasizing willingness and acceptance.) Does getting drunk like you did move you closer or further away from your goal of being a more responsible employee? What could you do that would be a step in that direction?

Any discussion of pursuing a value-directed course of action should also explicitly address barriers clients may encounter in adhering to their commitments. It may be useful to separate these into barriers that are internal (e.g., "I'd like to go back to school, but I'm afraid I'd fail and feel stupid.") versus external (e.g., "I probably couldn't afford to go back to school anyway."), although the latter often unravel into the former (e.g., going back to school would present the client with financial worries they wish to avoid). Additionally, a consideration of barriers should include not only those that are immediately obvious, but also those that potentially might arise in the process of seeking goals. Accordingly, I help clients engage in "trouble-shooting" and personal problem solving once they have committed themselves to a particular course of action:

Because you value education, you've identified going back to school and completing your degree as an appropriate goal for yourself. And you've committed yourself to taking at least three courses next semester as part of that process. In doing so, we've talked about how you will experience unwanted thoughts and feelings along the way and how you can accept them when they occur. Can you think of any other obstacles or barriers that you might encounter that might make it difficult for you to keep your commitment? [Respond to whatever barriers are cited (e.g., "maybe I'll become really depressed again"), by asking how the barrier could be dealt with and if the client could keep the commitment *and* have the barrier occur. Suggest additional possible obstacles not mentioned by the client (e.g., "What if your car breaks down and you can't drive yourself to school?").] Suppose I offered you a million dollars if you finished three courses next semester, could you do it? Suppose I offered you a million dollars if you could jump off a 10-story building and fly, could you do it? So it's clear you are able to keep your commitment, the only question is whether you choose to do so.

At the point in time when the patient has the opportunity to seek valued life ends and inhale obstacles, I find it useful to get the ACT question into the therapeutic dialogue:

> Given a distinction between you and the things you've been struggling with and trying to change, are you willing to experience those things, fully and without defense, as they are, and not as they say they are, *and* do what takes you in a valued direction in the situation?

This question summarizes the entire ACT approach, integrating the positive aspects of self-as-context and self-as-process, acceptance, defusion, exposure, and focus on the present moment, into focused behavioral activation. ACT thus increasingly turns into a behavioral activation approach, with targeted behavioral goals and behavioral homework. In this phase it is important to keep homework linked to values and not to a secret method of escaping feelings or thoughts. The point of valued action is living, not self-manipulation. Accomplishing these ends requires that behavioral exercises be "held lightly." If a goal is sought and not immediately reached, it is not a tragedy. Those challenges are instead merely part of the process of living.

CLINICAL CONSIDERATIONS

The most general and objective way of assessing the response of depressed clients to ACT is through regular assessment of depression severity. With the exception of emergency or crisis situations, I see clients on a weekly basis, although in today's managed care environment, that may not be feasible. At the start of each appointment, a Beck Depression Inventory (BDI) is administered; either the original version (Beck, Ward, Mendelson, Mock, & Erbaugh, 1961) or the BDI-II (Beck, Steer, & Brown, 1996) can be used. Both versions provide an objective and convenient means of tracking client levels of depression (by the total score) as well as a way to specifically monitor any changes in suicidal risk via items 2 and 9 on the inventories. Item 2 assesses pessimism/hopelessness (i.e., "I feel that future is hopeless and that things cannot improve."), while item 9 directly evaluates suicidal intent (i.e., "I would kill myself if I had the chance.").

Although one concern is that clients might initially become more depressed during the early stages of ACT when inducing creative hopelessness is the goal, this has not occurred during my clinical and research experience. In general, most clients experience the creative hopelessness component as compassionate and validating. The degree to which this may be attributed to the strategy, discussed earlier, of titrating the level of creative hopelessness interventions is not clear and I have not systematically investigated this question.

The most common outcome trend is that clients respond favorably to ACT and display fairly consistent reductions in their BDI scores over the course of therapy. At pretreatment, most clients will report levels of depression in the moderate (BDI = 20–28) to severe ranges (29–63) that have been reduced to the mild (14–19) or minimal ranges (0–13) by 10–12 sessions of ACT. Clients who fail to show some decrease in their BDI scores by 3–4 weeks of therapy, or worse, who display an increase in their levels of depression, should be a cause for concern. The same can be said for clients that show reductions in depression over the first month of therapy, then become "bogged down" and stabilize at that level for the next month or so.

Several contributing factors, some occurring within therapy itself and others happening externally, should be considered when clients fail to show an initial or continued favorable response to therapy based on tracking their BDI scores. If the failure to respond is near the beginning of therapy, more "doses" of creative hopelessness (clients may not have yet abandoned the agenda of digging their way out of the hole) may be called for as well as more work on cognitive defusion and willingness (they metaphorically may have thrown down the shovel, but are still not in a position to respond appropriately to being given a ladder). Although I don't normally administer the believability version of the Automatic Thoughts Questionnaire (ATQ-B) on a routine basis, doing so in this case might provide some insight into clients' non response. As mentioned earlier in this chapter, depressed clients who were treated successfully with ACT showed significant reductions in their ATQ believability scores independently of similar changes in the frequency of depressive automatic thoughts (Zettle & Hayes, 1986). Having access to repeated ATQ scores might help identify clients continuing to report high levels of belief in depressive thoughts. These clients are probably still in the throes of cognitive fusion and presumably should benefit from defusion interventions.

"Shit happens" and sometimes it not only occurs before clients begin therapy, but also while they're in it. For example, clients may suddenly lose jobs, experience interpersonal break-ups, or be faced with an unexpected death in the family. Many clients will spontaneously bring these events into the therapy session, but others hide out with these events because of shame, guilt, and the like. For this reason, you as the therapist should directly question clients about recent negative life events if the progress they were making in therapy comes to a halt, or they begin to show elevated depression scores. Whatever reactions clients display in therapy to contemporary negative life events provides a rich clinical opportunity. Unwanted thoughts and feelings concerning the life event can be readily identified, the client's typical ways of engaging in experiential avoidance may become more obvious, and alternative ways of coping can be introduced and closely monitored.

Another set of external factors that may negatively affect response to ACT treatment are the continuous messages in the mass media that medicalize psychopathology, in general, and affective disorders, in particular. Clients may be exposed to talk shows, television specials, news segments, printed articles, and an increasingly aggressive campaign of direct marketing of antidepressants. These appeals typically portray affective disorders as genetically based, neurochemical disorders of the brain that require somatic treatment. As any experienced therapist knows, many patients come into treatment already taking antidepressants or convinced that they have a chemical imbalance that can only be corrected with medicines. How to integrate this common perception within the ACT framework is not a simple matter, because in many respects, the ACT model of depression is not really based in a syndrome way of thinking.

The biomedical model of depression and its treatment perpetuates a framework of reason giving that is in strong conflict with the ACT framework. I agree to work with depressed clients who are already taking antidepressants when they present themselves for therapy, but (if my recollection is correct) I have never referred a client for medication. Simply put, the goal of antidepressant therapy is to help the client feel good; the goal of ACT is to live a healthy, vital purposeful life. Furthermore, recently analyses of the entire FDA database on the SSRIs show that these medications produce only a 2 point improvement over pill placebos on the Hamilton Depression Scale (which is a 50 to 62 point scale depending on whether the 17 or 21 item scale is used) and even that tiny gain is before controlling for penetration of the blind that comes in most patients since these studies fail to use active placebos (Kirsch, Moore, Scoboria, & Nicholls, 2002). Thus, if one has a strong commitment to empirically supported treatments, the state of the evidence simply does not demand the use of antidepressants. I do not actively encourage clients who are already taking medications to stop taking them. However, the process of ACT tends to bring up the whole issue of how symptom elimination strategies fit with a model of change that encourages an acceptance of symptoms, as symptoms. Many of my patients independently decide to stop taking antidepressants for this reason, in addition to the fact that ACT seems to be a comparably effective treatment.

A somewhat different strategy may be used for the clients that believe their depression is caused by an inherited neurochemical imbalance and want my opinion on whether they should use an antidepressant. Quite understandably, such clients begin to seriously question the relevance and appropriateness of ACT (e.g., "How is any of this going to help me if I my depression is caused by a brain disorder?"). My usual tact is not to question the scientific integrity ("the literal truth") of this view, but instead to question the utility of knowing the cause of a problem versus solving it. I will often use the following metaphor to make the point:

> So you had the thought after watching the program on TV last night that your depression is caused by a neurochemical imbalance in your brain. That's an interesting thought. Suppose when you left here today you got out to your car and found that you had a flat tire. How useful would it be to correctly answer the question of why the tire is flat? Could there by any number of things that might have happened to cause the tire to become flat? Suppose you took the position that figuring out why the tire went flat had to occur before it was changed. How useful would that be? Is it possible, at least as far as this particular flat tire is concerned, that you might never know what caused it to go flat? Even if you hired a flat-tire specialist to look at the tire and determine why it went flat. If so, I guess the tire would never be changed. Which is more important here—figuring out why the tire went flat in the first place or changing it? Do you need to know what caused the tire to become flat in order to change it?

I think that, in fairness to clients, the ultimate decision about whether to use an antidepressant is theirs. Even if a client elects to try antidepressants, I can reframe the function of that treatment so that the goal is more realistic than what the pharmaceutical advertisements imply. The pill is not the answer for how to make your life work better. Antidepressants might help reduce symptoms that might impede functioning. If symptoms go down, there is still a need to face unwanted experiences, give up on self-defeating coping strategies, identify and choose valued actions and build new patterns of more effective behavior. There has never been a study that shows medicines can accomplish these more fundamental life objectives. Most clients understand this message implicitly and it allows us to operate with fidelity to the ACT model.

CONCLUSION

The first ACT studies done, now nearly 20 years ago, were done with depression, and thus the primary ACT protocols fit very well with the needs of depressed patients. Now that ACT has reached a wider audience, additional systematic applications of ACT to depression seem likely. For the individual clinician, this model gives a number of new and creative alternatives for the alleviation of this form of human suffering.

Chapter 5

ACT with Anxiety Disorders

SUSAN M. ORSILLO, LIZABETH ROEMER,
JENNIFER BLOCK-LERNER, CHAD LEJEUNE, AND
JAMES D. HERBERT

Anxiety disorders are the most commonly experienced mental health problems in the United States. Narrow, Rae, Robins, and Regier (2002), combining data from the National Institute of Mental Health Epidemiologic Catchment Area Program (ECA) and the National Comorbidity Survey (NCS), conservatively estimated the one-year prevalence for any anxiety disorder to be 13.1% for adults aged 18–54. These conditions tend to be chronic. Three year remission rates range from 16 to 23% for social phobia, generalized anxiety disorder, agoraphobia, and panic disorder with agoraphobia (Keller, 2000, in Barlow, 2002). In one longitudinal study, within the first 22 months following the onset of an episode, only 18% of individuals diagnosed with panic disorder and agoraphobia and about 43% of those with panic disorder without agoraphobia had recovered in comparison to approximately 80% of those with major depressive disorder (Hirschfeld, 1996). Functional status of patients with anxiety disorders is diminished as evidenced by higher rates of financial dependence, unemployment (e.g., Leon, Portera and Weissman, 1995), poorer quality of life (Massion, Warshaw, & Keller, 1993), and increased risk for completed suicide (Allgulander, 1994).

Given the prevalence, chronicity and cost associated with the anxiety disorders, it is not surprising that a great deal of effort has gone into developing effective treatments. For instance, cognitive-behavioral treatment for panic disorder has yielded large effect sizes (.68–.88; Gould, Otto & Pollack, 1995) and a review of several studies indicate that between 41% and 100% of clients are panic free up to 12 months following the termination of treatment (Barlow, 2002). Exposure treatment for specific phobia is associated with extremely high rates of success (e.g., Öst, 1989). Cognitive-behavioral group treatment for social phobia or social anxiety disorder (Heimberg, 1991) has also received strong empirical support (e.g., Heimberg et al., 1998) with exposure interventions yielding the largest effect sizes both alone (.89) or in combination with cognitive restructuring (.80; Gould, Buckminster, Pollack, Otto, & Yap, 1997). Exposure and response prevention (ERP) and cognitive therapy have been shown to be reasonably effective in treating OCD (Abramowitz, 1997). Finally, cognitive-behavioral approaches for GAD have been shown to yield significant changes (with large effect sizes) that are maintained or improved at six to twelve month follow-up (Borkovec & Ruscio, 2001).

Despite the abundance of clinical research available on the treatment of anxiety disorders, and a seemingly optimistic record of success, there is much room for improvement in current treatment approaches. An over-reliance on narrow measures of symptom reduction as the primary indices of treatment success and the limited study of long-term maintenance of gains may limit the generalizability of these findings to clinical practice. Even when provided with state-of the-art intervention protocols, a significant number of clients fail to respond to treatment and many of those classified by categorical indices as "responders" continue to evidence symptoms, remain functionally impaired, and seek additional treatment. This is particularly true when individuals with severe psychopathology or co-morbid conditions are not excluded from the treatment under study (e.g., Barlow, 2002).

A number of efforts are currently underway that are aimed at increasing the effectiveness (including the acceptability) of treatments for the anxiety disorders. For instance, given the aversive nature of exposure and response prevention for OCD, cognitive therapy has been investigated as a potential alternative. However, these efforts have been associated with mixed results (e.g., Cottraux et al., 2001; McLean et al., 2001), which is not surprising given the mounting evidence that cognitive therapy has failed to achieve its intended impact as an adjunctive or alternative approach to behavior therapy for anxiety disorders (Orsillo, Roemer, Block Lerner & Tull, in press). Given the strong empirical support for exposure therapy, we argue that treatments for anxiety disorders that retain and enhance the exposure component are most likely to produce clinically significant and meaningful results.

Acceptance and Commitment Therapy (ACT; Hayes, Strosahl, & Wilson, 1999) seems to show significant promise as an approach that is in many ways consistent with exposure therapy, and that directly addresses issues of comorbidity, fear and avoidance related to exposure, and concerns about quality of life. The main goal of ACT is to increase non-avoidant contact with the present moment, and the full range of private events that might occur, in the service of living a meaningful and valued life. Further, ACT is an integrative treatment approach in which symptoms across a range of psychological disorders (e.g., substance use, self-harm, behavioral avoidance) are conceptualized as serving an experientially avoidant function (Hayes, Wilson, Gifford, Follette & Strosahl, 1996). Thus, ACT can be used with individuals with complicated, comorbid conditions who might be considered poor candidates for traditional CBT. Fear and avoidance associated with exposure are directly addressed in ACT through methods aimed at decreasing fusion, building self as process, contacting self as context, defining valued life directions, and building patterns of committed actions. Indeed, an acceptance rationale drawn from ACT seems to increase the willingness of patients with panic disorder to experience panic symptoms (Levitt, Brown, Orsillo & Barlow, in press).

In this chapter, we will discuss the application of ACT to the treatment of anxiety disorders, specifically panic disorder, specific phobia, social anxiety disorder, OCD and GAD (the application of ACT to PTSD and trauma more generally is discussed in the next chapter). There is compelling evidence for the role of experiential avoidance and cognitive fusion in the development and maintenance of these disorders, and the core psychological processes targeted by ACT interventions (decreasing emotional control/avoidance, decreasing fusion, building self as process, contacting self as context, defining valued life directions and building patterns of committed actions) seem to be making their way into many of the new anxiety disorder treatment protocols. Thus, we believe that the ACT model may be able to supplement or facilitate existing empirically-supported treatment, particularly where we know something about the effective components of empirically-supported treatments and these components are consistent with an ACT model. Sometimes existing empirically supported packages include elements that cannot be combined with ACT (e.g., cognitive restructuring). In these cases it seems to make more ethical sense to use ACT treatment protocols where the existing empirically supported alternative treatment is refused, unavailable, or unsuccessful. ACT is part of the empirical clinical tradition, and this conservative approach is the same as with all emerging technologies within that tradition.

These recommendations reflect the current state of the evidence, and the fact that ACT is a general model, within which a variety of specific protocols can be developed. As a general model, the empirical support is currently stronger than it is as a specific protocol or set of protocols within the anxiety disorder area. That empirical state of affairs seems likely to change over time. There are a number of successful case studies (Carrascoso, 2000; Huerta, Gomez, Molina, & Luciano, 1998; Luciano, & Gutierrez, 2001; Zaldívar, & Hernández, 2001), and small but generally successful controlled trials using ACT protocols with anxiety disorders (e.g., Block, 2002; Block & Wulfert, 2002; Twohig & Woods, in press; Zettle, 2003). Successful randomized controlled trials also exist in the related area of stress (e.g., Bond & Bunce, 2000; see Chapter 11). A number of other studies are currently underway, so we will soon know much more about the utility of ACT with these populations. In what follows, we will assume that these ethical aspects have been followed.

FORMULATION

Generally speaking, the ACT formulation of the anxiety disorders is relatively straightforward. Various anxiety problems occur when: 1) Clients are unwilling to experience the symptoms of normal anxiety (pounding heart, vague fears) or private experiences that give rise to normal anxiety (fear of making a social error, worrying about an outcome in the future, having a recurrent "irrational" though); 2) Clients instead view normal anxiety related events as a basic threat to health that must be controlled and/or eliminated; 3) Attempts to control anxiety related events directly actually escalate anxiety to unacceptable levels; 4) Clients initiate emotional escape/avoidance strategies of a psychological (rumination, worry, hypervigilance) or behavioral (checking, situational avoidance) nature that exert some short term control over unwanted anxiety states, but create an anxiety rebound effect; 5) Emotional escape/avoidance is applied more frequently to keep up with the rebound and are reinforced by short term relief from anxiety; 6) Continued widening of the pattern of emotional escape/avoidance responses leads to severe psychological and behavioral constriction in core areas of functioning, loss of quality of life and, eventually, end state diagnoses (GAD, Agoraphobia). Below we briefly overview the presenting symptoms associated with each anxiety disorder and discuss how one might conceptualize these symptoms from an ACT perspective.

Panic Disorder

Panic disorder is defined in DSM-IV by the occurrence of unexpected intense episodes of fear that are accompanied by physical and cognitive symptoms (American Psychiatric Association [APA], 1994). While panic attacks are common across most of the anxiety disorders, in panic disorder they are accompanied by worry about future attacks, worry about the consequences of attacks (e.g., going crazy, having a heart attack), or behavioral change related to the attacks (e.g., job change to avoid driving across a bridge). Individuals with panic disorder often engage in "interoceptive avoidance" or the avoidance of behaviors (e.g., drinking caffeinated beverages, exercise, sexual relations) that may produce somatic symptoms that are similar to those experienced during a panic attack (Rapee, Craske, & Barlow, 1995).

Models on the origin of panic disorder underscore the contributory role of evaluating somatic symptoms as extremely dangerous. Individuals who experience panic attacks are more likely to have observed panic symptoms in their parents, to have had chronic illnesses in their households, and to have received more parental encouragement for sick-role behavior during their own experiences of panic-like symptoms than those without such symptoms (Ehlers, 1993). Thus an early learning history emphasizing the potential dangers of physical sensations may be common among those with this disorder. Prospective studies offer some evidence for the relationship between anxiety sensitivity, or the belief that anxiety and its associated symptoms have harmful consequences, and the later occurrence of panic attacks (e.g., Hayward, Killen, Kraemer & Taylor, 2000).

From an ACT perspective, this fear of bodily sensations drives the unwillingness to have them and initiates a pattern of experiential avoidance that may foster panic disorder. A number of externally based control strategies may be present including "safety behaviors" (e.g., carrying water, crackers, or medication) that are thought to protect the person in case of the onset of panic. Men in particular may use alcohol or nicotine in efforts to avoid or endure their panic symptoms (Kushner, Abrams, & Borchardt, 2000). Suicide attempts, the ultimate experiential avoidance strategy, occur more frequently in panic disorder patients with co-morbid affective, substance use, eating and personality disorders (e.g., Warshaw, Dolan, & Keller, 2000). Finally, in the case of panic disorder with agoraphobia, the avoidance or endurance with extreme distress of situations from which it might be difficult to escape or gain assistance in the event of a panic attack (APA, 1994), clients can become derailed from pursuing valued aspects of their lives in the service of avoiding situations that may cue uncomfortable somatic symptoms.

Specific Phobia

Specific phobia involves the significant fear of an object, animal or situation that causes marked distress and life interference. The DSM-IV (APA,

1994) specifies four main types, in addition to a residual "other" type: animal (e.g., spiders, snakes, dogs), natural environment (e.g., heights, storms, darkness), blood-injection-injury (e.g., seeing blood, watching surgery, receiving injections), and situational (e.g., flying, driving, bridges).

While experiential avoidance has historically not been as clearly linked to specific phobia as behavioral avoidance, several findings related to the focus of apprehension for individuals with specific phobia support the role of this process. For example, in one study that incorporated a panic induction challenge, Craske and Sipsas (1992) found that individuals with claustrophobia were as fearful of a hyperventilation challenge as they were of being in a closet, their fear-relevant stimulus.

Thus, from an ACT perspective, individuals with specific phobia are unwilling to experience the symptoms of anxiety (particularly physiological arousal) that arise when they are exposed to the objects or situations that they fear. While it may not be difficult for some people to avoid situations or objects that they fear (e.g., floods if one currently lives in the desert), many individuals' lives are constrained by their fears and this may prevent them from living in accordance with their values. For example, if one values helping others and has dreams of becoming a doctor, a fear of the sight of blood may prevent the individual from realizing that goal, unless he or she is willing to sit with and "hold" the fear and associated thoughts and bodily sensations that may accompany valued action.

Social Anxiety Disorder

Social anxiety disorder is characterized by a significant and persistent fear of social or performance situations in which embarrassment may occur. Individuals with this disorder fear the internal experiences that may occur in a social context (e.g., feelings of anxiety, negative self-evaluation, symptoms of arousal). This fear is often associated with high degrees of self-focused attention that has been demonstrated to be associated with impaired social performance (e.g., Norton & Hope, 2001) and to diminish the person's ability to attend to and to connect meaningfully with others. Consistent with an ACT model of experiential avoidance, once the relationship between the internal experience of anxiety and poor social performance is established, persons with social anxiety disorder typically become vigilant for internal cues of anxiety and may engage in a number of cognitive (e.g., self-talk, distraction) and behavioral (e.g., averting eye contact) escape responses directed toward controlling this anxious response.

One of the important core principles of ACT is that persons to a certain extent can "purchase" a measure of control over feared private events but the purchase price is one's quality of life. This is very clear in social anxiety disorder. Individuals with social phobia often engage with others in an innocuous and superficial way, politely smiling, appearing agreeable, nodding often (Leary, 1983, Leary, Knight, & Johnson, 1987, Patterson & Ritts, 1997) and making excuses and apologies (Edelman, 1987; Schlenker, 1987). In their pursuit to escape uncomfortable thoughts and feelings that arise in the context of social relationships, those with social phobia settle for poor interpersonal connection (e.g., Antony, Roth, Swinson, Huta, & Devins, 1998) and impairment across life domains that are socially-based.

Obsessive-Compulsive Disorder

Obsessive-compulsive disorder is characterized by the presence of thoughts, images, or impulses (obsessions) that are evaluated by the individual to be unwanted and dangerous. The content and form of obsessions in people with OCD tend not to differ from unwanted thoughts experienced by most of the population. However, individuals with OCD tend to experience their unwanted thoughts as more distressing, longer lasting, and more intense than those without the disorder (Rachman, 1997). In an attempt to manage (or escape from the anxiety associated with) these thoughts, individuals with OCD engage in behavioral or cognitive rituals (compulsions) designed to neutralize the negatively evaluated internal event. While these escape responses provisionally alleviate the distress associated with the obsession, they reinforce the ritual response and prevent the client from letting go of the struggle with internal experiences. Excessive use of alcohol and/or certain anxiolytic, hypnotic or sedative medications is also common (e.g., Dimitriou, Lavrentiadis, & Dimitriou, 1993), and can be conceptualized as additional attempts at experiential avoidance and escape.

Shafran, Thordarson, and Rachman (1996) used the term "thought action fusion" to describe the common belief among individuals with OCD that thoughts can directly influence external events (e.g., "If I imagine my son being hit by a car, it will happen") and that having negatively evaluated intrusive thoughts (e.g., "I want to stab my children") is morally equivalent to carrying out a prohibited action. While individuals with OCD differ in the degree to which they believe their thoughts to be true and their behavior unreasonable (Foa & Kozak, 1995), there is some evidence that poorer insight is associated with more severe symptoms and a worse prognosis (Solyom, DiNicola, Sookman, & Luchins, 1985).

From an ACT framework, cognitive fusion with negatively evaluated thoughts, images and emotions perpetuates experiential avoidance. The perspective that internal experiences are causal and dangerous strengthens the unwillingness to experience them. Deliberate attempts to suppress an unwanted thought or urge can paradoxically increases the importance, behavioral regulatory power, and even the rate of these thoughts or urges, further amplifying the vicious cycle.

Significant deficits in quality of life are apparent with individuals diagnosed with OCD, likely due to the restricted lifestyle those with the disorder adopt in order to avoid stimuli that might elicit obsessions and related anxious feelings. For instance, a person with obsessions about running over animals in the road might avoid driving at night, limiting their ability to engage in social activities after work. The rituals of OCD also can infringe on quality of life in that their completion requires an inordinate amount of time and energy.

Generalized Anxiety Disorder

The centrally defining feature of generalized anxiety disorder (GAD) is excessive worry. The process of worry typically involves a flood of future focused thoughts about potentially negative outcomes. This primarily verbal-linguistic form of anxiety has been conceptualized as a strategy of avoidance that diminishes the full impact of negative emotional experiences (Borkovec, Alcaine, & Behar, 2004). Research supports the notion that worry may function to temporarily diminish or avoid internal distress (e.g., Borkovec & Roemer, 1995). Thus, the most notable form of avoidance in GAD may be experiential; that is, individuals with GAD may be strategically and/or automatically avoiding unpleasant internal experiences by worrying about multiple future events. Ironically, in GAD, worry itself becomes an unwanted internal experience, prompting attempts to avoid it, which may paradoxically increase its frequency (Wells, 1995; Roemer & Borkovec, 1993; but see Purdon, 1999 for a review of inconsistencies in this literature). In this way, individuals with GAD are trapped in a cycle of experiential avoidance, perpetuating negative internal experience through their attempts to end this experience.

GAD is also subtly associated with behavioral restriction. Ironically, worrying about the future seems to result in procrastination, not successful, concrete problem-solving (Borkovec, Hazlett-Stevens, & Diaz, 1999).

CLINICAL APPROACH

When considering ACT in the treatment of a client diagnosed with an anxiety disorder, we start by explaining our treatment model to the client and discussing alternative approaches to ensure that the client is able to give informed consent. For instance, in treating a client with social anxiety disorder, we might say,

> One approach to treating social anxiety disorder that has some research support is cognitive-behavior therapy which is focused mainly on changing the nature of your thoughts. For instance, if you were to think you weren't good enough to ask someone out on a date, that approach would work on looking at the evidence supporting that thought, and would try to replace it with a more rational thought. CBT also gives you homework assignments during which you are asked to practice things that make you anxious with the assumption that your anxiety will eventually go down. Our approach to therapy shares some similarities with CBT, but there are also some differences. Basically, we think that direct attempts to change your thoughts don't always work and that sometimes they can even make the thoughts stronger and lead you to feel more and more out of control. We think that fear, sadness, and self-doubt are all part of the normal human experience and that it might be how we react to those thoughts and emotions—rather than the thoughts and feelings themselves— that cause us so much distress. We also think that your anxiety and related avoidance pulls you away from living the kind of life that you really value and so our treatment focuses on helping you to reconnect with what really matters to you. Part of this means examining alternative ways of coping with the barriers that have held you back from living the kind of life you really want to lead.

As demonstrated by this brief description, we find it useful to introduce the concept of values before we actually even begin treatment with the client. Clients with anxiety disorders almost invariably present to treatment with a clear conceptualization of their problem and with the goals of treatment: they have too much anxiety and they need to get rid of it. They are quite certain that the primary goal of treatment is anxiety reduction. Thus, we suggest in our initial contact with the client that we will be asking them to reconsider that goal and to consider alternatives. We are particularly mindful of this issue when we are treating clients in the context of an anxiety disorder treatment clinic, when our clients have had previous trials of cognitive-behavioral treatment, or when they have done considerable research into the treatment of anxiety. Often, we include an assessment of behavior in valued domains (Wilson & Murrell, in press; an earlier version of this is in Hayes et al., 1999, pp. 222–228) in our pretreatment assessment to underscore the prominence of this area in our treatment.

In most cases, some form of an exposure procedure is the most empirically supported component of treatment for anxiety disorders and these strategies are woven seamlessly into our application of other ACT methods. In our experience, it is common for clients initially to be unwilling to engage in exposure, to be willing only if they can do so without experiencing significant distress, or to find that they revert to various forms of avoidance and cognitive fusion during exposure. In such cases, we find that ACT often creates a therapeutic context that can encourage and mobilize the client to take action and to do so in a way that is more flexible and effective. Depending on the nature of the anxiety disorder and the course of treatment, exposure might be fairly traditional (for instance, in the case of OCD) or might be created through the assignment of valued actions (for instance, in the case of GAD).

Below we will highlight some methods of ACT that we believe to be particularly useful in the treatment of anxiety disorders. While we find the vast majority of ACT methods to be useful in the treatment of each disorder, a full description of the complete treatment of each disorder is beyond the scope of this chapter. Instead, we present some general techniques that may be useful for clients with any anxiety disorder before discussing a few disorder specific issues. One of the struggles in describing a treatment approach, especially a psychotherapy with a heavy experiential focus such as ACT, is that the description is inherently linear and generic, while the practice of therapy involves implicitly and explicitly weaving a number of concepts together and integrating them into one's interactions with the client. Nonetheless, we hope to provide an overview of some information that will help you the therapist use ACT in the treatment of these common disorders.

Assessment Strategies

Following our description of treatment to the client in the informed consent stages, we typically begin with a process designed to assess the client's conceptualization of his or her presenting problems, expectations for therapy, previous attempts to cope with the perceived problem, and overall quality of life. Our assessment often includes a structured clinical interview, questionnaires that assess constructs relevant to our conceptualization of anxiety, symptoms, and life satisfaction, and a clinical interview focused on exploring the client's valued directions and the ways in which control efforts and avoidance have served to disconnect the client from activity in these domains. The specific measures that we use vary from case to case and disorder to disorder but often include the Anxiety Sensitivity Index—Revised (Taylor & Cox, 1998), a measure of fear of anxiety sensations, the Affective Control Scale (Williams, Chambless, & Ahrens, 1997), a measure of fear of loss of control when experiencing strong affective states, the Difficulties in Emotion Regulation Scale (Gratz & Roemer, 2004), a measure of acceptance-based emotion regulation, the Thought Control Questionnaire (Wells & Davies, 1994), a measure of strategies for controlling unpleasant and unwanted thoughts, the White Bear Suppression Inventory (Wegner & Zanakos, 1994), a measure of thought suppression and the Acceptance and Action Questionnaire (Hayes et al., in press), a measure of emotional avoidance and emotion-focused inaction. The Valued Living Questionnaire (Wilson, 2002) is used to assess the importance of specific life domains (e.g., intimate relations, work) to a particular client and the consistency with which he or she is acting in accordance with personal values about each of those domains.

Intervention Strategies

Challenging the control agenda. An exploration of the client's conceptualization of the presenting problem often uncovers the belief that "controlling the thoughts and physical sensations I experience when I come in contact with X is necessary in order for me to move forward with life." In order to set the stage for a radically different approach to the client's problems, we begin treatment by helping the client contact directly the futility of previous attempts to mount this agenda. The client is encouraged to describe the ways in which he or she has attempted in the past to cope with anxiety, panic, worry, obsessions, and so forth such as distraction, suppression, cognitive change efforts, avoidance, and substance use (prescription and recreational). The costs and benefits of these strategies are discussed with particular attention to the fleeting effects of such strategies, the painful thoughts and feelings associated with repeated failure to control anxiety, and the resulting restricted lifestyle. In many cases, clients are already painfully aware that avoiding anxiety-eliciting stimuli is somehow taking them away from life pursuits that matter to them. For example, a client with a specific phobia of flying might present to treatment because action consistent with her values in the family relations domain (i.e., "being there physically and emotionally for family members") is impeded by the phobia when her daughter and grandchildren move across the country. With more severe and chronic anxiety disorders, the relationship between anxiety control efforts and reductions in valued actions in life may be less apparent to the client as behavior motivated by avoidance has become habitual and subtle. Throughout the discussion of previously attempted solutions, the therapist gently distinguishes between beliefs the client holds that these methods *should* work ("I should be able to gain control over my anxiety") and the client's actual experience of how they work.

During this initial stage, clients are naturally curious about the alternative to direct efforts to control anxiety. It is important, however, that you refrain from providing premature answers to clients' inquiries in this regard for several reasons. First, by moving too quickly you may fail to appreciate the client's unique experiences. Second, providing a "quick-and-dirty" solution such as "the goal is to learn to accept your thoughts

Table 5.1. Examples of Clinical Issues and Treatment Implications of ACT with Anxiety Disorders

Clinical issues	Treatment implications
Client expresses the goal to be free of anxiety and anxiety-related thoughts	Validate as a reasonable wish and explore the possibility that it is unworkable. Consider metaphors from the Creative Hopelessness phase of ACT (*e.g., digging to get out of the hole*). Review the efficacy of past and present attempts to reach this goal and costs associated control efforts (in session and through homework).
Client reports that control efforts are working/ useful.	Introduce metaphors (*e.g., polygraph, love*) to open up the possibility that while internal control efforts may sometimes appear to work, they often fail when really needed. Have client monitor efficacy of control efforts in anxiety provoking situations.
Client minimizes interference of avoidance in daily life	Use "feed the tiger" metaphor to illustrate cumulative consequences of avoidance. Monitor daily action and obstacles to potential actions in valued domains.
Client is unwilling to take action that may elicit anxiety-related thoughts and feelings	Use mindfulness exercises and other defusion methods to decrease the threatening nature of internal experiences. Review willingness as a behavior rather than a feeling. Use experiential exercises to help client reconnect with values.
Client asks for more explicit instructions on "how" to accept thoughts and feelings	Use "Tell me how to walk" exercise to demonstrate the limits of verbal instruction

and feelings" is unlikely to have much impact, and may even be perceived as simplistic or trivializing. Perhaps most importantly, even if accepted by the client, such statements are likely only to encourage further cognitive entanglement and rule-governed behavior, thereby undercutting one of the ultimate goals of ACT. Failing to provide immediate answers to the client's questions about alternatives to experiential control can sometimes be awkward and uncomfortable. We have found that simply letting clients know that we will work together to find ways of dealing with anxiety that will allow clients to live a valued life generally assuages the need for immediate answers.

The next phase of treatment typically involves offering the client our conceptual model of the development, maintenance, and treatment of anxiety disorders. This presentation covers two distinct concepts: the adaptive function of emotion and maladaptive consequences of attempts to control emotional and cognitive experiences. Drawing from traditional cognitive-behavioral treatments for anxiety and other acceptance-based treatments such as Dialectical Behavior Therapy (Linehan, 1993), we discuss how emotions are adaptive in that they communicate important information to an individual about his/her reaction to a context (e.g., "I feel fearful when a car is moving toward me," "I feel sad when someone I care about tells me they are moving away"), and they motivate behavior (movement away from the car; taking action to stay in contact with the friend). Emotions may sometimes produce an uncomfortable state, but attempting to ignore or change them can have significant negative consequences. We use the *Stove Metaphor* to highlight the analogy between physical pain (another unwanted, but adaptive internal experience) and emotional pain. We suggest that if one experiences physical pain when touching a hot stove, attempting to stop that internal signal of pain or distract oneself from it can have significant consequences (e.g., you may leave your hand on the stove and continue to get burned). So, while the experience of pain is unpleasant, it is adaptive in that it sends the message that an action is needed (moving one's hand). Further, if one avoids using a stove for fear of the possibility of experiencing physical pain, then the value of self-care (e.g., nourishing oneself) becomes secondary to attempts to avoid the internal experience of pain.

In this discussion of the function of emotion, we also differentiate emotional experiences that are clearly responses to a specific situation (e.g., "I feel anxious when I give a speech") and those that are muddied by reactions to that initial emotional response (e.g., "I feel anxious when I give a speech and I shouldn't feel this way; here I go again; I can't control this feeling; I am a failure"). We refer to these as "clear" and "muddy" emotions, drawing from the concept of "clean and dirty" emotions in ACT. We prefer the term muddy emotions to dirty emotions for two reasons. First, for some of our clients, labeling an emotional state as dirty increased the negative association they had with their internal experiences and seemed to perpetuate avoidance efforts. Second, we find the term muddy to more concisely describe the process that occurs when one has a complex reaction to a clear, emotional response. For instance, we include under our description of muddy other factors that may diminish clarity of an emotional response, such as poor self-care leading to emotion dysregulation, reminders of other emotionally evocative contexts that may lead to an exaggerated response to a particular context, and leftover responses to previous emotional events that may again lead to exaggerated responses in a particular situation.

We suggest that the first clear, response reactions are normal and adaptive. In some cases, they may communicate that an action is needed (e.g., "I feel fear when a stranger approaches me with a gun"). In other cases, they may signal that you are engaging in an activity that is difficult, and that you have deemed important (e.g., "I feel anxious when I stand up for myself with my boss"). In the latter case, one would note the emotional reaction and take action consistent with the valued direction. In contrast, muddied emotional reactions may signal the need to increase awareness and defusion (discussed later in therapy, and more fully elaborated below).

The second concept that we present is a description of the functional relationship between anxiety and behavior. We stress that worry, compulsive responses, rituals, safety behaviors and avoidance are all examples of the client's effort to *control* or *"get rid of"* anxiety. Through the use of examples, we explain how as humans we grow accustomed to controlling our environment and eliminating experiences that we find unpleasant. Eventually, this will lead to a discussion of the ACT "rule of mental events":

> Because of our ability to think, plan, and problem-solve, human beings are able to control their environment to a very large extent. For example, if I am too warm, I can take off my sweater. If I spill this glass of water, I can get a towel and wipe it up. In other words, if I don't like something, I can usually 'get rid of it'. It sounds like the same thing happens when you experience an anxious thought or feeling. You feel anxious, so you take actions designed to get rid of the anxious feelings. This gives you a sense of control. But notice there is something funny going on here. From what you've told me so far, your direct experience is that the harder you try to control your anxiety, the worse it gets. So, I'm wondering if there might be a difference in how deliberate control works in the outside world as compared to in our own minds and bodies.

Once the control function of avoidance/compulsions/ safety behaviors is presented, the therapist can offer the client the following paradox: While these responses are an apparent exercise of control over the environment and/or internal experiences, the client often experiences the responses themselves (e.g., worry, compulsive rituals) as *beyond* his or her control. The question to be explored at this juncture is "Who is really in control? The client or the anxious thoughts and feelings?" This question is examined across a number of sessions through discussions, in session experiential exercises, and between sessions self-monitoring.

The *Man in the Hole Metaphor* (Hayes et al., 1999, pp. 101–104) is often used to illustrate how the apparent success of control in the exterior world makes it very difficult to give up applying this strategy to internal experiences, even in the face of a lifetime of evidence of its futility.

If the client reports instances where attempts to control anxiety worked (i.e., my anxiety really comes down after I have a couple of drinks), an examination of the limits of control and the potential costs of control attempts can be useful. Thus, we acknowledge that there may be occasions when one can temporarily reduce one's anxiety by redirecting attention or engaging in an activity such as alcohol use. At the same time, we invite the client to acknowledge the growing sense of vulnerability that comes with such temporary solutions, and to note that when they felt they really needed to control anxiety and were unable to do so, sometimes control attempts actually amplified their distress. The *Polygraph Metaphor* (Hayes et al., 1999, pp. 123–124) can facilitate contact with this concept, as can homework assignments that involve the client monitoring anxious thoughts and feelings, control efforts, and resulting thoughts and feelings.

The *Passengers on the Bus Metaphor* (Hayes et al., 1999, pp. 157–158) is another useful metaphor that can illustrate how the client's attempts to gain control have actually resulted in the loss of control over his or her life direction. In the metaphor, the client's anxious thoughts (e.g., "Did I leave the stove on?" "Is the door really locked?", "Do I look like a fool in this interaction?") are presented as "passengers," and avoidance, compulsive responses and rituals as "side streets" that take the driver off course (e.g., rather than leaving one's apartment to attend a job interview, several hours are devoted to rituals designed to eliminate thoughts about danger).

Willingness as an Alternative

Once a client begins to experience the futility and cost of anxiety control efforts, the possibility of allowing oneself to have such experiences while moving forward in the direction of valued goals is presented. Both the *Chinese Handcuffs* metaphor (pushing yourself farther into them is what it takes to give yourself room to move around) and the *Tug of War with a Monster* metaphor (rather than struggling to pull against the monster on the other side of the rope, perhaps the best way to stop yourself from being dragged into the pit by the monster is to let go of the rope) are offered to introduce the idea of acceptance as an alternative to the cognitive and emotional control agenda (see Hayes et al., 1999, pp. 104 and 109 respectively).

The *Two Scales Metaphor* (Hayes et al., 1999, pp. 133–134) can be an effective way to introduce the relationship between willingness and anxiety. In this metaphor, we suggest that the client has been trying to turn the volume of their "anxiety reaction" scale down, but that it is stuck on high because of the low setting of a second, overlooked scale we call the "willingness to have anxiety" scale. Whereas movement on the reaction scale is beyond the client's control, the client can determine the setting of the willingness scale. Clients are often in a situation in which the willingness scale is set low, and this low setting is locking the reactions scale on high (anxiety). We suggest to clients that if they choose to turn up the willingness scale, reactions will be freed up and can vary to include happiness, joy, sadness, anxiety, surprise etc. In other words, while choosing willingness will not necessarily result in reduced anxiety (e.g., it is not an anxiety control method), it will unlock the reactions scale and allow an individual to experience range of emotional experiences that occur in the living of a valued life.

Often, willingness and acceptance are initially misunderstood to be synonymous with resignation—the idea that the client needs to accept the inevitability of constant anxiety and a restricted lifestyle. This misunderstanding is addressed by spending some time defining the qualities of applied willingness and illuminating the relationship between willingness and commitment to valued action.

For instance, willingness is clearly delineated from wanting as is illustrated in the *Joe the Bum* (Hayes et al., 1999, pp. 239–240) or, as we sometimes adapt it, the *Joe the Annoying Neighbor* metaphor. In this story, the client is asked to imagine hosting an open house to which all the neighbors are invited. The party is an enjoyable success and then Joe arrives with his annoying voice, his complaints and put-downs and his embarrassing clothing and mannerisms. The choice is to welcome Joe to the party, even when you hold a very strong negative opinion of him, or to spend the rest of the party attempting to get rid of him and preventing him from returning. Either you engage in the party along with Joe and your negative evaluation of him, or you miss out on the party while attempting to keep Joe away. The poem, "The Guest House" by Rumi (printed in Segal, Williams, & Teasdale, 2002), often used in mindfulness-based interventions, can also be used to communicate the quality of willingness.

Anxious clients frequently attempt to negotiate limits on willingness, especially when contemplating exposure exercises. For example, a client with agoraphobia might proclaim a willingness to venture to the mall, but only on the condition that his or her heart does not begin racing. True willingness cannot be limited by the quality or quantity of one's internal experiences. An ice skater in an ACT workshop described it this way: "I can decide whether to do a single-axle or a double-axle, but if I am going to do either jump, I have to commit to *jump*." Willingness can, however, be limited behaviorally by controlling the amount of time one allows oneself to come in contact with anxiety provoking stimuli, and the specific stimuli one is willing to confront. Clients can usually be persuaded to experience complete willingness either for a very brief period (e.g., 30 seconds or 1 minute initially), and/or in a relatively safe setting (e.g., the therapist's office) despite their common and understandable initial reluctance. The therapist can then build on such experiences to extend the settings and the durations during which the client is willing to be willing.

One of the primary goals in the application of ACT to individuals diagnosed with anxiety disorders is to facilitate the experience of anxiety, obsessions, and worry in a new context of willingness and defusion, thereby changing the nature of the experience from an unwanted, dangerous event to a thought or feeling that one is willing to have. It is not the *content* of a thought or feeling that makes it problematic, but rather the "unwillingness" to experience it. One way to demonstrate this idea (using OCD as an example) is to describe how others might experience the exact same thoughts that the client finds distressing. You can help the client see that when others are willing to have these thoughts and do not engage in rituals to "get rid of" them, the thoughts are simply experienced as thoughts, and do not evolve into obsessions. This is true, even if the thoughts are experienced as disturbing or anxiety-provoking. This point can be demonstrated with an example like the following:

> Two individuals are driving to work one morning along an identical route, each in his own car. Driver #1 has OCD, while Driver #2 does not. After driving through a school zone, both have the following sequence of thoughts: "I may have accidentally hit a small child with my car, even though I did not see or feel anything to suggest that. If this is the case, I might be dragging the child beneath the body of my car even now." While this might be an unusual thought for Driver #2 to have, all people have unusual thoughts from time to time. Both individuals find this thought disturbing and anxiety-provoking. Because Driver #1 is unwilling to have this thought and the anxiety that accompanies it, he pulls the car over and gets out to look underneath it. He may even drive back to the school zone to look for any bodies that might be lying beside the road. This "checking behavior" is an attempt to "get rid of" the disturbing thought and anxiety. Driver #2, while certainly not pleased with the thought, is willing to have it and continue driving to work. In both cases, the thought is the same, and even the anxiety level associated with the thought may be the same. The only difference between Driver #1 and Driver #2 is the willingness or unwillingness to have the thought as a thought.

Willingness is always discussed as something that will allow the client to choose valued life activities that have been abandoned in the name of controlling anxiety. We do not ask clients to experience distress for its own sake but only *in the service of* being able to pursue valued life ends. In fact, this link between willingness and committed action is one of the key features distinguishing ACT from traditional experiential approaches to psychotherapy. Like ACT, many humanistic, existential, and Gestalt psychotherapies also emphasize an accepting stance toward unwanted or distressing private experiences. As a general rule, however, these approaches emphasize experience for experience's sake, without explicitly linking willingness to values and specific behavioral goals. ACT blends experiential openness and acceptance on the one hand with work toward specific valued goals on the other.

We actively present the client with the conflict between wanting to engage in a valued and fulfilling life and wanting to avoid uncomfortable experiences. While both of those wishes are entirely valid and understandable, the client's personal experience suggests that they cannot be achieved simultaneously. The client's negative experiences with living a behaviorally restricted life, or attempting to control inner experiences while engaging life, is contrasted with the possibility of living a valued life while being willing to experience the inevitable thoughts, feelings and bodily sensations that accompany action. Typically, at this point in therapy, clients are cautiously open to the possibility of exploring the previously untried option of willingness, defusion, and valued action.

Methods to Facilitate Willingness

Willingness to take action that is consistent with personal values requires that the client make experiential contact with values and the committed action that they stimulate. Often, connecting with values produces pain that comes from recognizing how attempts to control anxiety have interfered with living a vital, purposeful life. Methods that encourage contact with a transcendent sense of self and that defuse or deliteralize thoughts can be useful in removing barriers to willingness.

Self-monitoring of thoughts, emotions, bodily sensations, and behavior can be introduced following the first session as a means of increasing the client's awareness and labeling of internal experiences. For instance, a client with GAD who initially reports "I am a worrier who feels terrible all the time" can instead notice that he had a thought about the safety of his children on Wednesday that was accompanied by a feeling of anxiety. This distinction becomes important as the client begins to consider taking action that may elicit thoughts and feelings that are perceived as negative.

We typically introduce the concept of mindfulness—nonjudgmentally observing one's experience without attempting to change it—early on in therapy and continue to revisit and practice it throughout. Initially, we practice mindfulness exercises directed at observing bodily experiences such as breathing, muscle tension, and the perception of sound. Once the concept of willingness is more fully understood and the client has gained some expertise in the practice of observing internal experiences, we introduce the more difficult mindfulness practices of observing one's thoughts and emotions. The *Leaves on a Stream* (Hayes et al., 1999, pp. 158–162) exercise, during which the client is asked to try and place each thought that is noticed on a leaf and watch it flow down a stream, is one practice that can be used to facilitate this process.

One client with OCD likened the process of observing his inner experiences to watching scrap metal go by on a conveyor belt. His temptation was to reach into the scrap metal as it moved by in an effort to sort it out. Some of the scrap metal was judged to be "good" and salvageable, while other pieces were regarded as flawed or even dangerous. But, the problem with sorting out scrap metal is that our bare hands and forearms get scraped and cut. The objective of mindfulness is to stand aside, watching, but keeping ones hands off of the scrap metal, simply letting it continue to move by.

The *Observer Exercise* (Hayes et al., 1999, pp. 192–196) can also be a powerful experience that illuminates a sense of self that remains constant, regardless of the thoughts, feelings, memories, bodily experiences and roles that come and go in the course of one's life. The *Mountain* and *Lake Meditations* from Kabat-Zinn (1994) can also experientially strengthen a sense of self that experiences daily and seasonal changes on the surface while remaining constant below. A number of metaphors such as the *Box with Stuff* and *Chessboard* (Hayes et al., 1999, pp. 136–138 and 190–192) also illustrate a sense of self as the context in which the content of anxious thoughts, images, feelings, and sensations reside.

Cognitive defusion and deliteralization techniques are also directed at helping the client to gain some distance from his or her internal experiences. From an ACT perspective, it is cognitive fusion that ultimately underlies experiential avoidance, so all of the work on willingness is also work on defusion and vice versa. Many of the techniques described throughout this chapter are at one level defusion techniques. Defusion procedures are only now being independently evaluated, but the initial results with distressing and anxiety-provoking events is positive (Masuda, Hayes, Sackett, & Twohig, in press).

One simple, but potentially powerful intervention is to begin to verbally label thoughts, feelings, and sensations as such when describing them in and outside of sessions. For example, you can have the client preface obsessional thoughts with the phrase "I'm having the thought that . . . " Other methods include singing the thoughts, saying them in silly voices, or observing them in silly script (such as bubble letters). This convention can be developed in session and applied outside of session as a habitual reminder of the separation between self, internal experiences, and behavior.

Another important issue addressed in this phase of therapy is the common use of thoughts and feelings as causes of behavior. For a client with an anxiety disorder, the most frequent reason given for not engaging in some valued activity is "I was too anxious." Statements such as "I wanted to go to the party, but I was anxious" and "I left the mall because I had a panic attack" essentially define these disorders. We adopt a few verbal conventions that undermine this assumed relationship. Specifically, we ask our clients to replace virtually all self-referential "buts" with the word "and" (e.g., "I wanted to go to the party and I was having feelings of anxiety"). We also ask clients to replace the word "can't" with "am choosing not to" such as "I can't give a presentation at work" with "I am choosing to not give a presentation at work." Both of these changes are designed to weaken the established link, often supported and maintained by the client's environment, between internal experiences and behavior. Thus, these methods are also defusion procedures.

Values

Although values clarification is the last phase of ACT discussed in this chapter, facilitating the client's ability to engage in valued activity is the ultimate purpose of therapy and it is addressed throughout the course of treatment. As discussed above, we assess behavior in valued domains at the outset of therapy and inform our clients that our treatment is aimed at increasing valued activity. When discussing the problems of attempting to control internal experiences and the possibility of becoming willing to allow those experiences to be present, behaving consistently in valued domains is the benchmark against which we compare these approaches to living. Once the idea of willingness is presented, the remainder of therapy is focused on two themes: revisiting values and building patterns of committed action, while teaching and reinforcing the use of methods designed to facilitate willingness.

We use a number of discussions, metaphors, exercises, and homework assignments designed to convey the idea that valuing is the process of purposeful action that brings vitality and meaningfulness to life. Early on in therapy, we sometimes give clients a writing assignment based on one developed by Wilson and Murrell (in press). Clients are asked to write for 20 minutes three times over the course of a week and to "really let go and explore your very deepest emotions and thoughts about the topics listed below." Topics for potential inclusion in this writing are a description of their valued domains, an exploration of the potential barriers to value-consistent action, and their deepest thoughts and feelings related to not acting consistently in accordance with those stated values.

In subsequent sessions, clients are asked to consider a number of life domains (e.g., family relations, career, recreation, spirituality) and to identify any values they may hold in any or all of these areas. In session, a number of issues related to the idea of valuing are presented to facilitate this assignment. For instance, clients can respond to the initial presentation of values with a list of goals that they think they should achieve in order to justify their being and/or to gain approval or acceptance from others. In ACT, work is done to clarify the differences between goals and values, to underscore the role of choice (as compared to reasoning or figuring out) in valuing, and to help the client gain "ownership" over values such that social influences do not entirely control choice in behavior. A number of in and out of session exercises are available to facilitate this work. For instance, the *Skiing Metaphor* (Hayes et al., 1999, pp. 220–221) helps to clarify the relationship between values and goals as process and outcome. One is asked to "imagine being poised on skis at the top of a mountain and having a helicopter pilot fly you to the bottom each time you are about to ski down. While you have achieved the goal of getting to the bottom of the mountain, it is apparent that the process of skiing is what makes getting to the bottom matter." The client can be asked to state and defend their favorite flavor of ice cream to experientially demonstrate the concept of choice, which reflects an action one can take without needing to provide reasons, explanations, or rationalizations.

Once clients identify some values that they hold, we ask them to self-monitor on a daily basis whether or not they engaged in an activity consistent with this value and, if not, what obstacles prevented such action. This homework exercise often results in several useful observations. For some clients, their use of thoughts, behaviors, bodily sensations, and emotions as reasons for not taking action becomes clearly evident through this process. Other find they actually *are* engaging in values consistent activities, but their struggle with worry, self-doubt, or anxiety prevents fully participating in and enjoying these activities.

Once clients have a better sense of their values and are open to the idea of action in valued domains, we ask them to make a commitment to action. This phase of treatment can be done in a number of ways. For instance, in our treatment of GAD, after discussing the idea of commitment in session, we again ask our clients to engage in an out-of-session writing assignment about their deepest thoughts and feelings related to making a commitment, including past failed attempts at commitment. In group treatment of social phobia, we have asked our clients to stand and make a public commitment to the group. This offers clients a chance publicly to "take a stand" with regard to what matters to them. It also provides an opportunity for *in vivo* exposure to anxiety eliciting stimuli and a chance to notice immediate and secondary reactions to the anxiety and discomfort that ultimately arises during the process of sharing one's intimate desires.

The *Garden Metaphor* highlights the importance of choosing a valued direction and the need to recommit to that direction even in the face of obstacles. This metaphor suggests that in order to grow a substantial crop such as beets or potatoes, one must pick and stick with a garden plot despite noticing all the faults of the plot (too little sun, too many rocks) and seeing or imagining a plot with better drainage and more sunlight. At this point, and continuing throughout therapy, we continue to suggest that commitments reflect an intention to act consistent with one's values and that failures to carry though with intended actions are expected. We often use a metaphor described by Marlatt (1994) to differentiate lapses (or failures at engaging in valued activities followed by a re-commitment to action) from relapses (an assumption that a failed attempt at action reflects a irrevocable failure and continued rumination over the failure). In this metaphor two monks who have taken vows of silence, as well as vows not to touch or even look upon women, come across a woman who is unable to cross a muddy creek. The first monk quickly picks up the woman, carries her across, puts her down and continues the walk. The second monk is incredulous over this behavior, ruminates over it for as long as he can until he finally breaks his vow of silence to admonish the first monk for his breach in behavior. The first monk replies, "I put her down hours ago. It seems as if you are still carrying her."

Although it can be helpful when a client identifies one or two valued domains to focus on through the remainder of therapy, more commonly clients settle on some interpersonal value that cuts across a number of domains such as intimate relationships, parenting, relationships with co-workers, and building/improving social connections. Often our clients continue to explore and rediscover their values throughout the course of therapy. External demands often require more or less focus on a particular valued domain and since a key goal of ACT is the establishment or more psychological flexibility, we encourage our clients to respond flexibly to those environmental exigencies. Some of our clients, particularly those with GAD, report that the importance of too many valued domains elevates their stress and anxiety. In such cases, careful analysis of the pliance related to particular values ("I should be spending more time working;" "a good parent would attend every PTO event") can help the client make freer choices about behavior. Our clinical stance is that it is the process of valuing that is critical to success in therapy rather than rigid adherence to behavior in a particular domain. Consistent with this emphasis on living a life worth living, we often have our clients monitor daily engagement in valued action across all domains as a way to helping maintain attention to their daily valuing.

Throughout the remainder of therapy, we continue to collaborate with clients to come up with potential valued activities for the week and we monitor successes and failures in keeping those commitments. When clients are having a difficult time following though with commitments, we have a number of suggestions for them to consider. For instance, we may have them write about, discuss, or imagine the personal relevance and importance of the chosen value. We suggest a number of mindfulness or defusion practices designed to provide some distance from perceived internal barriers. We may experientially explore the pain associated with engagement in the valued activity as well as the pain associated with avoiding it. If the client returns to the hope that control efforts will make valued behavior easier, we conduct mini-experiments to test out that hypothesis.

In some cases, values work provides adequate "exposure" to treat the anxiety disorder. More typically, however, especially in cases of OCD, social anxiety disorder, and panic disorder, some type of systematic exposure such as that practiced in traditional cognitive-behavioral treatments becomes a central focus of treatment. However, when exposure is conducted within the framework of ACT, the rationale is slightly altered. Rather than encouraging the client to engage in exposure with the goal of reducing anxiety, we emphasize engagement in valued activity as the rationale. The "exposure" we seek is to the domains in living that the client matters about. This gives the client the sense of direction needed to make room for anxiety experiences while engaging in valued actions. We don't predict that anxiety symptoms will get better or worse, nor is that the goal of exposure of this kind.

DISORDER SPECIFIC CLINICAL CONSIDERATIONS

Panic Disorder

Cognitive behavior therapy, particularly panic control treatment (PCT; Barlow & Craske, 2000), has been shown to be highly effective in the treatment of panic disorder (e.g., Barlow, Gorman, Shear, & Woods, 2000). In this approach clients are taught that the experiences they label as panic attacks and evaluate as catastrophic are normal and harmless bodily sensations. Clients are encouraged to participate in interoceptive exposure, or deliberate exposure to internal cues and sensations of panic, with the goal of reducing the likelihood that a panic attack will occur. Once the fear of internal sensations is targeted, the focus shifts to in-vivo exposure directed toward any accompanying agoraphobic avoidance. Cognitive restructuring is also an integral part of this treatment package as currently offered.

ACT is consistent with most of the core elements of this approach, particularly the elements that are known to be most central to its success.

For example, interoceptive exposure involves a willingness to experience uncomfortable internal reactions. Other elements, such as cognitive restructuring interventions, seem more in conflict, but even here a key part of the traditional CBT message is that one can take action even while experiencing negatively evaluated thoughts and sensations. Conversely, as evidenced by the very name of the intervention (panic *control* therapy), the explicit goal of treatment is a reduction in anxiety, including anxiety triggering internal sensations, while ACT does not emphasize the elimination or reduction of anxiety symptoms as a primary treatment goal. Seeing anxiety for what it is, distinguishing self from the symptoms of anxiety and doing what will promote a valued life are at the heart of ACT.

While it is not yet known if removal of the control-focused elements of traditional CBT are helpful or hurtful, some experimental work offers preliminary support for the utility of an acceptance rationale for enhancing exposure therapy among clients with a panic disorder diagnosis. Levitt and colleagues compared the physiological arousal, self-reported anxiety, and willingness to participate in a second carbon dioxide inhalation challenge of participants diagnosed with panic disorder who were randomly assigned to a suppression, acceptance, or control instruction condition before engaging in a CO_2 inhalation challenge (Levitt et al., in press). The acceptance rationale was drawn from the original ACT manual (Hayes et al., 1999). Although the groups did not differ in their physiological response to the challenge, clients in the acceptance group reported less anxiety and a greater willingness to participate in a second challenge than did the other two groups. Similar results have been shown by Eifert and Heffner (2003) with anxious females selected by the AAQ who were exposed to CO_2 enriched air following diaphragmatic breathing training or the use of an ACT acceptance exercise (an overt version of the "Chinese Finger Trap" Hayes et al., 1999, pp. 104–105). This study compliments Levitt et al. because a different specific ACT component was used, with the same result, and it was successfully compared to a condition (breathing training) of known value to anxiety disordered patients.

The results of these studies and other correlational or analog studies along the same lines (e.g., Felder, Zvolensky, Eifert, & Spira, 2003; Karekla, Forsyth, & Kelly, in press) suggest that we should continue to examine the potential utility of ACT in the treatment of panic disorder. It should be noted that no component analyses of PCT have shown that its few ACT-inconsistent elements are key to its effects. Indeed, trials are currently underway comparing PCT with PCT cast in an ACT-consistent manner (e.g., with acceptance rationale instead of control-linked rationales), which will determine how an ACT consistent form of exposure compares with a traditional CBT use of the same intervention.

Specific Phobia

Given that many individuals with specific phobia may not experience dramatic life altering impact related to their fears and may be ambivalent about treatment, the first issue you have to address is whether or not it is worth it to the client to "wade through the swamp" of his or her fears. Thus, treatment would initially focus on clarifying what gives the client's life meaning and how his or her avoidance of feared objects or situations might be impinging on his or her quality of life. We have found that the *Tombstone and Eulogy Exercises* are very effective methods for increasing motivation to commit to treatment.

Individuals presenting with one specific phobia will often meet criteria for additional phobias (e.g., Curtis, Magee, Eaton, Wittchen, & Kessler, 1998) or the index phobia may be causing interference across multiple contexts (Antony & Barlow, 2002) such as in the case of a claustrophobic who may avoid elevators at work, flying to visit relatives, and healthcare appointments that involve an MRI. Thus, you should conduct a broad assessment of functioning status in all relevant life domains.

Given the circumscribed nature of specific phobia, it is easy to underestimate the potential presence (and pervasiveness) of experiential avoidance. The client may not readily identify bodily sensations, thoughts, or feelings as the focus of his or her fear. Most often, clients relate their behavioral problems to being in the presence of the phobic stimulus. Nevertheless, we routinely assess how clients are "managing" their private experiences associated with fear. This is an important clinical variable because research suggests that fear of physical sensations varies across specific phobic types with situational phobias (including claustrophobia) being associated with the higher reports of anxiety sensitivity (Antony & Barlow, 2002). In addition, about 1/3 to 1/2 of individuals presenting with a primary diagnosis of specific phobia meet criteria for an additional anxiety or mood disorder (e.g., Brown, Campbell, Lehman, Grisham, & Mancill, 2001; Sanderson, DiNardo, Rapee, & Barlow, 1990) suggesting that there may be more pervasive problems with emotional avoidance than are readily apparent. The Acceptance and Action Questionnaire (Hayes et al., in press) and the Anxiety Sensitivity Index (Taylor & Cox, 1998) are good ways to assess the extent to which the individual fears the private experiences brought about by the feared stimuli.

Social Anxiety Disorder

Cognitive behavior therapy programs for social anxiety disorder typically stress several distinct treatment components, including graduated, systematic exposure (using both simulated interpersonal and/or performance exercises as well as in vivo assignments), cognitive restructuring, and social skills training (Cohn & Hope, 2001; Kashdan & Herbert, 2001). With the exception of the cognitive restructuring component, which must be modified to de-emphasize changes in content in order to fit with the ACT model, each of these treatment strategies can be readily incorporated into an ACT framework. Cognitive approaches to the treatment of social anxiety disorder typically focus on addressing the content of anxiety-related thoughts immediately prior to and again immediately following exposure exercises. In ACT, we modify this procedure by encouraging clients to take a few moments before and again after exposure exercises to notice current thoughts, feelings, and bodily sensations (perhaps describing these aloud) and notice that they can act *with* all of these, without needing to change anything about them. There is some preliminary support for the treatment of social anxiety using an ACT approach, particularly in group format (Block & Wulfert, 2002).

One aspect of the values clarification and goal setting work with this population deserves mention. From an ACT perspective, you should not assume that eliminating all social avoidance is necessarily the client's goal. Your goal is to help the client explore and clarify his or her own values, and discuss the extent to which avoidance of feared situations may interfere with movement toward these values. In our experience, most clients will come to recognize the negative impact of social avoidance. They can then conceptualize avoidance as a barrier to effective action toward chosen values, and begin taking steps to confront it. Allowing clients to come to their own conclusions permits them to take ownership of the goal of reducing avoidance, and reduces the possibility of potentially dysfunctional pliance.

OCD

Prolonged exposure to situations that typically elicit obsessive thoughts and the prevention of behavioral and mental rituals designed to reduce or ameliorate anxiety (Exposure and Response Prevention, ERP) has been shown to be an effective treatment for OCD (e.g., van Balkom et al., 1994; Steketee & Frost, 1998). Cues related to obsessions and compulsions that can be presented as exposure might include stimuli (holding contaminants, looking at a disordered room) or behaviors (turning off the stove, locking the door). Exposure can include in vivo exposure to actual stimuli or situations associated with obsessions and compulsions or imagery based exposure to images or thoughts. One of the frequently discussed shortcomings with ERP is the relative high patient drop out rate observed in clinical studies. Many patients with OCD are simply not willing to commit to this type of highly intrusive exposure treatment.

Our experience is that blending in ACT interventions sometimes makes the ERP treatment more acceptable to clients. For example, we often use a variant of the "take your mind for a walk" exercise. In this exercise, we will walk behind the client chattering obsessive thoughts while the client avoids engaging in the compulsive behaviors associated with the thoughts. Alternatively, you can simply chatter commands about where to walk, while the client chooses where to walk independent of the chatter. In either case, this defusion exercise provides an opportunity for the client to see his or her thoughts as "just" thoughts rather than as something more. Another ACT exposure technique is to have the client assign obsessive thoughts to each of his or her house keys. The client is instructed to think the thought whenever each key is handled during the day. The emphasis here is on experiencing the thought as a thought, and handling it, or carrying it, just like the client carries the keys.

Since the objective of exposure is to allow the client to experience obsessive thoughts as well as the anxiety that accompanies them, any responses that function to reduce anxiety should be prevented. This includes both overt behavioral responses like hand-washing or checking as well as subtle responses such as attention shifting or seeking reassurance from the therapist. Experiential avoidance in clients with OCD can be quite subtle, and is often not overtly behavioral. Foa and Kozak (1986) provide numerous examples of cognitive avoidance that arises even during exposure exercises. They found that patients imagined that they were elsewhere, focused on non-feared aspects of a situation, or actively distorted fearful images. In one example, a client with fears of contamination by urine showed an uncharacteristically rapid decline in anxiety after urine was placed on several places on his arm. Afterward, the client explained that in his imagination, he "froze" the contaminated spots to prevent them from "spreading" and was thus able to stop attending to them. In this example, ACT interventions would emphasize the importance of being willing, not only to be exposed to the urine, but to experience the thoughts of contamination and "spreading" that are related to the exposure. Willingness as an all-or nothing concept could be discussed here to underscore the consequences of insidious but subtle avoidance and escape behaviors.

GAD

Our approach to treating GAD combines traditional cognitive behavioral strategies with strategies taken from ACT and other acceptance-based interventions, all delivered in the context of an ACT-consistent conceptualization of GAD (described above; see also Roemer & Orsillo, 2002). The general description above illustrates the way we use ACT strategies to address the experiential avoidance and behavioral restriction that characterizes GAD.

We emphasize a variety of mindfulness-based strategies in our treatment of GAD. We believe that mindfulness is particularly beneficial in the treatment of GAD for several reasons. First, individuals with GAD focus excessively on the future; mindfulness facilitates present moment awareness and attention to current environmental contingencies, which can increase adaptive responding to the environment (Borkovec, 2002). Second, individuals with GAD have difficulty identifying and differentiating their emotional responses (Mennin, Heimberg, Turk, & Fresco, 2002); mindfulness interventions may increase contact with emotional experience in a non-threatening way and lead to better emotion differentiation. Finally, mindfulness may be particularly helpful in reducing clients' identification with their worry content.

To facilitate mindfulness, we provide psycho-education regarding the nature and skills of mindfulness and provide extensive opportunities for practice both within and between sessions. We use cognitive behavioral strategies such as diaphragmatic breathing and progressive muscle relaxation (Bernstein, Borkovec, & Hazlett-Stevens, 2000), as well as more traditional mindfulness exercises such as mindful eating, and breathing space (Kabat-Zinn, 1990; Segal et al., 2002). All of these exercises are practiced in a context of noticing and allowing one's internal experiences (e.g., breath, muscle tension, emotions, thoughts), rather than judging, changing or avoiding them. We address the potential risk of using relaxation strategies as rigid control strategies, while acknowledging that such strategies (as well as mindfulness exercises) may in fact lead to pleasant internal experiences at times (and the appearance that control over worry/anxiety is possible). We emphasize that the goal is not to eliminate or diminish anxiety in order to engage in life. If these strategies result in decreased anxiety, so be it, and the reverse holds true as well. The real aim of mindfulness practice is to increase contact with present moment experience, whether it be pleasant or unpleasant.

GENERAL CLINICAL CONSIDERATIONS

As is apparent from our description of treatment, ongoing assessment of the client's experiences and behavior through homework assignments is an integral component of our ACT applications. This provides us and the client with critical information related to behavior changes that have occurred and their clinical significance. We generally conduct a weekly assessment of relevant symptoms (e.g., anxiety, depression, suicidal ideation) as significant changes in either direction may merit examination and discussion in session. Finally, we frequently assess changes in the processes we consider key to ACT (e.g., acceptance, willingness) by asking clients to rate the percentage of time each week that they behave in a way that is consistent with these constructs.

While this assessment information can be considered a measure of treatment response, it should be interpreted with caution. It is our experience that response to ACT is not linear and that symptom reduction and intensification over time is expected as clients struggle with connecting to internal experiences and behavior. We have had a number of experiences in which our clients have experienced early symptom reduction that appears to be related to a sense of hopefulness about treatment and a preliminary, but limited, experiential understanding of acceptance. When clients are asked to engage in behavior that is associated with anxious thoughts, feelings, and bodily sensations, they may instinctively return to previously established habits aimed at anxiety reduction and experience a worsening of symptoms. We view this ebb and flow of symptoms as to be expected in the course of ACT treatment and address this with clients from the first session onward. It is one thing to be willing to be accept internal experiences in theory and quite another to do it in real life when challenging situations arise. We use the *Path up the Mountain Metaphor* (Hayes et al., 1999, p. 221) to remind our clients of the "switchbacks" that are an integral part of mountain trails that eventually allow us to get to the top. Our clients demonstrate the greatest treatment gains following these periods of struggle, likely because they are applying the concepts of ACT in a very real and painful way.

Another issue that deserves consideration is determining when to terminate ACT treatment. We believe that the most important work in ACT begins once therapy ends as clients continue to make choices about willingness and valued action. We often taper treatment from weekly to biweekly sessions once the client demonstrates a working understanding of the problems associated with attempts at experiential control, an openness to willingness, and a demonstrated commitment to valued action. In the last sessions we ask clients to come in with issues that they feel need additional attention before treatment ends. All along we set the stage for treatment being the very first step in a lifelong process that involves noticing attempts at avoidance, responding to experience, and making choices about behavior. We provide clients with handouts and exercises to use during difficult post-treatment experiences and encourage them to contact us for booster therapy on an as needed basis. We explicitly predict the possibility of "lapse" and help clients prepare for challenging times in the future, identifying exercises they can return to in order to remind themselves of key concepts. We encourage some form of consistent mindfulness (or defusion) practice in order to help them continue to practice experiential acceptance without therapy as a reminder.

Conclusion

Elements of current empirically supported treatments (ESTs) that are known to be critical to their effectiveness are compatible with ACT as are many recent treatment developments in the anxiety disorders arena. This includes a growing emphasis on the role emotional avoidance in the genesis of anxiety disorders and the important role that acceptance based interventions should play in the enhanced treatment models of the future. In addition, ACT brings to the table a set of interventions that are more unique (values based action, defusion), that have some empirical support, and that may enhance the effectiveness of current ESTs.

Whether ACT per se will be an evidence based treatment for one or more of the anxiety disorders will be determined by the clinical studies that are underway or are sure to come, but the link between ACT and anxiety seems likely only to grow. ACT was originally developed for use with anxiety disorders and that lineage is very evident throughout the current chapter. Perhaps it is not surprising then that the relevance of the ACT model to anxiety clients seems to be on increasingly strong empirical ground, and offers innovative and coherent approaches for clinicians working with this important population.

Chapter 6

ACT with Posttraumatic Stress Disorder

Alethea A. Varra and Victoria M. Follette

Epidemiological studies conducted in the United States indicate that prevalence rates for exposure to traumatic stressors may be as high as 70% of the adult population (Norris, 1992; Resnick, Kilpatrick, Dansky, Saunders, & Best, 1993). Trauma related experiences come in many forms: criminal victimization (rape, assault, armed robbery), domestic assault, childhood sexual abuse, natural catastrophes (tornado, fire) and combat related dangers, to name a few. Normal human responses to trauma (numbing, derealization, depersonalization) probably have significant adaptive value and over time tend to phase out of existence as the person integrates the impact of trauma in functional ways. However, for some trauma survivors, this adaptive integration does not occur. Instead, the impact of the trauma enlarges in their lives to the point that serious impairment in psychological, social and behavioral functioning occurs. Studies suggest that about 8% of the general population ultimately develops Posttraumatic Stress Disorder (PTSD; Breslau, Davis, Andreski, & Peterson, 1991; Kessler, Sonnega, Bronet, Hughs, & Nelson, 1995). Many trauma survivors seek therapy not only to address their private struggles with the aftermath of trauma, but also to help repair elements of their lives that are not working.

The diagnosis of PTSD fist appeared in the Diagnostic and Statistical Manual of mental disorders, third edition (DSM-III), with the intention of describing the characteristic symptoms that occur in individuals following exposure to extremely traumatic events (American Psychiatric Association [APA], 1980). PTSD is often characterized by high levels of anxiety and depression, but its distinctive symptomatology includes (1) reliving experiences such as intrusive thoughts, nightmares, dissociative flashbacks to elements of the original traumatic event, and psychophysiological re-activity to cues of the traumatic event and preoccupation with the event; (2) avoidance of thoughts, people, and places that resemble the traumatic event, emotional numbing, and an inability to feel the range of positive emotions; and (3) symptoms of hyperarousal, including heightened star-tle sensitivity, sleep problems, attention difficulties, hypervigilance, and irritability, anger, or rage (DSM-IV, APA, 1994).

In addition, necessary to a PTSD diagnosis is the first diagnostic crite-rion (Criterion A) which states that a person must experience or witness an event that involves "actual or threatened physical harm" and have an im-mediate subjective response to this experience that involves "intense fear, helplessness or horror" (APA, 1994). However, it is important to keep in mind that the experience of a traumatic event is necessary but not sufficient for the development of PTSD. As is obvious in the epidemiologic studies, only a fraction of those exposed to a potentially traumatic event develop PTSD. To explain this, trauma theorists have appealed to individual dif-ferences. A vast body of research (e.g., Dohrenwend & Dohrenwend, 1981; King, King, Foy, & Gudanowski, 1996; Fontana & Rosenheck, 1993) shows that the effects of life trauma are dependent upon such characteristics as (a) the stimulus component of the traumatic event, (b) the ongoing situational context within which the event occurs, and (c) the personal characteris-tics of the victim (e.g., age, pre-existing biological or psychological factors, exposure to previous traumatic events, social support, and individual's coping style).

While all of these factors are helpful in *predicting* who will develop PTSD after exposure to a potentially traumatic event, personal characteris-tics (especially individual coping styles) seem to be most salient to *treatment* because these response are susceptible to influence and change.

As this applies to ACT, there is a growing body of literature ex-ploring the relationship between acceptance, experiential avoidance and PTSD (e.g., Boeschen, Koss, Figueredo, & Coan, 2001; Pistorello, Follette, & Hayes, 2000; Walser & Hayes, 1998). While these papers examine the theoretical and empirical relevance of ACT relevant concepts, there are relatively few resources describing the direct clinical application of ACT to this disorder (Follette, 1994; Follette & Pistorello, 1995). The goal of this chapter is to conceptualize PTSD from the ACT perspective and to describe an ACT treatment protocol that can be applied to a variety of patient pop-ulations that present with PTSD. One of the major clinical challenges in delivering a treatment for PTSD is the heterogeneity of the trauma popula-tion. Because trauma is to some extent an act of chance or fate, the range of trauma seen in treatment is incredibly broad, and the time frames involved can be vast. Because of this, we will attempt to highlight certain core themes and general clinical considerations that seem to apply to most, if not all, trauma survivors.

FORMULATION

One problematic way of coping that has become increasingly emphasized in the trauma literature is avoidance. This term has been used to describe many different ways of coping and reactions to stressors and there is certainly no uniform definition operating in the literature. However, variations of the avoidance theme have been shown to influence the development and maintenance of PTSD across theoretical approaches and models. Examples include thought suppression (Shipherd & Beck, 1999; Guthrie & Bryant, 2000), avoidance (Shalev, Peri, Canetti, & Schreiber, 1996), rumination and suppression of intrusions (Steil & Ehlers, 2000), emotional numbing (Litz, Orsillo, Kaloupek, & Weathers, 2000), and experiential avoidance (Boeschen, Koss, Figueredo, & Coan, 2001; Follette, 1994 Hayes, Wilson, Gifford, Follette, & Strosahl, 1996; Pistorello, Follette, & Hayes, 2000; Walser & Hayes, 1998). Experiential avoidance is unique among this list because it (a) incorporates all of the phenomena above by encapsulating cognitive, emotional, and behavioral avoidance and (b) it is not specific to trauma-related sequelae but is instead conceptualized as a dimension found across a variety of psychological problems.

Experiential avoidance is central to the application of ACT to clients with PTSD. With trauma survivors, experiential avoidance generally centers on maladaptive behaviors used to avoid trauma-related thoughts, emotions, memories, and bodily sensations. The emotions, thoughts, and memories of traumatic events in and of themselves are not pathological. It is the attempt to avoid or eliminate these emotions, thoughts, and memories that results in dysfunction (for an in depth discussion of the relationship between experiential avoidance and trauma see Walser & Hayes, 1998). Examples of such maladaptive attempts to avoid trauma-related stimuli can include behaviors with dissimilar topographies such as substance use, somatization, compulsions, self-injurious behavior, and social isolation.

Several recent studies have begun to provide empirical support for the prominent role experiential avoidance may play in the etiology and maintenance or trauma-related psychopathology. Using a clinical interview in a sample of 61 combat veterans, Roemer, Litz, Orsillo, and Wagner (2001) reported that the tendency to inhibit emotional responses was associated with PTSD when covarying level of current psychological distress. In another study, Polusny, Rosenthal, Aban, and Follette (2002) found experiential avoidance mediated the relationship between adolescent sexual victimization and psychological distress. In a third study, Boeschen, Koss, Figueredo, and Coan (2001) found that experiential avoidance was detrimental to overall psychological outcomes for women survivors of rape. These findings provide preliminary support for the role of experiential avoidance in the development of trauma related psychopathology.

In the ACT model, acceptance and willingness is offered as an alternative to emotional avoidance. ACT is a viable therapeutic approach for trauma survivors specifically because the technology employed undermines the avoidance/change agenda and provides a context from which the trauma survivors can accept their personal history, private events, self, and others. This allows them to have a trauma history *and* make changes in their lives that are consistent with their values and goals.

The ACT conceptualization of PTSD symptoms shares some similarities with traditional cognitive-behavioral models in positing that dysfunctional adaptation to traumatic experience is dependent upon core cognitive processes (Horowitz, 1986; Horowitz & Becker, 1971) such as: (1) the extreme ease of retrieval, or hyper accessibility, of trauma-related memories (e.g., intrusive thoughts and feelings about the trauma), and (2) maladaptive efforts to defend against, or avoid these painful unwanted memories (e.g., avoidance of associated cues).

In order to successfully address the effects of trauma exposure in treatment it is necessary to properly assess: (a) the client's history, current life contexts, and general patterns of avoidance; (b) the client's presenting complaint and how this complaint relates to their traumatic experience; (c) factors that may be perpetuating maladaptive behavior and avoidance; (d) the presence of skills necessary to promote healthy coping responses and (e) the client's motivation to change.

We have found that the assessment portion of treatment may take longer with trauma survivors because it is necessary to spend more time developing a therapeutic relationship. This relationship is particularly important as you will be asking your client to share details of the traumatic material early on in treatment. Furthermore, many trauma survivors experience difficulties with trust, safety, and creating and maintaining close interpersonal relationships. These problems are often the reason such patients seek treatment in the first place, and they will be operative throughout your work with the client.

For treatment planning purposes, it is important to gather a thorough history from your clients. This should include a trauma history (both the most recent or most troubling event and any previous history of trauma or abuse), how the trauma has effected their life (e.g., are they avoiding certain activities, situations, or people), ways that they have tried to deal with their experience (e.g., drinking, not thinking about it), and ways that they have tried to understand or explain their experience (e.g., feelings of responsibility, feelings that people are bad). If the trauma took place in adulthood, it can be helpful to ask what their life was like and what ways they coped with experiences before they experienced the trauma.

Understanding the client's concerns, complaints, and goals may be more complicated for trauma survivors, given the wide range of post-traumatic behavior patterns that may be involved. Clients may come in complaining of depression, anxiety, sexual dysfunction, trauma-related intrusions, hypervigilance, general relationship problems, or problematic substance abuse to name a few. One of the first assessments you must make is to what extent the presenting problem is a way of coping with their negative trauma-related stimuli. If the complaint appears to function in the service of avoiding trauma-related stimuli, then you should also assess what specific content domains are avoided (e.g., specific thoughts or physical places) and what clients expect as a consequences of contacting those domains (e.g., helplessness or terror). Furthermore, it is likely that there will be other, non-trauma related domains in which clients are using similar avoidance strategies. Often, a theme will emerge that the client has an excessive need for control, or a maladaptive fear of unpredictability and change. Understanding what themes are present for the client will help you select particular ACT metaphors or treatment techniques to focus on, and will help your client generalize treatment gains by seeing how emotional avoidance operates across specific domains. In addition, by focusing on your client's entire life rather than just trauma related material, you begin to create a larger context that can help promote change and understanding. Trauma survivors often have constricted their life space to the point that avoiding trauma symptoms is what their life is about. Broadening this narrowed view of what life is all about is part of the goal of ACT itself.

It is equally important to explore the client's treatment goals to assure that you are not being drawn into an eliminative agenda. For example, it is not uncommon for a trauma survivor to want to "get better" so that they can forget what has happened to them or to make it go away. You should explain that while this is understandable, it just is not possible. Instead, you want to work to find a treatment goal that is both feasible and in the client's best interest. If the client wants to eliminate memories or symptoms of trauma as a pre-condition for getting on with life, you must point out that you are not in a position to change personal history. While this may seem obvious, it is important to emphasize early on that the ACT agenda is not one of "getting rid of things" including trauma-related thoughts memories or emotions. Without this emphasis, the course of treatment can be very confusing and frustrating for a client with a trauma history.

There are several factors that can perpetuate maladaptive behavior for trauma survivors. The factors are important to assess early as they can often influence the order and course of treatment. One of the most important factors to consider is whether there are short term benefits associated with maladaptive behavior. The obvious short-term benefit is the ability to avoid experiencing incredibly painful trauma-related stimuli. Moving straight into creative hopelessness with such a client can mean the end of therapy or a seriously damaged therapeutic relationship. We have found that it is generally more helpful to begin with values clarification in the service of creating a larger context for therapeutic change. Helping your client identify valued life goals will later allow you to address the impact of maladaptive behaviors on valued life outcomes. Asking a trauma survivor to make contact with frightening stimuli without such a context can be confusing, horrifying, and potentially re-traumatizing. Using values as a starting point can provide the necessary context to understand that willingness is in the service of moving in a desired life direction.

Trauma survivors may also believe that change is not possible. For example, a Vietnam veteran or childhood sexual abuse survivor may have this belief based on decades of experience with PTSD and the accompanying chronic symptomotology and psychosocial losses (e.g., problems with family, friends, vocation etc.). Your clients may be fused with the idea that they are defined by their trauma and associated distress, or must be the way that they are because of their trauma. In this case, you may first want to emphasize defusion strategies and self-as-context exercises. These strategies can help the client take a step back, start thinking about who they are, and make contact with the price of believing that change is not possible. In addition, you may want to begin with small behavioral experiments to demonstrate that they have the ability to behave in different and more adaptive ways.

A third factor that can perpetuate maladaptive behavior in trauma survivors is the conviction that emotional avoidance will eventually work. This belief may be difficult to address as it is frequently reinforced strongly by the client's friends and family and the short-term gain often associated with avoidance strategies. Likewise, these beliefs are sometimes based on specific confirming experiences and are even occasionally true. The two strategies frequently associated with this belief are the idea that "time heals all wounds" and the appeal of the "geographical cure" (everything will be better if the client moves, changes jobs, gets new friends etc.). In this instance it may be helpful to begin with creative hopelessness and to spend extra time dedicated to undermining the change agenda.

When creating a treatment plan for clients with PTSD, it is also important to assess whether or not the client has sufficient skills to participate fully in the ACT treatment. Extreme emotional dysregulation and serious deficits in personal problem solving or interpersonal skills may make it difficult for the client to attend to what you saying or to remember things after session. ACT treatment can appropriately include first order change strategies such as skill building interventions. If this is an issue, it may be useful to integrate a skills training focus in your treatment plan. Linehan's (1993) Mindfulness, Interpersonal Effectiveness, Emotion Regulation, and Distress Tolerance skills modules may be especially appropriate to work with trauma survivors. These particular skills can help clients with trauma-related negative emotions, thoughts, and memories in an ACT consistent way. You must be certain, however, that skills training is not put into the service of your clients control and eliminate change agenda. You need to make it clear that you are not teaching strategies that will clients to change, stop, or avoid their thoughts, feelings, or memories.

The client's motivation to change can be crucial to the success of ACT with trauma survivors. Two specific factors that might positively or nega- tively impact motivation to change are the strength and importance of the therapeutic relationship, and the clarity and importance of valued ends that are not being achieved due to current behavior.

As mentioned previously, the development of a supportive and safe therapeutic relationship is extremely important in the treatment of trauma survivors. It is necessary to integrate direct positive support and feedback with each stage of ACT. This usually involves validating the pain associated with traumatic life experiences and the difficulty in addressing previously avoided experiences. We use self disclosure frequently to legitimize the difficulty of the moves we are asking the client to make. For example, we will share our own reactions to what the client is saying whether it is sadness for what they have been through or excitement for something they have done. We may share difficulties we've experienced with one of the ACT exercises or metaphors. Our goal is to humanize the client's struggles. This often has the effect of reducing some the shame and humiliation that trauma survivors often experience.

The clarity and importance of valued ends that are not being achieved is a very important component of our motivational assessment. This issue arises in many ways over the course of treatment. One of the most com- mon motivational issues is the existence of service connected disability for combat related PTSD. For some veterans, service connection is their sole source of income. The client may believe (even if their service connection is permanent) that improvements in PTSD symptoms will result in a loss of livelihood and other negative consequences. For many veterans, disabil- ity has become somewhat of a life style and changing to a value driven, functional life plan is a major conceptual shift. For such patients, we nearly always start the assessment process with some type of values clarification work. Seeing the discrepancy between a valued life plan and the demands of a disability life style can help create motivation to change in the face of powerful short term incentives to stay unchanged.

All of the information gathered in the assessment process should be considered when formulating your treatment plan. The basic goals at this stage of treatment are to (a) set (and agree with the client on) specific goals for therapy, (b) select interventions and set the course of treatment considering the client's goals, specific symptoms, and individual strengths and weaknesses, (c) anticipate probable barriers to treatment success both in and outside of therapy, and (d) use the anticipated barriers as a guide for emphasis and order of interventions and metaphors.

CLINICAL INTERVENTIONS

The majority of ACT intervention strategies are appropriate for work with trauma survivors. We have found that certain ACT interventions can be modified to increase their effectiveness, while others may be less helpful if applied mechanically because of issues they might provoke around trust, safety and re-traumatization. Since ACT is not a sequentially driven treatment, but is instead defined by a set of core processes, core processes can be addressed in various orders.

For most trauma survivors, it is helpful to begin treatment with a full exploration of values. There are two clinical reasons. First, PTSD clients often have difficulty with trust and feelings of safety, so a direct challenge to their coping strategies (e.g., through creative hopelessness) can make them wary and even afraid of what ACT has to offer. Values work provides an opportunity for the therapist and client to develop a stronger relationship and safer context that will eventually allow you to gently challenge the workability of emotional avoidance strategies. Second, clients with chronic PTSD have usually been through therapy that has had only a modest (at best) impact on their lives. They may be less willing to commit to a therapy that immediately asks them to abandon safety behaviors and apparently carries the risk of great suffering. Values work is far less threatening, is very salient for clients and may help them to commit to therapy even when it is difficult and scary.

An additional consideration in the treatment of trauma survivors is how to incorporate paradox, confusion, metaphors and experiential exercises in the treatment package. These methods are common throughout much of the ACT protocol and are typically quite useful in undermining the clients need to understand, control, and evaluate with language. When working with trauma survivors, it is important to consider individual history to ensure that such techniques do not reenact certain aspects of the traumatic event(s). For example, survivors of childhood abuse may have experienced a home environment where the verbal behavior of the family did not match the physical behavior (e.g., daddy says "I love you" while molesting daughter) or the child's thoughts and feelings were consistently discounted and contradicted (e.g., parents ignoring hunger or insisting that the child is not really sad). Due to these concerns, it is important to make sure that you have a strong relationship with the client, understand the client's trauma history, clearly explain the use of such techniques to the client, and regularly check in to determine how your client is responding to these interventions. We believe these strategies are effective with trauma survivors provided there is a sensitivity to their potentially negative impacts.

Our clinical experience is that trauma survivors have very strong reactions to interventions that seem emotionally intrusive and they will simply leave therapy if they get too frightened. It is not uncommon for beginning therapists to become instructive or directive with some of the ACT technology and the hierarchical nature of such an approach can be intimidating for clients with a trauma history. Furthermore, the prevalence of dissociation in this population requires that you check to assure the client is psychologically present and tracking the material. Depending on the level of the client's distress, it may be helpful to give tapes of the sessions for the client to listen to.

Values

Beginning ACT treatment by returning to values can actually serve as an extended version of the "What does the client want?" discussion that has transpired in the initial assessment. The traditional ACT approach to values is usually not changed. The exception is that we are careful to avoid using the tombstone or funeral metaphors with clients that have recently experienced an event in which they thought they were going to die. This can be unnecessarily upsetting for a client and the funeral metaphor can easily be changed to a celebration dinner in their honor.

One of the challenges in values work with trauma survivors is that they often have a difficult time articulating what it is they really want. Sometimes a sense of foreshortened future is involved and the client cannot really imagine living long enough to accomplish concrete goals. Other times, they may have spent the time since the trauma thinking about what

Table 6.1. Clinical Issues and Recommended ACT Interventions for Clients with a History of Trauma

Clinical issue	Recommended ACT response
Patient complains about constantly struggling with feelings, memories, and thoughts about the event or that their history prevents any progress	• Ask client to identify the goal of the struggle (understanding, explanation, making the pain go away, future prevention) • Explore the workability of the struggle for that goal • Items in the box metaphor • Ask client to write autobiography and then rewrite it several times retaining the facts but changing the consequences • Ask the client what they would do tomorrow if today you determined that their history would always be the same and always be painful. What would they want to work on/live for then?
Client is repeatedly angry in session	• Reframe anger as in the service of avoidance • Discuss the concepts of clean and dirty emotions • Ask client to identify what thoughts, feelings, and memories are unacceptable and require fighting back • Ask client to evaluate the short and long term workability of their anger • Physicalizing exercise • Metaphors such as Tug of War with the Monster and People on the Hook, and What are you playing for? (Being right vs. Living Life)
Client repeatedly dissociates during session	• Spend time working with the client to increase their contact with the present moment • Help the client to build skills (e.g. mindfulness and distress tolerance; Linehan, 1993)

Client is repeatedly late or misses sessions	• Determine if these behaviors are in the service of experiential avoidance
	  — discuss the workability of this behavior both in terms of present circumstance and past experience
	  — determine what the client would need to be willing to face in order to engage in treatment
	• Determine if these behaviors are a result of a tenuous therapeutic relationship, lack of trust, or feeling of being overwhelmed
	  — if so, acknowledge that you may have misread the difficulty of what you are asking them to do
	  — spend more time building therapeutic relationship
	  — determine if there is a skills deficit and spend time building skills repertoire.

Table 6.1. (*Continued*)

Clinical issue	Recommended ACT response
Client stated that they are unsure that they are willing.	• Revisit the workability of their current approach • Focus on willingness—If you don't want it, you've got it. • Focus on Values and bring client in contact with what the suffering you are asking them to do is in the service of • Lower the difficulty of behaviors or activities you are asking them to engage in. (Begin with something small that they are willing to do) • Determine if the client has the appropriate skills needed to engage. If not—spend time building skill level. • Validate and normalize the difficulty of what the two of you are working on

happened and why rather than what they want to happen in the future. Each of these factors may increase the amount of time and effort it takes to develop a valued living plan with the client. You should simply be aware of this and help the client work through these concerns.

Some trauma clients are initially unwilling to consider what they want to be about because their conceptualized self is defined as being "broken" as a direct result of the trauma(s) they have endured. Thinking about desired life directions such as becoming a parent or engaging in an intimate relationship may be associated with trauma-related stimuli and too frightening to consider. If this is the case, it may be helpful to cut down the size of the intervention and focus on one or two domains that seem particularly important to the client. The rest of the domains and values work can then be moved to later in the protocol and a time when the client is more stable and ready to discuss issues so closely related to the self.

Creative Hopelessness

In ACT treatment of the trauma survivor, we use various creative hopelessness interventions to establish a context from which the client is willing to consider alternatives to emotional control and escape. We try to transition into creative hopelessness once the process of clarifying valued life goals has been completed. The context for creative hopelessness is to play valued life directions off of the use of unworkable emotional avoidance strategies. This way, your client will gradually discover the cost of

emotional control in terms of being able to pursue valued life ends. We review with the client all of the methods previously tried to exert control over
unwanted thoughts, emotions, and memories and then examine how well
these behaviors have worked to produce outcomes in living that are valued.

When introducing creative hopelessness to a client with a trauma history, it is important not to insinuate that the ways that they have coped
or responded were wrong. Most clients with trauma histories had no control over what was happening to them at the time of trauma. They may
have used dissociation and experiential avoidance to simply survive the
experience intact. When repeated trauma is part of the picture, such as
with child abuse or combat, these coping mechanisms developed over a
long period of time and probably gave the client some semblance of functionality. It is important for the therapist to validate what the client did to
survive. At the same time, the therapist must work with the client to understand how those same strategies are working in current life. In essence, the
problem the patient has to come to grips with is that emotional avoidance
strategies that may have allowed the client to function at one point in time
are now suppressing the client's chances of living a valued existence.

The balancing act between validating past experiences and making
contact with the unworkability of emotional avoidance strategies results
in creative hopelessness dialogues that are more subtle and less intrusive
than might otherwise be the case. Rather than just asking the client to
consider whether what they are doing is not working and offering no
explicit alternative, you are asking them to consider the role that their
values would play in the choice to explore willingness and acceptance.
The amount of time and effort put into values work emphasizes that the
therapy is not *only* about abandoning current strategies.

Many of the metaphors used to engender willingness are also quite
easily adapted to the experience of trauma. For example, the *Person in the
Hole Metaphor* (Hayes et al., 1999, pp. 101–104) easily incorporates the idea
that they were pushed (or marched) into the hole rather than just falling
in. In essence, it is helpful for a trauma survivor to see that their history is
understandably involved in how they got to where they are. We often will
modify the original structure of the metaphor by saying:

> So you were just walking along minding your own business and someone ran-
> domly (or someone you trusted) took your arm and threw you into a hole. That
> is pretty much what has happened to you. You had this experience, and now
> you find yourself in a hole with nothing but a shovel. You have tried to under-
> stand how exactly you got in the hole and why *you* were thrown in the hole in
> the first place, but that isn't helping to get you get out. You have tried digging,
> but that doesn't change the fact that someone threw you in a hole. In fact, it just
> makes the hole deeper.

This approach allows us to acknowledge the fact that the client has been victimized by events beyond control, but that analysis beyond that simple fact is probably not going to be helpful. Recognizing that understanding the past does not actually get them out of the hole leaves intact the conclusion of the metaphor; the client must still make a choice as to what they want to do. Do they want to keep digging or are they willing to consider another way?

Another creative hopelessness metaphor that can be quite helpful is the *Feedback Screech* metaphor (Hayes et al., 1999, p. 108). Trauma survivors can often strongly identify with this metaphor because they have often stopped participating in activities that they enjoy, interacting with people that they love, and experiencing life to the fullest in order to "live quietly." The goal of quiet living is to avoid any possibility of stimulating trauma related thoughts, emotions, or memories. In using this metaphor, we will often mention some of the research concerning avoidance of trauma-related stimuli to make the point that this is not just an interesting metaphor but also supported by science.

To overcome the cost of "living quietly," we try to reconnect clients to their values, so that any willingness goal that is developed does not lead to unnecessary or drastic suffering. For example, a veteran who sits alone all day might consider two alternatives to his form of "living quietly." The first alternative may be to invite his children to go to dinner at a local restaurant. The second alternative might be to attend the downtown fireworks display on the fourth of July. Both are examples of willingness, but the first may relate to the value of being an interactive father and the second is more likely to involve pure suffering. While ACT therapy asks clients to be willing to make room for unwanted psychological events, this is not suffering in the traditional sense, because there is a valued goal that makes any pain part of a purposeful act.

Another intervention we like to use is the *Tug of War with a Monster* metaphor (Hayes et al., 1999, p. 109). Clients with a history of trauma will sometimes identify the monster as their trauma-related thoughts, emotions, memories, physical sensations that remind them of trauma, the experience of the trauma itself, the perpetrator of abuse or even someone that enabled a traumatic event. Normally, struggle to maintain emotional control over these types of experiences, because they set off a chain reaction of stimulus equivalence processes. Of course, the harder the client tries to clamp down on the occurrence of these stimuli, the greater the shrinkage in meaningful life pursuits and the more out of control things seem when these monsters show themselves. In any case, this metaphor helps to emphasize the ACT agenda of willingness and detachment from thoughts and helps the client understand that willingness is truly about letting go of the struggle.

Control Is the Problem

With time, trauma survivors will give you signs that they trust the therapy process and feel safe in approaching more basic emotional avoidance problems. While introducing a name for the problem, we remain focused on validating a client's experience and the short-term effectiveness of emotional control strategies in the client's past life. However, we begin to shift the focus to current workability and this allows us to more directly challenge the client's current use of emotional avoidance strategies. Discussing the historical and learned etiology of control, as well as the observation that control strategies work in many circumstances, contributes to the normalization of this strategy. This allows the patient to feel accepted and not criticized, which in turn leads to a greater sense of safety. Thus, we typically take a more direct approach to attacking the control and eliminate agenda once we reach this stage of treatment.

The *Box Full of Stuff* metaphor (Hayes et al., 1999, pp. 136–138) can help a client to understand how the traumatic event they experienced has taken over their entire life. Conversely, the metaphor allows them to see the event as an object and as only a portion of what goes into their metaphorical life. The standard metaphor is well matched to traumatic experience and needs very little change. However, you should not be afraid to put something truly disgusting in the box to highlight the high negative valence of the traumatic event.

Cognitive Defusion

Most clients with PTSD come in with a well-developed story of what has happened to them, why it has made them the way that they are, and what they are no longer able to handle as a result. The extent to which clients are fused with the elements of this story is a strong predictor of dysfunction. The tricky part of working with the story of a trauma survivor is that there is a factual basis to much of it and so there is always a need to avoid implying that the entire story is false. This would be tantamount to denying that traumatic events even happened. Our goal in using cognitive defusion interventions is allow clients the opportunity to step outside of their story, to see it as at least partly arbitrary and to assess how well the story is preparing them for a valued life in the future. There are several cognitive defusion exercises that are very well suited to working with clients with PTSD. That may be related to the fact that this is also usually the first set of exercises after values that make intuitive sense to clients. It is in this stage that clients begin to see how some of the previous material fits together with both values and life change.

The deliteralization of thoughts, feelings, memories and physical sensations can be a powerful exercise for trauma survivors in many ways. First, intrusive private experiences are at the core of the PTSD diagnosis and reframing these experiences as signs of an inherent mental disorder to just psychological experience can be uplifting in itself. Second, undermining the reality of trauma-related self-judgment can help clients realize that they are not bad, dirty, or broken. Third, seeing these experiences for what they are and choosing whether or not to buy into them offers the trauma survivor a true sense of response-ability for picking a workable stance.

Deliteralization exercises in ACT address many of the core problems specifically related to PTSD (fusion, evaluation, and avoidance). We typically spend a fair amount of time educating clients about the nature of the mind, thinking and feeling as forms of behavior and so forth. Most trauma survivors are so fused with their minds and are so on the lookout for feared stimuli that it takes special effort to get them to really appreciate the concept of fusion. The amount of time may vary from client to client, but before moving on the client should be able to at least conceptually understand the importance of the observer perspective. Most of the exercises and metaphors provided are not content specific and are therefore simple to use without change. However, there are some exercises that provide particular opportunities for the client to explore their trauma-related thoughts.

Once the client gets used to the idea of labeling thoughts as thoughts, it can be helpful to walk the client through their trauma related thoughts using the "I'm having the thought that" prelude. Begin by talking about a recent situation in which the client became overwhelmed by trauma-related thoughts and emotions and ask them to notice what thoughts they had. As they report on thoughts or feelings, have them adopt the ACT verbal convention: "I had the thought that," or, "I'm having the evaluation that."

The *Passengers on the Bus Metaphor* (Hayes et al., 1999, pp. 157–158) offers another opportunity to closely examine trauma-related thoughts, emotions, and memories and how those factors influence the client's life. For example, we first go through the metaphor in its entirety using thoughts, memories, bodily states, or emotions that are relevant to the trauma related symptoms that plague clients. Then, we will ask the client to name as many passengers on the bus as possible. If time permits, it can also be helpful to ask the client about what each passenger is wearing and what he or she looks like. This exercise objectifies the client's provocative psychological content and, at the same time, functions as a type of exposure treatment in a safe environment. Both of these can also be true when asking client to express their difficult thoughts in an unusual manner such as singing or talking in a silly voice.

Another aspect of deliteralization that is particularly useful with trauma survivors is undermining the utility of reasons. If a client believes that a reason (usually their trauma) is responsible for their suffering, then they may be less willing to experience negative trauma-related stimuli or try new behavior. Integral to almost every story is the built in assumption that past negative events are causing current dysfunctional behavior. However, if we can get clients to see that reasons are not causes, they may be more willing to respond differently to trauma related stimuli and in a manner that is more in line with their values.

One ACT exercise we use frequently involves asking the client to state reasons for recent maladaptive behaviors, followed by a request for false reasons that might also explain their situation. This exercise can be expanded to address the use of a traumatic event as the reason for the clients suffering in a specific domain. For example, the therapist may ask the client why she thinks she is having difficulties with intimate relationships (her presenting complaint). The goal would be to track the reasons back to the chain of causes. Usually it will not take long to reach the client's traumatic experience. An example of how this dialogue might work is:

THERAPIST: So let's do a little exercise. Tell me in a sentence or two why you think you have difficulty with your intimate relationships.

CLIENT: (pause) Well, It is hard for me to trust people and I'm not very good at opening up.

THERAPIST: OK, so why else?

CLIENT: I don't know, I suppose I'm afraid that I might get hurt, or that I'll scare them away.

THERAPIST: So why do you think you have trouble trusting people and why do you think that you might get hurt or scare them away?

CLIENT: (pause) Well, I've been that way since the rape.

THERAPIST: Ok, so the rape has caused you to have trouble trusting people and makes you afraid to get hurt and those things make it hard for you to have strong relationships. Is that the general idea?

CLIENT: Yes.

THERAPIST: I understand that. Those sound like really true reasons. What I'd like for you to do now is to try to think of some fake reasons. Can you tell me some other reasons why you might have trouble trusting people or with intimate relationships?

CLIENT: Like made up?

THERAPIST: Sure. They can be realistic or silly, but I just want you to try to think of another way that you might have gotten in this hole-even without the rape.

CLIENT: Ok. So like if my parents had a horrible marriage and messy divorce. That might make me leery of relationships.

THERAPIST: Good. What else?

CLIENT: Or if I was paranoid and thought the government was watching me.

THERAPIST: (*after the client has provided several more reasons*) Wow. There a lot of ways a person can come to having trouble with trust and relationships.

When talking about the effects of trauma in such a broad sense, it is probably not useful to challenge the client's story line at the content level. Instead, we use this exercise as an opportunity to generally undermine trauma as a reason. However, if specific trauma-related stimuli are given as reasons for specific behaviors (e.g., I drank because I thought about the accident) then a more direct approach can be taken. You might challenge the idea that the thought "caused" the client to drink. One strategy that is very effective is to unhook the cause and effect by having clients use the word "and" instead of conditional causal words like "because." This convention is easy to instill in the session structure and has general usefulness in helping clients understand that private experiences do not cause behavior, although they may be occur in the same time frames as behavior.

Self-as-Context

The idea of self-as-context is that people are not their thoughts and feelings but rather the context in which they occur. For trauma survivors, this can take two forms. One is that many clients with trauma histories develop a conceptualized version of self that is heavily imbued with the past and current effects of trauma. Asking such clients to adopt a more functional, accepting stance toward life can trigger a variety of behaviors that function to protect the story. A second problem is that trauma survivors often deflect psychological experience in the here and now. The have troubles making contact with the self as ongoing process, i.e., they have trouble getting "present". Clients with an abuse history experience continued reinforcement of avoidance of self-as-ongoing-process because being present has been paired with difficult trauma-related thoughts, feelings and memories (Follette, 1994). Additionally, other family dynamics unrelated to the trauma may have led to problems in developing a sense of self. The goal of self-as-context interventions in ACT is to help client make contact with a type of self that is safe and consistent and allows for non-judgmental awareness of immediate private content.

In our experience, the *Observer Exercise* (Hayes et al., 1999, 192–196) works very well to show clients the essential continuity in their basic awareness of being both before and after the trauma experience. The goal is to show clients that they can be aware of private content without being defined by it. Trauma survivors really believe that they have been fundamentally changed by the experience, so it is important to take time and to try to do the entire exercise. The impact of this exercise may also be affected by factors such as the type of trauma or the age of the patient when traumatic events occurred. For example, it may be less effective with clients who have experienced childhood abuse because they may have engaged in such extreme traumatic deflection that their sense of self as context is very precarious. Typically, clients with severe abuse histories also tend to exhibit more serious forms of emotional avoidance (i.e., dissociative disorders, self mutilation). However, we have found that you can address the same concept using the *Chessboard Metaphor* (e.g., the trauma is a piece on the chessboard; Hayes et al., 1999, 190–192) or the *Box Full of Stuff Metaphor* discussed earlier. Ultimately, their self is still the box and the trauma and other events are just stuff in the box.

If the client is able to find the observer in the observer exercise, this can also be a helpful way for the client to practice focusing on the present rather than thoughts or memories of the past. Like most mindfulness exercises, the focus is on helping the client get in touch with the "observing self". We typically help the client relax and then instruct them to notice qualities in the immediate environment, thoughts, thoughts, memories and bodily sensations without allowing their mind to engage in judgment and evaluation. We usually instruct the client to practice some type of mindfulness exercise daily and especially when feeling distressed by trauma-related stimuli.

Willingness and Acceptance

Willingness and acceptance work with clients with PTSD is functionally a form of exposure treatment. During this stage of treatment the goal is to have clients engage in behaviors that tend to elicit various emotional barriers and practice acceptance rather emotional avoidance. Ultimately, willingness and acceptance will be needed as clients attempt to engage in value actions. Clients are encouraged to notice their internal experiences and practice moving toward difficult thoughts, and feelings rather than trying to avoid them. For example, we ask clients to talk about situations that might frighten them because of their trauma-related stimuli. At the same time, we instruct clients to notice the thoughts and feelings they are experiencing, particular the "mental chatter" that might lead to emotionally avoidant responding. Eventually, we will have clients talk about the actual trauma in the same manner. If we are having difficulty getting into contact with some basic trauma related stimuli, we will physically expose clients to trauma-associated locations (e.g., a restaurant or bank) or have them engage in activities that are associated with traumatic event (e.g., driving with a car accident survivor).

Some of the traditional willingness exercises such as the *Physicalizing* and *Tin Can Monster* exercises (Hayes et al., 1999, 170–172) can provide an opportunity for exposure work that is less direct or trauma specific. This can be helpful if the client experiences a great deal of distress with more direct exposure exercises or we may simply use the exercises to introduce exposure work in general. One of the most important willingness interventions is the *Eye Contact* exercise (Hayes et al., 1999, 244–245). The reason we like it is that it almost always "pulls" for trust and safety issues and these are at the core of PTSD for most patients. You should be very cognizant of the client's reaction to this exercise as it is an intrusion into personal space. You should explicitly and thoroughly explain the exercise and then get the client's permission to continue. We don't demand that clients do this exercise. If they remain uncomfortable about it after we've described it, we generally will just move on to another type of willingness intervention. When doing the exercise, we tend to sit a bit further away from the client than usual and we are careful not to touch the client. We use the exercise as a way to promote greater awareness of the knee jerk reactions trauma survivors have around trusting others and feeling safe. This material is bound to come up during the exercise and we will often debrief the exercise with a focus on what they did with trust and safety type content. In some respects, this is a perfect metaphor for what clients will run into if they commit to valued course of action in are domains of relationships, family activities or social relationships.

As cautioned previously, it is important to note that all of these activities should be in the service of moving clients toward valued life ends. If clients are willing to experience some of negative psychological content that is associated with willingness exercises, it should be framed as assisting them to act in accordance with their values.

CLINICAL CONSIDERATIONS

Given the philosophical distinction between the ACT approach to trauma and more traditional cognitive behavioral and exposure based approaches, a significant clinical issue is how to define success. Is success defined by the reduction or elimination of PTSD symptoms? Or is the measure of success the extent to which trauma survivors are willing to have symptoms and proceed in valued life directions? The two factors we choose to assess when evaluating response to treatment are (1) changes in measures of experiential avoidance, and (2) changes in patterns of valued behavior. As with ACT in other diagnostic domains, we want to see a decrease in experiential avoidance across the span of treatment. In addition, the client should begin behaving in new ways with the final goal of consistently acting in accordance with their chosen values.

Measures of PTSD symptoms may also help to evaluate changes during treatment, but we generally do not expect a steady reduction in symptom severity scores. When clients are asked to be more open to their experience, they may in fact report the mere presence more trauma-associated symptoms over time. For this reason, PTSD measures should be accompanied by a measure of the symptom's impact (e.g., how much did this bother you?) and a measure of the client's ability to function (e.g., were you able to do what you valued even while having the specific symptom?). Some interviews do ask about the impact of symptoms on the client but do so by asking how easily the client was able to put them out of their mind, think about something else, and so forth. These measures are defining success in ways that are the anti-thesis of ACT philosophy. Therefore, these factors should be considered when gauging success in treating PTSD symptoms per se.

SUMMARY

Acceptance and Commitment Therapy shows potential as a treatment for PTSD for several reasons. First, ACT addresses the emotional and behavioral avoidance and associated problems that are part of the sequelae to trauma. Second, ACT allows clients to improve their life and move in a valued direction with their history rather than to live a life driven and tormented by their history. Finally, the process of ACT treatment provides a safe context as well as sufficient reason (in the form of values) for clients to participate in exercises that will expose them to their trauma without unnecessary suffering. Although there is a great need for treatment outcome research and dismantling studies in this population, ACT as a philosophy and a technology is a promising addition to existing treatment approaches.

Chapter 7

ACT for Substance Abuse and Dependence

KELLY G. WILSON AND MICHELLE R. BYRD

Drug dependence and abuse have reached epidemic proportions. The 2002 National Survey on Drug Use and Health (NSDUH) estimated that 22 million or 9.4% of Americans over age 12 meet diagnostic criterion for substance dependence or abuse. The individual and social costs of drug and alcohol addiction are staggering. The total indirect costs of alcohol and drug abuse paid by the government, persons using, and their families, is conservatively estimated to be $245.7 billion per year (National Institute on Drug Abuse/National Institute on Alcohol Abuse and Alcoholism, 1992). These costs include addiction treatment, healthcare expenditures, lost work productivity and lost earnings due to work disability.

During 2002, approximately 3.5 million people were treated for substance problems in a variety of settings (not mutually exclusive) (NSDUH). The majority (2 million) received treatment in a self-help group format such as Alcoholics Anonymous or Narcotics Anonymous. It is worth noting that almost half a million people received treatment by emergency room providers and a quarter million received treatment while incarcerated. Despite the staggering prevalence of substance abuse problems, only 10% of those people needing treatment receive those services. The takeaway message in these statistics is that we need to develop intervention models that motivate substance abusers to seek treatment in the first place and better methods for retaining such individuals in treatment. While some barriers to treatment are financial and systemic, the underlying characteristics of chemical dependency treatment models may function as barriers. These include the extent to which clients are treated with respect and dignity, the extent to which treatment is sensitive to client values, and the extent to which treatment connects the client to existing community resources.

There are empirical data suggesting that experiential avoidance plays a role both in the development of addictions and as a deterrent to entering treatment. For example, studies that use random sampling of mood, cognitions, and substance use show that getting high tends to be both stimulated by negative private events and used to regulate them (Armeli, Tennen, Todd, Carney, Mohr, Affleck, & Hromi, 2003), and levels of acceptance measured by the AAQ relate to substance abuse (Forsyth, Parker, & Finlay, 2003).

The possibility that substance abuse may be driven by experiential avoidance, combined with the life numbing consequences of addiction, suggests that ACT may be a potentially effective treatment with this population. Indeed, there is a small but growing empirical literature that suggests ACT is an effective treatment for substance use and abuse. In a recent randomized controlled trial, ACT was shown to reduce drug use (both objectively assessed and self-reported) in polysubstance abusing opiate dependent individuals and was significantly more effective than methadone maintenance alone at the of a six month follow up (Hayes, Wilson, Gifford, Bissett, Piasecki, Batten, Byrd, & Gregg, in press). The clients in this study were fairly difficult: most were unemployed or underemployed. Fifty-two percent of the subjects met criteria for a DSM Axis II disorder; 40% for a mood disorder and 42% for an anxiety disorder. On average, clients in this study had been through 6.5 prior chemical dependency treatment regimes. This study provides preliminary support for the value on ACT with relatively severe substance abusing clients. On the other end of the spectrum, ACT has been shown to be significantly more effective than nicotine replacement therapy in smoking cessation at the end of a one-year follow up (Gifford, Kohlenberg, Hayes, Antonuccio, Piasecki, Rasmussen-Hall, & Palm, in press). Furthermore, ACT is well suited to the clinical environment in substance abuse treatment since it shares common ground with 12-step approaches (Wilson, Hayes, & Byrd, 2000), motivational interviewing (Budney et al., 1997; Miller, 1996), and relapse prevention/harm reduction models (Carroll Rounsaville, Nich, & Gordon, 1994; Marlatt & Gordon, 1985).

CASE CONCEPTUALIZATION

Understanding the inner workings of substance abuse as a primary experiential avoidance strategy will do much to help you, the clinician, formulate an effective ACT treatment approach. Although the following

ACT case conceptualization model is focused on the chronic, severe, multi-problem addict, these same principles can be modified to fit other, milder forms of addiction. When conducting that initial assessment with a chronic substance abuser, you should gathering information in the following areas:

1. Avoidant repertoires
   a. Pattern of substance involvement—especially shifts in substance abuse patters over time and in differing situations.
   b. Avoidant behavior patterns other than substance involvement.
2. Avoided events
   a. Contexts that precipitate experiential avoidance strategies.
   b. The degree of fusion with specific thoughts, emotions, memories, bodily states, and behavioral predispositions in the substance abuse triggering contexts.
   c. The role that substance abuse plays in helping to regulate or eliminate unwanted private events.
3. The immediate reinforcing effects of these experiential avoidance strategies or the extent to which the client believes that substance abuse "works" to eliminate or control unwanted private events.
4. The client's valued life directions in various domains, assuming that these life directions could be freely chosen.
5. The workability of substance abuse as a primary strategy when measured against the clients' valued life directions. Is substance abuse contributing to the embodiment of these life directions, or is it detracting or distracting from, or even quelling value consistent behavior?
6. The degree to which the client sees a "discrepancy" between valued life directions and current reality as a source of "concern" that might warrant trying something different.

To illustrate, a 30 year old man with a long history of poly-substance involvement and major depression entered treatment precipitated by the stormy end of his second marriage. He reported persistent depression with suicidal ideation dating back to adolescence. His suicidality had accelerated during life crises, such as the current relationship breakup.

The client reported a history of shifting among substances abused, modes of administration, and density of use. While initial use appeared to involve a mix of use for positively reinforcing effects of the substances, many instances of use seemed associated with experiential avoidance, including managing social discomfort, increasing a sense of belonging with a drug using cohort, and being a "big-shot" by having and sharing substances. Shifts in patterns of use sometimes involved the discovery of more effective drugs or different means of administration, like a shift from intranasal to intravenous use of cocaine. This phase of the case conceptualization suggested that the client had a very long history of mixed substance abuse that was associated with positive self related consequences, despite the appearance of a life destroying problem. In addition, substance abuse had emerged as the primary way this individual managed negative private content.

Substance involvement caused problems in virtually all areas of living. For example, unreliability forced him to remain in menial jobs and caused serious problems in his relationships with his parents, both spouses, and with his daughter (8 years old at the time of treatment). As is frequently the case, difficulties in one area had negative effects on other areas. Problems at home disrupted work. Problems at work caused even more problems at home. All of these failures in adult development themselves became aversive. Substance involvement became, over time, a singularly reliable source of relief in a world that had less and less to offer and more and more to avoid.

In the short term, drug use is functionally related to lessened contact with an increasingly painful world. However, over the long term, this client found himself further and further from the things about which he cared most deeply. Making experiential contact with this discrepancy was also a "trigger" for substance abuse. For example, a core value for this client was his relationship with his 8 year old daughter. His unreliability had driven his ex-wife to minimize his contact. That same unreliability also led the daughter herself to be reluctant to spend time with him. Whenever he called, or even considered calling on the telephone, he would be filled with self-loathing, negative evaluations of his past acts, and a certainty that he was incapable of sustaining that relationship even if it were available.

Chronic substance abusers, such as one just described, have problems that go beyond their substance involvement. They often come from highly dysfunctional family environments that leave them with significant life skills deficits. A core part of the case conceptualization is to determine the extent of these deficits in areas such as interpersonal effectiveness (i.e., social skills, conflict resolution skills, assertion skills), personal problem solving, and personal goal setting. Even in the presence of serious skills deficits, it is important to determine whether and how cognitive fusion and experiential avoidance interact with such deficits. For example, if a substance abuser has social skills deficits, social interactions are likely to fail, producing feelings of humiliation, incompetence, and hopelessness. When the substance abuser retreats from interactions into the world of substance abuse, opportunities to have social behavior shaped are further reduced. This creates a vicious cycle in which social failure and isolation becomes more and more likely.

Likewise, many substance abusers engage in substance use in order to control or eliminate other negative affective states such as anxiety and depression. From an ACT perspective, the basic role that fusion and emotional avoidance play in any of these psychological struggles is thought to be similar. They are "birds of a feather". Thus, ACT treatment for substance abusers with co-morbid disorders is fairly straightforward. Indeed, some community based ACT treatment programs specifically target both substance abuse and other problems (e.g., trauma, depression).

ACT Intervention Strategies

Building the Therapeutic Contract

There are frequently coercive events surrounding a person's entry into treatment for addiction. In the most extreme cases, clients are ordered to treatment under threat of incarceration. Even with these extreme cases, a solid therapeutic contract is typically possible. In order to forge the contract, all that is needed is a shared value between the therapist and the client that can dignify the work of treatment. The ability of the client to make their own decisions can be a place to begin. The following vignette demonstrates one way to approach this very important issue:

> THERAPIST: I understand that you came to treatment under court order. I don't know about you, but I don't much like being ordered to do anything. So I want you to know that I expect you to have some negative thoughts about being here.
>
> CLIENT: No. I told the judge that I really wanted treatment. Getting high has caused a lot of trouble.
>
> THERAPIST: That's great and if it is clear to you that getting high isn't moving you ahead in life, then I want to support you in working on that. However, I want you to be entirely clear that we can do very important work together, even if you hate the idea that you have to come. In fact, if you are mad, or if you have mixed feelings about being here, I will be most useful to you if you say that straight out. And, I am going to make a couple commitments to you here and now. First, I will not report that you are doing badly in treatment if you tell me that you are mad about being here. In fact, I might be likely to say that we are doing well, because it will mean that you and I are able to talk about what you care about and what you

want in your life, and that is what the treatment is about. I also commit, here an now, not to try to convince you that you should be in treatment, or even that your drug use is bad and should be stopped. I do not see it as my job to tell you such things. Now, I might think that if I were in your shoes, I would definitely seek treatment, but so what. What possible difference could *what I think* make? It is *your life,* not mine, and it will be *your direction* we take, not mine. I am sure that the judge is not the first person to tell you what to do in your life. If that were going to work, I assume that it would have already worked. Instead, this treatment will be about your deepest desires. Also, I don't expect you to necessarily believe what I am saying right now. What I do expect is that a sense of direction in this treatment will emerge out of your own experience and that whether I am useful to you will also show up, not as a thought, but in your direct experience of moving forward in your life.

Normally, as is shown in this transcript, it is a good idea to get these ACT "messages" into the process of treatment almost immediately. Negative thoughts about treatment are not the enemy. Feelings of ambivalence about drug use are not the enemy. Thoughts and feelings will be important to notice, but will not be the deciding features of treatment. Instead, treatment will be about values, commitment, and an appeal to the client's direct experience of workability. The client will not recognize these components at this point in treatment; but ACT philosophy is promoted from the initial interaction forward.

What Goes Wrong in the Initiation of Treatment?

A number of difficulties may arise that can defeat your attempts to form a therapeutic contract. Some substance abusers may be overtly compliant. The transcript above illustrates some of the ways that compliance is managed. You should not attack it or label it. Simply set it to one side and commit yourself directly to the person before you. Clients may also present with a sort of sullen disengagement. As with compliance, set the presentation to one side and make the contract. Both of these presentations are assumed to be functional repertoires that lead in ordinary social interactions to disjointed relationships based on pretense or the coercive effects of withdrawal. In either event, to become engaged with "the act" allows the act to create a fracture between the actual human being who has presented for treatment and genuine engagement in that treatment.

The sullen, self-righteous, angry client is treated in an entirely similar way without defense, and without arguing with the anger:

CLIENT: It is just bullshit that I have to be here.

THERAPIST: Yes, I can't say that I like being told what to do. It's probably why I got this job. At least while I am in this room, I am my
own boss. I would hate being made to come to see me. Let me make
something entirely clear though. I am working for you here. Unless
you leave treatment, I am going to work ceaselessly, unrelentingly
in your service. I have no doubt that we can find at least one thing
that we can agree on as a goal of treatment. Right now, you *have* to
be here or you will go to jail. I don't like being told what to do, and
I don't like anyone else being told what to do, and in my world, a
great outcome would be that therapy could deliver you into a position in which treatment would be a choice. I do not expect you to
believe me. I am, after all, a part of the machine that is holding you
in place. Nevertheless, here and now, I declare that I am working in
your service and the only way you can stop me is to leave and not
come back. I am not asking you to believe me. This is not about what
you believe or not. What I am saying is what I am up to. Watch me.
Let your own experience tell you whose side I am on here. Let me
ask you this: Imagine that I had a switch right here. If you flip this
switch being in treatment is entirely your choice. *The switch does not
take you in or out of treatment, it just makes it so that it is entirely your
choice.* Would you flip the switch? If it were possible that I meant exactly what I said, and that working for you in this way could make
it so being here was a choice, would that be something you value?

The underlying assumption here is that these repertoires, both
compliant and defiant, have not worked. If you the therapist reinforce
overly compliant behavior or attempt to confront sullen defiance, you
are likely responding like the legal and therapeutic community and will
probably see the same poor results. Our working assumption in ACT
is that even the most chronic substance abusing clients are capable of
valuing and choosing. If treatment is to be successful, the substance abuser
must "show up", identify valued life directions and make choices. The
entire thrust of workability is tied to the notion of valued life outcomes.
If you believe that a chronic substance abuser is "broken" and incapable
of contacting values and making choices, that message will be implicit in
your therapeutic interactions.

Creative Hopelessness and Addiction

Once a therapeutic contract is forged, the next task is to begin to
foster a sense of creative hopelessness. A long career of addiction often
means a stream of losses: lost jobs, lost time with family, lost friends, lost

Table 7.1. Comprehensive Substance Involvement Worksheet: Part I

Write down a history of your drug use (alcohol too, of course). On the worksheet write your age, types of drugs used, frequency of use (# of times per week, month), and how used (smoke, eat, inject, etc.). Include a section for the following substances:

1. Alcohol
2. Marijuana
3. Hallucinogens (LSD, mushrooms, peyote etc.)
4. Depressants (Xanax, Valium, barbiturates, etc.)
5. Stimulants (speed, cocaine, ecstasy, ephedrine etc.)
6. Inhalants (glue, gasoline, Pam, etc.)
7. Opiates (heroin, Vicodin, codeine, OxyContin, Percodan, etc.)

Begin with the first time you remember using any mood altering substance no matter how little of the substance was used. It is important that you be painstakingly thorough in this task. Use the following format:

Stimulants

Age	Quantity/Frequency	How Used
12 years to 15 years	Amphetamines 2–3 tablets/6–8 × per year	Oral
16 years	A few lines of cocaine/about 4 × that year	Snorted
17 years	About 1/4 gram of cocaine/about 3–6 × per week	Snorted/some smoked
	etc.	

This may well seem like a long and difficult task. It is. It really is doable though. Just pick a substance and work your way through from first use to present. Take your time. If you find yourself unable to remember for one substance, or time period, switch to another and work on that for a while. Sometimes working on another area will help you remember more about the one you are having trouble with. If, in the end, you find that you simply cannot remember for certain substances or time periods, make your best estimate. Your thoroughness with this task will have an important impact on the effectiveness of your treatment.

opportunities. The losses themselves are painful and any sense that one has participated actively in them is doubly painful. The first step in this process is to get in touch with the client's patterns of substance involvement. The Comprehensive Substance Involvement Worksheets (CSIW) presented in Tables 7.1 and 7.2 will help facilitate this process.

The purpose of the CSIW is both to provide assessment information and to increase psychological contact with the troubled substance use history that most addicts commonly avoid. There is no way to get clean without contacting the costs of use. In essence, the CSIW exercise functions as a form of exposure treatment for the client. Just as in an exposure for anxiety, you need to be sensitive to the client's level of arousal, and strategies (both

Table 7.2. Comprehensive Substance Involvement Worksheet: Part II

This section should be completed *after* completing Worksheet I. Write down any problems or changes in your life that were associated with using in each of the listed areas. If there were no consequences, write none. However, we would encourage you to list consequences even though they may have been small. For example, you may not have been fired from a job, but you may have gone to work hung-over and been less effective in your work as result. This need not have been ineffectiveness that others noticed. What is important is whether you see yourself as having been less effective. Number each section and keep the 10 areas separate from each other as much as possible. What we are looking for here is any cost of using. Pay special attention to places where, as result of using (or drug seeking) you did things that violate your personal values (concealing, rationalizing, being secretive, being violent, etc.). *Give descriptions of specific events in each area.*

1. Intimate relations (wives/husbands/girlfriends/boyfriends)
2. Family (include family of origin and your own children)
3. Friends (changing to using friends, isolating, conflict over drug use)
4. Education/training (fail to start, perform poorly, or quit school/training program)
5. Occupation/employment (lost jobs, chronic unemployment)
6. Legal problems (include all arrests and their outcomes–conviction or not, incarceration, probation, parole, fines, living secretively)
7. Physical/health problems
8. Engaging in dangerous/risk taking behaviors
9. Recreation
10. Spirituality/religious practice
11. Taking advantage of treatment

obvious and subtle) for "checking out" psychologically from the content of the session (see Chapter 5 for more on ACT and exposure). The goal is to foster and maintain more open and flexible contact with the client's actual experience.

The CSIW-I, typically given as homework and then reviewed and elaborated in the subsequent session, simply asks the client to recount in detail their patterns of substance involvement. The inventory works through each substance type independently and details amount, frequency, mode of administration, and shifts in patterns of these features.

The historical review of substance use should be conducted in excruciating detail but without judgment or interpretation on the part of the therapist. You should attempt to appreciate the nuance, ambiguities, and paradox present in these stories, without drawing conclusions (e.g., "So that attempt to cut down on pot smoking in 1979 didn't really pan out.") These kinds of conclusions at this stage of treatment will probably elicit either compliance or defense—neither of which will be helpful. Rather, you the therapist should adopt a posture of active interest: "So it looks like you temporarily reduced your use of pot in 1979. What was going on around the time of that shift? Can you remember the reasons you decided to cut down? Can you remember the reasons you didn't want to cut down?" Pay particular attention to times when use patterns have shifted, since these often reveal renewed efforts at experiential avoidance or attempts to replace experiential avoidance with other behavioral strategies.

Once the CSIW-I has been completed (which may take more than one session, depending on the extent of substance use history and client age), give the CSIW-II as homework and review it in the next session. The CSIW-II asks the client to broadly define and list any costs associated with having used alcohol or drugs to particular areas of functioning, such as in their family life or in their employment. Costs to include in this analysis may be financial costs, opportunity costs, and costs to their relationships, to name but a few. Clients are asked to detail consequences ranging from small or mild (e.g. felt a hangover; arrived 5 minutes late to work) to serious (e.g. ended friendships with non-using buddies, injured someone they care about; overdosed). Do not allow the client to write about costs in terms of broad categories. Instead elicit specific incidents that bring you and the client into contact with the cost. Thus, if the client writes that they endangered family, ask for specific instances. The CSIW is assessment, but it is also exposure. Specific instances where the client drove with his daughter in the car while intoxicated will better serve now and later in treatment than a generic acknowledgement about endangering others.

When debriefing this comprehensive exercise, substance abusers will often express a sense of wonderment at how long/how much they have used during their lifetime. The therapist should adopt a circumspect, nonjudgmental, and respectful approach to this type of comment. Clients will commonly attempt to manage the pain of making contact with the costs they have experienced. One manifestation of this process may be to "swear off forever." If addicts can convince themselves, even momentarily, that they are finished with using, the emotional pain of making contact with personal history is momentarily lessened. It can be tempting to join the addict in demonizing drug use, but this has likely been tried repeatedly by the addict and by others. An open, defused, accepting posture is usually more effective. The second likely strategy will be to avoid it entirely, by minimizing, rationalizing, or if all else fails, by sinking into despair and relapsing. Your job is to help the client stick with the task long enough to contact what is underneath these responses, and to roll this into treatment itself.

When done well, the combination of the CSIW I and II is likely to elicit a strong emotional response in clients and bring them into contact with the unworkability of using (often as both an antecedent *and* a consequence of substance involvement). This is the core of the "creative hopelessness" phase: facing the workability of what has been going on, realizing that the easy solutions have been exhausted, and allying with the validity of that experience by opening up to the possibility of real change.

What Goes Wrong with the CSIW?

There are a few patterns of behavior that can emerge during this exercise that can present some clinical challenges. The most common is despair and hopelessness in its traditional fused form; however, anger may also emerge. Both of these presentations may lead to missed session or sessions in which the client arrives intoxicated or coming off a recent relapse. This work is painful. If the client becomes fused with the thought that the pain is without point, they will defend themselves. If they cap off a session of anger or hopelessness with a relapse, it should not be a surprise: getting high works.

THERAPIST: It is hard isn't it? Hard to look. Hard to stay with it.

CLIENT: I've looked before. It has never made a difference. What's the point?

THERAPIST: When you have looked before, what did you see? Did you see a problem?

CLIENT: Look, I want things to change, and I have convinced myself before that things had changed, but always, always, I end up right back where I started. One more trip around the wheel. Best just to get out of the way—try not to take anyone else down with me.

THERAPIST: And are both of those familiar to you—hoping, wishing, trying to make yourself believe, on the one hand. And then collapsing in a heap, giving up, retreating into using, on the other. And can you feel any life in those? In either of them? What if this work is about something else? Something besides trying and quitting and trying and quitting, hoping and giving up, hoping and giving up, over and over and over again.

CLIENT: Like what?

THERAPIST: Sometimes getting where something isn't can help, even if you don't know where the thing is. Does it feel, sometimes, as if you are being buried alive? It is as if your own history is your enemy and each day it gets a little bigger and weighs you down just a bit more. Like the more times you hope even, right there in the hope is your sense of the next cycle—hope, collapse, hope, collapse. What if it is the case that the reason this keeps coming back around is that there is something in there for you? What if, in the middle of that muck, there is something of extraordinary value? What if it is the case that at the center of all that pain there is something that could transform your life? What if there is something that could happen in our work here that could change your pain into an extraordinary asset?

CLIENT: I've been hopeful before.

THERAPIST: I am not talking about some kind of sunshiny "keep your sunny side up" pitch. I am not telling you to think, or hope, or believe anything. You have tried that. You get it: this isn't about what you believe. Not about believing in Santa—like maybe I am him. And, not about believing that I am full of crap. It's not about believing at all. I mean really—acting on what you *believe* got you here—stuck in treatment with me. I have believed in all kinds of stupid things. So what? All I am asking is whether it is *possible* that there is something of extraordinary worth in the center of your pain. Not that you think it is *believable*, or *true*, or even *likely*—just whether it is possible.

CLIENT: Well sure, it's possible. But I don't think so.

THERAPIST: Of course you don't think so, why should you? But this isn't between me and your thoughts—this is between you and me as persons. Heck I don't believe it myself sometimes—so what? But here is what I will do, and what I will ask you to do: don't believe it, assume it. Like that door over there. If we want out of the room, and assume it is locked, we just sit here. If we assume it is not, we go turn the knob. We can always just sit here later—let's go turn the knob. If treatment runs on belief—yours or mine—we are screwed. Sometimes I have a bad day. I don't believe I can do anything. Don't like 'em, don't want 'em, but they come along. If we go by what I believe, some days I would just come in and tell all my clients to just go home—there is no hope. Beliefs come and go and we don't seem to get to chose them. Now assumptions—assumptions are cool. We can choose our assumptions, even when they collide with our beliefs. Like if you really, really, believed the door was locked, could you assume that it was not and go turn the knob? Let's see—let's go turn the knob? And as far as looking in the middle of all that pain for something worthwhile—why not—you've looked everywhere else. You looked in the bag and the bottle, in hope and despair? What the hell—if I am wrong, I promise to refund you misery in full at the end of treatment.

As is demonstrated in this vignette, it is very important to attack fusion with self deprecating and hopelessness engendering evaluations, and to help the client "make room" for the profound sense of personal pain that often is present. Believing is heavily discounted. Moreover, unlike a cognitive therapy, where you might challenge the client's beliefs as distorted, the approach is to hold ALL beliefs (including those of the therapist) lightly.

Values: Setting a Course

For the chronic drug addict, breathing a clean and sober breath can be excruciating. Discontinuing drug use can often be part of removing the veil that keeps the substance abuser out of full contact with the pain of everyday life, including pain that is the result of events over which the individual had no control (i.e., sexual abuse as a child) and pain this is a consequence of addiction (i.e., a failed marriage, loss of a parenting relationship). It is difficult to imagine the degree of emotional damage that is frequently seen in the histories of severe substance abusers. Asking them to get "clean and sober" is really the same as asking them to get in direct contact with this wreckage. Very few client will make this move unless the stakes are high enough to make voluntary exposure to this negative content a legitimate, purposeful, life promoting act. The most powerful motivating force in this regard is the client's values. The original ACT values protocols (Hayes et al., 1999, pp. 222–228) were first developed to help severe substance abusers contact that sense of purpose that would dignify an acceptance path in the midst of such pain.

We assess values in ten domains: (1) family (other than parenting and intimate relations), (2) marriage/couples/ intimate relations, (3) parenting, (4) friendship, (5) work, (6) education, (7) recreation, (8) spirituality, (9) citizenship, and (10) physical self-care (Wilson & Murrell, in press). This expands the original list in the ACT book by dividing family relations into parenting and other family relations, since parenting values are often particularly important to clients and warrant a separate assessment. We have also developed a Valued Living Questionnaire (Wilson & Groom, 2002) that can be used for values assessment.

From an ACT perspective, values are not *things* so much as dynamic ongoing patterns of engagement in different life domains. Most critically, values function to organize behavior and provide a certain sense of direction. As discussed in the original ACT book, values must be differentiated from life goals. Goals are achievable outcomes that might be the embodiment of values (i.e., getting married might be one achievable outcome in pursuit of the value of pursing healthy intimate relationships), but ideally, a value provides a life course that never ends. So, for example, marriage might be a goal; however, the value might be to have a rich and loving intimate relationship. No matter how positive a relationship is, there is always more that can be done to create intimacy.

A potent sense of life direction is a powerful ally with clients who have gotten into difficulties by living their lives according to how they feel and what they think. The problem with using how you feel and what you think to run your life is that thoughts and feelings can be incredibly transient. Consider even the most committed parent child relationship. At one time or another, every parent thinks hard about whether having children was such a good idea. By contrast, personal values tend to be extraordinarily stable. Our clients may have abandoned valued domains over time, but typically, the underlying sense of direction has not been abandoned. Consider the following transcript from the male substance abuser described above in which the therapist inquires about the client's relationship with his nine year old daughter:

THERAPIST: How long has it been since you called Olivia?

CLIENT: It's been a couple months.

THERAPIST: Months. (pause) A long time. I know what she means to you. Must be painful.

CLIENT: You know, I promised myself I would not wait this long. I should just disappear. She has had enough of this from me. I call, and then I just disappear. Sue, her mom, stopped even telling her when I was planning to visit. I used to get drunk and show up days late. She told me Olivia would just sit on the porch waiting for me to get there. "When will Daddy get here?" She just got sick of cleaning up my messes.

THERAPIST: Yes. It is so sad, just thinking about that little girl, sitting on the porch, waiting for her Dad.

CLIENT: I thought that it would change once I got sober. I'm not drunk, but I am as worthless as I ever was. Sue is right: Olivia would be better off without me.

THERAPIST: Do you have a picture of her? (Client shakes his head— no). Close your eyes a second Tim. (Speaking very slowly and deliberately) Now, I want you to picture that house where you daughter lives (long pause). Let yourself *see* her sitting on that porch (long pause). Let yourself notice what she is wearing (long pause). Notice her hair Tim (long pause). Notice the look on her face Tim (long pause), as she waits for her Dad. OK Tim, now I want you to open your eyes and look at me. Notice how you are feeling *right now*.

CLIENT: I feel sick. I hate this. I feel this way whenever I talk to Sue. She kicks my ass, and I get mad, but I know I deserve it. I feel this way whenever I think about Olivia. She doesn't deserve this.

THERAPIST: Yes. But, let me ask you this Tim: What if I could give you a choice? I am not saying that I can give you this choice. I cannot.

But, I want to present the choice so that we can get clear what you care about. What if in this hand, I offered you the possibility that you would never, never, ever feel the way you feel right now again for the rest of your life. There is a price to be paid though—the price is that you sever all ties to your daughter. You turn away today and never, never look back. She sits on that porch waiting, forever. In the other hand, I have a different choice. In this hand, Dad shows up, he finally gets there. I mean *really there*. I mean there like she knows that Dad is someone she can count on, thick or thin, no matter what, he will love her and he will be there for her. But, again, there is a price to be paid. What if putting you in your daughters life—richly, meaningfully, not just on that porch, but at graduation, when she gets married, when your first grandchild is born. I mean *THERE*. But in order for that to happen, you have to feel what you are feeling, and more, like ten times more. If feeling that made being her Dad possible. Which would you chose Tim?

CLIENT: I don't like the choice.

THERAPIST: Of course not. But if this *were* the choice Tim, what would you chose.

CLIENT: I don't think I can do it.

THERAPIST: I don't give a damn what you think, Tim. And, know what? I also don't give a damn what I think. I care what you value Tim. I care about what you would have your life be about. And the same goes for me. I am not here doing this work because of something I *think*. I am here because of something I *value*. Of course you don't think so. But I am not asking if you think so. I am asking what you would choose. In a world where you *could* chose Tim .... which would you chose?

CLIENT: I would choose Olivia.

THERAPIST: Yes. OK Tim, so here is the deal. What if this therapy could be about making a rich, meaningful relationship with Olivia possible? Not certain. I don't know the future Tim. But possible. What if this could make it *possible*. Let's have the therapy be about something you'd want on your tombstone Tim. Tell me this: if you could have on your tombstone "he dedicated his life to not using drugs" or "he dedicated his life to not feeling bad" or "he dedicated his life to being a father to his daughter," which would you chose? There is a guy in my tradition Tim, named Og Lindsley. Og had a saying about working with people. Never chose a goal that could be done better by a dead person. So something like "not using drugs" or "not feeling bad"– well a dead person could do that—perfectly in fact. Dead people never get high; they never feel bad. But a dead person couldn't be a Dad. No way! Can you be a dad? Maybe? Maybe? You don't think so, but have you ever thought something, and later found out you were just wrong? Ever believe, really believe, there was a Santa? We can't be certain how this will turn out Tim, but we can decide what this treatment will be about. Is Olivia worth betting your time on, worth betting your pain? Which will you chose Tim?

CLIENT: I choose Olivia.

THERAPIST: Yeah man. I think we have a contract here. Here is what I will promise you Tim. If we do this, really do this it will be painful, I mean painful like detox will look like a picnic. But let me promise this too. We will not do anything painful that is not *for* something *you* value. For something that *you* would say is worthy of your pain. And, one last thing Tim. I promise you that I am going to hang in there with you through this. Can you hear me Tim? Do you get that this matters to me? I have not taken your path Tim, but I know that showing up for life is hard. I get how important this is to you and I am committed to working on your behalf.

In this vignette, the focus of the therapist is to find some value that can inspire and direct the activities of both the therapist and the client. The treatment contract forged in this session defines the direction of treatment. It provides motivation. In Tim's world and in ours, Olivia is a bigger prize than abstinence from drugs.

This direction dignifies the pain that will surely come. Tim's value is likely to provide a much more stable compass heading than thoughts or feelings. There were times (at her birth, for example), when he thought he would always be there for his daughter. There have been other times, (when his wife moved out, for example), that he was certain that he would never be worth anything to anyone. His values about parenting, by contrast, have been stable over the same time frame.

What goes wrong in values assessment? There are many potential clinical challenges to be confronted when conducting values based assessments and interventions. Fortunately, most of these pitfalls present you with the opportunity to use acceptance, defusion and to return to the ultimate workability of the client's reactions. Common problems that emerge in values work include compliance with actual or perceived social convention (which is well treated in the ACT book and will not be repeated here), confusion about values, switching values in the service of emotional avoidance, and the absence of values in key areas.

Confusion about values and switching values are often functionally related to emotional control and avoidance. If one is confused about one's values in a certain area, then inaction is a sensible and relatively safe option.

Confusion is also produced by fusion with evaluations about being "right and wrong". If one stands up and declares a valued course, then all of the self defeating behavior that has come before will seemingly make the client "wrong". This type of evaluation and reason giving should be targeted using conventional ACT defusion and experiential exercises. Values switching is another reasonably common response pattern and it may either be indicative of a clinical problem or a benign, positive event. You and the client might be working with a specific stated value and find that it is connected to some larger value. This is a golden clinical opportunity to expand the therapeutic contract. So, for example, the value of being in a richer relationship with a daughter could be connected to a larger value of being connected to people. The contract might then expand so that the relationship with the client's daughter was a part of a larger pattern of committed action. The same behavioral topography could also be connected to backing up from the relationship with the daughter, however, and as the therapist you need to take a careful look at the functional determinates of the shift from one value to another. When therapy has an unfocused, diffuse quality, and lacks a strong sense of direction, it often indicates that client is shifting the values focus in the service of emotional avoidance.

Clients will sometimes present as if they value nothing. As ACT therapists, we assume—even in the absence of evidence—that the client is either misrepresenting their experience, or that they are so trapped in their pattern of emotional avoidance that they are on "auto-pilot". This assumption is not ontological or naïve—it is strategic. If it is the case that the client literally values nothing but getting high and not getting caught, there is nothing to work on in therapy. By contrast, it is entirely *possible* that the person does value something, but is so frightened, demoralized, resigned, that values have been pushed out of awareness. Assuming that the client has values and proceeding in that direction clinically gives you the therapist the best chance of unlocking this pervasive pattern of experiential avoidance.

Strategies to reveal avoided values could include things like asking back through time: "Was there a time when you wanted something, to be something, to do something?" Or, we might ask, "In a world where you *did* care about something, what would that be?" People don't start life wanting to be a drug addict. Often, as we push back in time, we find long abandoned hopes and dreams. The client lives inside of a story about what is possible and what is not. We are absolutely *not* asking what they think is possible, what we think they are capable of, what they think the world will allow, or what they think can be done given their history or life circumstances. We are asking what they want—in a world in which what they really want is possible. For example, in discussing values with an addict who had at various times been homeless and engaged in prostitution in exchange for heroin, we were surprised to learn that she had always dreamt of becoming a nun. Whether or not this client becomes a nun, the underlying values of service and spirituality can be lived and expanded.

Acceptance and Defusion

Acceptance and defusion based interventions are to a significant extent different methods of exposing the client to feared and avoided stimuli. However, ACT employs exposure in a constructional, not eliminative way. ACT is not typically focused on decreasing the likelihood that feared private content will "show up." The goal is to help the client generate more flexible psychological responses in the presence of previously avoided events. If understood in that way, it is quite proper to say that ACT is in part a method of exposure or even of extinction (which can also be analyzed as a method of producing more response flexibility, Wilson & Murrell, in press), but the historical linkage between these concepts and eliminative goals is very strong, so we need to be mindful of the clear differences of meaning. From an ACT perspective there is no particular virtue to approaching a feared object per se. There is virtue in fostering the freedom to approach when approaching serves a client's values. It is the inflexibility generated by experiential avoidance repertoires that are the target of acceptance and defusion methods.

Addicts experience many events that generate inflexibility. Some are inherent. For example, stopping drug use may generate sensations and emotions (e.g., drug cravings) that can only be eliminated quickly by more drug use. Methods incorporating exposure to such interoceptive sensations already has some preliminary support as a drug treatment approach (Pollack, Penava, Bolton, Worthington, Allen, Farach, & Otto, 2002). Other kinds of events are the result of "dirty suffering", or the attempt to avoid situations that engender appropriate but painful psychological content. You will often identify these sources of inflexibility when conducting the CSIW and values assessment (i.e., avoidance of relationships, or parental responsibilities, because of the fear, guilt sadness they bring up). You can use acceptance and defusion interventions to address both of these sources of psychological inflexibility. It is not a matter of "logic", but rather "standing for something" that will legitimize the work that needs to be done and the discomfort that will come along for the ride while the addict does it.

In the example of the addict above, it was no coincidence that Tim did not have a picture of his daughter in his wallet. When Tim brought a picture of his daughter into therapy, and sat looking at the picture, he made psychological contact with his history of trauma around Olivia. He remembered the day his ex-wife packed up Olivia and left. He remembered his wife, Sue, telling him that Olivia had asked if Dad was gone because Olivia had been bad. The only way Tim could control or eliminate the pain associated with these memories was to avoid Olivia and any cue associated with her. In therapy, we had Tim practice *in vivo* exposure with photos of Olivia, letters from her and a baby cup that Tim had bought for her to celebrate her first birthday.

We also had Tim participate in "eyes closed" exercises—taking him back in time to particularly painful moments. When conducting such experiential exercises, it is critical that you closely monitor the client's reactions. For example, you might observe that the client is tensing up physically. This might involve such observable signs as tightened jaws, tightened voice quality, or the clinching of hands and arms This typically signals that emotional arousal is rising and the any predisposition to emotional avoidance is going to present itself in the exercise. As the wave of arousal and emotional avoidance grows, you need to help the client stay present and hold both the original pain and the desire to run from it in awareness. Help the client "just notice" the various emotions, thoughts, and sensations that emerge. The goal is to maximize contact with the avoided event and with all of the internal and external participants of that psychological moment. It is learning to hold still in the face of provocative psychological content that builds acceptance and flexible and effective responding.

Consider the following experiential exercise with Tim that begins by looking at a picture of Olivia and evolves into an imagery based exercise in which Tim visualizes himself at his home on the day that Olivia and Sue moved out. The vignette begins when Tim is in the room looking at Olivia as his wife tells him that she has to take Olivia and leave. The therapist has gleaned from Tim the precise words that he recalls from that day:

THERAPIST: Look at Olivia's face Tim. Notice her hair, what she is wearing. Listen to Sue Tim: 'We have to go Tim. Olivia is not safe here.' Look into Olivia's eyes Tim. Is she crying? Stay with her Tim.

CLIENT: (*quiet*) Not crying. She looks confused—sort of blank.

THERAPIST: Tim, notice your arms and hands right now. Feel that tension in your arms. Scan your arms and notice where it is greatest. See if you can let go of that tension for just a moment. (*pause*) See if you can just let go of that resistance Tim. Now come back to Olivia's eyes. Let yourself *be* in that room with her. Tell me where you feel it in your body Tim.

CLIENT: In my chest and throat. Tight.

THERAPIST: OK Tim. I want you to focus on that tension for a moment. Try to picture the areas that are tense . . . . the shape of those areas. Imagine that the areas of tension are red, and that the areas with the most tension are brightest. (Pause) Let your self notice the tightness you feel there. A tension that is like you are about to be hurt. Readying yourself for some injury. (pause) And, now I want you to gently let go of the tension. (long pause) If it could serve Olivia Tim, could you let yourself hurt? Now gently come back to Olivia's face, her eyes. See if you can let yourself feel what Olivia feels . . . . as if you have a direct connection to her.

Note that the thrust of this exercise is not to lessen Tim's sadness regarding this very sad day. His sadness is inextricably connected to his love for his daughter. Rather, the therapist is trying to produce flexibility in Tim's responding, so that when this sadness and memories occur, he has the flexibility to remain psychologically present and to do what needs to be done to promote valued life outcomes. When you do acceptance and exposure work of this kind, you should look for signs of freezing or flexibility: constriction or openness in the client's posture, expressiveness, voice quality, and so on as markers that progress is being made.

Tim did reestablish a relationship with his daughter, and after many years of failing to meet his responsibilities, he had to face many reminders of these memories and emotional reactions before his daughter actually felt safe enough to spend time with him. If contacting these psychological events were unacceptable, then pursuing his values with respect to Olivia would be impossible.

Experiential exercises, both in vivo and imagery based, help the client develop both breadth and flexibility in response to cues involving direct aversive conditioning experiences. An additional clinical problem is that fusion processes create fearful events that occur only in the world of ideas. For example, a serious substance abusing client will often have thoughts such as "No matter how hard I try, no matter what I try, nothing ever really works or ever will." This thought itself will be avoided. Using various defusion exercises is often a necessary first step to enable the client to see these thoughts *as thoughts*. There is no literal future present. What is present is a story about the future.

When disturbing thoughts cry out for avoidance, non-judgmental, openness, appreciation and acceptance represent the kind of broadening of repertoire that is a central aim of ACT. For example, you the therapist can begin each session with a brief mindfulness exercise prior to any intervention involving strong exposure components. In order for experiential exercises to work, the client has to be psychologically present, and this type of mindfulness exercise helps the client learn to stay in the present moment as a conscious human being. This is no less true for the therapist than for the client, and thus it is usually best to do the exercise along with the client. You the therapist also need to be *in the moment* if you want to stay in touch with the client's reactions during particularly challenging sessions. For example, in the previous vignette, the thoughts of the therapist are defused in the same way as the thoughts of the client (e.g., I don't give a damn what you think, *or what I think.*"). ACT defusion interventions, such as *Milk, Milk, Milk* (Hayes, et al., 1999, pp. 154–156) can be readily adapted to substance abuse content. For example, the therapist might take a well worn bit of self-talk such as, "I can't stay clean," and say the phrase over and over again with the client. You can use more playful variants to help clients develop an experiential appreciation of defusion. For example, the therapist and client could say the phrase very, very slowly for two minutes; then very, very quickly for two minutes; then in a low voice for two minutes; then in a falsetto voice for two minutes; then say it in the voice of a cartoon character for two minutes. This odd interaction with thoughts of incompetence violates the social verbal context that gives thoughts of incompetence their potency. Saying these seemingly frightening words out loud violates the normal social/verbal context. Repetition violates the context. Playing with voice quality violates the context. Goofiness definitely violates the context. Before you start the exercise, describe what will be done and get agreement to proceed. The following vignette demonstrates how to start such a playful defusion intervention.

> THERAPIST: OK, Tim, we are going to do the exercise now. We are going to take your sense of inadequacy and play with it and I want you to watch what happens. (Therapist gets very serious.) Listen: Tim, you will never, ever clean up. You are completely inadequate. Even though you hope that you will some day, you *know* deep down that you can't do it. Let yourself feel it Tim.

You the therapist should maintain direct eye contact say these words as if you really *mean* them. This will let you get a baseline response to this sense of inadequacy when it shows up for the client. Note your own emotional, physical, cognitive reactions, and behavioral predispositions and then those of the client. As soon as you are confident that both of you are psychologically present, begin the exercise. During the exercise, watch the client. If the exercise is pushed far enough, you will see a broadening of the client's reactions to the disturbing thought. Often, the client will physically relax; laughter is not uncommon and is a particular good sign that defusion has occurred. You can also use this intervention with great impact in a group setting, since the tweaking of the social/verbal context is more profound when done at a group level. If being playful with regard to difficult content violates the context of literality, being playful in a group does so doubly.

You should continue these exercises until you see some visible markers of flexible responding on the part of the client. After concluding, it is worthwhile to debrief the exercise by contrasting the physical and psychological constriction present at the beginning of the exercise with the flexibility that emerges in the context of the exercise. If the client begins to back up psychologically from the difficult material (i.e., refusing to continue, reverting to talking about the content of the repetitive thought), you need to do the same sort of gentle coaching that you would do in any experiential exercise or exposure session.

With severely addicted clients, ACT defusion exercises need to be thought of in terms of shaping and successive approximations. Just as in any shaping procedure, the more intimate the contact with the client, the less likely it is that we will proceed too rapidly in the shaping procedure. As described above, the therapist needs to remain very mindful of the minutia of client behavior, watching for changes in posture and voice quality that will tell us whether we are holding the challenging material in place, but at the same time not running ahead of the client. If a client seems to be psychologically immobilized, "re-upping" the value that justifies getting present with avoided content can move the process along. For example, asking the client "If it moved you closer to Olivia, Tim, could you step forward?"

Committed Action

All ACT interventions are ultimately in the service of committed action. Two variants of committed action are worth examining with regard to substance abuse. First, some committed acts will be commitments that are in the service of other commitments. These second order commitments are more central to the work. For example, Tim might commit to staying clean, not because of the virtues of staying clean in and of itself, but rather because staying clean makes other commitments possible. Tim's access to his daughter was limited by his willingness to stay clean. More critically, Tim had a history of substance involvement interfering with his ability to make and keep commitments at work, at home, and in social situations. A description of the process of making commitments is contained in the original ACT book, including a transcript with a client that is making a commitment to stay clean (Hayes et al., 1999, p. 243).

With a client like Tim, you the therapist might ask him if he would be willing to make a commitment to responsible fathering and, if the answer is yes, you would use the Values, Goals, Actions, Barriers worksheet

Table 7.3. Clinical Issues and Recommended ACT Interventions for Clients with Substance Abuse

Clinical issue	Recommended ACT response
Treatment is mandated or coerced	• Defuse objections to treatment as an obstacle to effective work • Defuse both compliance and defiance • Values intervention—find a value that can be agreed upon as a basis for a therapeutic contract. For example, self-determination, making therapy a choice as a therapeutic value.
Relapses and slips	• Defuse thoughts and feelings of failure, and especially around past failures, and thoughts of "permanent" or "ultimate" failure • Reconnect to values and link exposure and defusion to values • Do discrimination training contrasting experienced vitality of values-driven suffering in defusion and exposure exercises as compared to suffering experienced while attempting to suppress thoughts and feelings of failure
Fear of commitment (e.g., to living sober or to other values)	• Distinguish commitment as an object or an outcome from commitment as a process. Commitment is not to the outcome. Commitment is to the process. In essence the commitment is to commit and recommit as many times as is necessary. • Distinguish belief from assumption. Beliefs come and go; however, we can choose our assumption even as belief waxes and wanes.
Client says that they do not care about anything	• Get present in an experiential exercise to not caring about anything. Ask if the client could **choose** to be someone who cared or not, what they would choose. If they choose no, work on self-determination as a value (see above). • If they choose yes, ask "What if this therapy could be about creating a space where valuing"?
Client is convinced that they are irretrievably bad: "I haven't told you the everything. Some things are so bad they cannot be told."	• Empathize. Therapist should get in psychological contact with the level of isolation the client is experiencing. "It must be so painful for you, so isolating." • Client and therapist should use experiential exercises to make contact with and defuse the client's altogether human longing to be known and accepted. • Defuse "must" be able to tell in order to know if one is acceptable. • Make it clear that there is no special virtue in telling or not telling. The question is, what value is served by telling. • Ask: "What if our work here could be about creating a space where even the most horrific things could be told, if telling could make a difference in what you value?"

(continued)

Table 7.3. (*Continued*)

Clinical issue	Recommended ACT response
Irreversible losses or harm caused (i.e., loss of parental rights, vehicular manslaughter)	• Use experiential exercises to get psychologically present to the pain. • Defuse content that emerges in exercise. • "What if part of what we do here is to find a way to honor the loss or harm?" • "If the loss could guide activity you could value, what things, even very small things might you do this day that could honor the loss?" • Do discrimination training around vitality involved in even the smallest honoring of the loss as contrasted with the lack of vitality of working to suppress thoughts of the loss.
Client comes to therapy intoxicated	• Intervention should be sensitive to the meaning of the intoxication and whether it is the first time, or one of many. • The meeting should not be business as usual and the intoxication ought to be noted at minimum. Bear in mind that people in the addicts life have both ignored intoxication and rejected the client in anger over intoxication. Take a moment to get present to the different reactions the client has gotten to intoxication in the past. • If first time, to the extent possible, get present to the cost. This must be done in a thoroughly nonjudgmental way. • With some severely addicted individuals, meeting them at some level of intoxication may be our only opportunity to intervene. • With the client who is capable of coming to sessions clean, the therapist should allow their own feelings of vulnerability and incompetence be present in the meeting. Make the therapist' sadness **and** ongoing, unremitting commitment apparent, then send the client home.
Therapist is mad at client.	• Take a moment of silence. Ask the client to focus on her or his breathing. The therapist should use this time to become mindful of anger, noting thoughts, images, memories, and bodily sensations as they emerge (therapist defuses own anger). • Therapist should attempt to make contact with the value and vulnerability underlying the anger. • Therapist may note the anger that occurred and ask client about previous experiences where a person working for or with them became angry. • Therapist should make their unremitting commitment apparent in this exchange.

from the ACT book (Hayes et al., 1999, p. 227). Tim identified several goals connected with this value. Regular quality contact with Olivia was one of the goals. The action involved buying a dozen post cards, addressing them, and writing on each one "Hi Olivia. Just thinking about you today and wanted to write to say how much I love you." Tim committed to send one card a week. The committed action assignment allowed him to write more than this on the card, but any card had to be mailed regardless of the content. Exercises in committed action often raise issues that can be addressed with acceptance and defusion interventions. For example, you might ask Tim to bring a postcard to session and conduct an experiential exercise that helps him get in psychological contact with his love for his daughter. You could walk with him to a mail box, doing a mindfulness exercise all along the way. You could have Tim get present with, and describe outloud, his bodily sensations, thoughts, memories, and emotions in relation to the act of sending the post card. Alternative, you could have Tim "take his mind for a walk", where you the therapist plays his mind and pesters him with well worn statements that emphasize his failures, the possibility that Olivia will never care for him and so forth. Tim's job as the "human" is to listen to your pestering while completing his commitment to mail the post card. Interventions such as these are designed to help your client acquire a rich and articulated pattern of responses to actions that might seem small in scale, but serve to "trigger" large networks of avoided private stimuli. In this way, you can use committed action assignments, acceptance and defusion interactively to build psychological flexibility.

What goes wrong with committed action? Substance abusers with a long history of making and breaking commitments will have a very difficult time with this component of treatment. Two major clinical issues need to be addressed. First, you the therapist needs be clear about the definition of a commitment. Substance abusers are often reluctant to make a commitment because they are afraid that, one more time, they will make a promise and then fail to keep it. You the therapist need to explain that the type of commitment you are talking about is not an outcome commitment. It is engaging a valued commitment over time that may well *include* failure. So, for example, the commitment to abstain from drug use does not mean that the addict will never use again. One cannot really commit to such a thing, because the future (and the past) are not in our personal control. Emphasize that the client can only act with purpose in the present moment, with intention at the 100% level. In the face of failure, remind the client that it is possible to commit to getting back on track as rapidly as possible. The commitment to stay clean means that the client will not use, *and*, if relapse occurs, the client is committed to stopping. How many times? As many

times as it takes. You have to be clear that the commitment of interest is in
the here and now.

Sometimes simpler domains can clarify what is meant by commitment
from an ACT perspective. For example, if you were teaching your child to
walk, you would help them to their feet when they fell. You could commit
to teaching them to walk, even knowing they would fall. How many times
do you help them stand up in the process of teaching them? Answer: however many times it takes. In ACT committed action has the same quality
of engagement with a valued direction over time. The outcome at any particular point in time in not as important as the quality of committed action
itself.

SPECIAL CLINICAL CONSIDERATIONS

Treating substance abusers is a very complex and challenging clinical
task. A plethora of factors may complicate treatment: decisions about in-
patient/outpatient care as the appropriate venue, whether to detoxify the
client, responding to intoxication in session, addressing co-morbid conditions, integrating 12-step programs and treatment philosophies, correcting
skills deficits, addressing couples distress, mixing methadone and other
psychotropic medications, to name a few. As if all that weren't enough,
you are likely to see a near infinite combination of these features. In addition, decisions about these matters are often made with near religious
conviction—often without compelling clinical evidence or with an eye towards practicalities. Ultimately, many of these issues are empirical questions and you the therapist need to be aware of the evidence and manage these decisions in a way that is consistent with the best evidence. In
some of these areas, there is as yet no convincing science to guide decisions. It is in these areas that we will make some recommendations,
based upon our experience with using ACT to treat substance abusers.
These recommendations are not "truths" but rather seem to be sensible first
steps in the effort to develop effective, efficient, and acceptable treatment
strategies.

Adapting ACT to the Inpatient Treatment Setting

The initial scientific results suggest that ACT is a promising outpatient
treatment model for substance abusers. Much less is known about how to
adapt ACT to the inpatient setting, whether it be in an intensive treatment facility or a halfway house. However, it seems logical to assume that
incorporating ACT into the in-patient milieu could have salutary effects

on treatment outcomes. In such settings, trained staff could build an ACT model at the core of the treatment program or integrate ACT principles into the existing treatment program. For example, integrating interventions that focus on identifying valued directions and making commitments to action in the service of those values could easily be integrated into a substance abuse treatment group. The behavioral literature suggests that public commitments tend to be more predictive of behavior than private commitments (Hayes, Rosenfarb, Wulfert, Munt, Zettle, & Korn, 1985). If the treatment is inpatient, the public aspect of any commitments made is intensified, since the person can't go home after group and forget about what they have said.

Do You Have to Detoxify First?

Historically, many treatment facilities required a brief period of abstinence prior to admission. Treating fully detoxified individuals has some advantages. Treatment requires that the individual be psychologically present, not just physically present. Intoxication can be a substantial barrier to being in the present moment. In addition, the presence of intoxicated individuals may pose dangers for other individuals who are in treatment. However, the benefits of a prior detoxification come at a cost. Requiring detoxification may function as a barrier to entering treatment, most likely for those clients with the most severe addictions. Ironically, a requirement for detoxification may select for more treatment-motivated individuals (and make the job of treatment easier), but may exclude the individuals least likely to recover given contingencies that are naturally occurring in their native environment.

Depending on the substance and the client's health status, medically supervised detoxification may be a necessity. However, when it is not indicated for medical reasons, riding out a difficult detoxification process can provide many opportunities to practice acceptance and mindful noticing of the ebb and flow of urges and the discomforts associated with the abstinence syndrome (what Alan Marlatt calls "urge surfing", Marlatt & Gordon, 1985). The context of an uncomfortable detoxification can also provide opportunities to examine the workability of the solutions the "mind" will offer (i.e., the best way to feel good right now is to use). Finally, although you may be tempted to lower your demands during a distressing detoxification, doing so may contribute to the fusion with the thought that the symptoms of abstinence are unbearable. It is in the presence of this physical and mental discomfort that you the therapist might consider focusing on bold committed action. If clients can commit to staying clean and practice defusion from thoughts such as, "later would be a better time to clean up", they stand a much better chance of staying clean during less turbulent moments. To expand on Marlatt's metaphor, if clients can learn to ride the big waves, the smaller ones are less likely to throw them.

Addressing Intoxication in Session

It is interesting that substance abuse is nearly the only area where we would even consider sending a client home for showing symptoms of the difficulty that brought them into treatment. You, the therapist need to take a pragmatic view, rather than moralistic view, on this issue. There are times when treating an intoxicated client is the only chance you will have to gain a foothold. If so, we would recommend that you seize the opportunity, and begin working with the client on how coming to session intoxicated might be an example of the emotional avoidance that characterizes the client's functioning in so many areas. You might even ask the client to describe how being intoxicated right now is "working" to promote to promote valued outcomes. If the level of intoxication is sufficient that the individual cannot process this type of information at some level, then we regretfully send the client home. When the individual returns to treatment, it is important to examine how showing up high is working for the client. You the therapist also need to monitor your own acceptance level with such clients. Many therapists are tempted to engage in retaliation, lecturing, confrontation, or moralizing in an attempt to be "right" and make the client "wrong". Obviously, injecting this dynamic into the therapy process simply re-invigorates the trap the client has been in for many years.

The Role of Agonist Treatment and Antidipsotropics?

We have an initial demonstration of the additive benefits of ACT for clients receiving agonist treatment for opiates (Hayes et al., in press). In this, we trained therapists to remain agnostic with respect to methadone treatment and reframe its use as a matter of personal choice. If clients wanted to wean themselves from methadone, we did the hard work around that. If they chose not to, we supported them in that choice. The use of such medicines is ultimately a matter of values for the client. Perhaps methadone use can function in the service of experiential avoidance strategy, but you should always remember that experiential avoidance is not the enemy *per se*. Nor is experiential avoidance an all or nothing matter. We all engage in forms of experiential avoidance, and ultimately, its impact can only be judged by the extent to which that avoidance interferes with lived values.

We have also used antidipsotropic medications in combination with ACT. For example, we treated an alcoholic client who took antidipsotropics as a part of his treatment agreement with the judicial system. We turned adhering to the medication agreement into an exercise in committed action. The individual being treated was married. In session, the client was asked to remember the day that he took his wedding vows. We asked him to view his wedding ring as a physical symbol of that commitment. He then made the commitment to take his Antibuse each morning, in his wife's presence, in the same spirit that he made his wedding vows. In this case, the focus of the intervention was to make something as simple as taking a medication an action that was based in values and done with a purpose. The focus was not on casting Antibuse as a way to eliminate drinking (though it has that effect); it was a means of positively affirming a commitment to relationship and responsibility.

The Role of Other Psychoactive Medications

As with agonist treatment, our recommendation is to be agnostic with respect to psychoactive medications. Medications have benefits and costs, and your job as the therapist is to examine these costs and benefits with reference to the client's ability to live a valued life. It is worth noting that this is a matter to watch with particular care with substance abusers, since they have very often used substances in order to manage experience. You should be willing to discuss the role psychoactive medications might play in supporting experiential avoidance and have the client assess the workability of this strategy. For example, far a schizophrenic client with a history of stopping medications, staying on medications might be a form of committed action. In other cases, the medicine might be promoting a symptom control and elimination strategy that is all about feeling "good" rather than doing good.

Compatibility of ACT with a 12-Step Model

In some prior publications, we have pointed out the numerous areas of compatibility between ACT and traditional 12-step programs (Wilson, et al., 2000). The best way for you to integrate ACT philosophy with 12-step treatment philosophy is to learn about Alcoholics Anonymous at some considerable depth. In the United States, 12-step programs are everywhere. You should not dismiss this community resource or regard it as a nuisance. Such programs are a fact of life and can play a major supportive role for many substance abusers.

Ernie Kurtz has written the most scholarly, authoritative, and exhaustive account of AA available today (Kurtz, 1979). In it, Kurtz speaks of AA culture as multi-faceted. One can find in AA members that are entirely

dogmatic, disease-oriented, and confrontational. These stereotypic attributes of AA are rarely seen in the actual AA seminal texts: *Alcoholics
Anonymous* (Alcoholics Anonymous, 1976) and *The Twelve Steps and Twelve
Traditions* (Alcoholics Anonymous, 1953). Orienting clients to relevant pas-
sages of these two core texts can go a long way towards insulating clients
against the more dogmatic versions of AA that they may encounter in a
particular AA support group.

To highlight this compatibility, we have challenged rooms full of 12-
step oriented treatment providers to identify for us the place in these two
core AA texts where the words "confronting denial" appear. We have
never received an answer, because this phrase is never seen in either of
these texts. While "confronting denial" is taken as a given in AA, it is, in
fact, wholly contrary to the traditional AA literature and is more a product of 12 Step treatment centers than AA itself. These texts do speak of
self-deception, but most psychological theories (including ACT) acknowledge the human capacity for self-deception, rationalization and other
means of avoiding psychologically challenging material. The AA texts
say that alcoholics are confronted by life, not by sponsors or in meetings.
In fact, *Alcoholic Anonymous* is entirely clear that it is a mistake to even
diagnose someone as alcoholic, let alone confront them regarding their
alcoholism.

> We do not like to pronounce any individual as alcoholic, but you can quickly
> diagnose yourself. Step over to the nearest barroom and try some controlled
> drinking. Try to drink and stop abruptly. Try it more than once. It will not take
> long for you to decide, if you are honest with yourself about it. It may be worth
> a bad case of jitters if you get a full knowledge of your condition. (Alcoholics
> Anonymous, 1976, pp. 31–32)

This position is entirely consistent with an ACT perspective. We want
to bring the client into intimate contact with the workability of what they
are doing, what they value and the interaction of those two things. Some
AA sponsors and AA meetings will be highly dogmatic and incompatible
with ACT treatment. It is worthwhile for you to cultivate a relationship
with the local AA community so you can direct clients that are interested
in using AA to meetings and sponsors that are more consistent with an
ACT perspective (and with core AA literature). Most communities have
a wide variety of AA meeting groups, including some meetings open to
interested individuals without alcohol problems. Anyone can attend an
open AA meeting as long as they are respectful of the anonymity of the
individuals who go to those meetings. Good knowledge of 12-step core
texts can also aid in cultivating an ACT friendly perspective when training
traditional 12-step oriented treatment staff.

Combining ACT with Other Substance Abuse Treatments

In principle, ACT can be combined with a variety of other commonly used substance abuse treatments. For example, Marlatt's harm reduction interventions (Marlatt & Witkiewitz, 2002) and Miller and Rollnick's (1991; 2002) motivational interviewing are very compatible with ACT principles. In a stepped care model of treatment, you might employ Marlatt's psycho-educational and motivational approach as a very brief, sensible first step. If this fails to address the problem, you might begin a more in depth interventions using emotional avoidance, acceptance, defusion and workability, which would be more characteristic of an ACT intervention. Likewise, there is no fundamental incompatibility between ACT and multifaceted approaches such as the Community Reinforcement Approach (Meyers, Miller, & Edwards, 2001). Serious substance abusers will frequently have isolated themselves from situations that build and maintain basic life skills such as grooming, appropriate engagement in employment and educational settings, and in social activities that are not centered on intoxication. ACT can contribute to these treatment programs by adding motivational components, based in values work, or through the application of acceptance/defusion interventions when psychological obstacles emerge as barriers to skills training activities.

CONCLUSION

The application of ACT to substance abusers does not differ substantially from ACT with any other population. As is true of ACT in general, we assume that substance abusers find certain thoughts, emotions, memories, bodily states and behavioral predispositions unacceptable and use various strategies to eliminate, attenuate, or reduce these private experiences. The result of these experiential avoidance strategies (substance use being the most prominent in this case) is the loss of flexibility and vitality in our clients' lives. Eventually, the loss vitality itself becomes something further to avoid, the circle closes. Avoidance begets avoidance, and at some level, any contact with a sense that we are propagating our own degraded existence, "demands" escape. And, deeper and deeper we sink into meaninglessness and despair.

ACT provides a way out of the self cycling negative results that are produced by excessive experiential avoidance. The way out of the trap is to winnow some sense of direction out of the chaff of an avoidant lifestyle. Initially this sense of direction may be quite meager—a vague sense of wanting more, wanting something bigger, richer, more vibrant. Then, we help the client begin to move in the direction of a bigger life. As the client begins the move towards a bigger, richer, more vibrant life, psychological obstacles inevitably crop up. To address these obstacles, the ACT therapist employs acceptance, defusion and mindfulness interventions to create freedom of movement, even in the face of seemingly insurmountable obstacles. As the client moves forward in the face of these obstacles, a life begins to take shape that shows signs of meaning and purpose. Pain may not disappear, but it is now pain with a purpose. This is the core of the ACT model.

Chapter **8**

ACT with the Seriously Mentally Ill

PATRICIA BACH

Psychotic disorders in general and schizophrenia in particular have generally been regarded as disorders that are relatively difficult to treat. While psychopharmacological treatments are widely available and effective compared to placebo controls (Davis, Schaffer, Killian, Kinard, & Chan, 1980), many patients with serious mental illness (SMI) are unresponsive to medications. Relapse rates are 20% per year among patients who receive psychosocial treatment and antipsychotic medication and twice that among persons receiving medication only (Gorman, 1996). SMI patients also tend to be treatment non-compliant with high service utilization and service costs, and to have significant family, financial, and social problems, even with available treatment (Miner, Rosenthal, Hellerstein, & Muenz, 1997).

Delusional beliefs and hallucinations are defining symptoms of psychotic disorders and in this chapter we will focus a fair amount on these "positive" symptoms. They are notoriously difficult to eliminate completely. About three quarters of SMI patients on continuous anti-psychotic medications continue to experience positive psychotic symptoms (Breier, Schreiber, Dyer, & Pickar, 1991). While newer atypical antipsychotic medications reduce negative as well as positive symptoms of psychosis their impact on psychosocial outcomes is mixed (Corrigan, Reinke, Landsberger, Charate & Toombs (2003). Perhaps for that reason, psychosocial treatments available for serious mental illness, including psychotic disorders, have generally emphasized skills training, problem solving, token economies, medication management, vocational rehabilitation, and when applicable family interventions (Kuipers, 2000). These psychosocial interventions

185

have not targeted symptoms of the illness so much as addressing skills deficits associated with serious mental illness.

In recent years more psychotherapies, and especially cognitive behavioral approaches, with empirical support have been developed for the treatment of delusions and hallucinations (Haddock, Tarrier, Spaulding, Yusupoff, Kinney, & McCarthy, 1998). Psychosocial interventions for symptoms of psychosis have generally emphasized reality testing, verbal challenges to belief, distraction, or improving perceived control over symptoms and symptom expression.

From an ACT perspective, the mere presence of symptoms of psychosis (positive or negative symptoms) is not necessarily the core of the clinical problem. Indeed, the majority of persons who report hallucinations have no mental health problem (Tien, 1991) and about one half of persons with schizophrenia make positive as well as negative evaluations about their experience of hallucinations (Miller, O'Connor, & DiPasquale, 1993). While delusional beliefs, by definition, have content that does not correspond to reality, at the level of process they appear to be no more difficult to modify than are culturally normative beliefs such as political or religious identity (Maher, 1988). Instead, as in other areas discussed in this volume, the problem is the role these symptoms play in the total behavioral repertoire of the patient. As in other areas, the most significant difference between ACT and traditional cognitive behavioral approaches is that ACT interventions do not target the *content* of perceptual experiences, beliefs, social withdrawal, and so on. Instead, the emphasis in treatment is on the *functions* of these events and the effectiveness of overt actions taken by the client in relation to them.

There is some empirical support for this ACT approach. Case studies have supported the efficacy of ACT for individuals reporting auditory hallucinations (Garcia & Perez, 2001), and a recent randomized controlled trial of ACT with psychiatric inpatients experiencing delusions or hallucinations, showed that participants exposed to only 3 hours of an ACT intervention were half as likely as treatment as usual (TAU) participants to be rehospitalized during a four month follow-up period (Bach & Hayes, 2002). Participants in both groups reported decreased distress in the presence of their symptoms at follow-up, and increase compliance with medication, so this did not explain the outcome. Participants in both groups also reported fewer symptoms at follow-up, but ACT participants were significantly *more* likely to report symptoms than were control participants. ACT participants were also less likely to believe symptom content when it occurred. These factors helped explain the outcome results. No ACT participant reporting hallucinations and no ACT participant reporting both delusions and decreased believability of those delusions were rehospitalized at follow-up. This suggests that the higher levels of symptom reporting in the ACT condition were due to greater acceptance and less denial of these symptoms, and perhaps also to lower levels of believability of symptom content. This study is currently being replicated in a dissertation and the post data and early follow-up comport with the first study (Gaudiano & Herbert, 2004).

Current thinking suggests that the disability that often accompanies serious mental illness is a result of a combination of factors including biological events, the impact of symptoms, and skill deficits that are often secondary to the impact of symptoms and to long periods of institutionalization. A psychiatric rehabilitation approach emphasizes the need for comprehensive treatment including pharmacological and psychosocial interventions, skills training and environmental and social supports. ACT may be uniquely suited as a psychotherapy that addresses both the impact of symptoms and the motivation to set goals and adhere to treatment regimens.

FORMULATION

Overall, most cognitive and behavioral therapies are aimed at trying to change or eliminate undesirable thoughts, feelings and bodily sensations. The emphasis is on changing the *content* of private events. In the case of delusions and hallucinations most cognitive behavior therapies emphasize eliminating delusional thoughts or hallucinations, testing reality, or getting the client to accept that their experience is not 'real'. Such approaches to the treatment of delusions and hallucinations are based upon an implicit assumption that it is false beliefs per se that are the problem, and that once the private events are no longer occurring, the individual will function normally. However, delusions and hallucinations appear to be highly resistant to change and tend to recur even after periods of remission. Many psychiatric patients enter hospitals experiencing delusions and/or hallucinations, and are unable to take care of themselves. Gross symptoms of psychosis often are rapidly reduced after the subject is medicated, and especially among those given a diagnosis of a depressive or manic episode with psychotic features. However, whether occurring in the context of a mood disorder or psychotic disorder, these symptoms tend not to disappear permanently or completely, but to continue at a lower level or to disappear and then recur even after years living of asymptomatically.

Since hallucinations and delusions are resistant to permanent elimination, a more pragmatic approach might be to teach individuals to respond differently to their own private events. From an ACT perspective it is the individual's interaction with these symptoms, not their occurrence or non-occurrence alone that leads to dysfunction. Responses to symptoms and to ideas about "mental illness," both overt responses to avoid or escape them, and thoughts that lead one to restrict one's life (e.g., "I have to make the voices stop", "I can't leave the house because I'm afraid people will stare at me", or "I'll never be able to get a job; who would hire someone with schizophrenia?"), often seem to cause more emotional pain and self-defeating behavior than symptoms themselves. Some negative symptoms of schizophrenia, such as avolition, and poverty of speech may be as much due to consequences of the disorder such as medication side effects, understimulation and demoralization, as to the disorder itself.

The avoidance and fusion model of psychopathology that underlies ACT seems to apply well to the positive and many of the negative symptoms of psychosis. Reactions to hallucinations are noticeably similar to reactions non-psychotic people have to intrusive thoughts; attempt to control them by trying to suppress the unwanted thought content. Delusions tend to be a means of avoidance rather than an object of avoidance. In this case, feelings of inadequacy (Bentall & Kinderman, 1999), loneliness, anxiety, cognitive uncertainty (Bentall, 2001) or other such private events often seem to be regulated in part by delusional beliefs. That is, delusions reflect an attributional style that functions to maintain the individual's self-esteem. Avoidance and fusion make these private events even more impactful. For example, the individual with the delusional belief that her treatment providers hate her may skip mental health care appointments in order to avoid experiencing unpleasant feelings associated with this thought, such as anger or fear. But this avoidance leaves her with less support and ultimately with more fear or anger. Similarly, the person with grandiose delusions about his identity or accomplishments may behave in ways that that lead to rejection, ridicule, and legal problems that increase feelings of inadequacy. Many negative symptoms of psychosis (e.g., social withdrawal, flat affect) could be reflections of chronic avoidance of difficult emotions and thoughts, particularly in a social context. In all of these cases "the solution is part of the problem." That is, attempts to control distress lead to more distress.

The amplifying effects of avoidance patterns that are characteristic of an ACT model of psychopathology fit several of the features of psychotic behavior. Persons with serious mental illness are known to make more frequent references to their own cognitions as compared to normal controls (Rosenburg & Tucker, 1979), and to experience more frequent hallucinations during periods of anxiety and stress (Slade, 1972). Hallucinators have a stronger belief that it is not normal to have intrusive or unwanted thoughts, more interest in consistency of thought, and less confidence in their cognitive processes (Lobban, Haddock, Kinderman & Wells, 2002). Struggling with psychotic content is not helpful behavior: when one tries to control private events in one domain of behavior, it is *more* difficult to exert conscious control over simultaneously occurring behaviors (Bargh & Chartrand, 1999).

Traditional interventions have attempted to convince the client that the voice is self-generated, teach distraction and other coping skills, encourage the client not to talk about hallucinations, or find a historical explanation of the hallucination in the client's history. All of these approaches are based on the assumption that the hallucination itself is the problem. In contrast, from a functional contextual perspective, the origin of the symptom is not especially important—what is important is the relationship between the symptom and overt behavior.

Considered functionally, hallucinations and delusional beliefs are not substantively different from other verbal events a person might experience. Responding to a paranoid delusion by writing a threatening letter to a public official, or responding to a command hallucination by skipping an appointment is functionally similar to writing to a senator to oppose a policy or deciding against seeking a promotion after having the thought that one is unqualified. Auditory hallucinations are on a continuum with negative thoughts about oneself and with intrusive thoughts. Delusions are on a continuum with any beliefs a person might have. Beliefs themselves are harmless, even when they do not appear to conform to reality, because thoughts do not cause behavior. It takes contextual features to link thoughts to behavior, such as support for the literal meaning of thought, or the need to avoid certain thoughts. ACT targets these contexts.

The rationale for this approach is that the real difference in patients' lives and level of functioning comes from behavior not from symptoms. In fact, symptoms themselves are poor predictors of outcomes important to the individual such as employment success (Rogers, Anthony, Toole & Brown, 1991). The person experiencing command hallucinations is not hospitalized because they are hearing voices, but because they act on the content of the hallucination, by attempting to harm themselves or another, by taking street drugs, or by discontinuing prescribed medications. The person with persecutory delusions in not hospitalized for bizarre thoughts, but for assaulting someone they believe intends to harm them, or pouring their "poison" medications down the drain, or repeatedly calling the police.

Negative symptoms of schizophrenia including flat affect and lack of motivation tend to be more 'treatment resistant' than positive symptoms. Many persons with schizophrenia are unemployed, have unstable living arrangements and live socially impoverished lives with about half reporting one or no social supports. The emphasis in ACT on behavior activation

Table 8.1. Examples of ACT Issues and Interventions

Client says they need to make voices stop	Feeding the tiger metaphor; Polygraph metaphor
Client says this IS real, (buying thoughts)	Just noticing thoughts. Two computers metaphor. Is it possible to think the thought AND do X?
Client says action with respect to voices/delusional belief is based on a value	Explore competing values. How does action with respect to symptom interfere with attaining goals important to the individual?
Client is stuck in a struggle with symptoms	Explore how overt responses to symptoms lead to aversive outcomes; Person in the hole metaphor; Chinese handcuffs exercise (consider making concrete)
Observing and distancing from thoughts	Soldiers in a parade exercise Play out Box Full of Stuff Take Your Mind for a Walk
Evaluating symptoms	Bad cup metaphor
Exploration of private events that arise in relation to symptoms	Physicalizing; Tin can monster exercise

through exploring values, goals, and choices and examining barriers to changing behavior can be a starting point for increasing opportunities for reinforcement and/or can be easily combined and integrated with psychiatric rehabilitation programming that tends to emphasize individual choice, goal-setting, and empowerment.

CLINICAL INTERVENTIONS

ACT with persons with psychotic disorders proceeds much as ACT with other populations, but strategies are modified depending on the degree to which symptoms, cognitive deficits, and communication skill may interfere with treatment (see Table 8.1). Persons with schizophrenia often have impaired social and conversational skills and varying degrees of thought disorganization. Individuals with severe mood disorders may also have impaired concentration and communication skills. The ACT therapist should proceed slowly and may need to be more directive with clients showing thought disorganization, severe symptoms or limited communication skills. Further, persons with schizophrenia have difficulty understanding abstract social cues while correctly understanding more concrete cues (Penn, Combs & Mohamed, 2001). You have to keep it simple when working with an individual showing such cognitive impairments or deficits. For example, in introducing the concept that the solution is part of the problem the *Person in the Hole* metaphor (Hayes et al., 1999, pp. 101–104) may be too lengthy and abstract. The *Chinese Handcuffs* and *Feeding a Baby Tiger* metaphors (Hayes et al., 1999, p. 104) are briefer while conveying the same idea that what one does to try to change a problem often makes it worse. Until an individual client shows the ability to handle more lengthy or abstract material, all of the exercises you use should be similarly simple and brief. Exercises should be active, rather that passive, so that you have a chance to assess whether the client is following the material. The use of physical props and more concrete exercises can also be helpful. There are many ways to approach this, for example, in exploring reason giving and undermining reasons as causes, you might find it helpful to begin with a fairly concrete exercise before asking the client to generate more personally relevant examples. The client is simply asked to generate as many reasons as they can for why someone might say "no thank you" when asked if they would like a piece of cake. Answers may focus on eating behavior, other environmental events, internal feelings and sensations, or attributions about the person offering the cake, e.g., the person is full; they don't like cake; they are going out to dinner later; the cake might be poisoned; they are on a diet; the person offering the cake is a lousy baker; they don't like eating in front of other people; they have a stomach ache; they are allergic to chocolate. Concrete exercises such as this help the client understand rather abstract material and helps the therapist assess the client's level of understanding. More physical exercises also seem to be useful. In working on defusing from cognitions the *Taking Your Mind for a Walk* exercise (Hayes et al., 1999, pp. 162–163) can be very powerful with clients experiencing hallucinations; many remark that they feel irritated, but not distressed by, the 'mind' that is following them around and chattering incessantly, and most clients quickly make a connection between this exercise and their experience of hallucinations.

Therapy may proceed more slowly and be somewhat more redundant than with other clients, particularly if the individual is experiencing thought disorganization or frequent hallucinations. While it is useful to do ACT while the symptoms are in the room, if a client is floridly psychotic or meets criteria for a manic episode with psychotic features therapy is usually not useful until symptoms remit somewhat. Each session should begin with a thorough review of the material covered in the previous session, and you should summarize material periodically during sessions themselves. If you have been talking more than listening you should ask the client to react to what has been said.

It is important to determine whether the client believes that the content of their hallucinations or delusional beliefs describes reality, while simultaneously not getting into a patronizing or critical stance linked to the believability of content. (A delusion is, by definition, a belief that is not congruent with reality, however, many consumers with psychotic disorders have insight into the delusional nature of their beliefs during non-acute phases of their illness when not actively psychotic.). The consumer who is aware that his or her hallucinations are not 'real' is often invested in avoiding the hallucinations themselves or discomfort that accompanies them, or makes negative self-evaluations based on the presence of symptoms. They may use social isolation as a strategy for avoiding stimuli that might occasion hallucinations or delusional thought content and accompanying negatively evaluated feelings, or abuse alcohol and other substances to self-medicate. In contrast, the client who believes that the thought content is real is often invested in avoiding a feared outcome. They may be worried that that something bad will happen to them, or that they will be forced to do something they do not wish to. Here avoidance strategies are usually different, such as obeying a command hallucination to make the thought stop, or acting on a delusional belief in order to avoid feelings such as fear or anger that might accompany the delusional thought content.

It is essential to bring outcome goals into the picture early on, because strategies for avoiding hallucinations or delusional beliefs, or the feared outcomes of them, may 'work' in the short term even though they interfere with an attempt to attain valued outcomes. Frequent hospitalization is often an outcome of maladaptive attempts to avoid symptom related distress. Hospitalization itself is distressing to many clients, and interferes with other valued goals such as maintaining employment, housing and significant relationships.

The initial focus of therapy is largely determined by the willingness of the client to participate in therapy. Persons with serious mental illness often enter treatment involuntarily through hospitalization, or at best semi-voluntarily through referral from a case manager or other mental health services brokers. One approach for engaging the involuntary client is to begin treatment with a focus on goals and values rather than creative hope-lessness. If the client can see that their own behavior stands between them and attaining desirable goals they may be more willing to engage in the treatment process, particularly if they can make a link between participation in treatment and attaining these goals. It is worth noting that ACT interventions emphasizing goals and values and identification of how present behaviors interfere with goal attainment shares some features with Motivational Interviewing (Miller & Rollnick, 2002). This approach has been shown to increase both insight and treatment adherence in persons with schizophrenia (Rusch & Corrigan, 2002).

Persons with serious mental illness may initially have a difficult time identifying and articulating goals. Those who have been in treatment for many years often have a history of being told by treatment providers what their goals 'should' be with little examination of values and limited emphasis on personal choice. For example, some consumers may describe the goal of having their own apartment, and upon attaining it find that they enjoy having someone prepare their meals and prompt them to keep appointments and complete activities of daily living. Also, some consumers feel resentment or futility when they find employment and learn that a portion their salary may be retained by their payee if their housing is subsidized. These are often viewed as disincentives to live independently or to work. It is helpful when the client can articulate values that might sustain behavior change rather than concrete goals alone, such as the value of having choices about where to live or the value of being productive or self-supporting. For example, the client who resents that her social security disability payment is decreased if she begins working may me more willing to continue in a job if employment is linked to the value of being self-supporting or being active in addition to simply the goal of having a job.

With more motivated clients, treatment may begin with creative hopelessness and proceed later to examination of goals and values. In this case, ACT can begin with an exploration of the subject's previous approaches to coping with symptoms of psychosis, and how successful these approaches were, and what the consequences of them were. The possibility that the attempted solutions to the problem are part of the problem can then be explored.

You should address the nature of hallucinations or delusional beliefs emphasizing that delusional or hallucinatory content is often not very different from thoughts many people have, and that the major difference between the client and others who experience fewer aversive consequences is in how they respond to these cognitive phenomena. Several examples of thoughts many people have that are similar to common delusional or hallucinatory themes should be presented such as fears that one is the target of other's animosity, thoughts of harming one's self or others, grandiose thoughts, and so on. Self-disclosure can be helpful if it seems to fit the relationship with the client. One of the advantages of ACT with this population is that the theory underlying ACT questions the value of cognitive fusion whether or not thoughts are negative or positive, normal or abnormal. Thus, there is a radically respectful and non-hierarchical feel to these interactions. Any sense of reassurance from a patronizing position (e.g., "there, there, poor dear. Your thoughts are not so strange.") should be assiduously avoided.

Typical versus atypical reactions to thoughts should be discussed, with an emphasis on the idea that the problem is not symptoms per se, but how one responds to them. Discussions should be open and non-judgmental, regardless of the specific content of the patient's psychotic experience. The goal is normalizing symptoms, that is viewing them as on a continuum and not all that different in type from the experiences of 'normal' people. Such a stance increases the chances of the client reporting symptoms to the therapist, and decreases any perceived need to defend ones' symptoms or symptom content as being 'real' (Turkington & Siddle , 2000).

You should explore symptom(s) in detail with your client. The client should describe the content of the hallucination or delusional beliefs, related thoughts and feelings that arise when the symptom occurs, and what the individual is inclined to do. You should use defusing and accepting language, but without self-consciousness. For example, you can ask about how the client responds "when you have the thought that [add specific content] . . . " but without any sense that you are trying to "convince" the client that this experience is "just a thought" as if to dismiss it. As this material is covered, bring out strategies that are being used to try to make the symptom go away such as shouting at voices, staying indoors, using illicit substances, obeying a command hallucination, or distraction.

You should thoroughly explore what has happened in the past when clients have tried these control strategies, since the client's own experience will be your best ally. As you identify the consequences of trying to rid one's self of unwanted thought content, the *Polygraph Metaphor* or *Chocolate Cake Exercise* (Hayes et al., 1999, pp. 123–125) can be used to illustrate the futility of trying to control unwanted private events. You may also at this point introduce the idea that "if you're not willing to have it, you've got it." It is important to link these ideas to the client's actual experience. You should ask the client to look carefully to see if his or her experience doesn't confirm the point. For example, ask if trying to rid one's self of voices or to stop paranoid thoughts really eliminated the voice or thoughts over time. If the individual reports that avoidance strategies 'work' because they alleviate symptoms you should push out the time frame, and also examine other consequences that follow attempts to suppress symptoms. If the individual cannot recall any, ask about the client's history regarding hospitalizations, legal consequences, housing, employment, and relationships. Typically, a number of negative outcomes will emerge that seem to be consequences of trying to suppress symptom content.

It can help to take a "matter of fact" and accepting tone in this part of therapy, implicitly normalizing the struggle as well. Simple metaphors, such as *Chinese Handcuffs* (Hayes et al., 1999, pp. 104–105) can show how normal and yet how unhelpful it is to struggle. To make this more concrete it can help to have actual finger traps of that kind to play with in session (they are inexpensive and readily available from companies selling "gag gifts" on the internet by searching on the term "Chinese finger traps"). Seeing how normal it is to struggle can be very validating for these clients who are so often "on the short end of the stick" in their interactions with others. It helps to see that they are doing what anyone would do with such content, and that the unworkability of these efforts is built in for us all.

The issue that normally comes up at this point in an ACT protocol is acceptance or defusion. Of the two, it usually makes sense to begin to work on defusion first with this population. It is important, however, not to allow the client to confuse defusion with the invalidating idea that their thoughts are thoughts because others think they are irrational or bizarre. This is one of the great advantages of ACT with this population, as compared to traditional CBT or other approaches that have to question thought content from the point of view of "my thoughts are rational while yours are not." In ACT, *all* thoughts are just thoughts—whether they are the therapist's or the client's. The only important issue about thoughts is whether what one does with them contributes to a successful life.

The *Message on a Computer Screen Metaphor* is a good place to start. Ask the person to imagine that there are two computers, side by side, that are identical in all details—same software, same data, same machine. Imagine that what is on the screen of both is a frightening image: say a picture of the walls of the room melting [if the client is delusional pick instead an odd thought, but in either case pick an item that is not the same as the clients]. In one case the operator of the computer is sitting close, and has forgotten that what he [fit gender to the client] is seeing is even on a computer screen. In the second case, the operator of the computer is sitting back quite clear that this is just something on the screen. Which operator do you think will be more frightened by that image—which one will work harder to change it?

This metaphor (which is widely used in ACT, but oddly is not in the ACT book) is used here to illustrate the difference between how one might react to content they believe to describe reality, versus content that is noticed without necessarily being believed. It will allow a gentle shift in how the issue of the believability of symptom content is addressed. In ACT the client is being asked to notice private events as if s/he were a mere observer, to notice which thoughts are more difficult to distance from, and to consider the workability of adjustments to thoughts instead of their literal truth. The *Soldiers in a Parade exercise* (Hayes et al., 1999, pp. 158–162) can be used to provide practice observing and distancing. In this exercise, the subject is asked to visualize their thoughts as words or images, and to just notice them without trying to stop them. It helps to have the client state them out loud so that you can guide the exercise and correct attempts to control, believe, or disbelieve these thoughts. As an alternative or addition, the exercise, *Taking your Mind for a Walk* (Hayes et al., 1999, pp. 162–163) can be used. In this exercise, go for a walk with your client, and take the role of the client's 'mind' chattering non-stop for the duration of the walk (five minutes is usually sufficient) in stream of consciousness fashion, e.g., "those flowers are pretty, I should get some flowers, but I need to get groceries first . . . darn! I'm out of milk . . . I'm so forgetful . . . ". This exercise can be especially powerful with clients who hallucinate because they can talk about the experience of a voice that was 'not their own' and that they could not stop, and explore how they felt and whether they 'believed' any of the content and if they were able to distance from it and merely observe it. Some clients may find the experience irritating or amusing, and it may allow them to consider the experience of hearing voices in a new way.

It is also helpful to present some concrete everyday examples of observing thoughts without acting on them in they way the thought tells one to. For example, a dieter may notice the thought that, 'I want a piece of that cake', or an employee may notice the thought that, 'my boss is a jerk and I want to tell her off' without acting on them, believing them, or disbelieving them. Everyday experiences (e.g., watching TV and hearing what commercials tell us to do without either doing it or arguing with ourselves about not doing it) can be used as defusion models. If the client continues to object to the possibility of noticing thoughts without acting on them, ask the client to consider what the world might be like if everyone acted on the content of every thought . . . we'd probably all be in a jail, hospital, or cemetery. Emphasize that thoughts and feelings—including hallucinations and beliefs—do not have the power to make one act; one always has the option of doing something other than what the thought tells them to. It can help to do a concrete exercise on this point—for example, by repeating "I can't pick up the pen" while picking up a pen.

The *Bad Cup Metaphor* (Hayes et al., 1999, pp. 168–169) may be used to assist the client in distinguishing between descriptions and evaluations of private events, and also to continue to normalize negatively evaluated thought processes, such as hallucinations. The distinction between the process and content of symptoms may be explored. You should introduce the verbal convention of saying, "I'm having the thought that . . . " when speaking about thoughts. There is less behavioral rigidity implied by "I'm having the thought that I'm a bad person" (or "I should kill myself," "I have a recording contract with a major record label," "the president is really Satan") than the same event described literally (e.g., "I am a bad person", or "the president is Satan.") This convention helps in recognizing that thoughts, even if experienced as powerful or as outside voices, are merely thoughts that may or may not correspond to reality. If the convention is applied, it is a good idea for you to adopt the convention as well (for example, when self-disclosing).

It is important to present the concept of defusion in the context of successful working: the notion that the client should engage in behaviors that work best in allowing them to reach their stated goals. When it comes to thoughts and feelings, you are asking the client to explore the idea that with some thoughts it may work best to just notice them and accept that they occurred without trying to change their content. This idea can be especially useful for clients who lack insight into the delusional nature of their beliefs. When working with such clients it is useful to consider that someone might choose to ignore a thought even if they really believe the thought content is 'real', because acting on the thought would prevent them from attaining a valued goal. For example, the dieter *really* feels hungry and *really* wants a cookie and he chooses to ignore the thought in the service of attaining the goal of dieting, and does not need to convince himself that he is not hungry or does not want a cookie. And the person with a delusional belief might believe that her boss doesn't like her and choose to go to work in the service of keeping her job or getting her paycheck without trying to convince herself that her boss really does like her. This can be experienced as validating, as the content of the belief is not challenged. This is an empirical argument, not a logical one, so there is no reason to be absolute about this. Some verbal events can be usefully examined, changed, and edited: writing a story, persuading others, or concrete problem solving might be examples. But none of these involve *avoiding* or struggling with thoughts. The clients own experience will provide an excellent guide for how to treat their own private events and thoughts over time, provided they can stay focused on workability. For persons with a serious mental illness the attainment of goals often requires experiencing disturbance from their symptoms in order to remain outside the hospital and pursue their interests. Seeing this can provide sources of behavioral regulation long after therapy is over, which may help account for the usually long lasting effects of ACT in early studies with this population.

The importance of treatment adherence may also be treated from the point of view of workability. Treatment noncompliance is very common in persons with serious mental illness (Gorman, 1996). If applicable, ask clients to describe objections to full treatment compliance, and then to examine these thoughts from the point of view of their experience of workability. Usually the client will be able to note that treatment compliance usually allows the subject to have the most behavioral options in pursuing other goals and interests. If that is not the case, do not argue the point with your client. Ask instead for the client just to continue to watch this issue very carefully and notice their actual experience. It may also be useful to explore the very notion of treatment 'compliance' and instead approach it as treatment 'adherence'. Compliance suggests following the orders of others and may be experienced as disempowering. Adherence suggests choice and following a plan. "Treatment adherence" is a better fit with facilitating empowerment to choose behaviors that work in the service of pursuing valued goals and interests.

Defusion and workability will provide a good foundation for learning acceptance. The *Tug of War with a Monster Metaphor* (Hayes et al., 1999, p. 109) is a simple and effective way to open the issue. In this metaphor a struggle to control thoughts or feelings is likened to a game of tug of war with a monster. The only real way to end the struggle is to drop the rope, rather than to struggle harder. You should describe acceptance as an action rather than a feeling, and link it to what would come up if they experienced their specific symptom without trying to change it or act on the content. Generally, the primary consequence is some degree of subjective distress. If the client is vague about what feelings occur an exercise such as the *Physicalizing* or *Tin Can Monster* exercises (Hayes et al., 1999, pp. 170–174) may be helpful for eliciting responses to the symptom, and practice more accepting stances to take in relation to negatively evaluated symptoms. Throughout ACT, the client is should be exposed to his own avoided private events through guided exercises. The point is to give the individual practice in experiencing the emotions they have tried to avoid in a safe, defused, and accepting context.

Many clients with serious mental illness are likely to struggle with acceptance of their illness and negative self-evaluations may arise during this work. For example a client might say, "if I accept hearing voices then that means that I'm crazy." Usually more defusion and acceptance provides a way forward. Often such worries are at their base social worries. Stigma towards and prejudice and discrimination against persons with serious mental illness are very real experiences. Defusing from the evaluations of others is not substantially different from defusing from one's own thoughts. One can refuse to 'buy' the evaluation even while acknowledging that it feels painful to be negatively evaluated. You might gradually increase the difficulty by saying something like, "if I told you the walls in this room were green would you believe me? If I told you that your name was not "Debbie" would you believe me? If I told you that it was 'bad' to be six feet tall (height of client) would you refuse to accept your height and start to slump when you walk or to only wear high heels? If I said that 'deep down there is something wrong with you' would you 'buy' that? And if so, what would you do to change it?" If it seems appropriate, you might also share a personal experience with being negatively evaluated by others.

Like workability, acceptance can and usually should be linked to issues relating to treatment adherence in this population, such as how they feel about their diagnosis, medication, and participation in outpatient groups and individual treatment activities. You can emphasize that acceptance of the need for treatment may give one more options in life. Clients should be assisted in generating new strategies for managing symptoms that focus more on process than content, such as talking to someone, making an appointment with a mental health worker, or practicing life skills—not to decrease the frequency of symptoms, but to learn to carry out daily activities with symptoms when they are present. It can be helpful initially to write down the strategies as a reminder if symptoms are frequent or if the client has cognitive deficits.

Goals and values should be initiated or revisited before developing concrete behavioral interventions towards goal attainment, and if applicable, relapse prevention. The behavioral component of ACT is very similar to standard behavior therapy, involving initially short term, concrete, and relatively small goals and building over time as behavioral patterns strengthen. One difference, however, is that all goals (not matter how small) are linked to an overarching value, and are considered to be opportunities to practice acceptance, defusion, and skill building. ACT fits in well with the wide variety of skills acquisition approaches known to be helpful with seriously mentally ill populations. In this stage of treatment it may be especially important to communicate with other treatment providers if applicable.

Many persons with serious mental illness who participate in individual therapy also participate in psychosocial rehabilitation programming, day treatment, supported employment or housing, or assertive community treatment. Communication among treatment providers can facilitate identifying goals and values, identifying opportunities to practice skills, addressing barriers to participation in other treatment components, and monitoring progress. In inpatient settings therapy may consist of only a few sessions given that average hospital stays are brief. Milieu therapy may be the primary setting in which the client has opportunities to practice defusing from thoughts and feelings. Communicating with other staff and educating them about conventions such as saying "I'm having the thought that" or asking a client, "are you going to buy that thought" can reinforce what is learned in therapy sessions if ACT concepts are repeated by other staff. Urging other staff to begin talking about 'treatment adherence' rather than 'treatment compliance' can also be useful. Finally, other treatment providers may believe that the client's symptoms should completely remit before they are discharged from the hospital. Many clients have learned to deny symptoms because they have learned that denying symptoms means they are more likely to be discharged while acknowledging symptoms means they are more likely to remain hospitalized. The ACT therapist can take a two-pronged approach in this situation. The first is to work with the client on goals and values where discharge is not seen as an end in itself, and to explore how remaining in the hospital might increase opportunities to learn more skills and put the client in a better position to attain valued goals. The second might be to act as an advocate on the treatment team and point out positive changes in the client's behavior (and if applicable, to educate staff about the utility of symptoms as a criterion for determining readiness for discharge).

In outpatient settings the ACT therapist may want to explore the client's engagement with others whether in the structured context of participation in other treatment activities such as psychosocial rehabilitation, day treatment, or group living arrangements, or whether the individual is employed or lives with other family members or roommates. The reason for this is that avoidance and barriers to attaining goals are most likely to be contacted in the context of interacting with others in treatment, family or community settings. If the individual lives alone and is relatively isolated your therapeutic task is all the more difficult, as the individual may have rather successfully 'escaped' negatively evaluated experiences and may be unlikely to report avoided content. In other words, ACT is most effective when the client participates regularly in structured activity such as mental health programming and/or regularly interacts with important others such as family members or roommates, as such experiences are the source of therapeutic 'content'. If the client is involved in other mental health programming it will be useful to be in contact with these other treatment providers. You may have a client who is self-referred and lacks significant contact with other persons and activities but if so it is likely that the client will be in distress about this condition which will itself be a focus of therapy.

In inpatient and outpatient psychosocial rehabilitation programs ACT can be effectively done in a group therapy setting with persons with serious mental illness (see Chapter 14 for more on ACT with groups). Group meeting time should be kept relatively brief, around 45 minutes. ACT can be used in both fixed and rolling admission groups and there are advantages and disadvantages to each admission procedure. In fixed groups all consumers are on the same page, and on the other hand in rolling admission groups more 'advanced' group members can model acceptance and goal setting. Alternately, ACT principles and exercises can be incorporated into existing groups. For example, it can be effective to introduce cognitive defusion and acceptance into a symptom management group, or willingness and values into medication management and goal setting groups.

Another important area is that of defusing from the conceptualized self and discovering other senses of self. A focus on self-awareness and mindfulness has often been regarded as beyond the capacity of persons with serious mental illness and especially those with schizophrenia. If regarded as skills rather than as innate capacities, however, ACT may offer a venue for persons with a diminished sense of self to learn to relate more effectively to self and to others.

There is evidence that persons with schizophrenia have an impoverished or impaired sense of self and also have an impaired ability to appreciate the perspectives of others (Penn et al., 2001). Mindfulness is a core component of ACT and other 'third wave' cognitive behavioral treatment approaches. Persons with schizophrenia and other serious mental illness may benefit from mindfulness approaches as much as other client populations do even while the relatively abstract concepts of 'mindfulness' and 'self' may need to be approached in a more concrete manner.

To introduce mindfulness, begin with exercises that increase self-awareness and have non-threatening/neutral content. For example, one guided exercise has the client imagine floating up from their chair in the room until they are high into the stratosphere and then to float down back to earth and settle back into his or her chair. Begins by asking the client (or clients if a group) to close their eyes and be aware of body sensations (e.g., the feel of one's feet on the floor, and one's body in the chair), and then to expand awareness to notice presence of others in the room (therapist if individual, all others if a group), and to notice noises in the room and outside. The client is then asked to imagine floating up to the ceiling and noticing the chairs, desk, floor, etc. . . . and then go right through the roof noticing the grounds, city block, cars, people, etc . . . floating higher and noticing all the buildings, and roads, and rivers, etc. . . . to seeing the whole city . . . whole region . . . oceans, mountains, continent, etc. and eventually the earth itself from far away [you should provide sufficient detail in each of these steps to describe the local region and then situate it on the earth]. The client is then asked to gradually float back down [direct attention to things to notice as this happens, essentially repeating what was said earlier in reverse order] and to settle into the chair.

Many clients finds this exercise relaxing. After the client or clients are settled in their chairs debrief about 'seeing' all the sights, how it was as if they were in two places at once, a part of them had the experience of floating up while they were still in their chair, and how the individual stays safe in the chair in the room knowing who he is and where he is even while his mind goes sight seeing. In essence this begins, in a non-threatening way, to help the client notice "the observer self."

A central metaphor in ACT for that sense of self is the *Chessboard Metaphor* (Hayes et al., 1999, pp. 190–192) which likens psychological content to the chess pieces and the observing self to the game board that is free to move in a valued direction while the pieces remain engaged in their various struggles. This metaphor may be suitable for some persons with serious mental illness and too abstract for others. If it is too abstract, more concrete methods can be used, such as acting out "the board" with props such as a writing tablet with small objects placed on it. If you used the *Box Full of Stuff* metaphor (Hayes et al., 1999, pp. 136–138) in cognitive defusion work this metaphor can be expanded to address issues of self. You might use a small wastebasket filled with papers and small items and say something like, "this is your illness/voices/symptoms and the box is full . . . what can you do if it's full with this stuff that you don't even like looking at?" Patients will often say "empty it" but the futility of that can be acted out by putting an item called "empty it" into the basket. They may say "not look at it" but you can point out "if you tried to keep yourself from seeing the wastebasket (move it) would it really be gone? Or would you still know it's there?" This can be acted out by putting it partially behind something and saying "now I want you to move around and tell me when you can and can't see it." Ask the patient to notice that they can only be in a small part of the room where they can't see the wastebasket. This metaphor can be expanded for consumers with social withdrawal or social fears by saying "now I want you to try to keep me from seeing the wastebasket." As you move about the room the patient will have to work to hide it from view, which can lead to debriefing about how exhausting it is to try to keep others from seeing it. You can then transition to the larger point: "if you can't hide it, empty it, or get rid of it, what can you do?" If the patient doesn't come up with anything suggest looking at the entire room and how there is so much more stuff than just the wastebasket: e.g., "look at the picture on the wall, the bookshelves, the view out the window; all the things in the room beyond the wastebasket full of stuff." You might point out how the client is talking to you even while the wastebasket is sitting here. Ask the client to imagine getting up and browsing at the books on the shelf or looking out the window or working at the computer or chatting with someone who enters the room, all while the wastebasket is sitting there. To link this experience to a sense of self, you might suggest that, in relation to the wastebasket and other contents of the room, sometimes the client is like a person working at the desk or chair (you can have the client actually move to a different chair, and look around the room). Then ask "is there a part of you that is like that—you could do lots of things in this room and sometimes you notice the wastebasket and sometimes you do not?" If asked sometimes clients will realize that if they have to keep the wastebasket hidden or keep trying to empty it they would have to stop everything else to do that. If the client does not have this insight you might point it out.

This physical metaphor can be expanded by having the client move to the door while you the therapist remains in the room. Say "pretend I am you and tell me what you are doing and saying" (make sure clients say "I", not "you"). Then move around the room, manipulating objects and occasionally speaking. The client generates a running description of this in "I" terms: e.g., "I am getting a book and I see the desk and the chair and the wastebasket. Now I am looking out the window and saying "it is a nice day." Now I am picking up the wastebasket and looking at it and saying, "yuck." Now I am yawning." This can then be debriefed by saying, "isn't it true that there is a part of you that is like that—that can see you doing things and looking at the bookshelf and out the window and at wastebasket, and notices you evaluate things as good or bad, and sees you memories of what you were doing in this room last week and last year, and sees you mind imagine what you will be doing and thinking here tomorrow." The relevance of this sense of self to acceptance should then be pointed out: e.g., "Sometimes you will be more like the person doing things in the room and sometimes more like the person looking at yourself and the stuff in the room, and either way, you will never be the wastebasket, only someone looking at it. Whether it is full or empty or looks bad or good or smells awful, it's not who you are. Can you imagine being in the room and AND looking at the wastebasket? Is that OK?" Specific material about symptoms can be worked into this. The two key points to be understood (experientially, not just intellectually) is that "you are not your content, and that struggling with the content takes a lot of time and energy and interferes with doing other things.

The above exercise can be slightly modified to be helpful for delusional clients who lack insight into the delusional nature of their beliefs. You can suggest that what is in the wastebasket is that content (e.g., "I'm a rock star"; "the president is Satan"; "he killed someone and should go to jail"). Use the physical metaphor of carrying the basket while trying to do thing (e.g., work at the computer, browse the books) versus putting it down where it still can be seen. This approach can work with delusional clients because the target is not whether the content is "real." The issue is that when 100% of their energy is focused on the wastebasket and keeping it close, they can't do anything else. This tiny crack in a delusional system can be enough to lead to large behavioral changes. For example, after this kind of work a client who had significant legal and social problems as a result of trying to prove that the governor of her state was a member of a cult decided that she had spent enough energy notifying criminal justice personnel of the governor's alleged illicit activity and decided it was time to focus on looking for a job and suitable housing. She changed her behavior dramatically, even though her delusional beliefs about the governor remained, and would have been vigorously defended had they been directly challenged.

Mindfulness work and especially the concept of the observing self may not go much further with clients who have significant thought disorder or other cognitive deficits. Others may benefit from further exploration. For example, the *Observer Exercise* (Hayes, et al., 1999, pp. 192–196) may be beneficial with modification, such as simplifying the roles to things actually done (e.g., smoking, watching TV), or not asking for recent memories if this challenges the patient due to poverty of speech, experience, or selective attention to negative experiences.

The point when clients begin to take action toward fulfilling goals is often a critical time in therapy. Many persons with serious mental illness lead very socially isolated lives and have rather successfully avoided contact with negatively evaluated experiences. In the initial defusion and acceptance work they may underreport important concerns because they are truly not aware of them. Increased feelings of fear, frustration and hopelessness and negative evaluations of self may not arise until they begin participating in treatment, move into a new living arrangement, or begin a job. Both SMI patients, staff, and significant others often underestimate how overwhelming such changes might be (Pratt, Gill, Barrett & Roberts, 1999). With any ACT client you need to be prepared to cycle back and forth between defusion and acceptance and committing to and pursuing valued goals, but this is likely to occur much more with persons suffering from SMI. At this point in therapy it may be useful to use the *Swamp Metaphor* (Hayes, et al., 1999, p. 248) and the *Looking for Mr. Discomfort* exercise (Hayes, et al., 1999, p. 247). In this exercise the client is exposed to negative private events in session and ask if she's willing to find "Mr. Discomfort" to sit with whatever shows up and renegotiate her relationship with whatever shows up. Once established as a working metaphor for negatively evaluated private experiences, therapist and client can talk about "Mr. Discomfort" showing up at work or in skills training group, and renegotiate the relationship with Mr. Discomfort every time he shows up. If the client does experience what they perceive to be failure this can be a useful opportunity for exploring commitment, if applicable, or for focusing on what the client learned from the experience. For example, if someone moves from an independent living arrangement and returns to a group home he might believe he has failed at being independent. You can help him consider what he values about living with others, and consider other ways in which he might work towards attaining the goal of greater independence (e.g., pursuing independent social, recreational and vocational opportunities while living in a group home).

CLINICAL CONSIDERATIONS

There are some special considerations you must consider when working with clients with SMI. Some considerations include examining the very definition of serious mental illness, examining one's own beliefs about persons with serious mental illness, working with involuntary clients, working with consumers dually diagnosed with substance use disorders and psychotic or mood disorders, and differences in working with clients diagnosed with psychotic disorders versus mood disorders with psychotic symptoms.

What Is Serious Mental Illness?

Unlike other diagnostic categories, the term "serious mental illness" is usually defined by state agencies rather than by health care associations, in part because this designation is often used to determine eligibility for various services and entitlements. Definitions of SMI may consider the specific diagnosis, the duration or intensity of illness, the degree of functional impairment in social and occupational functioning, subjective distress, or other factors. Thus, it is possible that a person with any given diagnosis might not meet local criteria for SMI. For example, persons with Bipolar disorder often do not meet state criteria for SMI due to shorter duration of symptoms or more periodic decrements in social and occupational functioning. This chapter, however, is focused on the individual experiencing positive or negative symptoms of psychosis, and functional impairment related to these symptoms, whether or not they are categorized as SMI within a given system of care. ACT interventions are sensitive to the symptoms, goals, opportunities, sense of self, and concrete versus abstract thinking abilities of the client more than either the diagnosis or legal designation as such.

Therapist Beliefs about Serious Mental Illness

When working with persons with SMI you need to examine your own thoughts, feelings and beliefs regarding this population. Stigma and prejudice about person with serious mental illness is rampant among mental health professionals as well as among members of lay society. For example, in a vocational rehabilitation presentation I gave, several attendees objected to the word "career" in reference to the vocational aspirations of their clients. They believed that their clients could only attain a "job" as opposed to a "career." It is not uncommon for clinicians to wonder at such basic life goals as having a significant other and or a job—even when these goals are specifically articulated by the client.

The clients themselves may believe that they are somehow defective and unable to achieve. Sadly, this belief is supported not just by much of the population but also by mental health professionals. Symptoms of psychosis are not legitimate reasons for not pursuing valued goals. There are plenty of examples of individuals with serious mental illness who are productive members of society and are able to maintain relationships, earn advanced college degrees, have desired careers and participate in recreation and leisure activities. Sometimes stigma on the part of the therapist cuts the other way and the therapist may be tempted to make negative evaluations about the choices the consumer makes, for example the choice to live in a residential setting as opposed to living independently. It is important to maintain a consistent stance of empowering consumers to pursue their values. ACT is helpful in this regard, since ACT principles are known not just to help clients but also to undermine the believability of stigmatizing thoughts and the behavioral impact of uncomfortable feelings in therapists themselves (Hayes, Bissett, et al., in press).

Working with Involuntary Clients

Clients with symptoms of psychosis seen in inpatient settings are often on an involuntary status and may have a long history of hospitalizations. Here it is important to examine the client's beliefs and attitudes about therapy. The involuntary, therapy-wise client is more likely to benefit from participation in ACT if it is clearly different from past approaches, and if it begins with an examination of goals and values rather than beginning with why the client has been hospitalized. This population may, in fact, be especially motivated to participate in ACT as opposed to traditional therapies that focus on symptom elimination.

Clients in this population may also tend to underreport and minimize symptoms because all too often a client who acknowledges hallucinations is kept in the hospital while the client who denies them is discharged. Unfortunately, many psychiatric hospital policies collude in maintaining the stance that the symptom is the problem despite growing evidence that this is not true. Family members and treatment providers who are also convinced that the problem is hallucinations or delusional beliefs may need to be educated about the relative independence of symptoms and behavioral functioning. In treatment, it is more powerful to focus on overt behavior, in the context of acceptance and defusion. Even very reluctant clients can be hooked into treatment if they see the possibility of attaining goals even if the symptom never remits.

Substance Abuse

About 50% of persons with serious mental illness are also diagnosed with a substance use disorder (Mueser, Bennett, & Kushner, 1995). Most persons in this population who abuse substances are opportunistic abusers who do not have a drug of choice and may not have the financial resources to purchase drugs and alcohol on a regular basis. Others show more in-grained patterns of use. Dually diagnosed individuals are often bounced back and forth between the mental health and drug and alcohol systems of care. "Integrated care" is helpful, but is often unavailable. Fortunately, the same ACT strategies that have been shown to work with psychotic problems have also been shown to work with substance abuse, so there is no reason not to provide a kind of integrated care for these patients by addressing both mental health and substance use targets (see Chapter 9). Very often substances are being used to address symptoms or to avoid some feeling such as boredom, and in these cases substance use can be treated as any other method of avoidance.

Cognitive Deficits

Schizophrenia is associated with cognitive deficits including deficits in abstract thinking and social cue recognition (Corrigan and Penn, 2001), and as a result abstract metaphors can be challenging to this population. Many therapists overgeneralize and avoid any use of metaphorical talk, but in fact metaphors and stories can be particularly useful to persons with cognitive deficits if they are simple, concrete, personally relevant, and specifically related to important clinical issues. One way to 'concretize' metaphors is to use physical props. Some common ACT metaphors described by Hayes and colleagues (1999) are elaborated and include props. Where they are not the therapist may be able to easily innovate. For instance, instead of merely describing *Chinese handcuffs* (Hayes, Strosahl & Wilson, 1999, p. 104) or the *Bad cup* metaphor (Hayes, Strosahl & Wilson, 1999, pp. 168–169), the therapist might have Chinese handcuffs and a coffee cup on hand while presenting these metaphors. When referring to social settings and situa-tions and to life-experiences it is important that the therapist use exam-ples relevant to the client's social history and functioning. For example, while many clients' relate to the metaphor of a person inviting *Joe the bum* (Hayes, Strosahl & Wilson, 1999, pp. 239–240) to a party, a client who is homeless or has lived in an institution much of his life may be confused by the metaphor having no experience with hosting parties or even relating more to "Joe the bum" than to the party host. When in doubt, the therapist can always get feedback about the client's understanding in the moment and review in each session.

Remission of Symptoms

Some clients will find that their symptoms quickly remit upon beginning a course of psychotropic medications. This may occasion early termination of therapy, but the processes targeted by ACT may help prevent relapse after the acute phase is completed (Bach & Hayes, 2002). You should engage the client around the issue of relapse, and about mood symptoms since these tend not to remit as quickly. The skills ACT establishes are not dependent on avoided content.

CONCLUSIONS

Psychosocial interventions with psychotic individuals are woefully underdeveloped, despite their value. Medications are helpful with these patients, but they are frequently not nearly enough. ACT provides a powerful new model for this work that is radically accepting, validating, non-hierarchical, and yet behaviorally focused. The ACT model deserves to be explored and evaluated by more providers working with these clients.

Chapter 9

ACT with the Multi-Problem Patient

Kirk D. Strosahl

Of the many types of presenting problems seen by mental health, chemical dependency and general health care providers, none is more challenging than the patient experiencing chronic mood disturbance, marginal social adaptation, high levels of interpersonal isolation, conflict and/or daily stress and, frequently, recurrent self-destructive behavior. These patients often receive a clinical diagnosis of "personality disorder," but it is probably more appropriate to describe them as "multi-problem" patients because of wide spread deficiencies in their cognitive, emotional, behavioral and social functioning. Such patients typically experience chronic negative emotional states such as depression, anxiety, apathy, boredom, loneliness, guilt and anger. This affect is a major driver of a plethora of maladaptive coping responses: chief among them are repetitious suicidal behavior, and addictive behaviors such as alcohol/drug abuse, eating disorders and/or chronic self-mutilation. Multi-problem patients also experience significant difficulties in social and interpersonal functioning. They have trouble forming and maintaining interpersonal relationships and often inject the therapy process with a conflict-laden set of issues around forming and maintaining both casual and intimate adult relationships. The number and magnitude of these behavioral, cognitive and emotional problems is a source of frustration for therapists. It is hard to conceptualize a plan of action in therapy when, at any given point in time, the patient exhibits generalized failure in so many areas of functioning. Further, the disruptive presence of chronic suicidal ideation, suicide attempting and various other forms of self-destructive behavior disrupts the continuity of treatment and can severely challenge the therapeutic relationship.

Not surprisingly, multi-problem patients tend to undergo multiple and ineffective regimes of psychotherapy and poly-pharmacy. Therapists often describe such patients as "therapy-wise," meaning that they can anticipate and counter the interventions of even the most skilled therapist. Multi-problem patients often show superficial "insight" into the cause of their difficulties, but seem unable to change unworkable behavior patterns. When a behavior change plan is put together, it is often not followed, leading the therapist to question the patient's motivation to change.

The goal of this chapter is to describe an ACT approach to understanding and treating the multi-problem patient. To accomplish this objective, I will review the genesis of the personality disorder construct and describe how it can be re-conceptualized within an ACT framework. This will allow you, the clinician, to identify the core processes underpinning the multi-problem behavior pattern and, in turn, better target your interventions. The remainder of the chapter will describe a coherent set of ACT interventions for multi-problem patients, including how to understand and address chronic suicidal and self-destructive behavior. Finally, I will offer some practical suggestions on how you can manage the interpersonal and motivational "space" when working with these clients, using very basic ACT principles.

The traditional notion of "personality disorder" as it is defined in the DSM-IV refers to "an enduring pattern of inner experience and behavior that deviates markedly from the expectations of the individual's culture, is pervasive and inflexible ... is stable over time and leads to distress and impairment." (American Psychiatric Association, 1994). The DSM taxonomy consists of 10 specific personality disorders: Paranoid, Schizoid, Schizotypal, Antisocial, Borderline, Histrionic, Nacissistic, Avoidant, Dependent & Obsessive-Compulsive. There are a number of criticisms of this taxonomy, including excessive overlap among symptom criteria, a high level of inference in defining symptoms, low symptom base rates and poor agreement between a priori definitions of disorders and observed symptom clustering in multi-dimensional scaling studies (cf. Widiger, 2001; Widiger, Trull, Clarkin & Frances, 1987; Livesley & Jackson, 1986). These objections have never been successfully resolved, but the labels and distinctions continue to be widely used.

The prevalence of personality disorders in the general population has not been properly researched, but estimates are approximately 1–1.5% for the more commonly diagnosed disorders (Livesley, 2001). Prevalence estimates in the mental health setting vary markedly but hover around 10–15%. This figure is misleading, however, because this group of patients consume upwards of 40% of all mental health resources (Strosahl, 1991).

Personality disorders were long neglected by behavior therapists in part due to controversy about the entire concept (see Strosahl & Linehan, 1983 for a review). In the last decade behavior therapy approaches to multi-problem behavior have begun to be published (Chiles & Strosahl, 1995; Linehan et al., 1991; Linehan, 1993; Strosahl, 1991).

Much of the growing emphasis on acceptance and change principles in "third wave" behavior therapy can be attributed to the early and pioneering efforts of behavioral theorists who were attempting to understand and treat multi-problem patients. The first randomized clinical trial of Dialectical Behavior Therapy (Linehan et al., 1991) has led to a wave of optimism about the potential of other contextual approaches. DBT should be regarded as the preferred treatment for woman with Borderline Personality Disorder (BPD), with or without substance abuse problems (see Hayes, Masuda, Bissett, Luoma, & Guerrero, in press, for a review).

More cognitively focused treatment models may also have significant clinical benefit for patients with Borderline Personality Disorder (e.g., Beck, Freeman & Davis, 2004; Young, Klosko & Weishaar, 2003). However, the data are still preliminary.

The only study of ACT with multi-problem patients was uncontrolled, looking at the efficacy of a 12-session ACT program with a total of 60 patients seen in an HMO outpatient mental health center. Most of these patients had undergone multiple regimes of therapy and medications, without much benefit. Group modules introduced participants to the core ACT concepts and interventions, using a patient education and home based practice approach. For example, patients entering this program were expected to develop a valued life goal and to take specific steps toward that goal between class sessions. Among program completers, we found a significant drop in self rated depression from pre-treatment to post-treatment. In addition, a large percentage of patients that completed the ACT classroom program indicated that they had made significant progress toward achieving the goals they had set for themselves (Strosahl, 1991). The lack of a control group makes this little more than a pilot study.

ACT has also been used in more controlled studies that contained significant portions of personality disordered patients. For example, Hayes et al. (in press) successfully applied ACT to patients with severe substance abuse problems, half of whom had a personality disorder (see also Strosahl, Hayes, Bergan & Romano, 1998).

CASE CONCEPTUALIZATION

Multi-problem behavior differs in degree, but not in kind, from many typical clinical problems. The key difference is that multi-problem patients are embedded in a self-amplifying network of these problems. There is a "private logic" to the world of the multi-problem patient, and it is a logic that is familiar to ACT therapists.

Multi-problem patients exhibit four distinctive features that, collectively, define the clinical challenge you must confront. They exhibit inflexible maladaptive behaviors that are:

- *Pervasive*: The same limited responses occur in a wide variety of seemingly unrelated situations
- *Persistent*: These responses continue over long periods of time and seem to gain habit strength
- *Resistant*: These behaviors do not seem to be shaped or modified by the huge negative consequences they bring for the patient
- *Self-Defeating*: Over time, these narrow response patterns constrict the patient's life space, quell value driven behavior and produce a paradoxical motivational deficit

In clinical practice, these functional processes seldom come in neat, clean, segregated packages. They are always interacting and it is easy to get confused about which process(s) is driving the patient's responding at any given time. Fortunately, the fact that these processes interact in a cyclical way means that there are many possible "points of access" into unworkable behavior patterns. Undermining one process is going to effect how the other processes function.

Examining these processes from an ACT/RFT point of view, we suspect that: 1) Basic functional properties of language have gone awry; 2) Higher order language functions such as rule governed behavior are overriding direct contact with experience that would shape more adaptive behavior; 3) Short term reinforcement is maintaining emotional avoidance behavior; and 4) Skills deficits preclude the ability to deliver more flexible responses.

Pervasive Dysfunction

Functionally speaking, multi-problem patients fail to make appropriate discriminations between situations that share a few but not many overlapping attributes. For example, any interpersonal conflict can evoke the same catastrophic response from the patient (i.e., avoidance/withdrawal, heightened negative arousal, suicidal ideation or attempt), no matter what it is about, whom it involves, or how serious it is. The patient responds in terms of broad rules and large equivalence classes, without contacting psychologically the myriad contextual features that are available to regulate the verbal relations that apply to disparate events. Experiential avoidance seems to feed this phenomenon. For example, if the patient experienced a traumatic interpersonal event such as sexual abuse, physical abuse, neglect or abandonment, the patient may avoid thoughts about these events to the point that they lack the ability to pull up specific negative memories, even when cued to do so (e.g., Pollock & Williams, 2001). What is left is a vague sense that people, perhaps all people (including the therapist) are potentially dangerous. Ruminative thinking is used to ward off possible harm, but it also undermines the specificity of autobiographical recall (Watkins & Teasdale, 2002). This set of findings provides an interesting parallel to an ACT case conceptualization of Generalized Anxiety Disorder (see Chapter 5).

The loss of specific memory in the service of emotional avoidance comes with a substantial price. Since the patient has a hard time recollecting and discriminating between safe and noxious situations, affect regulation is a problem. The vague and broad equivalence classes of dangerous events means that "danger" is almost constantly present, and the patient is chronically over-aroused.

In their early history, multi-problem patients have often been exposed to parents or other role models who respond to negative affect by drinking, abuse, skipping town, quitting jobs, punching out the supervisor, and so on. As adults, they possess limited skills available to address psychological challenges. In treatment, it is important to assess and remedy specific skills deficits that might be contributing to the patient's difficulties.

Often, multi-problem patients will exhibit both of these processes. For example, a female patient may report dissociative experiences after being greeted and smiled at by a male checker at the grocery store. She has a history of being sexually abused by her father; during these sexual encounters she would dissociate from the situation as a means of deflecting the emotional and physical pain of abuse. Although the situations appear to differ considerably, they both involve an interaction with a male that may have the potential properties of dangerous intimacy and thus evoke the same dissociative response. In addition, the patient lacks certain basic social skills and, when greeted by the male checker, cannot produce a socially effective response (i.e., smiling at the checker and offering a return greeting).

Persistent Dysfunction

Many patients report a long history of emotional, cognitive and behavioral dysfunction, despite the fact that they elevate the patient's suffering and, in the long run, lead to greater and greater disability. What accounts for this rigidity? From an ACT/RFT point of view, the major culprit is fusion with dysfunctional rules and thoughts and the short-term reinforcement associated with emotional avoidance. The lack of flexibility that results, leads to a kind of "behavioral trap" in which natural contingencies cannot shape more effective behavior.

Multi-problem patients apply rule-governed responses in a way that re-elicits the basic problem that engaged the rule in the first place. These rules gain such dominance in the patient's repertoire that it is hard to supplant them long enough to learn new, more effective behaviors. The ACT principle, "If you won't have it, you've got it", seems to apply here.

An example is the dilemma of the female patient described previously. If she is carrying a rule that says "Give a man an inch and he'll take a mile," the logical response is to protect herself from potential damage by quelling the interaction with the clerk. This might tie into a second augmenting rule that says, "If you are a good girl and don't get taken advantage of, you will be rewarded with a love that lasts a lifetime." The exact form the resulting rule-governed response will take is determined by the patient's learning history. In this case, her dissociative reaction is an over-learned, self-protective but also emotionally avoidant response. At the level of social outcome, the clerk won't develop any further interest in the patient, and she will remain isolated. However, viewed from the perspective of rule-governed behavior, she will have prevented the predicted damage to herself, remained a "good girl" and thus is still in line for the rewards promised in the future, and she will not have to experience the discomfort that new behavior would produce. The rule is self-supporting because she will remain interpersonally isolated, lonely, and mistrustful. She is less likely to begin to learn how to develop supportive, intimate relationships.

Emotional avoidance is inherently self-reinforcing (Hayes, Wilson, Gifford, Follette, & Strosahl, 1996). When you avoid or escape something that feels bad, the avoidance actions are negatively reinforced and emotional avoidance increases. This is a key feature of multi-problem behavior patterns. In the example above, the female patient will experience anxiety because she associates the smiling, greeting clerk with the dominant rule governed response and the associated augmental. After all, by definition, she is in danger of being taken advantage of and is in danger of not being a good girl. This will automatically (by learning history) introduce both fear and anxiety as immediate affective states. By not responding to the clerk, she promotes her social isolation (an unfortunate external result) but reduces her anxiety level (a positive internal result). This is not different in kind from other patients—multi-problem patients are simply in the trap deeper than most.

Resistance to Change

One of the more common findings in research on multi-problem suicidal patients is that they are poor problems solvers. They tend to generate fewer solutions, tend to generate less effective solutions, and rely more on passive strategies such a luck, others changing or just the passage of time. If you cannot solve the various problems that life presents, you cannot grow into a new set of problems. You spend your life dealing with the same issues over and over again. This is the normative state of affairs in therapy with the multi-problem patient.

These weaknesses in problem solving may be linked to the weak autobiographical recall mentioned earlier. Indeed, overly general recall is known to be strongly associated with deficits in personal problem solving (Pollock & Williams, 2001). If you can't recall the past, then you will be fated to repeat it.

A second and equally important mechanism is that excessive rule following produces relative insensitivity to direct contingencies. Contingency-shaped behavior molds over time to its consequences. Rule-governed behavior need not be controlled by direct consequences—it can be controlled by broad social support, or by verbally distorted "consequences" (such as avoiding "harm" from the store clerk when in fact all that was avoided was social contact).

Multi-problem patients are regulated by rules to the point of self-destruction. They are the most conspicuous victims of the "control and eliminate" change agenda that is so pervasive in western culture. This rule is heavily augmented in our culture (strong people can control their feelings, health is the absence of pain, normal people don't suffer very much) despite its bad outcomes. The patient carries this explanation for their difficulties: 1) The cause of my incapacity is the presence of (pick an aversive private event: chronic negative mood state, traumatic flashback, negative thinking) that has been caused by (pick one or more historical explanations); 2) To become functional again, I must gain control of my (aversive life event); 3) This will be achieved by understanding how I learned to be this particular way so I can change it; 4) I will know I'm in control when the aversive event does not show itself any more; 5) Then, I can go on with my life as a functional being; 6) *Until then, you can't expect me to live my life!*

The unique aspect of the multi-problem patient is that this cultural rule is followed to its logically absurd conclusion. You can stop literally every aspect of your life from working if you absolutely insist on not having negative internal states. Your life can literally be "about" not having certain experiences and you can go on this fools errand for decades without it ever dawning on you that the rule itself might be wrong! It is not unusual to hear multi-problem patients emphatically state (as a fact) that other people can control their depression, anxiety, flashbacks and so on. This is held out as proof that the patient is not a) trying hard enough; b) lacks the necessary will power or character to make a change or c) is inadequate and "broken." This process demonstrates the power that rule-governed thought can exert over contingency shaped behavior. Much of my approach to working with such patients is to call out rule following for what it is and to try to get the patient off "auto-pilot."

Maladaptive Behavior That Is Self-Defeating

There is logic to the world view of the multi-problem patient that most therapists seem to miss. When your life is in shambles, you are unable to sustain healthy relationships and you aren't contributing to society, you have some heavy explaining to do. Enter the "story". This is the patient's account of what has happened to cause the problem and what must be done to fix it.

The story is a very important part of the daily existence of the multi-problem patient, particularly in between episodes of runaway negative affect and self-destructive problem solving. The story both explains and justifies that patient's dreadful state of being. One thing I frequently hear from therapists who are working with a multi-problem patient is that he or she seems to have some "insight" into the causes of his or her difficulties. What the therapist is engaging is the patient's story and it usually has a sort of common sense logic to it: *These events happened at some point in the past and now cause me to be the way I am today. I am a victim of these circumstances and the thoughts, feelings and memories it produced in me are unacceptable. Everything I do seems to make these things worse. I've tried everything that a normal person would try, but it doesn't work for me. Left with no alternatives, I'm engaging in the only behaviors left to me. Therefore, I have good reasons for being what I am and doing what I do.*

The clinical impact of the story is that it allows the patient to sustain existing maladaptive behavior patterns and integrate negative life consequences into the story without having to examine what is working and what isn't working. Over time, the story becomes fused with the patient's conceptualized self—a form of self that dominates the experience of the multi-problem patient. For many multi-problem patients, it is extremely important that the story is "right" and more than one such patient has committed suicide to prove the point. To undermine the story at the level of content might remove the patient's right to be a victim, to claim that life is unfair, or to blame a perpetrator for all the patient's current suffering.

These are the verbally distorted "consequences" that sustain adherence to the story, and many multi-problem patients will defend the story as if their life depended on it. In my clinical approach, I place a lot of emphasis on attacking the story as a story, not as content that needs to be argued about in therapy.

There is another element of the story that plays an important role. It systematizes beliefs and instructions that essentially claim that facing feared mood states, memories, and/or bodily sensations is the same as inviting psychological annihilation. One of my patients once remarked, "If you're asking me to accept my mother's criticism and rejection, you're asking the wrong person. I'll kill myself before I'll allow that to happen." Thus, this patient was forced to avoid contacts with her mother and use drugs/alcohol to numb her unacceptable emotional states after any family get together. What is being avoided is an imagined reality that could (and probably would) be much worse than the one she is in, such as loss of sanity, uncontrollable rage, or ceasing to be.

Multi-problem patients are locked in a life and death struggle with the self as an ongoing process of knowing, in part because their sense of "self as context" is weak. They are capable of simple self awareness, as long as it doesn't involve making contact with uncomfortable thoughts, feelings, memories, or bodily sensations. When negative private content appears, they fuse with the unwanted experience to such an extent that their sense of self disappears into the process of experiencing. This is a very frightening experience that is often described by patients as disappearing into a black void. The irony is that when the patient lands at the bottom of this void, he or she would be squarely in the middle of "self as context." Instead of carrying the process through, it is aborted and the avoidance of uncomfortable content is seemingly even more a matter of life and death. This problem may exist because the life histories of multi-problem patients are often loaded with early trauma, before deictic frames have fully established a sense of perspective and "self as context." That continuous sense of self may even increase the clarity of autobiographical memory, and contact with aversive thoughts and feelings. As a result, they have never learned how to take a non-judgmental observing stance and let disturbing thoughts, feelings, memories or bodily sensations take their natural course.

Left with no other choice for addressing chronic aversive private experiences, multi-problem patients will turn to numbing strategies that can be employed very quickly and that have rather immediate, short term positive effects such as thinking about or attempting suicide, cutting on oneself, getting drunk or stoned, dissociating, binging and purging, and so on. In the world-view of the multi-problem patient, these behaviors "work" because the overriding goal is to get out from under the feared private content. The cost of these continuous numbing strategies is that value driven behavior virtually disappears. It is not at all unusual to ask a multi-problem patient the following question: "What would you be doing in your life if you didn't spend all of your time cutting on yourself?" And the common answer back is: "I don't know." The patient has settled for a lifestyle that has very little vitality, purpose or meaning other than the patient's current success in avoiding aversive private events. This lack of a valued life plan makes it extremely unlikely that a patient will risk any perceived point of psychological safety to make a behavior change. There is nothing *intrinsically* motivating about making a behavior change that will require acceptance of feared events. There must be a point on the horizon that legitimizes taking this risk.

CLINICAL INTERVENTION

Many of the basic components of the ACT conceptualization of multi-problem behavior lead directly to the staging and sequencing of various ACT interventions (see Table 9.1). My treatment approach can basically be divided into four discrete stages: 1) Contain, reframe and make contact with the cost of, high risk behavior; 2) Attack the basis of, and the patient's fusion with, the story; 3) Address barriers to change, mainly those produced by fusion with rule governed responses; 4) Make contact with values and engage in patterns of committed action. The goal of ACT is not just to eliminate self-destructive and/or blatantly dysfunctional behaviors, but also to help the patient find the "human being" inside. Because ACT does not regard such patients as "broken" or "defective," the global purpose of treatment is to help the patient discover the nature of the trap, rediscover long suppressed dreams and begin behaving in ways that promote vitality, purpose and being.

Address High-Risk Behavior

The calling card of the multi-problem patient is a pattern of self-destructive, high-risk behavior, chronic suicidal ideation, repetitious suicide attempting, and/or self-mutilation. This pattern may also be fueled by repeated episodes of drug and/or alcohol abuse. An uncontrolled pattern of high-risk behavior produces a number of negative results in therapy. First, unless the therapist finds a way to integrate this behavior into the process of ongoing treatment, there will be ongoing difficulties with treatment continuity. Second, the high-risk behavior pattern often is part of a "crisis of the week" syndrome that has the effect of putting the therapist is a highly reactive posture (Strosahl, 1991; Chiles & Strosahl, 2004).

Table 9.1. Clinical Issues and Recommended ACT Interventions

Clinical issue	Recommended ACT response
Patient expresses suicidal wishes or engages in suicidal behavior	1. Reframe suicidal behavior as problem solving behavior in the service of experiential avoidance; 2. Ask patient to identify what thoughts, feelings, memories or sensations are unacceptable 3. Ask patient to evaluate the short and long term workability of engaging in suicidal behavior
Suicidal behavior re-emerges in the course of treatment	1. Don't deviate from treatment model! Stay calm and matter of fact! 2. Continue to use problem solving and the emotional avoidance reframe 3. Try to functionally analyze situational triggers that produce unacceptable private events 4. Ask patient if he/she would be willing to have avoided private events, ever so briefly, just as experiment 5. Consider using suicidal behavior as target variable in willingness, suffering, workability diary
Patient exhibits chronic parasuicidal behavior pattern (i.e., repeated suicide attempts, self mutilation)	1. Focus on role of parasuicidal acts in the service of emotional control 2. Use the workability concept repeatedly, avoid getting into power struggles over suicidal acts 3. Analyze external reinforcements for suicidal behavior and create a case management framework to minimize them 4. Form a crisis plan with the patient that anticipates future occurrences of parasuicidal behavior (i.e., crisis card, agreement on after hours phone calls, random support calls) 5. Use various ACT metaphors such as shovel and hole, tiger on the porch or feedback screech to demonstrate the self amplifying nature of experiential avoidance and the need to stop suicidal behavior so as to practice new responses
Patient doesn't complete between session behavioral practice, misses sessions and/or shows up only when in crisis	1. Go back to issue of whether these behaviors are in the service of experiential avoidance. Has the patient engaged in this type of behavioral response before? How did it work then? How is this working now? 2. What would the patient have to be willing to face in order to stick with treatment? 3. Take the blame for misreading the magnitude of the changes. Take a pragmatic stance and cut back on behavioral practice to meet the patient's willingness level 4. Avoid using negative interpretations or labeling such as "resistance", "you must like suffering because you don't to want to change it", etc. 5. Steal the point of resistance by normalizing the difficulty of making any behavior change; play devil's advocate in favor of not making any behavior change 6. Emphasize that this is a matter of choice and only the patient can do it

(continued)

Table 9.1. (*Continued*)

Clinical issue	Recommended ACT response
Patient indicates a reluctance or refusal to make contact with certain "unacceptable" private experiences	1. Ask patient how this stance has worked up to now in terms of promoting effective responses 2. Begin values clarification, possibly using the what do you want your life to stand for exercise, the funeral exercise or writing on the tombstone exercise 3. Help patient see the "cost" of avoidance in terms of failing to move in valued directions 4. Work on small bits of willingness, i.e., limiting exposure to feared experiences so as to get a glimpse of what direct experience looks like when you are not running from it 5. Use contextual metaphors such as chess board, chairs on an ocean liner to highlight self vs. contents of self experience
Patient complains about constantly struggling with feelings, memories, thoughts, physiological symptoms (usually suicidality will be the "quick fix" when struggling ratchets unwanted private events)	1. Ask patient to identify what the goal of the struggle is (feeling "normal" "good" or free from pain) and how struggling has worked. Has it created control of feelings? Or a feeling of being out of control? 2. Ask patient to imagine what would happen if he/she just stood still with this event. Take the chain of outcomes as far as the patient's imagination will carry it. 3. Emphasize that willingness and acceptance are alternatives to struggle and rejection 4. Use willingness, suffering and workability diaries to highlight inverse relationship between willingness and levels of suffering and workability 5. Use experiential exercises such as the tin can monster to elicit and deconstruct feared events in session
Patient carries a story that emphasizes history of victimization, that life is unfair or provides reasons why normal living will never be possible	1. Ask patient to do the autobiography rewrite several times. Don't argue about the content of the story, or invalidate the patient's attachment (million stories can be constructed to describe the impact of the same set of facts) 2. What if this story were declared totally true? What would you want your life to be about tomorrow? 3. Emphasize that it is the patient's "right" to believe anything in the story. Each human being constructs a story by choice. Your concern is how believing any particular element is working to promote the patient's sense of vitality. 4. Point out that the most dangerous thing about stories is that they can make our past into our future. 5. Avoid attacking the story from the point of view of logic, inferential errors or distortions

Table 9.1. (*Continued*)

Clinical issue	Recommended ACT response
Patient starts to "deteriorate" when confronted with the likelihood of improved life functioning, achievement of valued goals or termination of treatment	1. Usually a sign that the patient is in the "corpus delecti" trap. Who would be made right if you got healthy and happy? 2. Use fishhook metaphor to highlight letting go of the aggressor is a pre-requisite for moving ahead 3. Talk about etymologic root of the word "forgiveness" as an act toward restoring self, not a denial of victimization 4. Use journey metaphors to highlight importance of making room for processes like anger, righteousness, revenge while continuing to move forward toward valued ends 5. Use session tapering booster sessions and field experiment reframe to reduce termination anxiety. Have an open door policy for return in the future for a "tune up"

This posture can produce rapid shifts in treatment goals and intervention methods, with the result that both the therapist and patient get confused about the focus of therapy.

High-risk behavior also elicits a variety of fears in therapists, mostly in relation to the adverse outcome of suicide and possible legal exposure. Often, therapists work in settings that have fairly demanding risk management protocols for addressing suicidality. On the one hand, the therapist is constantly hearing suicidal communications from the patient that technically fit risk management requirements for emergency evaluation and possible hospitalization. On the other hand, the therapist knows that there are few times when the patient is not at least thinking about suicide. This is not the same type of suicidal behavior that one might observe in a more functional patient experiencing an acute life crisis. The typical multi-problem patient has developed a suicidal "lifestyle" which creates an ongoing tension between the goals of risk management and the goals of effective treatment.

Ultimately, the therapist gets worn down from the stress of being in the "hot seat." This may lead to covert or overt attempts to terminate the patient from therapy. Even seasoned therapists can find themselves saying things like, "If you can't stop this suicidal behavior, I can't treat you." If the patient could gain control over the suicidal behavior as a pre-requisite for being in treatment, then why would treatment be needed at all? The typical patient has tried everything under the sun to get control of suicidal thinking, suicidal behavior and so on. The problem is that the methods used to control this behavior are cut from the same cloth that led to suicidality in the first place (i.e., control or eliminate suicidal types).

Space does not permit a full exploration of the many forms and functions of suicidal behavior, nor can all the details of an effective clinical management model be described (for that see Chiles & Strosahl, 2004). For present purposes, I will focus on the ACT conceptualization of suicidal and high-risk behavior and how to effectively respond to it.

The goal of any treatment for chronic suicidal behavior is to decrease its frequency, intensity and duration, so the patient has time to learn new, more effective responses. As exemplified by the *Man in the Hole* metaphor (Hayes et al., 1999, 101–104), it is very difficult to learn positive coping responses when all of one's time and energy are being sucked up engaging in negative coping responses. I will often use this metaphor to point out the futility of trying to experiment with more adaptive, life affirming behavior when the patient's daily routine is organized around struggling with suicidal and self-destructive impulses.

From an ACT perspective, suicidal and self-destructive behavior is an extreme form of experiential avoidance. It helps the patient gain temporary control over what are perceived as intolerable, inescapable, unchangeable private events. The sine qua non of suicidal crisis is trying to avoid or eliminate emotional pain that is viewed as:

- *Intolerable*: The patient has limited skills for tolerating negative arousal. This includes difficulties with reducing physiological over arousal and rule governed responses that emphasize running from, rather than facing pain.
- *Inescapable*: The patient experiences this pain at all times with only temporary periods of relief (usually in response to engaging in suicidal behavior/thinking, self mutilation or drug/alcohol abuse).
- *Interminable*: The patient does not believe that the pain will evolve naturally to some other form of experience. To the contrary, the patient believes that s/he is fated to be chronically suicidal until death occurs.

Faced with the Three I's, nearly any person would be capable of at least thinking about suicide as an option.

It is important to realize that suicidal behavior generally serves both an *instrumental* and *expressive* function (Chiles and Strosahl, 2004). The term instrumental means that suicidal behavior is used to solve any number of problems the patient might be facing. Usually, the consistent theme in suicidal acts is the desire to control and eliminate unbearable emotional pain, whether it is the result of grief, depression, anxiety, traumatic memories, loss, shame or anger. The expressive function of suicidal behavior is the "message" to the world, the therapist, or the abusive father. This can include the felt sense of panic or desperation (thus, the classic notion of suicide as a "cry for help") but it also often includes the sense that the patient is "right" and someone else (or the world) is wrong. This latter expressive function leads many therapists to label suicidal acts as "manipulative." This is little more than a way to morally rebuke the patient for engaging in the behavior and adds nothing to our understanding of it.

A final characteristic of suicidal behavior is that it is learned, shaped and maintained by either external and/or internal reinforcement. *External reinforcers* include changing the reactions and/or expectations of significant others, escaping from stress filled environments, maintaining disability benefits, getting extra therapy sessions, being hospitalized, or preventing the termination of therapy with a much beloved therapist. *Internal reinforcers* involve the ability of the behavior to control and/or eliminate intolerable aversive states. Behaviors which reduce unpleasant internal states can be strongly conditioned in a few learning trials, because aversive internal states are very potent motivators of escape oriented behavior.

As Kierkegard once remarked, "Thoughts of suicide have gotten me through many a dark night." With multi-problem patients, self-destructive behavior serves this same comforting function. The thought that one can commit suicide has a calming influence because it gives the patient a way out of an otherwise intolerable situation. In treatment, I elicit this theme by calmly and systematically deconstructing an episode of serious suicidal behavior. I will ask about the patient's mood states and how they were affected by self-destructive behavior. I will try to pinpoint private events that are particularly unacceptable to the patient in the process. In most cases (but not all), the private events that are most likely to produce suicidal behavior are negative emotional states such as anger, shame, depression, guilt and boredom. Normally, the patient will discover that self-destructive behavior helps regulate these mood states, at least in the short run. The paradox, of course, is that this behavior pattern has an extremely short half-life. It must be engaged in repeatedly to maintain its effectiveness.

Over time, the suicidal behavior pattern takes on a life of its' own. It swallows up more and more of the patient's energy and eventually becomes the dominant theme in the patient's daily life. Suicidal urges are very much like a "hungry tiger", a metaphor I often use at this stage of treatment. The more you feed them, the more oppressive and threatening they become. At the same time, patients get to know their suicidal behavior patterns so intimately that they can almost predict in advance what will and will not set these responses into motion. I will often say something like, "It sounds like suicidal thoughts and behaviors are your friends— they help you when you have to confront feelings that are painful to face. At the same time, like most friends, they want to be with you more and more and, if you let them, they might even move in with you. This doesn't make them bad; it just means they need some guidance from you about how much time you want to spend with them."

I generally don't want to focus the discussion on eliminating suicidal behavior because that is what the patient has already tried to do without success. I always try to come down on the side of living, but not in a way that is coercive or confrontational. I want suicidal behavior to be less mysterious, less romantic and more pedestrian. In ACT terms, suicidal behavior is what happens when you are completely unwilling to experience and make room for personal pain. Viewing suicidality in that way helps me put it in the same cloth as the patient's other emotional avoidance behaviors. This permits me to use any episodes of suicidality in therapy to promote discussions of the relative costs of willingness and acceptance versus struggle and avoidance.

The next thing I want the patient to discover is that chronic suicidality, while promising emotional relief, actually functions as an aversive mental state. It is emotionally painful to have self destructive urges and it should come as no surprise that acting upon the urge is one way to escape this pain. It is very common to hear comments such as, "I have urges to hurt myself all of the time and I just fight, fight, and fight to keep from doing it." In other words, the patient's struggle is no longer with the private events that *originally* triggered the use of suicidal behavior. Rather, it has now become a functionally autonomous focus of struggle. To complete the "friend metaphor", the friend has moved in with the patient without an invitation and is now with the patient constantly. This friend's companionship is getting tedious, but the patient doesn't know how to gracefully invite the friend to leave the house. I will often say something like, "It sounds like your suicidal urges are having you, rather than you having urges. What do you suppose would show up if you just let those urges be there, without trying to control or eliminate them? Doesn't your experience tell you that the harder you to try to suppress your urges, the stronger they become? I know your mind is telling you that the thing to do when the big bad thoughts show up is to get control of them ... and pronto. But which are going to believe here? Your mind or your experience?"

Another way I approach this is to use the *Man in the Hole* metaphor to help the patient realize that the only tool being used is "Urges to kill myself" or "Cutting myself." As long as the patient is busy using suicidal behavior to solve every personal problem, no new tools can be discovered and no new actions can be taken. I can then use little prompts in therapy like, "Are you digging right now?" or "Which tool are you pulling out of your bag of tricks right now?" Another, more provocative, way to push this issue is to say, "What would you be doing in your life if you weren't stewing in your suicidal urges all the time?" I don't discourage therapists from being provocative with such patients, as long as the communications are not condescending, pejorative or moralistic in tone. These are questions the patient has to come up against: "Are you going to spend all of your time and energy thinking about and trying to kill yourself? And what would you be doing in your life if you weren't doing that? And what monsters would you have to recognize and make room for to do that?"

When the patient gets "lost" in suicidality during a therapy session, I often use re-orienting strategies to undercut this automatic behavior pattern. One of my favorites is to carry a stopwatch that makes a loud clicking noise. As the patient slips into suicidality, I click on the timer and hold it in front of the patient. I will say something like, "Do you hear this sound? It is the sound of your life clicking away. The clock of your life is ticking. Can you hear it? Is this what you want to be doing with it?" I might also say something like, "There is one big difference between this stop watch and your life. When I push this button, the watch stops measuring time. In your life, you can't stop the watch from ticking away, until the end comes. So, despite all the reasons you have for not wanting to live and not wanting to pursue your dreams, your life doesn't care. It just keeps ticking, ticking, ticking." I don't try to be moralistic when speaking in these terms. I'm trying to be realistic and in a deep sense of the term, compassionate. Behind the veil of the patient's unworkable verbal behavior, a person's life is being wasted one second at a time.

I also will use the "clean" and "dirty" suffering intervention (Hayes et al., 1999, p. 136) to help the patient distinguish between the original "clean" aversive events (i.e. anger at an abusive mother) and the dirty suffering that is brought on by trying to control or eliminate the original private event. Suicidal ideation/attempting, self-mutilation is dirty suffering in action. This type of continuous pain is the cost of avoiding other more basic private experiences. I will often ask the patient, "Are we talking about clean or dirty suffering here?" or, "What do you suppose would happen to your suicidal urges if you just made room for your (avoided private event)?" I always try to portray the functional relationship between unwanted private events and emotional avoidance strategies such as suicidal behavior. At this stage of treatment, I seldom get into the validity of the patients anger, depression, guilt etc. I just accept it for what it is and instead focus my energy on reframing the suicidal behavior.

Alcohol, drugs, self-mutilation, binge eating and/or purging are also common high-risk behaviors that are heavily nested with suicidal behavior. One basic function of these behaviors is to "numb" or distract the patient from negative mood states. Multi-problem patients cut on themselves because the act of cutting creates a physical sensation of pain that distracts the patient from the emotional pain that is present. In essence, this constellation contains dysfunctional behaviors that are functionally identical to suicidal behavior. These behaviors differ only in form, not in function, so it should come as no surprise that drug and alcohol abuse and suicidal behavior co-occur in the majority of multi-problem patients. To make this point, I will say things like, "You know, there are an endless number of ways people can numb out, avoid or escape from things they don't want to face. You've told me about a number of behaviors that seem very similar from this perspective. They provide you with an instant outlet and you have to feed them all the time to keep them happy."

The final issue that has to be addressed is whether the suicidal behavior is "working." In ACT, the concept of workability pervades all six of its key components. Workability means that the patient's responses are building the patient as a human being and promoting a sense of vitality, meaning and purpose. This is a very tricky area to get into with multi-problem patients because it is very easy for the novice therapist to begin "bullying" the patient. Bullying means that the therapist has already decided what will work for the patient and what won't work. The patient senses this lack of openness and begins to say things to appease the therapist. However, the patient has not taken responsibility for choosing actions—rather, the patient is responding to plys issued by the therapist—so the exercise is empty.

It is very easy for therapists to bring their own agenda to work with the suicidal patient. Normally, the agenda is to have the patient stop suicidal and high-risk behaviors, because these behaviors are source of considerable fear and anxiety for the therapist. In order to use the workability strategy, you have to be relentlessly pragmatic and non-judgmental, and to truly mean it. This is not a verbal game, a trick or a form of therapeutic manipulation. Workability is a pragmatic concept that is measured on a patient-by-patient and situation-by-situation basis. It is not a moralistic or idealistic concept. To get into the issue of workability with a suicidal patient, I constantly have to check to make sure my own social conditioning is not interfering with the process. I have to have absolutely "clean hands" in terms of not pursuing my own hidden agendas for the patient.

I think the workability issue is so central to working with chronic suicidal behavior specifically and multi-problem patients in general, that I introduce it in the treatment process as soon as I can. With respect to chronic self-destructive behavior, it is not uncommon for a patient to say, "Yes, taking pills and cutting on myself works! It gives me some relief from this awful life and there is no way I can make it through a day without doing it." First of all, it is important to see the patient's initial view of what we mean by workability. To the patient, it often means feeling better or not experiencing some type of private event at all. Suicidal behavior is a notoriously effective method for engendering short-term relief from negative emotional states. So, in that sense, the patient is stating something that is true. When you cut on yourself, give in to the urge to drink, ingest pills, binge and purge, mainline drugs, there is an immediate sense of relief that looks superficially like effective emotional control. The problem is that the relief only lasts a short while and then the deeper process of "short term gain, long term pain" takes hold. This very process is commonly integrated into the story. Such patients will say things like, "I know I'll be suicidal for the rest of my life. Eventually, I'll get the job done."

Depending upon which lens one puts own, chronic suicidal behavior either works well (emotional pain management) or it isn't workable (hope for a different future, self-empowerment, vitality). I will usually accede to the first benefit of repetitious suicidal behavior and attack the second area. I might say something like, "I know how important this behavior is to you as a way of managing the extreme emotional pain you are in (a validating communication). I know that it works to numb that pain and in that sense, it makes your life more bearable. What I'm wondering is how does this make you feel about your prospects for a better life. Do you feel like you are increasing your chances of living a better life? Or do you feel like you are decreasing them? What I mean by workability is the sense that you are growing as a human being, and are moving yourself in the direction of living a valued, vital, purposeful life. In that sense, is this workable?" If I can get any glimmer of recognition that the long-term impact of these behaviors is negative, I will immediately introduce an ACT saying: Gain control of your feelings, lose control of your life. I can immediately say something like, "It sounds like the trade off you've made is this: You will use suicidal behavior to control how intensely bad you feel. In return, you are willing to trade in your chances of having a meaningful life. Is that how you see it? Is that a trade you would choose to make, if you had a choice?" The patient might say something like, "But I don't have a choice. I have to do something about these feelings (memories, urges) or I would go crazy." Then, I might say something like, "So, another thing your friends (suicidal thoughts, urges to cut) are telling you is that they are the only way out. That if you don't use them to deal with this situation, you will be eaten alive by your own feelings. Why do you think they would tell you that? What's in it for them?"

I keep the focus of therapy at this point on the "cost" of being in a suicidal lifestyle. There are an endless number of ways to approach this. For example, you can write out a belief that supports emotional avoidance (I won't express anger toward my mother), situations that put that belief into play (calling my mother, being at a family gathering), the behaviors the patient has to engage in to follow the belief (avoid talking about things that I'm angry about, artificially agree to things to keep from getting in arguments) and then the impact on what the patient values as an outcome (feel I'm hiding out instead of being genuine, I get mad at myself for being such a wimp). Sometimes, it might make sense to conduct a full bore values, goals, strategies maneuver, although when I do this early, it is usually with the goal of building some motivation to change.

Technical aspects of managing suicidal behavior. There are a host of technical considerations that every therapist should know when working with chronic suicidal behavior (Chiles & Strosahl, 2004). At the outset of treatment I always develop an understanding with the patient around such issues as emergency phone calls, hospitalization options, alternatives to hospital placement, suicidal communications during phone calls and so forth. Generally, I take an open approach to receiving after hours calls, as long as the patient understands that these will be problem solving interventions, not emotional venting sessions. I think the literature on the effectiveness of hospital treatment for chronic suicidal behavior suggests that hospitalization is a bad idea for these patients except in extraordinary circumstances. I look for alternatives to hospitalization with the patient. Does the patient have a supportive and competent family member/friend that they could stay with in a time of crisis? Is there a local crisis line that the patient could use? Is there a short stay respite facility that the patient can link up with in event of an emergency? Generally, I develop protocols that require the patient to act in a way that reinforces self-management and self-care behaviors. In a sense, I'm trying to structure the situation so that the patient is learning new, rule governed responses that emphasize self-control and better self-care.

In terms of case management, it is important to create a unified treatment plan if you are working in a clinic setting where multiple providers might see the patient over time. There should be one "principal therapist" who is in charge of the patient's care. If the patient has a history of presenting to various hospital and clinic facilities in suicidal crisis, it is important to create a uniform patient management plan. This may involve meeting with emergency room physicians, primary care providers, and emergency room social workers to explain the clinical management plan. Generally, I emphasize the importance of not reinforcing suicidal behavior, either negatively or positively, during a clinic or emergency room presentation. This means limiting the amount of interpersonal interaction involved and instead funneling the patient back to the primary therapist. I generally don't schedule extra therapy sessions when a multi-problem patient is in suicidal crisis for the same reason.

The primary therapist must be cognizant of several very important rules when addressing recurrent self destructive behavior:

1) avoid a moralizing, condescending or threatening stance about suicidal behavior; 2) avoid making suicidal behavior the focus of treatment, when the focus should be learning to make room for feared and avoided private experiences, and defusing from provocative thoughts; 3) emphasize that the patient is able to make choices about whether to engage in suicidal and self destructive problem solving strategies; 4) take an observational as opposed to evaluative stance with respect to suicidal behavior; 5) come down on the side of life whenever you can; 6) employ a calm, matter of fact approach when discussing self-destructive behavior; and 7) don't get into confrontations over suicidal behavior unless you are trying to get rid of the patient!

Undermining Confidence in and Fusion with the Story

In most cases, I will initiate the next phases of treatment when I think high-risk behaviors are decreasing to the point that it is possible to work with the patient's more basic issues. Each patient comes with a unique learning history and functions in a unique environment. Consequently, a therapist needs to conduct a relatively thorough functional analysis of core dysfunctional behavior patterns (see Chapter 3). This includes determining when and how often dysfunctional behaviors (i.e., drinking or self-mutilating) occur, the stimuli that trigger these reactions (environment, interpersonal factors, internal states), the short and long term consequences of these behaviors, how these behaviors have changed over time, the patient's beliefs and expectancies about these behaviors and so forth.

Initially, I like to develop an understanding of the scope and nature of the patient's problem using this ACT formula: What have you tried? How has it worked? What has it cost you? The first question generally elicits the types of control strategies the patient has used, and will give me a good idea of the amount of cognitive fusion that is occurring in the patient's private experience. It also lets me see conceptual/functional similarities between various unworkable strategies. The second question will generally elicit the "story" the patient carries to explain his/her history of pervasive dysfunction. The third question can be used to both assess and leverage the patient's commitment to valued living. It is also an opportunity to get the patient to connect with the ultimate price that has been paid for years of chronic self-absorption.

Sometimes patients may have developed more adaptive strategies for certain aversive states, but not for others. One patient had recovered from drug/alcohol addiction using 12 step oriented self-instruction and acceptance strategies. She had years of sobriety even though she had frequent urges to start using again. She rated the intensity and negativity of her urges to use alcohol at nearly the same levels as the depression and anxiety states that provoked her suicidal ideation and self-mutilation. Yet she was able to let go of urges to use again, while the same type of urge was experienced as irresistible when focused on suicide or self-mutilation. In this case, the problem is not one of repertoire as much as generalization across situations. Some digging around nearly always provides some examples of positive, acceptance-oriented coping in almost anyone's life. These skills can be an ally in treatment.

Many ACT therapists report obtaining significant clinical benefit when they initiate a values clarification component at the outset of therapy, at least in part. This seems most indicated when the patient apparently lacks any real investment in changing dysfunctional behaviors (which is often the case with multi-problem patients). Having the patient make contact with the real personal costs of dysfunctional responses may promote motivation to experiment with alternative responses. The key goal in using this strategy is to shift the "responsibility" for making valued choices and actions to the client, rather than letting therapy devolve into a series of sermons by the therapist. It puts the ACT question right on the front burner: "What do you want your life to be about and what are you doing to make it so?"

There are risks in using values clarification strategy up front. The client may return with an empty values clarification form or claim to lack any meaningful life goals. This is the "I don't know" reply that is a characteristic response to the question "What would you be doing in your life right now, if this problem were to suddenly vanish." One way I approach this is to reframe it as a direction the patient is choosing to take in life. I might say something like, "It sounds like not knowing what you want your life to stand for is a life direction you've been taking for quite a while. If you line up all the I don't knows you have used to define your life direction up to now, are you satisfied with the direction you are going? If you died unexpectedly today, would you be OK with the epitaph on your tombstone reading, 'Here lies Bill. Spent the majority of his life wondering what to do with it'. If I get any meaningful reaction from the patient, I will re-approach the values issue by saying something like, "Before this cloud descended over you, can you remember what you used to dream about your life becoming? Can you remember a time when you knew what you wanted your life to stand for?" For the more typical multi-problem patient, a values clarification components can help set up the difficult work of confronting the "story." My experience is that using values work early functions as a motivational intervention; because most patients do not yet have the skills need to accept feared content and engage in valued actions. Instead, it is just a peek at the horizon to indicate that there is something at stake in this work. It is my way of "waking up" the patient, often after years of deep slumber.

My major goal in this phase of treatment is to elicit the patient's story, get the patient to invest in it and then undermine the patient's confidence in it. Multi-problem patients normally have a series of explanations for their dysfunction, often inherited from earlier regimes of therapy. The most key components are: 1) How I got to be the way I am and 2) What attribute of my life that will have to be added and/subtracted in order for me to be able to function like others. This is dangerous territory, because the patient's story is going to be drawn from the verbal community of reason giving, meaning that it will have a certain logic to it that can trick you the clinician. Furthermore, the patient is usually heavily invested in it being "true." In ACT terms, the story is an exercise in "self as conceptualized content." Many patients will defend their story to the death, figuratively and literally.

The story should not be addressed with the goal of helping the patient modify its contents. At the level of content, the multi-problem patient is often "therapy wise" and frequently can draw the therapist into buying the patient's story as a credible factual analysis of cause and effect relationships in the patient's developmental history. Every element of the story may be literally (structurally) true—but if it is unworkable, it is functionally false (see Chapter 1 on the pragmatic truth criterion in ACT).

For example, one patient said simply: "I don't do anger." Instead, she would cut on her arms and legs, think about killing herself for hours on end, dissociate, hear voices and numb out emotionally. She maintained that her inability to do anger came from numerous aversive events with her mother, who would become verbally abusive at even the slightest hint of independence on the part of her daughter. The verbal and physical abuse described was truly horrific and no doubt had some type of influence on the patient. Unfortunately, the function (as opposed to the content) of the story was to provide the patient with a convenient rationale for avoiding any situation where she or any other participants might experience anger, hostility or criticism. The analysis fit with how the verbal community treats issues like this, and the elements were literally true, but if these reasons were taken as causes, we would somehow need to undo the patient's history in order to establish better functioning. To counter this pernicious dead-end, I will often say something like, "You know, with everything being said about what you went through as a child, adolescent or adult, I have two things to add. One is that I don't for a moment doubt that this was incredibly painful and traumatic for you (a validating communication). The other thing I have to say is that the most dangerous part of your history is that you are about to make it into your future."

When the story is "bought" in by the patient, it decreases motivation to try alternative responses. In fact, if the patient actually tries a new strategy and it doesn't work, the event provides further evidence that the story is true. The therapist may not realize that the client is facing two losses if a new coping behavior is tried and fails. In keeping with an ACT perspective, the story is probably representative of how the patient has tried to analyze and solve various life dilemmas, and thus dealing with it directly is likely to fail (as it has in the past). I might say something like, "It seems like you've been through this way of analyzing what has happened to your life before. Has this been one of the strategies you've used to get on top of this situation? What strategies does it suggest you should try? How have those strategies worked when you've put them into play in your life?"

I believe that contextual interventions are the only way to effectively undermine the patient's story. At the level of context, the patient needs to make experiential contact with the story as a constructed set of verbal relations, and the issue must turn from literal truth to workability. There are an endless number of stories available to describe any one person's life.

I will often initially elicit elements of the story quite deliberately using some strategies that are reminiscent of traditional insight oriented therapy. Unknown to the patient, my goals are completely different. I'm not interested in helping the patient acquire more insight. I want the patient to put the story on display and then to begin to see it for what it is. I will say something like; "Tell me about the pivotal events in your childhood, adolescence and adult life and how you think these events have made you into who you are today?" I might also ask, "Tell me what it is that you would have to eliminate in yourself or your life that would allow you to live like other people?" Another way to ask this is, "What do you think you need to gain in our work that will give you a chance to live your life better?" I want the patient to get invested in the story with me, so that when we begin to examine the workability of this story, the clinical impact will be greater.

One of my favorite ways to attack the story as context is the "autobiography rewrite." I ask the patient to write me a brief 1 or 2 page autobiography, citing key events in life that account for his or her current difficulties. Usually, the product will be fairly negative, self-focused and pointing to pivotal cause and effect relationships. Then, after reviewing the initial product, I will ask the patient to rewrite the story using exactly the same events, but this time with a different connotation. I do not require that the connotation be positive, only that it be different. Then I will repeat the process perhaps two or three more times. Usually, I will review each story and then ask something like, "Without saying that this version of your story is more accurate, better or worse, than the first one, do you think this story is at least credible? If you were reading someone else's story and this was it, would the interpretations of these key events seem at least plausible?" I never get into arguing with the patient about the "truth" of any particular story, nor do I imply that the original story is wrong (content wise). I am just helping the patient make contact with the mind's unending ability to generate stories and to link events together in various forms.

Another of my favorite interventions is the "pick an identity... any identity" game. I write out a number of negative and positive personality attributes (e.g., afraid of angering or disappointing others, asserts point of view in a clear and unafraid way, has a loving, compassionate feel for others) on slips of paper, put them in a hat and then have the patient draw 10 or so attributes. The game in session is to have the patient imagine that these attributes (randomly drawn) are real attributes and to imagine how this person would respond to a problematic life situation.

I use the concept of workability over and over again during this and all phases of therapy. Workability functions as my "safety valve." The following are but some of the therapeutic traps that activate that safety valve:

- I'm doing all the work in a session
- I'm arguing with the patient about some content (as opposed to context) issue
- The patient has lured me into the control and eliminate change agenda
- I'm telling the patient what the "right" thing to do is

I retreat into the following type of question: "And, assuming that you tried this before or have used this type of self-analysis before, how has it worked in terms of promoting your goals in life?" This question has a way of stopping the patient from living and reliving the story during treatment. I don't want to get into a confrontation about this tendency, but I do want the patient to discriminate between when the story is in operation and when the human being is in operation. Another related tactic is to say something like this: "Who am I hearing from right now? Your mind, or you?" Strategies that give you the clinician the ability to "retreat to the surface" are very important in working with the multi-problem patient. Even the most experienced ACT therapist will get tangled up in the patient's verbal jungle—that is what makes difficult patients "difficult." Throughout treatment, I'm asking myself whether I am approaching this situation from the perspective of the patient's change agenda, or from an agenda of what works in the world. While doing this, I'm at all times trying to be non-judgmental about what the patient needs to do to make life more workable. These patients don't need judging. Their story is full of self judgments and judgments of others. What they need most at this stage of treatment is someone who can stay out of the story, focus their attention on the costs of fusing with the story and do it in a way that communicates compassion, caring and concern.

Addressing Barriers to Change

There is no clear line of demarcation between one phase of ACT and another, particularly so with the multi-problem patient. At the same time, as the first two stages of ACT proceed, there is a natural shift in the topic of conversation. The initial phases of treatment focus on these core themes: "What have you tried? Does your experience tell you its working or not? Can you let go of things that don't work for you?" Later in the treatment process, the following types of themes typically emerge: "What do you want your life to be about instead?" "What barriers will you have to 'in-hale' to do something new, positive and more life generating?" "Are you willing to start moving in that direction, knowing that it will provoke all of your hidden monsters?" From an ACT perspective, multi-problem patients embody the FEAR model (fusion, evaluation, avoidance, reasons). They fuse with feelings, thoughts and other private experiences, tend to see the world and themselves in very judgmental terms, use avoidance as a primary coping response and have an elaborate set of reasons to explain and justify their dysfunction and misery. Once the patient demonstrates openness to admitting that current coping responses are never going to work, there is room to look at the alternatives.

As the tone of the therapeutic conversation changes, I introduce the patient to the idea that one can choose to "make room for" unpleasant events such as negative affect, suicidal urges, traumatic memories, negative self evaluations and the like. I want the patient to experience the relationship between elevated levels of willingness and a decreased sense of personal suffering. If the patient is willing to try this, I will usually set up a self-monitoring assignment that has the patient rate daily levels of willingness, suffering and life workability. I try to create visual images and metaphors that I can use in later sessions when the patient is in a low state of will-ingness. My preference is to use a limited number of ACT metaphors and strategies again and again (e.g., tug of war, quick sand, clean & dirty suffer-ing, experiencing feelings exercise), rather than barrage the patient with nu-merous different metaphors. This allows us to develop some "buzz words" that I can use when the going gets tough. These nonlinear communications help the patient detach from the moment and look at alternative response options. I can always ask the patient something like, "What are you in a tug of war with now?" "What kind of pain are we talking about here? The clean stuff or the dirty stuff?" "Are you having this experience or is this experience having you?" "Are you *feeling* this good or trying to feel *good*?"

At the level of content, the concept of willingness is easy to talk about. At the level of application, it is a fundamental act of choice that is deceptively difficult. To demonstrate this point, I like to use the *Eye Contact* exercise (Hayes et al., 1999, p. 244–245) to show how a simple act of willingness can lead to a host of unexpected challenges. This is an emotionally powerful exercise for multi-problem patients, in part due to the amount of content that gets stirred up about closeness, attachment, and abandonment. It also signals to the patient that I'm willing to share this type of intense exchange with him or her. Contrary to an often expressed fear of therapists that this exercise will create "boundary issues" with the multi-problem patient, I've found it to have a humanizing effect on the therapy process. It signals the following: I'm willing to show up and you are too.

One of my favorite ways to access underlying rule governed responses is the "rules of the game" exercise. This involves having the patient generate written "sayings about life" that apply to various moral or situational domains, for example, dealing with personal pain, how one is to act when the situation calls for seeking help from others, interpersonal trust, and so forth. These are the "clichés" that we all are exposed to at the cultural level. These are clichés precisely because they are so widely used. I ask the patient to write down his or her favorite sayings about life in several important domains: 1) How to set a life direction; 2) How to treat other people; 3) How to seek help from others; 4) How to deal with personal pain and trauma; 5) How to explain fate or luck when it is bad luck; 6) How wrongdoing by another is to be handled. Other areas are added given the particular circumstances of the patient. There are many ways to use the responses elicited in this written exercise. One is to just play with the wording of the cliché so that it becomes distorted. For example, the cliché, "no-pain, no-gain" expresses the idea that to grow as humans we have to be willing to go through pain. However, "no gain, no pain" has an interesting, different, and also useful meaning. I might generate the second twisted cliché and then ask the patient explain them both, focusing how the meaning shifts by the simple manipulation of a word sequence. This of course is a metaphor for the arbitrary nature of verbal constructions. A second intervention is related to the actual content of the clichés that are produced. For example, one patient produced this rule about seeking help and support from others in a time of personal crisis: "Smile and the world smiles with you. Cry and you cry alone." This allowed me to mention in an offhand manner how proscriptive and morally loaded some clichés are. Taken literally, as opposed to being seen as sayings, they can make adaptation easy or hard. I might say something like, "If this were a basic rule for how to address this type of situation, how would that really work for you? What if you just saw this as a cliché? Can you rewrite this rule so that it has a different meaning, any different meaning?" The point is not to get the right answer, or find the rational belief. The point is psychological flexibility—seeing rules as verbal processes that can be addressed in myriad ways, based on workability.

Typically, in this stage of ACT, I will address the same themes again and again. There is no point in pushing value based actions, for example, if the patient can't or won't make contact with willingness as an alternative to control, avoidance and struggle. My experience is that fusion, avoidance, rigid rule following and the use of reason giving are very solidly entrenched in the multi-problem patient. Years of practicing these behavior patterns suggest that learning new responses is likely to be an uneven process. Experiential contact with willingness and defusion as the alternative will probably occur in bits and pieces. I haven't had many multi-problem patients report an "ah ha" phenomena that turned their lives around.

Values Oriented Living: The Alternative to Struggle and Non-Participation

At some point in the therapeutic process, the patient will signal that he or she is ready to try something different. The form that this takes differs from one patient to another. In ACT, making room for traumatic memories, unpleasant effect, disturbing thoughts or unpleasant physical sensations is not a naval contemplation exercise. Being asked to stew in personal pain for the sake of stewing would be a form of therapeutic sadism. The purpose is try new responses that embody something the patient wants to stand for in life. If I haven't already done so, I will employ the ACT exercises that are relevant to values clarification, goal setting and journey, and if the earlier work of that kind was truncated, it will be revisited now. My favorite opening maneuver is the "what do you want your life to stand for?" exercise. In this exercise, I ask the patient to imagine that s/he has died suddenly, but higher powers allow him/her to attend the funeral in spirit. This allows the patient to listen to the eulogies of friends, family members, spouse and so on. I ask the patient to imagine what he or she would like each of these key players to say at the funeral. Then I debrief the exercise. This becomes source material for the full values clarification exercise (Hayes et al., 1999, Chapter 8). I often dovetail "epitaph" interventions linked to what the person has been doing as a counter foil in this process. So, for example, I might say something like, "Notice that most of what you imagined involved people remembering you for intangible, but important, personal values such as being a good friend, a good listener, someone who could be relied upon in hard times. So, imagine their surprise when they visit your grave at the cemetery and see this marker: "Here lies Joan. She spent her life waiting for mom to apologize." "Is that what you want your life to stand for? If you line up all of the choices you have made in this area of your life, do you like the direction you are taking? Is this where you want to go from here on out? There is a choice to be made here."

Choice is an interesting concept for the multi-problem patient, who is a specialist in "not choosing." Not only is the patient not choosing, but also the patient will make the claim that no choice can be made. Often, this claim is nested in the patient's story. It might read something like, "Every time I've tried to make something of myself or do something different, I fail." The implication often is that the world, luck or bad circumstance has (unfairly) removed the patient's ability to choose and/or there are no options available in a life situation. This stance, of course, is a form of choosing. Even the stance, "I have no choice" is a choice. I think it is important not to let the patient wiggle out of this knot because, much like the concept of workability, it is a key theme in treatment. I present this question over and over again during treatment, not as something to beat the patient over the head with, but rather to create an orienting response. I'm not going to buy the idea that the patient can't make choices, no matter how seductive the patient's story line is. Almost invariably, the real issue is that the patient is afraid to invest in " hope for the future" without some guarantee that a positive outcome will occur. The patient is over-invested in the outcome of the story, not what the process of living the story has to teach him or her. For this reason, I like to use journey exercises and metaphors that emphasize several points: 1) Choices have to be made; one cannot choose to not choose; 2) Any choice is made without guarantee of any particular result; 3) Taking a chosen direction begins a process of living that produces its own purpose and meaning.

One of my favorite interventions is to suggest to the patient that we take a walk and talk. After I lead the way for a while, I will suddenly stop leading and ask the patient to pick the next direction. When the patient starts to pick, I will begin putting forth worries, concerns or dangers that might occur if we walk that way. Usually, the patient will retract the initial choice and suggest another direction for the walk and I'll do the same with that direction. Quickly, the patient will begin to see that we are engaged in a physical metaphor about choosing based upon a guaranteed outcome. After a while, the patient might ask me which way h/she *should* choose, since I've put forth so many possible negative reasons for not walking any direction. Then, I might say something like, "Well, we could just stay right here and not walk any further, but that would be a choice and, you know, bad things might happen to us if we don't walk. Knowing that we can't make any choice here that doesn't have some downside, can you just pick a direction and begin walking?"

I think it is always important to avoid telling the multi-problem patient what the "right" course of action is. This is a temptation when the patient has finally dropped some patently dysfunctional responses and appears willing to experiment with new behaviors. Instead I emphasize that trying any new response is essentially an act of willingness. Neither of us actually knows what will happen if a new response is tried. All we know is what will happen if the patient continues using the same responses as before. That outcome is quite predictable. This helps me get around the patient pressing me to "guarantee" that if a new response is tried, the patient will feel better, have a happier life, and so on. Willingness the action means to choose to take a step without knowing what the outcome will be. No guarantees. Besides, any guarantees the patient is seeking are probably originating in the old change agenda. If you are using willingness and choice to "trick" feelings, thoughts, memories or physical sensations into going away, then you are not willing and you are not choosing. Patients will usually signal this reversion to the old agenda (e.g., "You mean if I just accept my suicidal urges, then they will stop plaguing me day and night?").

Another way I approach this key issue is to link the concepts of choice and play. Play is a useful intervention in therapy, because the typical multi-problem patient is all about "winning and losing", being "right vs. being wrong", being "worthy or unworthy" or situations being "fair or unfair." All of these themes combine to make the multi-problem patient overly fused with the abstract evaluations of living, as opposed to participation in life. The concept of play is the antithesis of this dominating, dichotomous approach to experiencing life. In play, the outcome is an arbitrary end point that has not been reached. When you reach it, the game is over. Children play all kinds of games that are made up on the spur of the moment. The rules often change in mid-stream and the delight the child receives is from the process of play, not just whether the game is won or lost. After all, if the child loses at one game, another one can be invented in a second that promises a chance to win. But truthfully, playing itself is a form of winning. The ACT saying is, "First you win, then you play." From a life journey standpoint, playing, not winning, is the pathway to vitality, purpose and meaning.

In therapy, a simple card game can serve as a physical metaphor for this. For example, I ask the patient to play a game of "spades" with me. In the middle of the game, I will suddenly declare that the game is "hearts" not "spades." If the patient objects, I'll say something like, "I said let's play cards, not what particular kind of cards we were going to play. Do you still want to play? I don't know what's in your hand; heavens, you might even win this game when I would have won the other game. Notice that when I change the name of the game, you have to change your strategies. That means there is no one right to play cards because it all depends on what the game is." I might change the game several times in clearly an arbitrary fashion, or I could change it in a way that clearly guarantees me a victory. The patient might say something like, "Hey, you're cheating; that's not fair." I might say, "Do you want to keep playing, knowing that I might change the rules? What if I changed them so that you won? Would that be fair? If fair is measured by who has the best chance of winning, then you could become more focused on the rules than on playing this stupid game of cards. So which do you choose right now? To focus on the rules and whether you win or lose or to just have some fun playing cards with me?" Other games that allow a contextual rule shift are equally useful. For example, one could start with a game of chess and turn it into checkers.

A unique and potentially treacherous feature of this phase of treatment is the interaction of pain, trauma, righteousness and forgiveness. Multi-problem patients often have very traumatic childhood and adolescent histories, involving physical, verbal and sexual abuse, parental mental illness and/or drug/alcohol addiction, divorce, domestic assault and so forth. The relational frames that get established in these traumatic environments are fairly primitive and rigid. One key manifestation of this is the patient's sense of victimization and the belief that "life is not fair." These scars can only be healed through corrective life experiences, but none of this can occur if the patient is standing on the sidelines of life crying, "Foul." This places the patient at the nexus of several core themes that can have a deleterious impact on therapy if they are not addressed.

The first and most important theme is to help the patient accept and move through various life traumas that function as barriers to vital, purposeful living. Multi-problem patients are often focused on gaining retribution from a perpetrator of sexual abuse, an alcoholic father, a cold and rejecting mother who left and so on. The patient's story often uses these traumatic life events as reasons why functioning in the here and now is impossible. To make sure the perpetrator stands accused, the patient usually adopts a "corpus delecti" posture. In legal theory, this doctrine means "no victim, no murder." Similarly, if the patient starts living a valued life, a core element of the patient's story is potentially challenged. After all, if the patient can bounce back from these horrific events, maybe the events weren't so horrific and the perpetrator might not be guilty of a vicious act.

In ACT terms, the patient has a choice between being "right" and being "alive." I am never surprised by the power of this psychology when I work with the multi-problem patient. The patient appears on the verge of engaging in valued life actions, only to relapse and become acutely suicidal. My goal is to help the patient stop living a life waiting for justice and retribution.

There are several ACT interventions that can be used to target this important barrier to healthy living. The first is simply to ask the patient, "Who would be made right if you moved forward with your life and started doing things that worked for you? Who would be made wrong?" Another powerful intervention is the fishhook metaphor. "It's like you and your father are on the same fishhook together. You are both stuck, but you were stuck first and later you stuck him. Now, for you to free yourself, you first have to push him off the hook. Then, and only then, can you slide off the hook." Another, more provocative way I dig at this is to say something like, "Listen, when you get to heaven, each person gets assigned a job for eternity. Make sure to tell God that you have lots of life experience being judge, jury and executioner."

A second major theme is getting the patient to use forgiveness as an act of willingness. The opposite of seeking retribution is to forgive the aggressor. This is a particularly thorny issue for patients who have lived their entire lives waiting for the perpetrator to acknowledge the deeds done and to ask for forgiveness. Of course, given the basic nature of abusive, sabotaging relationships, this type of "confession" and throwing oneself on the "mercy of the victim" is very unlikely to happen. In fact, additional abusive interactions are often triggered by the patient's persistent attempts to get the perpetrator to confess and apologize. A suicidal patient once told me that the only reason she had not killed herself was so that she could watch her mother suffer through her (the daughter's) multiple hospitalizations, so that the mother would know how badly she had hurt her daughter.

I use forgiveness in a very specific way to defeat this process. Most patients construe forgiveness to mean that they are letting the perpetrator "go free", which effectively amounts to denying the original event. The etymologic root of the word involves "giving what went before." The gift involved here is *to you*. It is literally letting yourself go free, so that your life can move ahead. I might say the following (in this version I am using the term "grace" for "gift" since they are etymologically variants of the same Latin root "gratis" meaning "free.").

"You seem to be at the crossroads of a major life choice. You could elect to restore the grace you had before these terrible events occurred in your life. This does not let anybody free of guilt if they committed some terrible wrong. We both know what happened and there will never be any version of your history in which these things did not happen. That's not the point. The point is that as long as you refuse to accept these events and move on, you are allowing the perpetrator to continue to rob you of your grace. So, the choice seems to be whether you will be willing to forgive and restore grace or be to unwilling to forgive and continue to be victimized. One choice lets you have your history for what it is; the other lets your history have you. This is not a decision based upon logic. It is a choice and only you can make it."

A final therapeutic principle is to get the patient to nibble at committed action, and in a way that incorporates sound personal problem solving and effective goal setting. Multiple research studies have shown that multi-problem patients lack effective problem solving and goal setting skills. They tend to set life goals that are unrealistic, give up prematurely, and/or measure success using the wrong benchmarks. At this stage, I will often expose patients to self-control behavior modification skills and models of personal problem solving. My goal is to help the patient acquire skills that will generalize to other situations in life, long after therapy is over. It is important to understand that ACT is essentially a "behavior therapy." Therefore, if the patient lacks the necessary skills to engage in a behavior that the patient is willing to do, you the clinician must engage in a skill training intervention. I emphasize that it is important to learn to set and achieve goals all through life. I try to help the patient understand that, just as playing cards requires a specific set of strategies; playing life requires the same type of approach. You don't reach life satisfaction; you can only strive toward life satisfaction. As the saying goes, "You never reach west, you can only head west. No matter how far west you go, there is always more west to go."

I don't want the patient to become overly focused on whether a particular goal is achieved. I want the patient to see goal setting as the means through which "aliveness" is achieved. So, I tend to encourage the patient to select small, manageable, positive steps. The magnitude of the committed action is not nearly as important as whether committed action occurs. To make this point physically, I will have a patient jump off a book that I've placed on the floor. Then, I will have the patient jump off a chair. I then ask the patient whether one of these actions was not jumping. The patient will usually look a little confused at this question, but will usually point out that one jump was big and the other was small. I then point out that the act of jumping is not measured by how far the fall is. It is the act of stepping off an edge with both feet. A jump can be big or small, but it is a jump just the same. This allows me to use jumping metaphors or sayings. For example, I will often talk about committed action this way: "You can't jump a canyon in two steps. It doesn't matter whether the crevice is a foot wide or twenty feet wide. To get from this side to the other side requires a single step. How big that step is depends upon how wide the crevice is, and the rule for success is always the same."

CLINICAL CONSIDERATIONS

In the big picture, I think there are three major process factors that lead to successful ACT therapy with a multi-problem patient: 1) forming a humanizing, motivating therapeutic relationship that maximizes the patient's responsibility for change, while minimizing the therapist's use of confrontation, coercion or manipulation; 2) integrating high risk and crisis generating behavior into the ongoing process of therapy, rather than allowing it to disrupt the therapy process, and 3) recognizing how the therapeutic community reinforces the patient's unworkable change agenda, while simultaneously challenging it and promoting an ACT consistent model of personal problem solving/healthy living.

We need to find a way to humanize our relationship with the patient (rather than to label, moralize, confront and criticize), communicate a sense of confidence in the patient's ability to make changes and emphasize that the entire work of ACT is to get the patient participating in life. To this end, it is a central ACT tenet that such patients are not broken, but trapped in an unworkable, culturally supported approach to dealing with personal pain. Similarly, I communicate my optimism about the possibility of finding alternatives that will work better. No matter how troubled the life, no matter how many futile regimes of therapy have gone before, I am always voting for the patient.

Continuity of treatment is of key importance with a patient who is experiencing daily life stress, social and emotional instability and on-going self-destructive behavior. If the therapist responds to the latest "crisis of the week" with conventional crisis management strategies, months or years of treatment can be consumed with little in the way of continuous intervention. Crises and unstable behavior patterns need to be brought into the normal course of treatment. ACT provides a powerful model for this, since the themes of emotional avoidance, cognitive fusion, valued action, and workability will reappear in almost every instance of self-mutilation, suicidal ideation, drug or alcohol abuse, or whatever the "crisis" may be. Thus the latest crisis can be but the latest example of key issues in ACT—rather than a sudden "brush fire" that needs to be dealt with in some other way.

The same issue occurs in a different way later in ACT treatment when the patient engages in new emotional avoidance behaviors that may not have been the focus of treatment to start with. For example, the patient with a history of chronic self-mutilation may gain a measure of control over that behavior pattern but begin to also engage in heavy drinking. The key to successfully handling the "second problem" event is to link it to previous emotional escape strategies and then treat it as part of an equivalence class of escape responses. Ordinarily, there will be shared "triggers" that control dysfunctional behavior, although the form of emotional avoidance may change. In most cases, these avoidance/escape triggers will be internal mood states (depression, boredom), physical sensations (shakiness, hypervigilance) or interactions with others that might trigger unpleasant outcomes (rejection, social humiliation) and associated negative mood states (anger, guilt). The emergence of "new" problems is such an opportunity. With each example, the possibility of generalizing acceptance and defusion strategies to the entire class grows. Once that begins to occur, therapy is over and life itself has become "the therapist."

The biggest value of ACT is that it helps the therapist avoid buying into the patient's (and the culture's) unworkable change agenda. Initially this can be uncomfortable for therapists. It means that we abandon "understanding" and "feeing better" as goals of therapy. Good ACT therapists have to be willing to experience that sense of discomfort and persist (which is why good ACT therapists are usually those who see the relevance of ACT to their own lives).

This is particularly difficult with "therapy wise" patients. Past therapy has almost always directly or indirectly reinforced the analyze-control-eliminate change agenda. Content-based treatments typically focus on the analysis of cause and effect relationships that are assumed to account for the patient's current dysfunction. This could range from an analysis of how early childhood trauma could later lead to pervasive concerns about trust, betrayal and abandonment, to eliciting the patient's core schemas with the intent of having the patient correct distorted and irrational core beliefs. I try not to be dismissive of past content-based therapies, because that would constitute being dismissive of the patient (who is using the same basic approach) and the patient's past experiences. It is best to be agnostic and to appeal to direct experience: perhaps these strategies work very well for some people, but what does the patient's experience say about the workability of these strategies? If the patient still feels stuck (which is almost always the case) then perhaps it is time to try something truly different.

Length and Intensity of Treatment

It is often assumed that "more therapy is better" and that, "patients with more problems need more therapy." This is not necessarily so (Howard, Kopta, Krause & Orlinsky, 1986). Multi-problem behavior patterns have been shaped, maintained and reinforced over years. They will not be undone simply through verbal analysis in the therapeutic context, but rather through practicing different responses in the actual environment. "More therapy" can actually delay this needed step if it conveys the hidden message that "first you get fixed in therapy, and then you start to live." We have used ACT successfully in a time limited classroom setting with multi-problem patients and have explored a variety of stepped care strategies (Strosahl, 1991). For example, individual therapy sessions can be widely spaced, supplemented by phone calls and home based practice using workbooks and other end-user materials, or enhanced by groups or classes. Individual sessions once or twice a week for years should not be the expectation, merely because these patients have multiple problems.

Self as Context Interventions

There is a belief in some theoretical circles that using self-observational strategies with "borderline" patients is not a good idea because they presumably lack a coherent sense of self. My experience is that mindfulness and/or self observation exercises that are tailored to the patient's level of functioning can be very effective. I've never had a patient decompensate or swing into suicidal crisis as a result of mindfulness exercise. This being said, patients do vary in their ability to understand acceptance and mindfulness concepts. For example, one patient may have been through Alcoholics Anonymous and is familiar with concepts such as "Let go, Let God." Another patient will have zero history with anything even remotely related to mindfulness. These differences can be dealt with by altering the pace of ACT. Part of my initial assessment involves determining if the patient has had any prior exposure to strategies such as willingness, acceptance or mindfulness. If so, these should be used as a base to build from. For patients with no previous experience with self observational strategies, it is important to avoid lecturing and intellectualizing about mindfulness. Instead, focus on having patients make experiential contact with this "space."

Conclusion

For all of the clinical challenges they present, multi-problem patients are an exceedingly interesting group of patients to work with. They bring into stark relief the humbling reality that the power of the therapist is limited. They highlight many of the chinks in the armor of socially promoted beliefs about emotional pain and what to do about it. In many important ways, I developed into an ACT therapist as a direct function of working with these patients. I discovered that I needed to get a foothold in therapy that was outside the box of traditional strategies. The non-judgmental pragmatism that is at the heart of ACT provides a powerful framework for working with difficult patients. Future research will show how far that framework can take us in the alleviation of the enormous suffering carried by these patients.

Part III

ACT with Special Populations, Settings, and Methods

Chapter **10**

ACT with Children, Adolescents, and Their Parents

AMY R. MURRELL, LISA W. COYNE,
AND KELLY G. WILSON

In contrast to the growing empirical support for ACT interventions with adult problems and populations, ACT applications with children, adolescents, and their parents are in relatively early stages of development. Our preliminary data, and data from other sites, suggest that ACT and its components can be successfully adapted for children in developmentally appropriate, therapeutically beneficial ways. Evidence suggests that ACT can be useful to parents dealing with the challenges children present. As with any new intervention, conceptualizing and using this approach is a trial-and-error process. Keeping this in mind, clinicians using the adaptations suggested in this chapter should be committed to measuring progress through the use of ongoing assessments.

ASSESSMENT AND CASE CONCEPTUALIZATION

The ACT formulation of suffering and distress for children is really no different than it is with adults, but the form it takes and the complexity of the child's context can be different. The key variables in the equation are the excessive use of emotional control/avoidance strategies, based upon cognitive fusion with unpleasant content, and the child's resulting inability to pursue valued life directions in the arenas of family, friends, recreation, studies and so forth. Particularly with children, a competent ACT case conceptualization assessment always begins with a functional analysis of the problem behaviors that bring the child to treatment in the first place. From a contextual point of view, it is very important that you the therapist understand the factors that are related to the appearance of problematic behaviors, as well as both internal and external "reinforcements" that might maintain those behaviors.

From an ACT perspective, the key factors to look for are the degree of experiential avoidance evident in a problematic behavior pattern as well as restrictions in valued life outcomes that are the result of such avoidance. Very frequently, we find that children spend a great deal of time engaged in experiential avoidance in attempts to reduce or control suffering that is often triggered by fusion with beliefs or expectancies. In children these efforts are often overt and behavioral, such as avoiding school or failing to perform tasks. While such efforts may eliminate painful events in the short-term, they undermine behaviors that will lead them in more meaningful, valued directions. Thus, ACT case conceptualization with children tends to focus on the following core areas:

1. The form, frequency and intensity of the problematic behavior
2. The situational triggers for these behaviors, both internal private experiences and external events
3. The distressing thoughts, feelings, memories, sensations or events that the problematic behavior pattern is helping the child avoid
4. The specific experiential avoidance/control strategies used to manage painful psychological content
5. The short-term reinforcers (e.g., feeling less anxious, feeling more accepted) that maintain these unworkable control strategies
6. An assessment of the client's valued directions in school, recreation, friendships, family, etc.
7. The extent to which problematic behaviors are interfering with any or all of these desired life outcomes.

For example, an 11-year-old boy was referred to a clinic for school refusal behavior. Presenting symptoms included pervasive worry, irritability, and somatic concerns; he was given a provisional diagnosis of Generalized Anxiety disorder. During the functional analysis interview, the child stated that, "being called a mama's boy shows up when I think about going to school". Once this painful content was identified, the therapist and client listed all the things the client did to avoid going to school. Working with children normally requires seeking information from the parents (and siblings if available), because the family unit forms an extremely important "context" in which problematic behavior is embedded. This is a major difference as compared to normal adult ACT work. In this case, the parents were less concerned about the child's school refusal and instead viewed their child's irritability as their biggest concern. Such inconsistencies in the definition of the "problem" are common in families and need to be assessed during the functional analysis. Next, during a values assessment, the client indicated that making friends was important and meaningful to him. Given that information, the therapist was able to help the child assess the degree to which emotional avoidance and control behaviors (e.g., such as fighting at school) might actually be undermining his ability to make friends.

ACT CLINICAL INTERVENTIONS

Informed Consent and Therapeutic Contract

Because it is in part an exposure-based treatment, ACT is often emotionally demanding and requires a willingness to explore and experience painful thoughts, memories, and situations. After the functional assessment has been completed and a set of treatment goals are developed and discussed, it is necessary to forge a therapeutic contract. The contract solidifies the therapeutic alliance by specifying the commitment needed to assure that therapeutic work will be done. Typically, this agreement is flexible, and continually changes and expands as treatment progresses.

You should include both children and their parents in these discussions for two primary reasons. First, children must make informed choices about their treatment. If treatment is undertaken at the behest of parents alone, children may be less likely to comply with treatment. Second, no parent desires to see his or her child suffering. It is important to discuss with parents that ACT treatment can be painful at times. Parents must understand that any such suffering may enable positive behavior change. The analogy of a visit to a physician may be useful: to find out what is wrong and facilitate healing, a doctor must press where it hurts.

ACT therapists often use metaphor to illustrate points, and such an approach may serve well to help children and parents gain an experiential understanding of the requirement of completing uncomfortable tasks in pursuit of better health. In this case, the analogy of exercising is a useful example as it is applied in the initial meeting of a children's therapy group:

THERAPIST: Is exercise healthy for you?
CHILD: We learned in science that it helps keep your heart working.

THERAPIST: Did you learn anything else about it?

CHILD: We learned that it helps you stay fit and maybe even live longer.

THERAPIST: Yeah. So it sounds like it is a healthy thing, right?

CHILD: Yeah.

THERAPIST: I want you guys to do jumping-jacks for me as fast as you can until I say stop. (After a minute, say): Was that easy?

CHILD: Yeah, really easy.

THERAPIST: What if you had to do it for a long time, or if you had never done jumping-jacks before, then would that have been easy?

CHILD: No, then it would be really hard.

THERAPIST: Right. The work that we are going to do is like exercise. Just like exercise, it is hard and might hurt or make you tired at first, but it might also be meaningful or helpful in the long run.

The "Mud in the Glass" metaphor also illustrates the painful treatment process. Children may be given a glass of muddy water that has been allowed to settle. The following transcript demonstrates the use of this metaphor with an 11-year-old foster child, removed from the home because of sexual abuse and neglect:

THERAPIST: Our work here is going to be hard. It will stir some things up. Your life is kinda' like this glass, and our work is to get this glass clean. How do you suppose that we could get the mud out of the glass?

CLIENT: We have to scoop it out with this spoon.

THERAPIST: Yep. What will happen?

CLIENT: I can probably get the mud out, but not without getting the water really dirty.

THERAPIST: That is right. Remember that I said that the glass is kinda' like your life? Do you know what I meant by that?

CLIENT: (pointing to the clear water in the glass) Well, now that I am with the Smiths, my life looks pretty good. I have nice clothes, and I get to school on time, and nobody can tell what my life was like before—the water is clear. The mud is hiding down there at the bottom. It is not gone, just not easily seen.

THERAPIST: (nodding) Uh-huh.

CLIENT: (pointing to the mud settled at the bottom of the glass): Except to me—I can only fool myself for a little while. I know that there is a lot of mud down there. I see it. I want it gone, but I don't want to make the water muddy. Then everyone will know that I am a mess, and it will really hurt.

THERAPIST: It will probably hurt more than it does now. You are right. What if scooping it out could make an extraordinary difference for you? What if getting the water messy was worth it?

CLIENT: I see that the only way to get the glass clean is to make the water a mess. All of the stuff about my real mom and her house will be right on the surface. It is scary, but I really want to stop having to hide who I am. It is really important to me. I will do it. (the client began scooping the mud out of the glass)

THERAPIST: That's cool. I want you to know how much your courage inspires me. And that is what I want for you too. I want to do everything I can do to help you work for a life where you can be with people and not have to hide yourself. I also want you to know that whatever pain you go through here, while we are working together, it will always be for that life you are wanting. I know that it is hard to experience that pain, and you just did it while we were cleaning the glass. That is really important.

ACT treatment should be collaborative and the temptation to lecture, advise and direct should be avoided. This seems to be especially true with children. It is often tempting to lead clients, particularly when they do not go along as easily as this girl did. Our clinical experience is that children "disappear" when this type of pressure is applied. While seemingly agreeing to a course of action suggested by the therapist, children will not "own" the course of action and are much more likely to stop when confronted with distressing private content. This client immediately saw the implications and agreed to treatment, even though she understood it would be painful. Other clients struggle with what the treatment process will be like. They may have difficulties understanding the concept of acceptance as an alternative to emotional avoidance, or cling to the idea that the therapy can be successful without hard work and painful experience. In these cases, you should use additional metaphors and exemplars. It is your responsibility to make sure the child and the parents understand that this type of voluntary exposure to painful private content is done in the service of helping the child attain a richer, more satisfying life.

ACT treatment consists of six core clinical components, and the ones we are most inclined to use with children include (1) valuing, (2) acceptance promoting interventions (creative hopelessness, control is the problem, acceptance as an alternative), (3) defusion, and (4) willingness and building patterns of committed action. To date, there are no data that can dictate order or length of time spent on components. Therefore, we allow the direction and shape of therapy to be client-driven and session-specific. It should be noted that we tend to use less of the "contact with the present moment" and "self as context" interventions that are also a central part of ACT. This modification is due the fact that many children are not developmentally ready to tangle with abstract concepts or issues. However, it is important to note that the ACT interventions we use do indeed have an impact on the child's development of self. Choosing and pursuing valued life directions, putting up with painful private content and learning to detach from upsetting feelings and cognitions are all pre-requisite experiences for helping the child develop a robust of self in the present moment as well as contact the sense of safety that resides in more basic forms of consciousness.

Valuing

In ACT, values are conceived as inherently motivating behavioral predispositions that, if properly framed, can serve as a counter-foil to self-defeating forms of emotional avoidance. We often employ values clarification work at the outset of treatment, because it helps establish the motivational framework for confronting distressing private experiences. For example, a child may value developing a stable, supportive peer group at school. In order to work towards that, the child must identify specific behaviors that are consistent with valuing friends. Sharing, listening, and taking turns are all consistent with making friends, while aggression, withdrawal, and interrupting conversations are not. These are not provided to the child as external or rigid rules. Instead, the workability of these ways of being is discussed in relation to whether they move the child towards what he or she values. Moving in a valued direction helps the client develop more adaptive behavioral repertoires, while also serving as a gauge of client progress.

When discussing valued directions with a child, it is important to short circuit talk about whether a valued life end is realistic or not. Instead, you should emphasize that it is not what is immediately possible to achieve that is the focus of treatment, but rather movement in the direction of chosen values. This helps the child learn that many values can never he "achieved" and put in stasis on a trophy shelf. Rather, the function of setting value based goals is to start a journey that may go on for decades. Simple analogies and metaphors can be used to make this point. Too often, children are already being "molded" to believe what they can and can't do in life by friends, family, relatives and teachers. Part of the power of values based work with children is that it can free them from these conceptual shackles, often with surprisingly powerful results.

When children make excessive use of experiential avoidance, it is not only difficult to pursue valued directions but also difficult to even recognize *what* they value. Simply put, short-term reduction of suffering may preclude working towards more distal, yet more potent reinforcement. In this way, values based goal setting may direct and dignify painful experiences in therapy. For example, a child with intense social anxiety may be willing to participate in an exposure exercise in the service of developing meaningful friendships. If this child withdraws socially to reduce anxiety, making friends becomes impossible.

Although the act of valuing is rather complicated and abstract, even for adults, it is crucial to the treatment. To help children comprehend valuing, it is helpful to introduce the concept of vitality. This transcript demonstrates a discussion of valuing with a group of children aged seven to ten:

> THERAPIST: (showing client a picture of a heart) I want you to write down or draw pictures about the important things that our hearts do. I can help you. Our hearts are vital. That means they are very important and keep us alive. Our hearts pump our blood.
>
> CLIENTS: Cool. We need our hearts to keep us alive. Is that what vital means?
>
> THERAPIST: Yes, that is right! (showing client a heart-shaped box) But this kind of heart is different. It keeps you alive in a different way. This kind of heart is about the things that are really important to you. They are not important for keeping your body alive, but they are really important for having and keeping special stuff in your life. This stuff is the people, things, and ideas that you really want in your life because you care about them a lot. These are called your *values*.
>
> CLIENT: My values are the people and things and ideas that are really important to me, like my family or playing ball with my friends every week?
>
> THERAPIST: Yep, those are some of your values. The things that we do that bring us close to our values are vital.
>
> CLIENT: I get it now.
>
> THERAPIST: (*showing client an empty medicine bottle with skull and crossbones on it*) Some things are like poison. They ruin or even kill what is really important to you. I want you to write down or draw pictures of all the things that you have done to fix your problems. Put the papers in the heart-shaped box if they are vital to you. Put them in this bottle with a poison label if they are not vital.

The Valued Living Questionnaire (VLQ; Wilson & Groom, 2002; Wilson & Murrell, in press) is a means to help clients contact their values and has recently been adapted for child, adolescent, and parent populations (Greco, 2002). The adolescent version incorporates teen-friendly instructions, while the parent version assesses how consistently children behave in accordance with their parents' values. It is important to discuss with parents that while inconsistencies between parental and child values may be important to resolve in the long run, they will not be an immediate focus of treatment. ACT treatment initially focuses on the values that the parents can endorse, rather than attempting to reconcile the differences.

Younger children may benefit more from physical metaphors related to valuing than from paper-and-pencil measures. For example, one might use a Velcro target with a label stating the child's value in its center:

> THERAPIST: (giving child a Velcro-covered ball) I want you to imagine that hitting the center of this target means living exactly as your values and your heart would tell you to live. I want you to put the ball on the target according to how things really are going right now.
>
> CLIENT: (placing the ball on the outer ring) Well, I guess about right here. I don't do most of the things that would show me or my family that they are really important to me. I don't spend time with them. I talk-back to my mom a lot. I don't help them out.
>
> THERAPIST: How does that feel—that you are so far away from the bull's-eye?
>
> CLIENT: It makes me feel bad, sad really. It is because I love my family. I value them, and I don't act like it at all.
>
> THERAPIST: Are you willing to do something different, even if it hurts, if there is a possibility that you could have great meaningful relationships with your family members?

Doing values work with children raises some developmental considerations. It is important for all clients, but particularly for young children, to note that values are rewarding but are not the same as rewards. Accordingly, it is necessary to clarify that valuing is not doing something simply to get a reward. Many children, especially those who have previously been in a behavioral treatment program, may state that they find things like video games or extra free time rewarding. While receiving a tangible reward is distinct from valuing, it can be used as an intermediate reinforcement when you are working with the child to develop new, more effective behaviors. For example, aggressive children who value friends may not have the skills to act accordingly. When incorporating values into a skills-training intervention, it may be necessary to provide small tangible reinforcers to help shape appropriate behavior.

Creative Hopelessness

Creative hopelessness is a sub-component of the ACT core process designed to increase acceptance. These interventions typically seek to undermine the dominance of emotional avoidance behaviors. In our work with children, creative hopelessness interventions serve two purposes. First, the therapist must understand and undermine clients' unworkable control strategies. This involves finding out what clients want, how they have tried to get it, and how their strategies are working. By helping children make direct contact with the unworkability of emotional avoidance behaviors, they may be more willing to try alternatives. Paradoxically, recognizing that it is not the child that is hopeless, but the strategies the child is using, can create a basic type of empowerment. This realization, while confusing, gives the child a "space" to move in a new direction. Then, you can begin the second step, which involves helping the child relinquish unworkable solutions.

We have found that some children have difficulty understanding the message of creative hopelessness. Since the child's construction of the problem may be based upon what parents and teachers have said, it may help to approach creative hopelessness from school and home contexts. One way to make contact with creative hopelessness is through activities that incorporate these contexts. This transcript demonstrates the application of creative hopelessness with an 11-year-old child. The child was given a worksheet with two non-gender-specific adults, with speech bubbles above their mouths and heads:

THERAPIST: *(pointing to bubbles)* Fill these in with thoughts and words that the adults in your life think and say about why you are coming to see me.

CHILD: *(pointing to a speech bubble)* Here my mom is saying, "Why are you always so hyper? Can't you sit still, even for one second?"

THERAPIST: Does your mom say that a lot?

CLIENT: All the time.

THERAPIST: What about this other grown-up? Who is this?

CLIENT: My grandma, because we live with her.

THERAPIST: *(pointing to the grandmother figure)* And what goes in these bubbles? What does she think or say about your problems?

CLIENT: *(pointing to thought bubble)* She thinks that my mom and I are going to live with her forever and that she will have to take care of me forever, because I will never be responsible enough to live on my own.

Once the presenting problem has been described, it is crucial to explore the personal thoughts, feelings, and behaviors that the child associates with it. Providing a life-size outline of a child may help. Consider this excerpt from the same session:

THERAPIST: (*showing child the life-size outline*) Now, I want to know what *you* think and feel about why you are here. Draw your thoughts near the head. Draw your feelings near the heart, and draw your behaviors near the hands and feet.

CLIENT: (*client writes in several statements and says*) Ok, I am thinking what a disappointment I am to my mom and my grandma. I am thinking that I never do anything right. I probably will end-up in some crazy hospital, or maybe jail. They are right. I can't take care of myself.

THERAPIST: What about the feelings?

CLIENT: Oh, I am guilty and really, really sad. All the time, well, almost.

THERAPIST: And what about your behavior? What do you do when this problem comes up for you?

Assessing the client's perceived problems in this way opens a discussion about attempted solutions. Through drawings, stories, or role-plays, children may describe all the solutions that they and their caregivers have tried. When children recognize that their strategies are hopeless, emotions surrounding these failures are explored through exposure. This offers opportunity for defusion and acceptance as well.

With older children, this discussion may surface more directly. For example, the parents of a 14-year-old girl often complained because she wore dark clothes and make-up. This caused a great strain in their relationship:

THERAPIST: Is there a reason that you choose such dark clothes and makeup?

CLIENT: I dress the way I feel. Ever since I can remember I have been depressed. I try hard to feel better, but nothing ever works. I just am not one of those people who have things turn out right for them. No matter what I do, it is useless.

She had tried drugs, alcohol, running away, skipping school, and had attempted suicide. She had also tried thinking positively and being compliant with treatment and her parents. Her emotions surrounding these unworkable solutions were extremely intense. She shook and cried through all of the first several sessions. This girl had attempted to get rid of her aversive internal experiences for a long time. During a creative hopelessness exercise, she recognized that moving towards these experiences might create more flexibility in how she lived. As she experienced what creative hopelessness meant, she spontaneously reported that for the first time, she had power in her own life.

Control Is the Problem

Most of the time, problematic childhood behaviors are just ill fated efforts to avoid or control unwanted private experiences. During this phase, you will try to help children understand the basic paradox of emotional control strategies: the more you use them, the more out of control things become. We focus on helping children directly experience how control strategies may work well in the short term but poorly in the long term. Because of the importance of peer pressure in children's social environment, it is also important to have clients understand that emotional control strategies are often learned from the culture rather than from personal experience. For example, our culture emphasizes that boys do not cry; that the proper response is to be "macho" and keep one's feelings buried inside. Boys who feel sad and want to cry may be left feeling like something is wrong with them. They may begin searching for ways to get rid of feeling sad and wanting to cry and this starts an unworkable process that makes such emotional experiences seem even more powerful and intimidating

Several metaphors and exercises described in the first ACT book (Hayes, Strosahl & Wilson, 1999) are especially useful with children. For example, many young clients enjoy the (don't think about) *Chocolate Cake* experiential exercise (Hayes et al., 1999, p. 124) and may be capable of generalizing it to other content, such as self-deprecating thoughts or sad feelings. The *Box of Stuff* metaphor (Hayes et al., 1999, p. 136) may also be appropriate. To make the exercise more concrete, you can use an actual box in which to place items symbolizing content from the client's life. Content is derived from the client's history and experiences, and there is usually something (usually an unwanted event or private experience) that the client wants to remove from the box. However, efforts to remove any unacceptable item themselves can be physicalized, put on paper and placed in the box. The following transcript demonstrates the use of this modified metaphor with a 15 year-old boy.

THERAPIST: (*placing an empty tissue box in front of the client*) This box represents your life.

CLIENT: (*very sarcastically*) Ok. That's pretty weird.

THERAPIST: I get that it seems silly to you. There might be something important that we can do here. Are you willing to try something with me?

CLIENT: (*again sarcastically and with a sigh*) I said ok.

THERAPIST: Well, I don't want to make you do anything. This is your treatment. I think that it might be useful, but this is up to you.

CLIENT: (*picking up the box and smirking*) Ok. So, this represents my life in some way. I don't get it, but I will play along.

THERAPIST: (*scribbles on some paper and hands to client*) These papers represent your mom and dad's divorce papers. They go in the box.

CLIENT: No way! It is my life, not theirs. I am not putting that in there.

THERAPIST: Your parents' divorce happened to you too. We can not change the things that happened in your life. Please, put them in the box.

CLIENT: (*throws papers on floor*) I don't want that in my life.

THERAPIST: I understand, and I understand that you probably don't like to think about the divorce.

CLIENT: No. I really don't. I would rather just throw those away.

THERAPIST: Yeah. I can tell. You looked pretty angry when you threw those papers. They represent some experience that is part of your life, so they go in your box.

CLIENT: (*putting the papers in the box*) Well, I am going to fold them up and stick them back here in the corner, that way I don't have to look at them or think about it.

THERAPIST: What else do you do when you don't want to think about the divorce, or other things?

CLIENT: Sneak out with my friends and go drinking. I regret it later, though. Even if I don't get caught, I feel bad anyway.

THERAPIST: Hmm. Let's write that down. It goes in your box too.

This continued for some time until the client had listed several avoidance strategies.

CLIENT: The box is jammed full.

THERAPIST: I see. I wonder if sometimes you feel like that—all jammed up with no room to move in a valued direction?

The *Mule in the Well* story also may lend itself to use with children and adolescents. In this story, a farmer has an old, useless mule that falls into a dry, abandoned well. Upon realizing that he is stuck, the mule becomes afraid and begins to bray. The farmer, who hears the mule crying, decides that instead of pulling him out, he will just bury the creature in the well. As the farmer shovels dirt into the well, the mule realizes that he is being buried alive. He shivers and shudders, shaking the dirt from his shoulders to down around his feet. He steps up on top of the dirt. The farmer continues to shovel, and the mule continues to shake and step up and up, eventually stepping right out of the well. The therapist helps children understand that the mule could not have gotten out without the very thing that was burying him alive.

Control strategies may also be physicalized with children as a type of game. To illustrate this, we have created a board game. Children roll dice to move through the game, landing on spaces designated either for answering questions, or for doing a role-play. A question card might say, "What do you do when you are scared?" or "How do you act when you don't get your way?" Examples of action cards should include things like "Act cool," "Act out being polite," and "Act mean." We tell clients that to earn a chip, they must tell whether their responses bring them closer or move them further away from what really matters to them. The chips serve as intermediate reinforcements and can be redeemed for candy, playtime, or some other reward after the game is over.

Such exercises help children understand that "being" involves choosing actions that vary on the line of workability. Moreover, children begin to make contact with the underlying function of such actions. For example, we had a group of 6 children, aged six to nine, play the game described above while discussing bullies at school (a topic suggested by the school principal). Several of the children acknowledged that they acted in some way to conceal a different emotion. One 7-year-old girl said that when she was afraid, she acted like a "tough-bully." She stated that she "argued and beat people up." A 9-year-old boy stated that he was an "clever-bully." He described this as blurting out answers in class to make other children feel less intelligent, in order to feel better about himself. An 8 year-old girl, said that she was a "trendy-bully." When asked to describe what she meant, she told the group that she dressed in fashionable clothing in order to make people like her. When asked about bullying, the girl described herself as "snobby" to other children, especially girls. She stated that she acted as if she were superior to them, making it seem as if she did not care if they liked her.

In a similar exercise, we gave these same children masks showing various easily recognizable emotions. We then asked the children to take turns wearing them and verbalizing what they thought the person in the mask would say. They were able to recognize that many children and adults act like different kinds of bullies but only because they all are afraid of being inferior and unloved. Then the children collectively (without any prompting from the therapist) said, "It is really sad, because even though you want people to like you they won't, because you act bad trying to get them to like you."

Cognitive Defusion

Like their adult counter-parts, children often respond to thoughts and feelings as though they are literally true. For example, if a client had the thought, "I am stupid," he or she might avoid all situations eliciting that thought. Of course, such a response would prevent the individual from discovering, based on their own experience, that he or she could be successful. One objective of this treatment component is to teach children to discriminate between verbal content (including thoughts) and their direct experience. As children progress into middle adolescence, we begin employing cognitive defusion to help them differentiate their views of self from verbal content and to begin making the discrimination between self-as-content and self-as-context. This is particularly important with respect to evaluation and behavioral responses to evaluation. For example, teenagers may choose *looking* good by wearing the "right" clothes, having the "right" friends, and so on to please their peer groups. This stands in contrast to *being* good, or treating others with kindness, and valuing friends for who they are rather than for the external trappings of popularity.

This component entails a great deal of exposure to avoided content and experiences. Experiential exercises, such as *Milk, milk, milk* (Hayes et al., 1999, p. 154), are great ways to show children how the psychological meaning attached to verbal content can be easily and artificially altered. This exercise helps clients understand that through experience, verbal content may lose its psychological functions.

Assisting clients in recognizing that they can view thoughts as thoughts is an important piece of deliteralization and defusion. The following exercise conducted with a group of 6- to 10-year-old children introduces minds and how they work:

> THERAPIST: Our minds are kind of like symbols for our brains. Sometimes we need them, like for figuring out math problems. Sometimes we really don't need them, like to know that we love our families, or to be glad to see a really pretty sunset. Please, make a list of things that you do need your mind for and make another list of the things that you do not need your mind to figure out.
>
> CLIENT 1: I need my mind to figure out the way for me to walk home. I don't need my mind to know that I love spending time with my best friend.
>
> THERAPIST: Ok, good. Keep going. Anybody else?
>
> CLIENT 2: I don't need my mind to tell me whether or not my parents love me. I can just feel it in my heart.
>
> THERAPIST: You guys are doing a great job.
>
> CLIENT 3: Sometimes I think that I need my mind, but it doesn't help me.
>
> THERAPIST: What do you mean? Can you tell us a time that that happened?
>
> CLIENT 3: Sure, just yesterday. I was trying to figure out if I should

tell my teacher that my friend in my class told me that his mom and dad both hit him last week.

THERAPIST: What was going on in your mind?

CLIENT: Well, I was thinking all the things that might happen-like my friend could get mad at me and not be my friend. I also thought that if I didn't tell then he could get really hurt.

THERAPIST: You said that it did not help to try to figure it out. Tell us what it was like.

CLIENT: I kept going back and forth about whether or not to tell. I got confused and tired of thinking, and I did not ever feel like I came up with a good answer.

THERAPIST: Sometimes, our minds look for ways that things or situations that are like other things or situations, especially ones that happened to us before or that we think might happen to us. They focus on the past and the future, instead of right now. Our minds talk a lot and try to tell us what to do and whether something is good or bad for us. That is called evaluation. You can tell your mind is working really hard if you have been trying to figure out something for a long time and you still don't have an answer.

The therapist can adapt the *Taking Your Mind for a Walk* exercise (Hayes et al., 1999, p. 162) by having clients draw a little comic strip that has pictures of them and big brains (their minds) with sound bubbles. The title of the comic, to be filled in by the children, can be whatever they value. Children are asked to fill in the bubbles with what their minds say when they voice their intentions to move in the valued direction. Another method is to represent the mind with a superhero action figure ("Super-mind") that tries to save the client (another doll or superhero) from painful feelings but actually prevents the child from doing heroic things. For example, rain is a metaphor for painful psychological content, and Super-mind might prevent the client from getting wet by keeping him or her inside at all times, even when the chance of rain is minimal. Meanwhile, whole villages may need saving, but the Super-mind is too busy protecting the child for him to save anyone.

It is helpful to assist clients in recalling painful experiences and to distinguish between evaluations of those experiences versus actual outcomes. The therapist can ask questions like, "What does your mind say to you if you make a bad grade even after you studied?", or "What did your mind do when your teacher says that you are really smart?" Eliciting reactions to these questions helps distinguish verbal content from experience. Moreover, it introduces the idea that behaviors do not have to be dictated by what our minds say to us.

Willingness and Committed Action

We focus considerable attention on getting children to understand that willingness to make room for feared content in the service of a valued goal is the alternative to their unworkable patterns of experiential avoidance. You will also want to emphasize that taking this alternative step is a choice. It is not something the client "has" to do. When the client perceives this form of exposure as a choice, then the context for contacting feared experiences is altered. Clients realize that they do not "have to" avoid struggle, and they may choose willingness to experience suffering if it is in the service of some value(s).

For example, we often use the following analogy to highlight the distinction between being willing (a choice) and wanting an unpleasant experience (an evaluation) and how it affects the ultimate quality of an experience. Suppose your school friends dragged you onto a very tall, scary roller coaster against your will. That would probably create fear that would be pretty hard to handle because you had not chosen to go on the ride. Now, suppose you made the choice on your own to ride the coaster, and made up your mind to step into the car without being forced by any-one. Then, you might still be afraid of that coaster because it is very tall, but you might also be excited or wonder what it will be like to be on this ride. In other words, your fear would feel different and you might have more experiences to report after the ride. We make a point of emphasizing the child's right to choose because that prerogative is often not available in the lives of children. This type of analogy also demonstrates that will-ingness and committed action are ongoing processes and that it is OK to have second thoughts, painful feelings and keep moving in the direction of a commitment. The following transcript demonstrates the application of these principles with a 10-year-old boy.

CLIENT: I feel like I am spiraling down a slippery slide. I want to climb up to a better place, but it is really hard to climb up a slide like that. I am committed to doing that, though.

THERAPIST: Yeah, that will be really hard, and you will almost cer-tainly fall and need to get up again. I think that it is very interesting that you did not even think about the steps to the slide. Sometimes different behaviors that are totally new, and maybe more vital, do not even occur to us as possible routes.

CLIENT (*who now was crying*): I never thought of it that way before. I really am committed to getting up, even if it means falling off. I am committing to make a difference for myself and for my younger sister.

Exposure exercises that focus on real and imagined failures to keep commitments are useful when working with children. Children and adolescents can be asked to write or tell a story about failing to live their values. The story can then be used to help structure exposure based interventions. For example, the following interaction involved a socially anxious adolescent who continually made commitments to build close friendships that she did not keep. When she had identified this behavior pattern as familiar and quite exhausting for her, she was asked to imagine two scenarios, described by the therapist as follows:

THERAPIST: (*following a brief mind clearing exercise*) Imagine that you are at your graduation with a lot of people who really know you. The person on either side of you is one of your friends, and you can look into the eyes of each person and see their warmth and pride in you. Imagine looking into the crowd and seeing a few people who are your closest friends. Imagine looking into the eyes of each person and understanding that they are with you, that they know everything that you are, and that there is nothing left for you to hide. Imagine them knowing you, knowing about your deepest fears and failings, and standing for you as your name is called and you stand and walk up to the podium to gather your diploma. Imagine that as your diploma is placed into your hands, the world lies open to you, and you may go in any direction that you choose. Now imagine looking down into the sea of faces—people who you know who have made this journey with you, to find your parents' faces, and as you look at them, you see them full of pride. Imagine holding their gaze and letting them see how hard this journey has been, and let them see that you have chosen a life that is important to you . . .

THERAPIST: (*after a brief transitional exercise*): Now imagine that you are at your graduation, but it is a different graduation. You are sitting alone in a sea of people who are strangers. You have seen the people sitting on either side of you, but you can't remember their names. The time has passed for getting to know them, and for them to know you, as though a door had closed. You are afraid to look at them, afraid to meet their eyes, so you look at your feet, and wait, dreading the moment when your name is called. You hear the people in your row begin to rise and walk towards the podium, and you know your turn is coming. You hear laughing, and wonder, are they laughing at me? Now imagine that your name is called, and you need to stand and walk to the podium, but you are so afraid that you can't make your feet move. But you have to get up or people will see how afraid you are—with great effort, you rise up, your heart is beating fast,

and you keep your eyes straight ahead—you do not look anyone in
the eye. Your parents have come, but you are too afraid to search
them out in the crowd.

THERAPIST: In a world where you could choose your graduation,
which one would you choose?"

CLIENT: The first one.

THERAPIST: What if it was possible to have that graduation, but you
had to have anxiety every day to get it—would that be worth it?

CLIENT: (*brief hesitation*) If that's what it takes, yeah. I would do that.

Making commitments concrete by writing them down and having the
client share them with parents, teachers, friends, and others often helps
maintain resolve follow through on commitments. One way to enlist this
type of social support involves "team building." In this approach, children
state their commitments out loud to important others who are asked to
provide help in any way that is reasonable. We have used this intervention
with several children and adolescents who have school-related difficulties.
The clients created their personal teams by asking the important people
in their lives, including family members and teachers, to support them
in becoming extraordinary students. It is beneficial to have children list
specific, operationalized behaviors that they and their parents can monitor.
In addition, children are asked to have each member of the support team
state what they are prepared to do to support the child in following through
with commitments.

CLINICAL CONSIDERATIONS

Working with Parents

When using ACT with children, it is typically helpful to engage their
parents (for more on this issue see the child section of Chapter 13). Most
behavioral and cognitive-behavioral therapies for children incorporate explicitly defined roles for their parents. Some require that parents assist
in altering the environmental contingencies purported to maintain problematic behaviors. Others cast them as members of a "team" relied on
for encouragement and support as a child progresses through sometimes
challenging treatments (e.g., March & Mulle, 1998).

We believe that parents' values and vulnerabilities play a huge role in
determining parenting behaviors, although these are often left untouched
in many existing parent-training programs for children. Since humans are
verbal creatures, we can expect that parenting behaviors are entangled

in our verbal knowing about them. Parenting research has shown that parents are sometimes like broken records: they continue doing the same things over and over—and continue to escalate them—even though they do not accomplish desired goals, such as attaining child compliance. In fact, impaired parents may continue to use these behaviors even when the actual result is an escalation of child behavior. While skills deficits certainly play a key role in impaired parenting, one might consider by what process or processes this occurs.

The narrowing of parenting repertoires may be the result of a narrow learning history, poor role models, or cultural support for negative parenting habits. In clinical work, we have also been impressed with the impact of cognitive fusion and its detrimental effects on positive parenting practices. For example, a parent may equate the following: My child is misbehaving now = he's bad; He won't listen = I'm bad. When such equivalence classes are formed and fused with, parents may engage in the same narrow repertoire with more vigor because more is at stake psychologically. When the strategies continue to misfire, the parent may think, "I'm working so hard at this, and I just can't do it. I'm a terrible parent." So parents respond not only to a child's behavior, but also to a network of psychological meanings that those behaviors stimulate, many of which are provocative and evocative in nature. Running on this psychological treadmill may promote emotional avoidance of these painful internal stimuli as well as the situations that elicit them (e.g., troublesome behavior by the child). Thus, many negative parenting behaviors that have been attributed to skills deficits may in fact function in the service of emotional avoidance and control of painful psychological events.

ACT offers many tools to address the verbal context in which parenting occurs. ACT interventions with parents can be used alone (e.g., Blackledge, 2004) or in conjunction with skills training programs (e.g., Singer, Irvine, & Irvin, 1989). Experiential exercises may be used to identify potentially problematic psychological content that impacts parenting practices in difficult situations. For example, values work may help to marshal a potent, longer term value that may help to focus parents' treatment efforts. Parents might be asked: "What if it were possible to help my child have a bigger, more meaningful, richer life than I did? Creative hopelessness may be used to bring parents into direct experiential contact with the hopelessness of avoidance and control based parenting practices, so as to encourage them to "drop the shovel" (*Person in the Hole Metaphor,* Hayes et al., 1999, p. 101). When confronted with emotionally laded, difficult interactions with their child, parents can use defusion strategies to maintain awareness of thoughts, evaluations and emotions without necessarily having to response to them. ACT acceptance/willingness interventions may augment parents' ability to do what needs to be done "in the moment", rather than act to avoid painful content that is elicited by child behaviors. Finally, committed action strategies may help foster treatment compliance and encourage a flexible and responsive behavioral posture towards parenting. Although parents may not know exactly what to do when new difficult behaviors arise, if they are committed to pursuing valued goals as parents, it is unlikely they will return as easily to negative parenting practices.

Lack of Generalization

It may be difficult for children to generalize information from one set of circumstances to the next. For example, a group participant might really "get it" one week and not the next. Multiple exercises, analogies, and metaphors are commonly used to target a core ACT process and the need for this type of repetition is even greater with children. This leads to a common clinical error that you should try to avoid: Lecturing on an ACT principle out of frustration that the child is not "getting it" across functionally similar, but superficially different situation. In a similar vein, it is often tempting to get very directive with a child and to try to dictate the form of a behavioral goal. Our clinical experience suggests that it is extremely important to allow children to make discoveries at their own pace. In order to be consistent with the model, a child should repeatedly be exposed to direct experience and permitted to draw personal conclusions. Many therapists have a "soft-spot" for children, which may actually impair the ability to "let the treatment take its course." As therapist, you should be on guard for the temptation to take over control of the treatment process, a move that will only make your client more withdrawn and passive.

Control Over Life

Another issue unique to children involves how little control they have over their everyday lives. Adults have more flexibility to respond when they realize that something is not working in the service of living their values. For example, a 14-year-old girl placed great importance on spirituality, and in particular, on practicing a certain religion. She knew what she valued and was prepared to live accordingly. However, her parents felt that her spiritual and religious choices were inappropriate, and required their daughter to attend their church. They prevented the child from worshipping and practicing religion as she wanted, and punished her when she failed to attend their church. The girl was distressed and offended by the teachings of her parents' religion. They conflicted with her values about relationships with other people and education. Even though the therapist and the child discussed these issues with her parents, they were unmoved. Remaining sessions were spent discussing what this meant for the client. While this eliminated some of her distress, she still was unable to live her spiritual and religious values fully, certainly not with respect to specific daily practices.

Child Abuse and Neglect

A related and very complex issue that may arise during treatment is the suspicion or tangible evidence of child abuse or neglect. Legal and ethical guidelines require that abusive and neglectful situations be reported to the appropriate authorities. It is difficult to empower a client when circumstances dictate that someone other than the child will make major decisions about the child's best interest. Children frequently avoid emotional contact with the experiential aftermath of abuse by fusing with self critical evaluations (i.e., I'm being hit because I deserve it) or proscriptive rule governed responses (i.e., If I love my daddy, I will keep quiet about this). It is a major clinical challenge to assure children that nothing is wrong with them and to tell them that they have the power to make choices and changes about their lives; when, in actuality, they do not have the power to do so. It does not seem to matter what the therapist's intention is, or how the report is worded or discussed with the child. At least initially, there is a distance created.

The following therapy exchange occurred when an 8-year-old client revealed after 5 months of therapy that she was being physically abused by her adoptive mother.

> THERAPIST: Sally, what happened here (pointing to red handprints and bruises on the client's arms and face)?
>
> CLIENT: Mom got really mad last night, because I wouldn't go to sleep. She came in about 10:00 to see if I was asleep, and I wasn't. She was really angry. I should have been asleep; my bedtime is 8:30. Anyway, she grabbed me out of the bed. She was yelling a whole lot and she shook me and slapped me too. It was pretty bad. I thought that she was going to go away, but she didn't. She just started slapping me again. She did it a whole lot, more than usual. Please, please, don't tell though. I can handle it. Please don't tell. I will just get taken away again.

This child had been in several foster homes, had even been adopted and then returned to foster care twice. She was fused with the belief that her parents were the only ones who cared about her, and the therapist suddenly became the enemy. Months had been spent supporting this child in seeing that she was not bad or unworthy of love—seeing that she had everything that she needed to live a meaningful valued life. All of these clinical gains were compromised as soon as the child reported the abuse. She "knew" it.

> THERAPIST: I am sorry that you feel like I betrayed you. I had to tell. It is the law, but I also would do whatever I have to do to keep you safe.
>
> CLIENT: I know. It isn't your fault. I am bad. I am bad for letting my mom hit me. I should not have been awake at 10:00. I shouldn't have told you either. That was stupid. I was stupid to tell you. I knew that I could not trust you not to tell.

This child felt that she was bad, because only mean people (i.e., the mother who abused her) and people she could not trust (i.e., the therapist who reported it) could love her. This was an extremely difficult therapeutic moment. Whereas some children view the act of reporting as an indication of their value as people, this was not immediately evident to the child. It took several months before the therapist and the child were able to work together in a meaningful way.

Defining Clinical "Success"

The clinical examples described in this section highlight a major issue in relation to assessing progress in ACT with children: sometimes environmental constraints or risks are so overwhelming that the best immediate result is to keep the client from deteriorating or to find some glimmer of personal valued action in an otherwise repressive situation. In these cases, the "results" of treatment may not be immediately seen or easily quantified. In fact, in some cases, parental ratings of child behavior may actually worsen as the child becomes more autonomous. Despite this, even though they may not come to fruition for months or years, a real and meaningful difference may have occurred for the client. To ignore this reality of childhood existence and look *only* for short term indicators of success is a mistake. Instead, progress needs to be examined in a broad context.

SUMMARY

ACT work with children and adolescents is just beginning, and it is an empirical question whether the core clinical processes and associated interventions of ACT will prove successful children. There are some understandable, although unfounded, concerns about the applicability of ACT with children. In general, critics of ACT may feel that it is limited to clients who are intelligent, insightful, verbal, and so on. Previous research, however, has shown that ACT has produced positive results with clients having clear cognitive impairments (e.g., Bach & Hayes, 2002). Furthermore, ACT relies on experiential exercises and metaphors to teach concepts that are often difficult to put into language—precisely the approach used in the education of young children. These features make it relatively easy to target ACT toward children.

A related concern may be that ACT is too complex or esoteric a treatment for children. However, children's relational learning is based in the same processes as observed in adults (e.g., Lipkens, Hayes, & Hayes, 1993). It is reasonable to assume that children acquire many of the same rules as adults, because all adults were at some point children. Therefore, we would expect that many of the culturally promoted rules about health, suffering, emotional distress and what to do about it will be operative in children, albeit perhaps at a more concrete, simplistic level. This may actually be a clinical advantage in that adults have had years to "practice" these unworkable rules and have integrated them into the context of reason giving. Children, on the other hand, are relative "newcomers" to these rules and the unworkable strategies they generate. For that reason, it would not be surprising if ACT results are even stronger with children and adolescents.

Empirical ACT work is underway with children in several locations around the world, so we will soon know how well ACT works with this population. Meanwhile there are a number of empirical reasons to suspect that the ACT model applies to children (e.g., Greco & Eifert, 2004) and we have some limited evidence that it applies to parents (e.g., Blackledge, 2004; Singer et al., 1989). This chapter will hopefully empower clinicians to begin to find ways to apply ACT techniques and principles to this important population.

Table 10.1. Issues and Treatment Implications of ACT with Children, Adolescents, and Parents

Clinical issues	Treatment implications
Parents are discouraged if they do not see immediate improvement in child's behavior or emotional state	Assist with consideration and choice of treatment-related values (i.e., FEELING well and living well as compared to feeling WELL looking good, etc.) Use mud-in-glass and/or exercise metaphor (sometimes it hurts AND there is possibility of something useful if willing)
Client who does not wish to be in therapy—parents want the child/adolescent to receive services but he or she does not want to be there	Discuss with parents that client's willingness may affect treatment process and outcome Assist and support client in standing for self and choosing personal treatment direction—make discrimination between forced and chosen ways to spend sessions Use response-ability focus Values clarification exercises
Client chooses an approach that is aimed at a bigger more meaningful life and begins the work (acceptance, mindfulness, valuing) but retreats to a symptom removal focus when treatment becomes more difficult	Question usefulness/workability of control strategies and return to willingness Use tug-of-war with monster metaphor Use box-of-stuff metaphor
Client is fused with negative content	Expand experience Make reference to thoughts as behavior not real and causal entities Defuse with the milk exercise
Client says that he or she does not understand	Look for lack of understanding as avoidance and address willingness State things in a number of developmentally appropriate ways, especially using client-relevant metaphors and exemplars Use person in the hole metaphor
Client says that he or she values having something, being something, or doing something that is perceived by the therapist as different from client's valuing (e.g., having money, being cool, doing well at video games—all for their own sakes when client has revealed or alluded to wanting more)	Assume that clients' values are perfect and that there is a potential (not definite) "deeper" value Discriminate between wanting or liking and meaningful action in the service of what the client matters about Discriminate between goals, which may or may not be consistent with valuing, and valuing itself Attempt to trace reported value backwards by asking questions like, "What is important about being cool?" Use tombstone metaphor

Table 10.1. (*Continued*)

Clinical issues	Treatment implications
Client reports not caring about anything	Assume that clients' values are perfect and that there is a potential (not definite) unreported caring Assess functional avoidance Discriminate between willingness to care, especially aloud, and believing that its outcome will be a certain way Choosing not to choose Tombstone metaphor
Parents are convinced that the child/adolescent client has problems that need to be treated while the client and the therapist do not perceive treatment as necessary	Consider termination of treatment with the child/adolescent as the identified client Assessment work with parents to examine possibility of own distress, especially in the context of parenting (treat or refer as appropriate and necessary) Emphasis on values and control is problem

Chapter 11

ACT for Stress

FRANK W. BOND

The purpose of this chapter is to show how Acceptance and Commitment Therapy (ACT; Hayes, Strosahl, & Wilson, 1999) can be used to reduce stress. Stress has generally been conceptualized as a relational context in which people believe that a particular event threatens their well being, because they evaluate it as taxing, or exceeding, their coping resources (e.g., Lazarus & Folkman, 1984). Based on this view, stress interventions have either targeted the *stressor* (the event itself) or the *evaluation of the stressor* as a threat to well-being and one's ability to cope with it. While primarily focused on the latter target, ACT can be used to address them both.

There are a multitude of situations, both traumatic and routine, that may elicit a stress response, but perhaps the most ubiquitous ones center around the workplace. Organizational psychologists have identified a number of work related stressors that reliably predict negative psychological and behavioral phenomena (e.g., anxiety, loss of productivity and absenteeism). These stressors include a lack of job control, poor social support, role conflicts, and work overload (e.g., Cox, Griffiths, Barlowe, Randall, Thomson, & Rial-Gonzalez, 2000). I will use work-related stress as an archetype both because it is common and because it allows some discussion of the use of ACT in organizations—itself an important topic. You can apply the ACT intervention strategies described here to almost type of stressful situation, however.

The breadth and impact of work-related stress is difficult to underestimate. Research from the United Kingdom's (UK's) Health and Safety Executive (2003) shows that one in five workers report that they are seriously affected by work-related stress. A ten year prospective cohort study of initially healthy workers revealed that those who experienced high job demands coupled with little job control—perhaps the most serious combination of work-related stressors—had double the risk of death from cardiovascular disease, compared with people who did not work under these stressors (Kivimaki, Leino-Arjas, Luukkonen, Riihimaki, Vahtera, & Kirjonen, 2003).

Research on the use of ACT for worksite stress is young, but the initial results are promising. Bond and Bunce (2000) compared the effects of a brief ACT intervention to a wait-list control group and a training program that taught workers how to reduce stressors at their source in a large UK media organization. The ACT intervention (Bond & Hayes, 2002) was group-based (see Chapter 14) and followed the "2+1" method of brief psychotherapy delivery (e.g., Barkham & Shapiro, 1990) in which participants receive three, three-hour sessions: two on consecutive weeks, and a third three months later. This format allows clients to practice ACT techniques in their work environments and troubleshoot problems in the final session. We will describe the content of the protocol later in the chapter.

Results indicated that ACT improved employees' general mental health, depression, and their propensity to initiate innovations at work, relative to the control group. In accord with an ACT model, process analyses demonstrated that ACT produced its improvements by increasing psychological acceptance and increasing participant's ability to act on their values, not by changing the content of people's thoughts. Indeed, there was no significant pre-test/post-test change for the ACT group on cognitive content. Thus, it seemed that psychological flexibility (see Chapter 1) was the mediator through which ACT altered worksite stress.

A second randomized controlled trial targeted burnout in drug and alcohol counselors (Hayes, Bissett et al. in press). Using a one-day six-hour workshop, ACT was compared to a control training (on methamphetamine abuse) and to multicultural counseling. ACT had a greater effect than the comparison conditions on worksite burnout, and process analysis showed that the effect occurred because of significantly reduced fusion with negative thoughts about difficult clients in the ACT condition.

There is also correlational support for an ACT approach to stress in the workplace. A worksite study using the Acceptance and Action Questionnaire (Hayes, Strosahl et al., in press) showed that higher levels of psychological flexibility predict, one year later, better mental health and improved job performance (using overt, behavioral measures as well as self-report) amongst telephone call-center operators in a UK financial organization (Bond & Bunce, 2003). This effect occurred even after controlling for three other variables that are traditionally linked to work-related mental health and performance: locus of control, negative affectivity

(Jex, 1998), and job control (Terry & Jimmieson, 1999). Thus, several items of evidence suggest that an ACT approach might be useful, in the treatment of stress.

AN ACT CONCEPTUALIZATION OF STRESS: CONTEXT OVER CONTENT

Traditional cognitive-behavioral therapy (CBT) approaches to treating stress-related problems have focused on identifying and challenging the distortions in people's cognitive content; that is, in what their beliefs say regarding their coping abilities and/or what affects their well-being. In contrast, ACT argues that no matter how distorted one's cognitive content might be (e.g., "I can't cope with this"; "I'm not going to be able to work here anymore"), it will not *directly* lead to stress-related disorders, such as mental illnesses, musculoskeletal disorders, ulcers, and cardiovascular disease. Rather, it is only when people hold this distorted cognitive content in a specific *context* that it will have harmful emotional, physiological, behavioral, and (even) cognitive effects. This harmful context is one in which people (1) are *fused* with, or completely buy into, the literal meaning of their cognitive content (e.g., if I have the thought, "I am a fool", then I am really a fool); that is, they cannot see this content as an essentially automatic, idiosyncratic reaction to certain types of stressors; and, (2) they *avoid the experiences* that come about, in response to their (distorted) cognitive content (e.g., anxiety). This context of cognitive fusion and experiential avoidance is as much the "cause" of stress as a stressor itself, because it helps to determine whether experience with one stressor (e.g., an unexpected job assignment that the person evaluates in a cognitively fused way as "not fair"), leads to stressful reactions (e.g., anxiety and anger) and even additional stressors (e.g., wanting to quit work, wanting to verbally attack supervisors).

The other aspect of an ACT conceptualization of stress is values. In order to accept (i.e., not experientially avoid) and move through stressors, there needs to be a reason for doing so. Just coping with stressors for the sake of coping is an unfulfilling enterprise. When people succumb to stressors and stress and engage in avoidance actions, they generally are not behaving in line with their values, often, perhaps, because these are vague and poorly articulated. To the extent that a worker is not aware of his or her personal values, there is a greater likelihood of falling prey to a negative stress response. Thus, we have the familiar ACT litany fully present in stress: fusion with unwanted private content, experientially avoidant coping strategies, and a lack of defined valued directions, together working to conjure up an unmanageable stress response. Thus, the goal of ACT for stress should be to teach people the following strategies: cognitive defusion;

the acceptance of, rather than the avoidance of, challenging events and the private experiences (e.g., anxiety) they stimulate; and, the ability to define values and engage in stress management behaviors that are consistent with those values.

An ACT Intervention Program for Stress

We have developed a validated (Bond & Bunce, 2000) group treatment protocol that applies this model to stress using an integrated sequence of ACT concepts, exercises, and interventions. The protocol is detailed in relatively brief form in Table 11.1. Because it is time-limited (a total of nine hours in three sessions) key ACT components are delivered in a very efficient form.

Assessing and Promoting Motivation to Change

We begin by having people consider the effectiveness and workability of altering noxious internal events that their stressors occasion. Only when people see the futility and damage of unworkable fusion-produced avoidance strategies, will they be keen to entertain alternative coping techniques that exist outside of the context of fusion.

To start session one, participants are informed that any personal information that is revealed or discussed in this or any session is confidential, and they should not share or discuss it with anyone at all outside of the room, including partners and family members. If anyone is not prepared to make such a commitment to privacy, then they are asked kindly to leave. After laying these and other basic ground rules, the trainer asks the group, "What are your symptoms, or signs, of work stress or stress in general?" Responses are noted on a white board. After several people provide some examples, a slide describing various symptoms of stress is presented. This slide notes many physical (e.g., sleep loss), mood (e.g., irritability), thinking (e.g., worry), and action signs (e.g., overeating) of stress. The following narrative would not be unusual at this point in the session

> TRAINER: Is anyone willing to discuss their symptoms of stress?
> PARTICIPANT: I know I'm stressed when I start to worry. I can worry about anything, but I particularly worry about not meeting my work targets, and this gets my stomach in knots, and I can even have difficulty sleeping if the worry is particularly bad.
> TRAINER: Have you tried to do anything to stop worrying and sleep better?

Table 11.1. The Order of ACT Stress Intervention Techniques, and Their
Clinical Goals

Clinical goals	Intervention techniques
Creative hopelessness	Questioning workability *"... And how has that worked for you?"*
Control is the problem	The paradox of control *"If you aren't willing to have it, you've got it."* Consequences of control *Polygraph metaphor*
Defusion/Acceptance	Costs of low willingness *Clean vs. dirty discomfort* Willingness as full experience *Quicksand metaphor* Just noticing exercise *Leaves on the stream* Identifying stress buttons *Write down stressors or triggers for stress. Used for homework* Buying thoughts *Blondes have more...*
(Session 2)	Get off your buts *Replace self-referential uses of "but" with "and".* Observer exercise *Promoting self as context* The willingness question *Promoting goal-directed action with willingness* Tin can monster exercise *Promote willingness of difficult internal events*
Values-based action	Eulogy *Write down what you would have wanted to stand for and be,* *once you were dead.* Values clarification *List values in work and personal domains.* The willingness question *Promoting goal-directed action with willingness.*
(Session 3)	The observer and tin can monster exercises are firstly repeated.
Willingness as a values-based action	Bubble in the road metaphor *Action with willingness* Goal, Action, and Barrier clarification *List value-directed goals, and the barriers to taking actions to* *accomplish them.* Public commitment to values *State intentions to valued-directed actions.*

PARTICIPANT: Oh, loads of things: I've tried to talk myself out of the worry by "thinking things through," going to the gym, playing with my boys.

TRAINER: Right. Good. Let me ask you this. Your mind says, "think things through, play with your kids, keep fit, and then you won't worry." Right?

PARTICIPANT: Absolutely.

TRAINER: OK, and how has that worked? For example, as you've done what your mind has told you to do, have you been able to stop worrying or even worry less; and, have you then been able to enjoy or be involved more fully in what you need to do?

PARTICIPANT: Sometimes, but not always, and even if I can stop worrying, it's only very temporarily.

TRAINER: Right, so, overall, would you say that you've been able to stop worrying unnecessarily.

PARTICIPANT: Not at all: I spend so much time trying to stop worrying that I become exhausted and can't focus on doing my job well, or even enjoying playing with my boys.

TRAINER: Isn't that interesting? It seems like a paradox, doesn't it? I mean, you do what your mind says: do something to stop worrying, think it through, go to the gym, play with your boys, but it doesn't work. You still worry.

PARTICIPANT: Well, you're right, but what can I do?

TRAINER: What does your mind tell you to do?

PARTICIPANT: A lot: relax, eat better, don't bring work home, go on a proper holiday, we even bought a holiday home at the sea last summer...

TRAINER: So, it sounds like you've really tried to feel less stressed?

PARTICIPANT: Too bloody right I have.

TRAINER: I can see that you have; that you have really given it your all. So, I'd like to ask you: 'How have these things worked?' Have your considerable efforts to feel less stressed paid off in a fundamental way, so that by doing them you have transformed the situation and you are no longer bothered by worrying, lack of sleep, or tummy aches? Or are you, unbelievably, sinking in deeper, worrying more, feeling worse?

PARTICIPANT: Oh, I'm definitely worrying more, as I can't seem to do anything to stop fretting.

TRAINER: Incredible, isn't it? I mean if we had an investment advisor with this track record we would have sacked him long ago, but here your mind keeps leading you into efforts that don't really, fundamentally pay off, but it keeps following you around, nattering on, and it is hard not to give it one more go. I mean what else can you do but go along with what your mind tells you to do? But maybe we are coming to a point in which the question will be 'which will you go with, your mind or your experience?'. Up to now, the answer has been 'your mind', but just notice what your experience tells you about how well that has worked.

Conversations such as these are conducted with one, or two, more members of the group, and it is emphasized that listening to one's mind is not always effective in relieving the effects of stress, worry, unhappiness, and the like. Further, it's not even always effective in helping people to achieve the goals that they wish to accomplish. After two or three of these conversations, something like the following is said:

> Isn't this interesting, we do what our mind tells us to do about our thoughts and feelings, but it doesn't seem to help. In fact, it can even make us feel worse. Why is this the case? Well, human language has given us a tremendous advantage as a species, because it allows us to break things down into parts, to formulate plans, to construct futures we have never experienced before, and to plan action. And, it works pretty well. If we look just at the 95% of our existence that involves what goes on outside the skin, it works terrifically. Look at all the things the rest of creation is dealing with and you'll see we do pretty well. Just look around this room; almost everything we see in here wouldn't be here without human language and human rationality: the chairs, the lights, our clothes, the buildings we see outside the windows. So, we are warm, it won't rain on us, we have light and lots of beautiful buildings: with regard to the stuff with which non-humans struggle, we are in good shape, really. You give a dog or a cat all these things: warmth, shelter, food, social stimulation, and they are about as happy as they know how to be.
>
> So, the really important things in our life, important to us as a species competing with other life forms on this planet, have been done with human language. In a very significant way, we human beings realize this, and this realization is encapsulated in a pervasive rule that most all of us buy into: if you don't like something, figure out how to get rid of it and get rid of it. Now, this rule works extremely well in 95% of our life. But, not in the world inside the skin: that last 5%. It's a pretty important 5%, as well, because that is where satisfaction, contentment, and happiness lie. I don't want you to take my word for this; look at your own life, and in your own experience, not in your logical mind, is it not the case that: in the world inside the skin, the rule actually is, if you aren't willing to have it, you've got it.
>
> For example, two of you note that you struggle with worry; you're not willing to have it. But, if it is really, really important not to worry or be anxious, and if you then start to worry or be anxious, that is something to worry and become anxious about. Let's put a name on this phenomenon. Let's say: in the world outside our body, conscious, deliberate, purposeful control works great. So, figure out how to get rid of what you want to get rid of and do it. But in the areas of consciousness, your life history, self, emotions, thoughts, feelings, behavioral predispositions, memories, attitudes,

bodily sensations, and so on, such control often isn't helpful. In this world under our skin, the solution isn't deliberate control, the problem is control. If you try to avoid your own history, your own worries, your own anxiety, depression, and their triggers, you are in a no-win struggle. See, what I am saying here is that we can't effectively and consistently control our thoughts and feelings, or anything that happens under our skin, in our mind, in our body.

At this point, we introduce the *Polygraph Metaphor* to show how attempts to exert conscious, purposeful control over private experience can have the paradoxical effect of increasing unwanted experience (Hayes et al., 1999, pp. 123–124). The purpose of this part of the protocol is to undermine fusion, and augment contact with the costs of experientially avoidant coping behaviors. In individual-based ACT stress treatment, therapists can use all of this information to tailor general ACT principles, and intervention techniques, to the life history, and needs, of individual clients. For example, therapists can help clients consider a number of examples of how their avoidance-type coping strategies have failed to help them to achieve a fulfilled and meaningful life. In group-based ACT, it is more difficult for the therapist/trainer to do such tailoring. However, the previous excerpt should show how this strategy of focusing on workability can help participants to develop their own formulation as to the consequences of their experiential avoidance. This self-developed formulation ideally will serve to increase their motivation to try new, more effective strategies for coping with the stressors that they encounter.

Cognitive Defusion, Willingness and Acceptance as the Alternative

After concluding our discussion of the *Polygraph Metaphor* with the participants, we are ready to take a different tact.

We've seen how trying to control our thoughts, feelings, and other products of our mind is not a reliable, or even helpful, strategy for reducing our problems. But what is the alternative? Well, it's called acceptance. That is, if one is willing to have an emotion or thought, and not get rid of it or alter it, then one can escape the inevitable, detrimental consequences of control: if you refuse to have it, you've got it. This is inescapably the case both because the control strategy doesn't reliably and fully work, and also because the strategy itself results in an increase in the events it is designed to prevent. That is, the more you don't want to be anxious, the more anxious you will probably become. "Don't be anxious! Bam, you're dead!" (In reference to the *Polygraph Metaphor*.)

One way to conceive of the different outcomes of acceptance and control is through the clean versus dirty discomfort intervention described in the first ACT book (Hayes et al., 1999, p. 136). The trainer modifies the discussion to focus it on the discomfort of stress.

> Clean discomfort is the stress that we all experience in our lives as a function of living. Clean discomfort varies in level; it might be relatively low at times, as when we feel irritated at someone for putting us down, or it may be high, as when we have a major argument with a colleague or we lose a job. Life serves up painful events, and our painful reactions to them are natural and entirely acceptable. It is when we are unwilling to experience these natural reactions–the clean discomfort–that we wind up with what we term dirty discomfort. Dirty discomfort is emotional pain created by our efforts to control the normal, natural clean discomfort that we experience. That is, when trying to avoid, control, or get rid of the clean discomfort, a whole new set of painful feelings, emotions, and thoughts appear and stress increases. This dirty discomfort is the unnecessary addition of pain on top of pain: fear of fear, guilt over guilt, shame over guilt, blame over fear, or blame over unhappiness, as in "you've only yourself to blame for being unhappy in this situation." This simple additive process results inexorably in an increased likelihood that people will use control/avoidance strategies and, thus, carry-on in a vicious circle of ever increasing control and stress.
>
> Acceptance involves moving in the opposite direction: towards the pain, rather than away from it; towards the emotions, thoughts, and feelings that we dislike. Consider this: suppose you were caught in quicksand. Naturally, you'd try to get out. But almost everything you've learnt about how to get out will create problems for you. If you try to walk, jump, climb, or run, you just sink in deeper, because you end up trying to push down on the sand. If you struggle, wiggle, push with your hands, or crawl, you sink in deeper. Often as people sink, they get panicky and start flailing about and down they go. In quicksand, the only thing to do is to create as much surface area as possible: to lay out on the quicksand, getting in full contact with what you've been struggling with, but without more struggle. That will be hard: not hard meaning effortful, because to apply effort is to struggle. No, I mean hard as in tricky. It is tricky, because your mind is telling you to struggle in a situation where using this strategy is counterproductive. But don't let us be too hard on your mind, as it has been taught that this control strategy works, and it can't see anything else to do. Furthermore, it has learnt this ineffective control strategy so well that you can't just tell it to stop using it and expect that it will.
>
> Now, we are going to practice some acceptance, or willingness, strategies; strategies that encourage you to get into full contact with your bodily sensations, thoughts, and emotions without struggling with them; without trying to control them: that is, without trying to make them go away or avoid them.

At this point in the discussion, we introduce the participants to an ACT experiential exercise that will help make clear the points we have been discussing, using the *Leaves on the Stream* (or its functionally identical variant *Soldiers In A Parade*) exercise (Hayes et al., 1999, pp. 158–162).

At the conclusion of this eyes closed exercise, the trainer asks, "How did you find this exercise", and if it has not come up during the discussion, the trainer then asks, "How does this exercise relate to what we have been discussing?" As is hopefully evident, this exercise shows the participants a way to be willing to get in contact with their thoughts, feelings, memories or bodily sensations, without having to alter them or stop them. The trainer also notes that this exercise is useful to do when people start to feel stress. After this exercise, the content turns toward another component of our attempts to promote cognitive defusion. This has to do with the arbitrary, automatic and programmed nature of thinking.

> How would you finish the phrase, "blondes have more . . . "? (Most trainees will invariably say " . . . fun.") That's right! Most all of us will have heard this statement many times before. So much so, in fact, that it is practically impossible not to finish the statement, once I, for example, have begun it. It comes to mind automatically, without effort. Now, raise your hands if you really believe this statement to be true. Okay, let's try another one. How would you finish the phrase, "Jack and the . . . "? (Again, most participants would say " . . . beanstalk"). Absolutely, again, we've heard this statement so many times before, we could hardly not complete it, once someone has begun it. So, raise your hands if you believe that there was a chap called Jack who really had a giant beanstalk? Okay none of you believed both of these statements, but you could all finish them.

I think that this phenomenon gives us two very important insights into our thoughts. The first is that, given our own unique histories, we can't help but to think certain thoughts in particular situations; for example, "blondes have more . . . *fun*"! You can't help it: the word just appears from out of nowhere, as if by magic. The second insight is that just because thoughts pop into our heads, it doesn't then mean we have to *believe* them. Our parents, siblings, films, TV, books, and the rest of society can teach us that blondes have more fun, and jack had a giant beanstalk, and we will never forget these ridiculous statements: they will instantly enter our minds in certain situations; likewise, because of our own unique histories, more personally relevant statements will enter our head in certain situations. For example, you might always think: 'I can't cope with this!' when faced with certain types of problems; but, as with 'blondes have more fun' and 'Jack and the beanstalk', we don't have to believe them to be true; and, because we don't have to believe them, we don't have to try to change them, or get rid of them, either."

Identifying "Stress Buttons"

Participants next are asked to list on a piece of paper the various "stress buttons" that they have. They are told that these are situations, thoughts, emotions, or sensations that "kick-off" the stress process. For example, a confrontation with a co-worker, tight deadlines, certain types of assignments, thoughts of failure, unhappiness, concern, or shallow breathing may trigger a stress reaction. Before they start writing down these stress buttons, participants are asked to share with the group examples of their own triggers, in order to model what is expected. After several people have identified some of their own stressors, questions are elicited, and then participants write down their own stress buttons.

We can complete these topics in the first, three hour session. For homework, participants are asked to do the following between session 1 and session 2:

1. Notice, in the week between sessions, how cognitive avoidance, cognitive struggle, and a lack of awareness of what they are thinking (or cognitive fusion) amplifies and/or helps to maintain the stress process, when their stress buttons have been pressed.
2. Spend at least ten minutes each day practicing the *Leaves on the Stream/Soldiers in a Parade* exercise.

A piece of paper with these homework assignments is handed out to each participant at this time, and any questions regarding the homework are taken and answered.

The second group session begins with a discussion about what participants noticed, during the previous week, concerning the relationship between control, avoidance, struggle, and stress, particularly in the areas related to their stress buttons. Following this discussion, any issues related to the "just noticing" assignment are considered.

The trainer then begins to introduce a word convention that we have found to be very effective in our stress intervention program. It is called the "Get Off Your Buts" intervention and is drawn from the ACT book (Hayes et al., 1999, p. 167)

I'd like to talk about the word, "but," for a moment. It's a funny little word that can draw us into a struggle with our thoughts and feelings, when we use it to explain our behavior in terms of private events (i.e., thoughts and feelings). In so doing, we end up pitting one set of private events (e.g., a *desire* to succeed) against another (e.g., I feel so *angry* with my boss). 'But' literally means that what follows the word contradicts what went before the word. It originally came from the words "be out." When we use it we often say, "this private event be out that private event." That is "I'd should be nice to her as she is my boss, but she is a nightmare; so, to hell with her, I'll say what I like!." As you can see, "but" is literally a call to fight, so it is no wonder it pulls us up into the war zone with our own thoughts and feelings, which makes us more stressed, as we saw from last week's assignment.

Let's consider some examples of this "call to arms": "I love my partner, but I get so angry at him." How about this one: "I want to do a good job at work, but I am anxious or upset right now." Notice that although both say, "one internal event (e.g., love) should be contradicted by another internal event (e.g., anger)" what the person actually experienced in both cases was two things: for example, love *and* anger. The bit of the sentence after the but, or "be out," part isn't a *description* of what happened—it is a *proscription* about how private events, thoughts and feelings, should go together. This proscription, however, is exactly what we are trying to back out of, as it does not align with reality. No one *experienced* that two private events have to be resolved; rather, two private events were experienced: love and anger, for example. If the word "but" is replaced by the word "and," it is almost always much more reflective of reality. So, in our examples, it is much more accurate to say, 'I love my partner *and* I get angry at him, or to say, "I want to do a good job at work, *and* I am anxious or upset right now." Both things are true: the wanting to do a good job at work, and being anxious and upset. So, I'd like everyone to be aware of when they use the word, "but", and then substitute it for the word, "and"; because, this switch may make you more sensitive to one of the ways that we get pulled into the struggle with ourselves, which makes us less willing and, hence, more stressed. What are people's thoughts on all of this?

As can be seen in Table 11.1, the *Observer Exercise* and the *Tin Can Monster Exercise* follow this discussion of the word *but*. These are not detailed here, however, as they are described in detail in the original ACT book (Hayes et al., 1999, pp. 192 and 171–174 respectively).

Value Based Actions

Once cognitive defusion and psychological acceptance concepts and strategies have been introduced and directly experienced, participants are better able to commit to the final two goals of the ACT stress intervention: values-based action, followed by willingness as a values-based action (see Table 11.1). In ACT, values are important because working towards them brings meaning and satisfaction to our lives. Willingness is not an end in itself but is a means to enable clients to move their lives in a valued direction (Zettle & Hayes, 2002).

To achieve these two values-directed clinical goals, it is essential that people first clarify the values that they have. This important process is accomplished using techniques that are modified to fit the format. Participants often find values identification exercises to be intense and intimate undertakings, and they may be reticent to share their values with other people, especially work colleagues. Thus, we modify values assessment exercises so that participants can do them privately, even though they are in a group session. Obviously, if you are seeing stress management clients on an individual basis, then the need to protect privacy is essentially a non-issue.

The first assessment exercise proceeds as follows: Participants are handed a piece of paper with a large, empty tombstone that covers practically the entire page. They are then told by the trainer: "I would like you to close your eyes for a few minutes and follow your breathing . . . just follow it coming into your lungs and back out again . . . " The trainer allows participants to follow their breathing for about two minutes. Then, the trainer says, "Imagine that you have died, and that you have miraculously wound up attending your own funeral, in spirit form: not seen by anyone else. You find yourself watching and listening to the eulogies offered by people about whom you cared mostly: they could be your partner, children, friends, colleagues, acquaintances, whomever. Now, in a minute-or-so, when I tell you, I'd like you to open your eyes and write down a few statements about what these people, who are most important to you, would remember you for. What would you like your partner to say about you, as a partner? Have him, or her, say that. What would you like a friend to say about you, as a friend? Really be bold here: It's your funeral! Let them say exactly what you would most want them to say, if you had complete control over this situation. Now, when you are ready, I'd like you to open your eyes and take 10 minutes to write down brief statements about what you would most like three or four people to say about you, at your funeral. No one will ever need to see what you have written, so be completely honest in what you write."

The therapist then asks, "How did you find this exercise", and if it has not come up during the discussion, the trainer then asks, "Did anyone notice a difference between what you wanted to be remembered for, and how you are currently living your life?" The aim of this discussion is not to cajole people to say what they wrote (although people do volunteer this occasionally), but rather, to help people to focus on any dissonance that they experienced between their values and current actions. From this position, people are often motivated to consider and commit to the values that they have.

To help them to do this, the trainer next conducts a values clarification exercise, which, like the eulogy one, is an important step in identifying valued life directions. The trainer distributes the *Values Assessment Ratings Form* (see Table 11.2) and reads the instructions at the top of it. After clarifying the definition of values that is provided, the trainer asks if there are any questions as to what the participants are being asked to do for this exercise. Participants are given approximately 15 minutes to begin completing this form, and, if they do not finish, they are asked to complete it over the next day or two. Because this is a brief intervention with a specific target this values rating form does not break down life domains into the several varieties that are typically found in the ACT literature (e.g., Hayes et al., 1999, pp. 222–229). In an individual protocol, however, broader exploration would be possible and useful.

After completing this values assessment rating form, the therapist reminds participants that it will be three months until the next and final

Table 11.2. Values Assessment Rating Form

Values Assessment Rating Form

A value is a direction in life that you would like to move towards (e.g., the direction of West), but that you cannot arrive at, once-and-for-all (i.e., you can always keep moving West). In contrast, goals are attainable destinations in your valued direction (e.g., going to American from Europe). Thus, being a loving partner or a helpful colleague are both values, because you have to keep living like one, or you will cease to be one. Values are important because working towards them brings meaning and satisfaction to our lives.

The following are two domains of life in which people have values. Not everyone has the same values, and this worksheet is not a test to see whether or not you have the "correct" values. Please list the most important values that you have in your work and personal (or non-work) life. In choosing your values, only write down those that *you* really want to work towards. In other words, before writing one down, ask yourself: "Would I write this value down, if nobody could know that I was working towards it?" If the answer to this question is no, then this is not a true value for *you*, and you should not write it down. For each value, *rate* how important it is on a scale of 1 (high importance) to 10 (low importance). Rate how *successfully* you have lived this value during the past month on a scale of 1 (very successfully) to 10 (not at all successfully). Finally *rank* these values in order of the importance you place on working on them right now, with 1 as the highest rank, and 8 as the lowest rank.

Domain	Valued direction	Importance	Success	Rank
Work				
1.				
2.				
3.				
4.				
Personal				
1.				
2.				
3.				
4.				

---

meeting. In the intervening time, they are asked to indicate on their form how successful they have been, at the end of each month, in living every one of the values that they have listed. To help them to focus on moving in their valued directions, they are asked to consider the following statement each day (which is provided for them on a sheet of paper): "*Given a distinction between you and the things you've been struggling with and trying to change, are you willing to experience those things as they are, and not as they say they are,* **and** *do what will take you in a valued direction in a given situation?*" Participants are also asked to do the *Tin Can Monster* exercise everyday for one week, and then to do it one time each week, until the next meeting.

When they do it, they are asked to use as their material the stress buttons that they wrote down in the first session. To assist them in this assignment, participants are given an audio tape, or compact disc, that guides them through the exercise. They are also asked to bring their *Values Assessment Rating Forms* to the next session.

Session Three (Three Months Later)

The primary goal of the third session in our ACT stress protocol is to undermine barriers to values-based action. This is accomplished, in part, by showing participants that willingness to experience unwanted psychological events is, itself, a value-based action that can help them to realize their other values. The session begins by helping participants directly contact willingness and a solid sense of self by redoing the *Observer* and *Tin Can Monster* exercises. After these are completed and discussed amongst the participants, we turn attention to the concept of willingness as a chosen, values-based action. The first intervention we employ is the *Bubble in the Road* metaphor (Hayes et al., 1999, p. 230). The trainer uses the bubble metaphor to discuss people's barriers to the valued directions that they listed in the previous session, on the Values Assessment Rating Form. Consistent with this metaphor, the discussion focuses on the nature of barriers to valued action: Some are internal events such as thoughts, feelings, memories and expectancies while others are external events that evoke unwanted private experiences (e.g., guilt, shame, and anxiety as a result of the boss' expressed disappointment; people's incredulity at your not taking a "fantastic" promotion that would nevertheless involve moving your partner and teenage children to another part of the country). Also discussed is how one barrier to valued action might be another conflicting value. For example, it may not be possible for a person both to value producing consistently innovative work and maintaining a loving, intimate, involved relationship. Regardless of what form the barriers to valued action take, the question remains: are participants willing to take valued action *and* to experience the unwanted internal experiences that will inevitably arise? Participants are now hopefully oriented enough to complete the *Goals, Actions, and Barriers Form* presented in Table 11.3. This allows participants systematically to catalogue any of their barriers, as well as to identify strategies for overcoming them, in the pursuit of their valued life goals.

The group ends with the following exercise that involves making a public pledge to committed value based action: "I would like to go around the room and have each person, if they are willing, tell us one of their valued directions, and an action that they will take to move towards it. Then, I would like each person to commit publicly to let go of the needless

Table 11.3. Goals, Actions, Barriers Form

Goals, Actions, Barriers Form

Please list some goals, actions, and barriers to values-based action for each of the valued directions that you identified on your Values Assessment Rating Form.

Recall that a **value** is a direction in life that you would like to move towards (e.g., the direction of West), but that you cannot arrive at, once-and-for-all (i.e., you can always keep moving West). In contrast, **goals** are attainable destinations in your valued direction (e.g., going to American from Europe). **Actions** are concrete steps that you can take to accomplish your goals (e.g., book a ticket from London to New York).

Valued direction (from Values Assessment Rating Form)	Goals	Actions	Barriers
Work			
1.			
2.			
3.			
4.			
Personal			
1.			
2.			
3.			
4.			

struggles, and change strategies, that are interfering with moving towards this value; but, I only want you to make such a commitment, if you are really prepared to choose to give up this struggle. If there is no value that you feel prepared to state here, then that is fine: try stating one to your partner, or a close friend or family member; and, if you find that you are not willing to do that, at least state one to yourself in the mirror. The goal here is to make as public a commitment as you can to letting go of the struggle that is getting in your way of moving in your valued directions."

Participants are encouraged formally to practice a willingness exercise at least three times a week, and to keep their *Values Assessment Rating Form* and their *Goals, Actions, and Barriers Form* updated.

I have noted throughout this chapter that therapists can apply this protocol in a one-on-one format that is either time limited or relatively open-ended. In either case, more focus can be placed on monitoring how individuals are responding to treatment. Based upon these assessments, the therapist can adjust the amount of time spent trying to achieve a particular clinical goal (e.g., increasing willingness), or test out the relative effectiveness of different intervention techniques.

CLINICAL CONSIDERATIONS

In this section, I wish to discuss the clinical issues that arise when conducting stress management interventions, particularly in organizations. In order to reduce stress, one can either target: the (1) *stressor* itself or (2) people's *evaluations* of (a) the stressors' impact on their well-being and (b) their ability to cope with the stressor. This chapter has discussed how ACT can address this second target. But what of the stressors, themselves? Many participants attending our program are very quick to point out that their organization should not try to "fix" the employees, but rather should focus on making their organization a less "toxic" place in which to work (e.g., by reducing job demands). There are both ethical and pragmatic reasons why a therapist needs to listen and respond to these nearly inevitable and ubiquitous complaints.

Firstly, there is now sufficient research to conclude that certain work and organizational characteristics, or designs, have an adverse impact on employees' physical health, mental health, and performance. Given these findings, maintaining that it is sufficient to teach employees how better to cope with these stressors is equivalent to instructing them how better to cope with asbestos, or second hand smoke in the workplace (e.g., use a breathing mask, keep fit, and take your breaks outside). In addition to deleterious physical outcomes of high job demands and low job control, longitudinal research shows that these work design characteristics also lead to worse levels of mental health, performance, and absenteeism (e.g., Bond & Bunce, 2001; 2003; Terry & Jimmieson, 1999). These direct effects of work design characteristics on physical/mental health and productivity certainly argue for the importance of redesigning the way people work, which is typically the focus of organizational, and occupational health, psychologists (see Quick & Tetrick, 2002). Redesigning the way people work does not diminish the importance of *also* improving people's ability to cope with both unreasonable, and reasonable, work and life stressors. Indeed, Bond and Bunce (2003) show that the longitudinal benefits of higher levels of job control, in terms of mental health and job performance, are actually increased when people have greater psychological flexibility. Thus, there is empirical evidence that suggests that targeting both work design characteristics, as well as individual ones (e.g., psychological flexibility, through ACT), may provide the best response to workplace stress.

From a purely clinical viewpoint, we have found that participants are less hostile about and more responsive to a stress management intervention if there is also an organizationally-directed (e.g., work redesign) intervention occurring along with it. Many therapists do not have the ability to get an organization to implement work redesign initiatives, but even in this case you need to acknowledge the deleterious effects of certain work stressors and not minimize worker concerns over them. You should studiously avoid any comments that suggest that stress is "all in the individual." This is a dubious and empirically false position that many therapists incorrectly assume. I have found that I need to address these concerns directly at the beginning of a workplace ACT stress intervention, if I am to keep people attending the ACT sessions, never mind actively engaging in them. To this end, I use the following rationale, from Bond and Hayes (2002). In a participative way, I first discuss with the participants how some sources of stress may not be completely avoidable (e.g., under-promotion, and surges in demands caused by client needs). Also, I use many of the creative hopelessness strategies, listed in Table 11.1, to show how workers' efforts to modify stressful situations may themselves be inhibited by poor psychological coping strategies (e.g., use of avoidance strategies). Finally, I point out that work related stress does not occur in a vacuum, and the coping styles that increase stress reactions at home (e.g., being over-controlling) may also result in feeling stress at work. The primary reason for engaging in the ACT intervention is to learn how better to cope with stress in whatever venue it is experienced. This simple rationale often works long enough for people to stay in the SMI program and derive great benefit from it. Indeed, we have found that ACT naturally leads to more efforts to take control of stressors in the environment (Bond & Bunce, 2000), presumably because it helps remove the emotional and cognitive barriers to overt action. ACT is about empowerment and action, not just passive acceptance.

The final clinical consideration that I shall discuss here is the need to provide a clinical environment that respects the privacy and dignity of the participants. Unlike those in non-work-based group interventions, participants in worksite groups are often closely linked, if not known directly, to others in the group. As a result, personal disclosure carries some true risk for those who disclose. For example, negative evaluations of a co-participant's ways of coping could conceivably impact that person's chance of a promotion. For this reason, we have ensured that the ACT protocol described here uses intervention techniques that allow people to benefit while maintaining privacy over their values, goals, and barriers to action.

Conclusion

There are a growing number of empirical studies that have examined ACT and its processes of change, and that is the case in workplace and stress interventions as well. So far, the findings seem to justify the considerable research efforts that scientists are bringing to bear on this philosophy and system of psychotherapy. Elaborated versions of the protocol described are proving effective in promoting mental health, in addition to reducing work-site stress (Flaxman & Bond, under review). We are beginning to investigate the usefulness of ACT in work redesign initiatives. The aim of these and other research activities is to make ACT the most empirically tested workplace intervention used to help organizations and their employees attain physical and emotional health while maximizing productivity and work accomplishment.

Chapter 12

ACT in Medical Settings

PATRICIA ROBINSON, JENNIFER GREGG, JOANNE DAHL,
AND TOBIAS LUNDGREN

ACT consistent interventions can be used by medical and behavioral health providers to help patients who are struggling to manage a chronic health condition or improve their general health status. The Acceptance and Commitment—Health Care Model (ACT-HC; Robinson & Hayes, 1997) is an approach to combining medical and psychological interventions within an ACT consistent framework. The goal of the ACT—HC model is to help medical patients successfully implement behaviors that are consistent with their values in the presence of difficult private experiences triggered by medical discomfort, chronic medical conditions or elevated health risk.

The goals of this chapter are to introduce the tenets of the ACT-HC model as a framework for conceptualizing ACT interventions at both individual and programmatic level. We will describe intervention strategies for patients with medical complaints who are at risk for developing chronic suffering, for groups of patients that typically are not responsive to more traditional treatments (e.g., somatization disorders, chronic fatigue, and children with ADHD), and for those who have multiple health problems with little hope of substantial, lasting improvement in health. We will conclude with some suggestions for how to train medical and behavioral health providers in this approach.

While it is useful to implement ACT in hospital settings, the greatest opportunity to impact the public resides in the primary care setting since that is where most members of the community come first with their social, psychological and medical issues. The primary care team usually includes physicians, mid-level providers (Physician Assistants, Nurse Practitioners), registered nurses, and support staff. In resource scare venues, the "team" may be one medical provider and a nursing assistant. The best developed and most successful model for integrative health care involves adding a behavior health provider to the primary care team as a core team member with the goal of increasing the effectiveness of primary care providers in addressing the behavioral health needs of patients (Strosahl, 2001). In this system patients see behavioral health care as part of primary care, and this often relieves patient concerns about receiving a "mental health" service. Many populations that have historically been reluctant to access specialty mental health care (i.e., the elderly, male adults, ethnic and cultural minorities) accept care more readily from an integrated behavioral health provider. ACT works very well in this team approach in primary care (Robinson, 1996a, 1996b), and it will be emphasized in this chapter.

An ACT-HC Model

From the point of view of ACT, the key processes that drive health care behaviors are fusion with private content and excessive use of experiential avoidance, both on the part of the patient and medical providers, and a consequent lack of effective action. The extent to which these processes are activated in a patient's health care trajectory predicts a variety of negative health outcomes, from excessive health care seeking to poor self management of disease. ACT interventions that disrupt fusion and experiential avoidance and empower valued action among both patients and their medical providers are likely to promote superior healthcare outcomes. For example, a somaticizing patient may persist in requesting various procedures in an effort to control intrusive thoughts concerning illness, disability, and death. A physician may participate in this experiential avoidance by ordering additional tests, as this may allow avoidance of unwanted thoughts and feelings about missing a diagnosis or failing to help a distressed patient.

There is a great deal of support in the culture for experiential avoidance, and this in turn influences both the structure and content of health care delivery. News and magazine articles teach patients not to trust medical providers or the systems of care they work in, which shifts more control to the public media. There television advertisements train adults to detect unwanted private events and to seek out a medical provider for medication that will suppress or eliminate them. As will be described in the next chapter as well, this has lead to systems of care that are heavily oriented toward the regulation of private events, even when this is not helpful.

All psychological events, for patients and their health care providers alike, occur in a complex context influenced by specific variables. Some contextual variables and current psychological events cannot be directly manipulated, such as the personal histories and current private experiences of patients and providers, or the reimbursement guidelines of a large insure company. Others can be directly manipulated such as the prescribing patterns of medical providers, self management behaviors for an acute and chronic illness, or increasing knowledge about health risk. The value of an ACT approach is that it tends to focus work only on those events that are readily changed.

From an ACT perspective, primary care and behavioral health providers need to focus on: 1) their interactions with patients, particularly when fusion or experiential avoidance is elicited in the provider by a patient's behavior and 2) patterns of utilizing healthcare in relation to a specific condition or perceived health risk that are driven by the patient's struggle with fusion and/or emotional avoidance. Patients who under-utilize and over-utilize care are key targets, as outcomes for these two groups are most problematic. Providers may stimulate appropriate health care seeking among patients who tend to under-utilize health care services by learning to (1) retain patients who use experiential avoidance strategies that deter them from seeking appropriate care and (2) design value driven interventions appropriate to the patient's gender, level of motivation, and cultural context. Conversely, with patients who over-utilize medical services, providers need to: 1) address the patient's issues with cognitive fusion and emotional avoidance and focus on valued outcomes and 2) teach medical providers to identify and manage their own sources of fusion and emotional avoidance.

Treating General Medical Patients

Table 12.1 presents a formulation of ideal and problematic events in an episode of healthcare. An episode of care begins when a patient initiates care concerning a specific health complaint and concludes when both provider and patient agree that the problem has been addressed adequately. All encounters involve a provider and a patient, dealing with three components: problem definition, treatment plan development, and treatment plan adherence. In any of these domains, the process can result in high levels of control or low levels of behavioral regulation. Low levels generally result from vague, missing or inclusive information that leaves the patient and/or provider susceptible to negative emotional arousal, negative self evaluations, ineffectively managed physical discomfort and so forth. Higher impact comes from clear and unambiguous information about diagnosis and treatment.

In the ideal episode of care, the patient articulates the problem clearly, asks questions that the provider can answer, participates actively in

Table 12.1. ACT-HC Functional Analysis of Ideal and Problematic Primary
Care Encounters

Elements of Encounter	Ideal Encounter/High Control		Problematic Encounter/Low Control	
	Provider	Patient	Provider	Patient
Problem Definition	Identifies organic basis	Articulates clear descriptions	Orders multiple tests	Presents multiple, vague complaints
			Finds no organic basis	Presents highly anxious about discomfort
	Gives specific diagnosis	Asks questions	Gives no diagnosis	Insists on diagnosis
Treatment Plan Development	Explains affordable, effective treatment	Comprehends plan	Gives general advice for coping	Does not understand, is dissatisfied with advice
		Has skills and resources to implement plan	Lacks skills needed to help patients address unresolved discomforts	Lack skills needed to cope with discomfort and perceived lack of control
Treatment Plan Adherence	Schedules follow-up	Attends follow-up	No follow-up scheduled	Insists on multiple appointments with multiple providers
	Revises plan as needed; discusses prevention issues	Has adhered to plan	Difficulties coordinating care among multiple providers	Focuses on any inconsistencies in opinions from multiple providers
	Schedules follow-up; ends episode of care	Satisfied with outcomes	Episode of care continues without coordinated plan	Adheres poorly to treatment plans
			Patient seen as difficult	Changes primary care providers

planning treatment, understands the treatment plan, and has the skills and
resources to successfully implement the plan. In follow-up visits, the ideal
patient keeps the appointment, reports adherence to the medical treatment
plan, and is satisfied with treatment outcomes. Providers enjoy participating in these ideal episodes of care. Under these circumstances, the provider
diagnoses an organic basis or non-organic explanation for the problem that
is acceptable to the patient. The recommended treatment is accessible, af-
fordable, and effective. The provider schedules a follow-up visit, reinforces

the patient for adhering to the plan, revises the plan as needed, addresses prevention and/or health maintenance issues, and ends the episode of care.

In a problematic episode of care, the patient presents with multiple and or vague complaints that are difficult to understand medically. The patient is anxious about her/his symptoms and insists on a specific diagnosis, but the provider is unable to give one. The process worsens if the patient does not understand or is dissatisfied with the provider's advice. The patient may lack the skills needed to cope with physical or emotional discomfort and may resort to various forms of experiential avoidance, driven by the inability to defuse from or accept uncomfortable physical or mental events. Multiple appointments with multiple providers may be sought. The patient focuses on inconsistencies in opinions between providers, does not adhere to the medical treatment plan due to a lack of buy in, and continues to shop for other doctors and services.

Principles of an ACT-HC Model

Use of ACT in health care can be guided by several principles. We will use a diverse group of patients to illustrate the principles, including patients who respond minimally to available treatments (e.g., somatization disorders, chronic fatigue syndrome), patients who are at risk for developing chronic suffering (e.g., recently injured workers, older adults), patients with multiple health problems with little hope of substantial, lasting improvement in health (e.g. frail elderly), patients with chronic disease (e.g., diabetics) and ill citizens who face many barriers to needed treatments (e.g., South African citizens with epilepsy).

Health care seeking is driven by physical discomfort, emotional distress, a need for emotional control and confidence in health care resources. Discomfort always plays a role in health care seeking. A patient's discomfort may arise from anticipated negative consequences (e.g., "I will contract the flu if I fail to take a flu shot") or from current discomforts (e.g., "My head hurts"). Patients vary considerably in their level of anticipatory anxiety about and tolerance for physical and mental discomfort. Patients also vary in the resources that will allow them to cope with their discomfort. This might include knowledge about the health condition, self-management skills, availability of support or the tendency to experience fusion and engage in experiential avoidance.

When patients experience discomfort, they employ self-management strategies to address them such as taking over-the-counter remedies, allowing time for bed rest, or talking to a friend about a distressing personal problem. When these strategies fail to provide relief, the patient's level of discomfort increases. Fusion with evaluations about their symptoms may increase, and or new symptoms driven by psychological distress may appear. Patients vary in their susceptibility to the specific physiological components of distress (e.g., increased heart rate, gastrointestinal upset, muscular tension) and in their beliefs about health care services (e.g., "The doctor knows best;" "Doctors are quacks."). When people experience excessive unwanted private experiences (e.g., somatic symptoms), and do not see health care services as a resource, their self-management strategies may exacerbate the problem, such as through substance abuse, misuse of food, and or excessive work. Secondary problems often result. For example, a depressed, obese person may avoid seeking care for a painful cough with a fever because she or he is unwilling to be confronted about over-eating. Another person might suffer from social phobia and use nicotine to dampen arousal when social interactions are required. In these circumstances, health may decline further, leaving the patient vulnerable to more invasive and costly health care treatments in the future.

Experiential avoidance increases as first order medical assessments and interventions fail to control or eliminate emotional or physical suffering. When medical services fail to meet patient expectations, the patient may employ more experiential avoidance strategies in a futile attempt to gain control. For example, a patient who experiences a panic attack and receives a thorough medical evaluation yielding negative findings may fuse with negative thoughts ("They cannot find out what's wrong with me, even with the best tests available. I must have a rare and awful condition, or my doctor doesn't know what s/he's doing. I must be more careful than ever before and probably find a better doctor—a specialist!") that in turn lead to even more experiential avoidance. The patient may sleep poorly, experience fatigue, take a medical leave from work, and avoid exercise, friends, being away from home, and being home alone—and still experience the unwanted private sensations of rapid heart beat, trembling, chest pain, sweating, etc.

Using experiential avoidance strategies appears to make medical patients more vulnerable to anxiety and depression. Patients who are attentive to somatic sensations and prone to worrying about health, experience increasing levels of anxiety as their avoidance strategies fail. Over time, this type of patient becomes exhausted, worry behavior becomes automatic and attentional processes impaired. Many such patients become depressed and seek anti-depressants to help control or eliminate their overwhelming feelings of fear and failure. Healthcare seeking is put into the service of emotional control, and they blame their providers for the poor results, leading to a cycle of fusion and emotional avoidance for both the patient and providers alike.

This ratcheting experiential avoidance pattern is definitive of many chronic disorders you will see in the primary care setting. Somataform disorder, present in up to 14% of primary care medical patients, involves significant concerns with control of bodily sensations, emotions, and thoughts. Hypochondriacal patients believe good health to be a state where they are relatively free of symptoms of sickness and are likely to view even common, benign physical symptoms as indicators of poor health (Barsky, Coeytaux, Sarnie, & Cleary, 1993). Heavy utilizers of health care are less able to generate reasons why a pathological explanation for a common bodily sensation might be untrue (Sensky, MacLeod, & Rigby, 1996), making them more susceptible to difficulties with cognitive fusion.

Emotional avoidance produces self-amplifying, negative health outcomes. Experiential avoidance carried over time produces negative, self amplifying effects on mood state, self efficacy, perceived health status and objective health outcomes. The patient also utilizes more health care services, tends to have more family problems, and performs less effectively at work. Emotional control/suppression increases physiological reactivity and stress (e.g., Thompson, Gil, Abrams, & Phillips, 1992), which in turn creates increased somatic symptoms such as gastrointestinal distress and the like, and reduces adherence to medical regimens (Amir, Kaplan, Efroni, Levine, Benjamin, & Kotler, 1997). Thus it is not surprising that avoidance based coping styles are associated with poorer health outcomes among patients with chronic disease (Greer, 1991).

These processes tend to be self-amplifying. For example, when a person with major depression or an anxiety disorder (both problems heavily influenced by avoidance—see Chapters 4 and 5) experiences a significant medical problem, he or she may resolve the acute medical problem only to be left with chronic hypochondrical worry (Kirmayer & Robbins, 1996). When well meaning providers attempt to provide reassurance, a worried patient may use this in the service of an emotion suppression strategy, even though this may further exacerbate the cycle.

Acceptance and defusion provide an effective method of reducing the self-amplifying negative outcomes generated by experiential avoidance. Acceptance, defusion, and willingness are the alternatives to experiential avoidance, fusion and emotional control. A primary goal of using ACT in health care settings should be to help patients accept the presence of physical symptoms, as well as the thoughts, feelings and memories that accompany them, and shift their attention to positive health behaviors.

Acceptance-based coping is associated with less distress and improved outcomes for medical patients with cancer (Greer, 1991; Paez, Luciano, Gutiérrez, Montesinos, & Gómez, 2003) and chronic conditions such as diabetes (Richardson, Adner, & Nordstrom, 2001). Acceptance-focused or more approach-oriented interventions also improve health outcomes in chronically ill patients (see deRidder & Schreurs, 2001 for a review). A good example is journaling about past distress, an intervention that improves health outcomes (e.g., Smyth, Stone, Hurewitz & Kaell, 1999) and positively alters underlying physical processes such as immune function (e.g., Pennebaker, Kiecolt-Glaser, & Glaser, 1988).

When using ACT in health care settings you need to promote acceptance for both the provider and the patient. The medical provider needs to accept the self evaluations that show up when the patient cannot be "cured," for example. The patient needs to accept that physical and emotional symptoms can be experienced as they are without struggle and amplification. The goal is to learn to live in valued ways in the presence of sometimes uncontrollable physical and mental experiences.

Use acceptance, defusion, and values to facilitate changes in health behaviors. You can promote positive health outcomes by enhancing a patient's acceptance of and defusion from unwanted thoughts, feelings, and sensations, and focusing them instead on behavioral goal setting generated by values clarification exercises. Most patients desire to have good relationships with loved ones, to make a contribution as a worker, to make independent choices, to achieve personal goals, and so one. As patients and providers accept the reality of a health condition, they are better able to develop value driven behavioral plans that move the patient, step by step, closer to these and other behavioral objectives.

It is the combination of these factors in ACT that is powerful. Providers often focus exclusively on behavior but in ways that undermine effective behavioral regulation in some patients. For example, providers may tell non-adherent patients that they must change their behavior or die. Some patients immediately change their behaviors (which may help maintain this provider behavior) but many others react by subsequently avoiding contact with providers, equipment or medicine in an effort to control unwanted images and thoughts about poor health, disability and death. When positive health behaviors are directly assigned by providers the results tend to be a combination of better outcomes for those stay in treatment and higher drop out rates (e.g., Wearden, Morriss, Mullis, Strickland, Pearson, et. al, 1998). By combining acceptance, defusion, and values work with assignments of difficult behaviors, more patients may be retained in treatment. All of the ACT protocols tested so far with chronic disease have combined traditional behavioral tasks appropriate to the specific problem and acceptance, defusion, and values work.

The studies assessing the impact of ACT with medical problems are just now being done, but the data so far seems to support this combination. For example, ACT with diabetes patients has been shown to improve self-management behaviors and blood glucose control more than patient education alone and do so through greater acceptance of difficult thoughts and feelings specific to diabetes (Gregg, 2004). The same pattern has been shown with smoking: greater compliance through acceptance and defusion (Gifford, Kohlenberg, Hayes, Antonuccio, Piasecki, Rasmussen-Hall, & Palm, in press). Similar results are being found in other conditions (e.g., Montesinos, Hernández, & Luciano, 2001). Chronic pain will be reviewed in the next chapter.

ACT INTERVENTIONS

In this section, we will describe ACT interventions for general medical patients, including those at risk for more complex problems, at risk children, high utilizers of health care, and those with chronic disease. Table 12.2 presents a general list of clinical issues that are seen in medical patients, and associated ACT intervention recommendations.

Interventions with At Risk Adults

From a population-based care perspective, primary prevention is crucial to positive health outcomes. ACT targets variables that seem clearly relevant to prevention. For example, patients who are candidates for new and uncomfortable screening procedures may fail to participate because they fear the procedures or the results that might come from them. Sigmoidoscopy screening is an example: less than half of patients referred for screening to detect early signs of colorectal cancer participate, in part out of fear of the procedure (Cockburn, Thomas, McLaughlin, & Reading, 1995). Similarly, early-stage interventions that encourage acceptance and value driven coping may help patients adjust to new diagnosis of illness. For example, ACT has been shown to reduce the psychological distress caused by cancer, empowering patients to improve their overall quality of life (Branstetter, Wilson, & Mutch, 2003).

As you initiate your intervention with such patients, begin by assessing the patient's health-related quality of life. This can be done by using an instrument such as the Duke Health Profile (Parkerson, 1996). In sharing results with a patient, you can invite the patient to look at their intentions and values, as well as the impact of stress on their quality of life. Patients who are stuck in unworkable change agendas often resonate very well to the idea of making choices that support valued directions. This can elevate motivation for behavior change.

After briefly exploring reported symptoms (e.g., insomnia, irritability, excessive worry, social withdrawal), you can explore precipitating factors

Table 12.2. Clinical Issues and Treatment Implications for Medical Patients

Clinical issues	Treatment implications
1. Patient beliefs about healthcare have a negative or positive impact on healthcare utilization.	Provide counter veiling information about healthcare providers and processes. Work to help patient defuse from evaluations as "truths."
2. Patients believe providers have the magic bullet that will eliminate suffering.	Focus on workability of past "magic bullet" solutions. Explore what patient's life would be like if a magic solution worked.
3. Patients are always seeking a new treatment for their medical problem.	Consider this as form of avoidance. Accept patients desire to eliminate problem, and encourage them to focus on their experience rather than their mind.
4. Patients fuse with their stories of suffering and display distress, without being present and with high impact on providers.	Use various defusion and showing up in the present moment strategies. Instruct patients in skills that facilitate creation of wanted sensations, and, then, observation of unwanted sensations with greater tolerance.
5. Patients are fused with language about pain, fatigue, righteousness, and failure.	Use ACT strategies that promote defusion, and development of self as context (Pain on the shelf; tired/tired/tired, self as context). Use forgiveness concepts.
6. Patients experience multiple access barriers and seek care from multiple providers.	Improve healthcare access and centralize care in the primary care setting.
7. Patients have limited contact with their values and lack motivation to change.	Conduct values clarification exercise; help patients identify 1 or 2 valued goals; start with small patterns of action.
8. Patients are lonely, as they are typically isolated and have limited social support.	Provide services in groups when possible, as this helps create a peer group.
9. Health care resources are limited and patients need more intensive services than are available.	Utilize the PC team to amplify treatment impact.
10. Patients have skill deficits and need on-going attention.	Provide on-going primary and secondary preventive, educational programs that are easily accessible and for which the HC system provides incentives for participation.

and introduce the Primary Care Patient (PCP) Values Plan (see Figure 12.1). With stressed patients, the PCP Values Plan is a tool that invites the patient to look up from what often amounts to a very narrow focus on a single problem to an expanded view of life that includes recognition of valued directions. A story describing the difference between Eagle and Hawk is useful in introducing the PCP Values Plan. Paula Underwood Spencer, an Oneida, describes this difference in the following way: "When hunting, Hawk sees Mouse . . . and dives directly for it. When hunting, Eagle sees the whole pattern . . . sees movement in the general pattern . . . and dives for the movement, learning only later that it is Mouse" (Garret & Garrett, 1996, p. 211). You can explain that the difference between the Hawk and the Eagle teaches us the difference between specificity and wholeness. Wholeness shows us the large context from which to view the specific problem, while specificity gives us a point of reference from which to view the whole. In the language of the original metaphor, with more of an Eagle view toward their overall values, patients can work with Hawk like focus to resolve specific problems in ways that are consistent with values. Both are important to developing a perspective that includes what patients want or don't want, and the relation of these wants to valued life directions.

Higher functioning patients may complete the PCP Values Plan during a visit or even as a homework activity. Figure 12.2 shows similar values assessment materials which can be used to engage the patient in assessing life directions and barriers. Other triage and treatment patients will need ongoing coping assistance, since sometimes examining issues of values can itself be challenging. For these patients, we recommend teaching the patient one or more brief relaxation techniques (e.g., belly breathing) in connection with the Hawk and Eagle metaphor prior to introducing the PCP Values Plan.

Not all areas of the PCP Values Plan need to be completed by all patients. Sometimes, you may focus on one or two areas—those that are most impacted by current life circumstance. For example, one of us worked with a woman in her twenties who responded to a diagnosis of diabetes with highly significant anxiety and depression. She immediately canceled her planned wedding date, withdrew from many of her usual social activities, and began to doubt her ability to continue to work fulltime. Her PCP Values Plan focus was on Family and Friends, Partner, Work, and Body. With a shift in perspective and some skill training that supported taking Eagle perspective, this patient chose to participate in an intensive diabetes education program. She, her fiancée, and friends decided to set new shower and wedding dates. Her primary care provider supported her work and followed her, as she initiated other behavior changes concerning diet and exercise.

| | Intention | Barriers | Plan |

1. Family and Friends

2. Partner

3. Work

4. Leisure

5. Spirit

6. Body

Patient Label   Provider Planning with Patient   Date(s)

_____   _____

_____   _____

Figure 12.1. Primary care patient values plan developmen sheet.

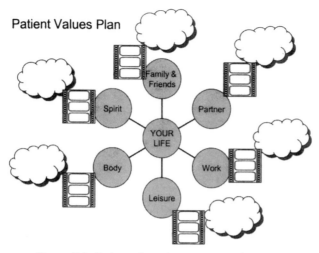

Figure 12.2. Patient values plan exam room diagram.

Injured workers often loose site of valued directions, as they struggle to cope with temporary pain and disability. In traditional care, these patients are invited to focus on their pain and to consume treatments that may not enhance their self-efficacy in coping with the injury. It is particularly easy for these patients to lose their way when they are provided economic incentives (i.e., paid leave) for living in ways that are not consistent with their values. They can easily fall into a harmful "thought-fest" frequently supported by the verbal community: they are a victim, they have been wronged, and poor functioning only shows how much this is so. Such reason-giving can further impair their functioning. Primary care providers are strategically positioned to identify these patients and to intervene to prevent disability. We recommend that providers avoid giving patients time off from work unless it is medically necessary and that they consider having patient's work half-days instead of full-days as an alternative to a medical leave. Then, patients are able to continue to receive the reinforcers—social, economic and occupational—that are available in the workplace, but not at home. We also recommend that providers screen injured workers by asking them if they like their job and if their employer reached out to them in a caring way at the time of their injury. Patients who don't like their job and feel unsupported by their employers are at higher risk for disability after an on-the-job injury. An ACT intervention for such patients will almost invariably include a values assessment intervention and work on accepting the physical pain or limitations imposed by the injury.

Table 12.3. ACT in a Preventive Population-Based Care for Older Adults:
A Nurse Phone Call and Psychologist Mind/Body Tea Program

Intervention timing	Clinical goals	Interventions
Week 1	Improve awareness of mind and body	Belly breathing and mind watching
Week 2	Encourage regular physical exercise	Self-monitoring exercise, body awareness while moving, stretching like a cat
Week 3	Encourage on-going efforts to build a strong social network	Clarify values concerning relationships with partner, relatives and friends. Preparation for death
Week 4	Optimizing consistency between daily activities and patient values	Acceptance or problem-solving concerning barriers to making behavioral choices consistent with values. Life is either a daring adventure or nothing at all. (Helen Keller) What lifestyle do you commit to now?
Monthly Calls 1, 2, & 3	Support Lifestyle Plan	Assess successes and corrections concerning lifestyle plan.

Prevention oriented ACT interventions for health care can also easily be adapted to the classroom format and can be applied in a variety of prevention pathways by any member of the primary care team. An example is the Health Improvement Project (HIP) for aging adults started by one us (PR) in a primary care clinic (Robinson, Del Vento, & Wischman, 1998). In order to age well, older adults need to learn distress tolerance skills and by self management strategies for common challenges of aging—pain, loss of friends, loss of function, and so on. The HIP is a population-based program delivered by a team comprised of a primary care nurse and a behavioral health provider targeting aging patients who go through a period of sustained high utilization of health care services.

In the HIP program, a medical nurse provides the basic service while the behavioral health provider offers back up consultation and classes on healthy aging. The program includes a series of seven brief phone calls to patients over a 4-month period and two HIP plans written collaboratively with the patient's primary care team to address any problematic health care process. Table 12.3 provides an overview of the content of the nursing calls. The first 4 phone calls occur weekly and address specific behavioral skills. The nurse mails a 1-page interactive brochure to the patient after each phone call. The brochure summarizes the skill discussed in the call and the skill development exercise planned with the patient. Any written behavior plan is shared with the primary care team and, then, placed in the patient's medical record. The nurse initiates three monthly follow-up calls during a continuation phase which follows immediately after the more intensive beginning of 4 weekly behavioral health assessment and change planning calls.

The HIP psychologist provides a weekly one hour body/mind class that is designed to expand on the content area of that week's nursing intervention. All patients are invited to attend in the first phone call, although attendance is optional. Typically, about half of the patients attend the class one or more times. About one third attend the group more than three times. During the first 20 minutes of class, tea is served while patients discuss community resources that they use to embellish daily quality of life. During the remainder of the class, the behavioral health provider gives a brief lecture on a health and wellness topic such as developing experiential acceptance, enhancing sensations of being in the present, or identifying and pursuing valued life directions in the pursuit of healthy aging.

Minnie is a good example of a typical HIP program patient. She was in her 80's and was living alone. She had spent years caring for her husband and had given up most of her valued activities during his last year of life. In an effort to save money, she had moved to the basement of her home and had rented out the main floor to her son and daughter-in-law. Unfortunately, she did not have a good relationship with the couple, so the few interactions they had were negative. During the initial nursing phone calls, Minnie indicated that meditation had once been helpful to her. We encouraged her to re-initiate her meditation practice and to attend the HIP Body/Mind Class. Minnie did attend the class and found it helpful. She learned breathing exercises and used them to help her relax during interactions with her live-in relatives. Minnie also resumed work on two books that she had started many years earlier. Over the course of her 4-month participation in the program, Minnie sold her house and moved to an apartment near a large library where she could attend writing classes and obtain materials easily. She practiced a chair aerobics program several times each week and developed more upper body strength. At a twelve month follow-up, Minnie indicated that she had submitted a book for publication and that she was attending a writer's group on a weekly basis.

ACT Interventions with At Risk Children

Children exhibiting patterns of problematic experiential avoidance go to primary care clinics often, and we need to recognize them and intervene early. Children with emotional disorders such as anxiety or depression incur health costs similar to children with physical conditions, such as diabetes and asthma—considerably higher than children with disruptive disorders (attention deficit hyperactivity disorder, conduct disorder, oppositional defiant disorder).

ACT work with children targets acceptance, defusion, and values using direct, concrete exercises, simple terms, and age appropriate metaphors. For example, one of us (PR) saw a 7 year old boy referred by his pediatrician for management of insomnia and abdominal pain with no discernable organic basis. The boy had witnessed domestic violence between his parents, and his father had been removed from the home. He was taught to watch his stomach as he breathed, filling and emptying it like a balloon, and to allow memories of the violence come and go like the an in his balloon. A 15 inch square "dream blanket" (provided by a circle of sewing women brought together by the Make-A-Wish Foundation) was used to support practicing this mindful breathing exercise at home. Values assessment work help him see a future where he played basketball, wore nice clothes, lived in a warm home, and was very involved with church, and behavioral steps were taken that might foster these goals. During the course of these various interventions, his insomnia and abdominal pain complaints ceased. Parents and teachers can also be mobilized to support acceptance and values work, and they themselves can learn to do similar work to deal with the challenges of an ill child (for an empirical example of a parent training package that used ACT to foster such outcomes see Singer, Irvine, & Irvin, 1989). We will amplify this approach in more detail in the next chapter as it applies to children experiencing pain (see also Chapter 10).

ACT with High Utilizers of Healthcare

There is small group of adult primary care patients who use a large proportion of primary care services. As a group, these "frequent fliers" are fused with beliefs that they have an undiscovered illness. They experience inordinately high levels of stress in their normal environment, have significant health issues, and some suffer from personality disorders. Primary care providers tend to order very costly procedures for such patients to rule out an organic basis for what is often a dynamic, ever-growing, ever-changing list of stress related complaints. ACT is ideal for work with such patients. The case of Maria suggests interventions that are helpful with high utilizing, distressed primary care patients.

Maria came to the clinic with a complaint of head pain. Her internist ordered a series of lab tests and provided specialty referrals during her first visit. She presented again within a week complaining of dizziness, insisting that this was a symptom of epilepsy. She reported having received medicine from an Emergency Room provider that helped temporarily, but caused her to feel tired and "out of it." She insisted that the date for planned diagnostic tests he moved up, as she was worried that she might have a tumor in her head.

An initial assessment of her health related quality of life indicated she had very poor perceptions of her general health and reported numerous psychosocial stressors, most of which were related to interpersonal problems. In order to speed treatment and reduce the stress of unexplained medical symptoms, we offered the patient access to same-day appointments and supported her efforts to obtain medical records from another state where she had previously resided. Her records indicated that she had demonstrated a similar pattern previously and that no organic basis had been found for her complaints. The patient returned for several same-day appointments with the primary care behavioral health provider and learned psychological acceptance techniques in 15-minute visits. She made no further emergency room visits over the next month and agreed to work with the behavioral health provider and the internist to develop a PCP Values Plan to help her move through her difficult situation with dignity.

The patient also attended the Quality of Life (QOL) Class, a seven session one-hour class based on the ACT principles that accepts up to 20 patients and "takes all comers"(see Robinson, 1996, for class content). Because of its size, the QOL Class is a fairly low-cost service that can readily be provided in the context of a primary care clinic. Table 12.4 provides an over-view of the content and sequencing of this curriculum. Patients can repeat the QOL class series as many times as they like, and they have the opportunity to assist in the class after a few repetitions.

In the class, Maria learned additional psychological acceptance skills and applied them, along with problems solving skills, to long-term family problems. She became less concerned about seeking out medical tests and, instead, became more appreciative of her health care providers and more focused on her behavioral goals. Her same day visits dropped off very quickly over the course of the intervention.

ACT for Patients with Chronic Disease

The term "chronic disease" is used to denote medical conditions that are prolonged, do not resolve spontaneously, and are rarely cured completely. Chronic diseases vary greatly, but in general they are common, serious, and costly for individual patients as well as society as a whole. The number of individuals living with chronic disease continues to increase, despite advances in medical technology and information about prevention (Narayan, et al, 2000). The management of chronic disease requires the patient to engage in a variety of self-management and

Table 12.4. Quality of Life Class

Class	Clinical goals	Interventions
1	Initiate focus on values, increase behavioral flexibility	Making a behavioral health plan that fosters hope for a valued life
2	Improve ability to notice avoidance and acceptance continuum	Self-monitoring of willingness, Behavior change to improve social support for valued living directions
3	Improve ability to observe body and mind and notice connections	Breathing exercises, body scan, BOSE
4	Address current distressing problems	Review of problem solving skills
5	Address interpersonal deficits	Understanding conflict in living a valued life, self-care skills for conflict situations, clarification of values concerning conflict
6	Clarify long-term directions	Climbing a Mountain Personal Assertion Planning A Commitment to Creativity
7	Plan an intentional lifestyle	Relapse prevention skill training Health care team collaboration plan

lifestyle change behaviors, but these are often not well addressed by conventional medical care or patient education interventions (e.g., Clement, 1995).

Table 12.5 provides a summary of clinical goals and possible ACT interventions for use with patients with chronic disease. One consideration when applying ACT with such patients is that they have a different mind set than patients seeking psychotherapy. Many of these patients are emphatically not interested in psychological therapy per se. They generally want help managing their disease. This means you may have to trim down ACT interventions like Creative Hopelessness to fit patients who are less insight oriented and use more straightforward exercises, directly linked to facilitating values-related behavior in health-care related areas.

The management of epilepsy provides an example. Epilepsy is a chronic and sometimes debilitating disorder that can be self managed to a significant extent. Some patients with epilepsy also have mental health problems, but many do not. In disease management terms, the key issue is how the patient responds to the life stress and self-evaluations of neurological symptoms that their seizures occasion. The seizures have an organic etiology, and the predisposition to seizures is not likely to change over time. When patients with epilepsy fear and avoid seizures, however, they become psychologically rigid and vigilant, and their life tends to constrict. Paradoxically, this posture increases the likelihood of experiencing a seizure and considerably amplifies the negative psychological, social,

Table 12.5. A Sample of ACT Interventions with Chronic Disease

Clinical goals	Interventions
1. Increase self-management behaviors (compliance with recommended exercise, diet, monitoring directives)	Health-related values work; focus on willingness to experience private events related to being sick
2. Identifying and understanding ways in which controlling private events gets in the way of self-management behaviors	Control as the Problem (Polygraph metaphor, Jelly doughnut metaphor, Fall in love metaphor
3. Conceptualizing self as context rather than content in the service of not buying thoughts and feelings related to chronic disease	Control as the Problem Chessboard metaphor Observer exercise Box with stuff in it exercise
4. Acceptance of negatively-evaluated fears of being sick, being disabled, and dying	Willingness Exercises (Physicializing Exercise, Tin can monster, Two computers, Little Dutch Boy, Monsters on the Bus
5. Defusion of negatively-evaluated thoughts about: being sick, being disabled, and dying	Deliteralization exercises (Take your mind for a walk, Milk exercise, Labeling thoughts/feelings, Distinguishing description, Tell me how to walk
6. Enhance commitment to behavior change in the service of disease and health risk management	Choice versus decision, Willingness as choice and act, Jumping exercise, Eyes-On

and behavioral impact of seizures (Dahl, Brorson & Melin, 1992). While not all seizures can be controlled, most can be influenced in fairly simple and direct ways (Dahl, 1992). The ACT approach is to teach patients to accept their predisposition to seize and the emotions and thoughts that trigger seizures, while continuing to behave effectively. This entails being willing to risk the embarrassment or psychological distress of having seizures (e.g., while engaging in social activities), as well as being willing to accept needed behavioral restrictions (e.g., driving restrictions for poorly regulated epilepsy). Fusion with negative reactions and judgments (i.e., I'm brain damaged; I'm never safe) is reduced, and the self-amplifying process associated with emotional avoidance and fusion is undermined. ACT interventions with epilepsy are currently be evaluated experimentally.

RECOMMENDATIONS FOR TRAINING PRIMARY CARE PROVIDERS

Primary care providers have a very difficult job. On average, primary care providers work 52.8 hours per week (Howard, 1992). When they go through a week with numerous problematic encounters, as defined in the

ACT-HC model, they may struggle with their thoughts and feelings. Behavioral health specialists need to be prepared to help providers experience the painful and difficult aspects of primary care work. Primary care providers welcome self-care workshops that emphasize acceptance and commitment strategies. When providers become highly skillful in these areas, they are empowered to use these strategies directly with more patients and to recommend behavioral health programs teaching these strategies to patients. ACT provides a theoretical structure for addressing the needs of providers and patient educators. The data on this claim are appearing with behavioral health providers (Hayes et al., in press). There seems to be no reason that it will not work equally well with medical providers or patient educators.

There is a great deal more to do to learn how to fit ACT into treatment in medical settings. This chapter was meant as a beginning. Already, however, it seems clear that ACT has a lot to contribute to the medical patients, their providers, and the system of health care.

Chapter 13

ACT with Chronic Pain Patients

PATRICIA ROBINSON, RIKARD K. WICKSELL,
GUNNAR L. OLSSON

Pain that persists for months and years has a profound impact on the sufferer's life. Many chronic pain patients develop co-morbid depression; they utilize medical care excessively and feel wronged by the care they receive; many leave their jobs; obtain disability and settle into a lifestyle that, at best, bears faint resemblance to that they once imagined was possible. Chronic pain is influenced by numerous psychosocial factors, including biological factors as well as the patient's socio-cultural background, beliefs, expectations, and emotions (Turk & Okifuji, 2002). Medical treatment success rates are high for patients with acute pain, but are disappointing for patients with chronic nonmalignant pain. The most common sources of non-cancer-related pain include (in decreasing frequency) back, head, joints, extremity, chest, abdomen and other areas. Since most chronic pain patients experience pain in multiple areas, most medical providers struggle to assess and treat all sources of pain and remain within the time constraints of busy primary care practices. Many patients are referred to specialists and undergo expensive, unsuccessful, invasive procedures—often repeatedly. The problem is not restricted to adults: children and adolescents also develop pain symptoms that are refractory to treatment and that lead to severe disability (Kashikar-Zuck, Graham, Huenefeld, & Powers, 2000). Research is more extensive with adult populations (Morley, Eccleston, & Williams, 1999) than with pediatric pain.

The psychosocial treatment of chronic pain typically begins after traditional medical care has failed to regulate the problem. General psychiatric approaches have little empirical support. Both operant behavior therapy (OBT: Fordyce, 1976), and cognitive-behavior therapy (CBT: Turk, Meichenbaum, & Genest, 1983) have empirical support, particularly with chronic pain syndrome and chronic low back pain (e.g., Puder, 1988; Turner, Clancy, McQuade, & Cardenas, 1990). When the two have been compared in adult populations OBT has been slightly more effective (Nicholas, Wilson, & Goyen, 1991; Turner & Clancy, 1988). In children, relaxation, biofeedback, and CBT all have some support (Eccleston, Morley, Williams, Yorke, & Mastroyannopoulou, 2002; Holden, Deichmann, & Levy, 1999; Janicke & Finnev, 1999), but results vary with the type of pain. In some areas (e.g., generalized musculoskeletal pain with children) there are no successful controlled studies on effective non-pharmacological interventions. There clearly is a need for new approaches.

Acceptance and Commitment Therapy (ACT) (Hayes, Strosahl & Wilson, 1999) offers a novel approach that may help behavioral health and medical providers prevent and treat chronic pain. There is a growing body of evidence that acceptance as the term is defined and measured in ACT (using a pain specific measure modified from the Acceptance and Action Questionnaire, Hayes et al., in press) is a key issue in the development and maintenance of chronic pain (McCracken, 1998; McCracken, Vowles, & Eccleston, 2004). Acceptance accounts for more of the variance in outcome on pain, depression, anxiety, disability, vocational functioning, and physical functioning than existing measures of coping with pain (McCracken & Eccleston, 2003). ACT interventions improve the tolerance of pain in normal populations more so than CBT interventions (e.g., Gutiérrez, Luciano, Rodríguez, & Fink, in press; Hayes, Bissett, Korn, Zettle, Rosenfarb, Cooper, & Grundt, 1999), while attempt to suppress pain tends to increase it (Cioffi & Holloway, 1993). There are supportive case studies on the outcome of ACT on pain with adults (Luciano, Visdómine, Gutiérrez, & Montesinos, 2001; Montesinos, Hernández, & Luciano, 2001) and children (Wicksell, Dahl, Magnusson, & Olsson, under review). Uncontrolled studies of ACT-based pain programs are also supportive (Robinson & Brockey, 1996). Finally, controlled clinical trials are beginning to appear. For example, in a small randomized trial (Dahl, Wilson, & Nilsson, in press) comparing four sessions of ACT to treatment as usual with workers who were taking excessive sick leave due to pain, large differences were found in the number of work days missed by the end of a six month follow-up.

In this chapter, we will consider gaps in current services as groundwork for consideration of ACT as a model that will enhance prevention and treatment efforts. In separate sections for adults and children, we will suggest specific interventions and offer methods for anticipating and addressing common obstacles to successful ACT treatment.

CASE FORMULATION

Pain + unwillingness to have pain = chronic pain. That, in a nutshell, is the core of the ACT model of chronic pain. This does not mean that relatively continuous pain only comes in the context of unwillingness—but rather that the life crushing effects of pain that we see in chronic pain syndrome requires more than pain per se. The goal of ACT is to help patients with chronic pain consistently act in ways that are aligned with their values while making room for all of the private experiences that go into having pain, as pain. Four areas need to be assessed when developing an ACT formulation of a chronic pain patient: (1) overt behavioral avoidance, (2) emotional control strategies, (3) fusion with pain related thoughts, and (4) life direction issues. Chronic pain patients vary widely within and among these dimensions. At one end of the continuum, we have the highly functioning patient with a shoulder problem of 6 months duration who works fulltime at a high-paying job that she likes. At the other end, we have a depressed patient with multiple health problems and a history of sexual abuse whose life has been blown up for decades by the experience of pain.

Behavioral Avoidance

Pain sensations are demanding, and all individuals with the ability to perceive pain avoid inducing it most of the time. However, individuals differ in the overt behavioral strategies they employ when pain sensations are present. These behaviors can be grouped into at least four groups:

1. *Isolating behaviors.* Most chronic pain patients distance themselves from work, leisure and social activities. They may leave their jobs, even when they like them, and avoid participation in volunteer jobs no matter how minimal the physical requirements. They fail to maintain friendships, or avoid contact with neighbors. They avoid exercise in response to the thought, "If I walk half way down the block, I'll start hurting and I can't stand it." So, they isolate, retiring to the couch or bedroom, where they often engage in health risk behaviors, such as smoking, overeating, or sedentary activities such as excessive television-watching.

2. *Interpersonal engagement behaviors.* The chronic pain patient engages the interpersonal world in ways that support "being a chronic pain patient." These behaviors may include irritability, self-disparaging remarks,

or excessive sharing of catastrophic thoughts about pain. Initially these produce various forms of engagement from others (e.g., anger, encouragement, reassurance) but in the long run they undermine social relationships.

3. *Medication, equipment, and procedure behaviors.* The use of pain medications and various devices (e.g., injections into trigger points, insertion of a plate into the back, use of wheel chair) initially may produce a positive result, but the effect is transitory and new medicines, procedures and/or surgeries are tried and tried again.

4. *Comfort behaviors.* Warm baths, self-massage, applying ice or heat packs, stretching, and the like may provide the patient with temporary relief from pain and may facilitate improved functioning when done with a willingness to experience pain sensations, thoughts about pain, or emotional responses to pain. If performed as behavioral avoidance strategies, however, the long term impact is not likely to be positive because—like all forms of experiential avoidance—they may strengthen the control exerted by such sensations, thoughts, or fears. As with all areas of ACT, it is the function, not the form, of these behaviors that is more important.

Assessing these various functions can be accomplished through verbal interaction with the patient, but using checklists saves time, improves communication, promotes more collaboration in forming treatment goals, and provides a means of evaluating whether treatment is working. The degree to which pain is associated with both the reduction of needed activities and the unwillingness to experience pain or private events associated with it can be assessed through the Chronic Pain Acceptance Questionnaire (CPAQ: McCracken et al., 2004), which yields scores in these two areas.

Emotional Avoidance Strategies

Chronic pain patients employ numerous psychological strategies for controlling their emotional responses such as suppression, distraction, emotional numbing, or avoidance of certain topics. They may focus on negative experiences with medical providers, or on the need to have pain go away. These emotional avoidance strategies tend to spread. Chronic pain patients who are most likely to experience depression are those most committed to controlling their cognitive and emotional responses. Experiential avoidance correlates as high as .72 with the Beck Depression Inventory (BDI) in clinical populations (Hayes et al., in press), and similarly acceptance of pain correlates −.52 with the BDI in chronic pain patients (McCracken et al., 2004). Catastrophizing beliefs about pain also predict depression in chronic pain (Turner, Jensen & Romano, 2000). Perhaps as an extreme extension of emotional avoidance, many long-standing chronic pain patients experience suicidal ideation, and the possibility of suicide needs to be assessed on an on-going basis. ACT offers excellent strategies for working with suicidal ideation, and this is discussed in more detail in Chapters 4 and 9.

Fusion

The literal negative evaluation of physical pain sets up the struggle to avoid and eliminate it. A chronic pain patient can report a current pain rating of 6 and note that such is lower than the average of 7 for the past week, and, five minutes later, start to cry and rub a body part, explaining that, "I can't take this pain anymore." The psychological path that produces such effects is cognitive fusion with thoughts about pain. Pain patients are more likely to associate neutral events with pain and to recall more sensory and affective pain-related adjectives in comparison to persons without chronic pain (Edwards & Pearce, 1994). The relational networks that result can be dramatically unhelpful. One of us (PR) recently asked a mother who suffered chronic severe headaches to relate her internal experience when she was asked to rate her pain. She cried, held her head, and stated that she feared that her children would soon have no mother and would be alone in the world.

Fusion with this type of catastrophic thought process is a core target in an ACT approach to chronic pain. Catastrophizing, which refers to an exaggerated negative mental set brought to bear during the experience of pain (Sullivan, et al., 2001), is associated with higher pain, poorer functioning, higher use of analgesics, and more difficulties with treatment (Jacobson & Butler, 1996; Robinson, et al., 1997; Thorn & Boothby, 2002; Ulmer, 1997). The Pain Catastrophizing Scale (PCS: Sullivan, Bishop, & Pivik, 1995), which takes just a couple of minutes to use and score, can be used to assess this area. Patients who obtain a total score above 38 (80th percentile) are particularly likely to experience adjustment difficulties and to progress poorly in rehabilitation programs (Sullivan, Stanish, Waite, Sullivan, & Tripp, 1998). Since the ACT treatment model is less focused on the content or presence of pain related thinking than on fusion and willingness, an additional measure can be added to PCS. The instructions to patients are as follows: "Everyone experiences painful situations at some point in their lives. Such experiences may include headaches, tooth pain, joint or muscle pain. People are often exposed to situations that may cause pain such as illness, injury, dental procedures or surgery. We are interested in your *willingness to experience* the thoughts and feelings that you have when you are in pain. Listed below are thirteen statements describing different thoughts and feelings that you may have when in pain. Using the following scale, please indicate the degree to which you are willing to have these thoughts and feelings occur when you are experiencing

Table 13.1. Paradigm for Conceptualizing Catastrophization and Willingness Levels among Chronic Pain Patients and Treatment Implications

			Willingness		
		Low	Treatment suggestions	High	Treatment suggestions
Catastrophization (Private Experience)	Low	Intensive	Full ACT Protocol Adjusted pace PCP	Less Intensive	Psycho-education about emotions Strengthen cognitive acceptance skills
	High	Most Intensive	Full ACT protocol Pace adjusted Significant Others involved Close coordination with PCP	Somewhat Intensive	Psycho-education about emotions Strengthen cognitive acceptance skills Chronic pain inoculation training

pain—without struggling and without attempting to avoid them." Patients then respond to the 13 statements on the PCS using a 5-point scale: 0 = not at all willing, 1 = to a slight degree willing, 2 = to a moderate degree willing, 3 = to a great degree willing, 4 = willing to have and experience completely.

Table 13.1 presents a method for conceptualizing treatment based on the level of the patient's catastrophization experience in relation to pain and his or her willingness to have the experience. Patients that are low in catastrophization and high in willingness may require relatively little treatment unless the low catastrophization score is an underestimation due to avoidance or even dissociation. Usually this can be ruled out using any exercise involving contact with direct emotional experience. In the more typical case, therapeutic activities for this group include education concerning emotional experiences in pain, and strengthening the acceptance strategies the patient is already using.

Patients with high catastrophizing and a high level of willingness may also require relatively little treatment, but they are at higher risk for developing prolonged suffering in response to injuries, particularly traumatic injuries. It is important to help this group strengthen their observer self and defusion skills. We often use a psycho-educational approach with these patients and will encourage the patient to participate in community activities that further strengthen acceptance skills (e.g., meditation classes, yoga, Tai Chi).

Patients with low willingness are more likely to be experiencing co-morbid emotional problems, such as depression, anxiety and worry. They will often have more functional impairments, such as interpersonal problems (including problematic relationships with their medical providers), unemployment, and difficulties with independent self-care. This group contains the "classic" chronic pain patient. Given this, they will probably need a full ACT protocol, close coordination with medical providers, and the involvement of significant others. Patients with low willingness and low catastrophization scores may progress more quickly than patients that are high in both catastrophization and unwillingness. However, be aware that low levels of catastrophizing can be produced by cognitive avoidance and/or primitive moves like dissociation.

Low levels of willingness are sometimes associated with a history of trauma, which can make chronic pain more complicated and difficult to treat. When a patient has a story involving having been wronged or traumatized, he or she may be fused with thoughts, images, and memories relating to their perceived victimization. If the trauma is related to the pain itself, or if compensation is being sought, more complications should be expected (Turk & Okifuji, 1996).

Fusion is also evident in the patient's story about pain and suffering. Fusion with right and wrong evaluations (e.g., "my employer made me ... " or "my doctor should have ... ") are both common and predictive of en-trenched difficulties. These patients are often the most faithful and rigid subscribers to the verbal community's notion that no one should have to suffer pain ... and they tend to have the most pain. It can useful while lis-tening to these stories to note the verbal relations that structure the story and how they connect to the patient's change agenda (e.g., physical pain = danger; physical pain = less acceptable person; physical pain = seek help; physical pain = take medicine; physically damaged person = burden to others, and so on).

Life Direction

While ACT attempts to undermine the verbal control exerted by un-workable catastrophic beliefs about pain, it tries to build verbal control as well by encouraging the patient to identify their values and engage in patterns of committed action that are consistent with these values. Chronic pain patients are often out of contact with their values, and often confuse them with concrete goals rather than qualities of action that can only be instantiated, not "obtained." Discussing values early in treatment may enhance motivation for treatment. The Valued Living Questionnaire (Wilson & Murrell, in press; see Hayes et al., 1999, p. 226 for an earlier version) can be used as part of the initial assessment of pain patients. In treatment planning, we highlight areas with significant inconsistencies between what the patient values and what is being done in life, and invite the patient to choose a beginning point. Chronic pain patients as a group respond well—often with a great deal of emotion—to discussion of values once they understand the difference between goals and values.

CLINICAL INTERVENTIONS

Table 13.2 provides an overview of the clinical goals and treatment activities typically employed in working with chronic pain patients. The amount of time spent pursuing each of these goals depends on the individual patient, and the order can vary. ACT is a flexible model and session length can also vary, down to the 15 and 30 minute appointments characteristic of such work in a primary care medical team (the focus of many of the clinical suggestions in this chapter).

Assessment

In addition to the questionnaires already mentioned as part of case formulation, health-related quality of life should be assessed. Session by session use of the Duke Health Profile (Parkerson, 1996) is good for this, particularly useful are the Physical Health, Mental Health, Social Health and Perceived Health scaled scores. Patients can complete the Duke prior to the start of the visit in less than five minutes, an assistant for the behavioral health provider can calculate scores in 2–3 minutes, and results are then available for discussion with the patient at the start of the appointment.

ACT can be introduced by explaining that scientists are continuing to do research to increase our understanding of pain and problems patients have when pain continues for a long time. Some of the most recent findings contradict previous assumptions about pain and ACT treatment may seem confusing at times for this reason. Since ACT treatment involves questioning some very basic assumptions (that the patient may have staked his quality of life on), it is useful to highlight how ACT is different than what the patient may be expecting, and that confusion or distress may come up because many of the concepts are counter-intuitive. Other treatment options should be discussed and a contract negotiated with the patient concerning minimum treatment length (e.g., 2–23 months) and methods for

Table 13.2. ACT Treatment Phases, Goals and Recommended Interventions for Chronic Pain Patients

Treatment phase	Goals	Clinical interventions
Creative hopelessness	Help patient perceive the lack of workability of current approach to pain. Help patient open to alternatives ways of responding to pain	What have you tried, how has it worked? Scientist-talk about pain. Coach vs. Reporter. Shovel and hole Metaphor. Valued actions vs. real actions discrepancy. Pain catastrophizing assessment
Control is the problem	Help patient see pain elimination as an unworkable strategy. Help patient see relationship between control & suffering	The rule of private events/donkeys. Polygraph Metaphor. Clean and Dirty Discomfort. Daily pain willingness diary. Two Scales Metaphor. Alphabet Soup Metaphor
Defusing Language	Help patient notice thoughts and feelings, including reason giving, at the level of an observer. Help patient weaken the social/verbal context of controlling pain	Your mind: Crown of diamonds, crown of thorns. Finding a Place to Sit Metaphor. Passengers on the Bus Metaphor. Take Your Mind for a Walk. Reasons as Causes. Cubby holing. BOSE
Observing Self	Help patient see self as separate from his or her mind; establish a "safe" place to have pain related experiences	Chessboard Metaphor. Pick an Identity Exercise. Observer self exercise
Valuing	Help patient identify valued life ends. Provide motivational force to function with pain	Taking a Stand Exercise. Letter to Provider/Loved One(s). Gardening Metaphor. Path Up the Mountain Metaphor. Riding a Bike
Patterns of Committed Action	Help develop and implement life-changing behavior plans	Choice vs. Decision. Jumping exercise. Swamp Metaphor

evaluating progress. Using the ACT modified version of the PCS provides an opportunity to introduce concepts related to simple awareness, willingness and self-as-context. Patients often seem confused but they also sense that we are talking about something different from what other providers have said, and this arouses some curiosity.

Not all patients choose ACT as a method of treatment when it is offered the first time. Some patients will decline ACT in favor of continuing narcotic medications and working with their primary care physician, for example. For such patients, you may want to help the physician develop a physician-patient narcotic pain management contract that includes a method for determining the effectiveness of treatment such as a health-related quality of life measure. Often it becomes obvious over time that narcotics reduce pain somewhat but at the cost of further worsening the patient's quality of life. This discovery can lead the patient to return for further discussion of the viability of an ACT approach. Patients need not stop using medications in order to do ACT but some patients do choose to taper from medications during ACT treatment.

Creative Hopelessness

After listening to the patient's story about his or her pain problem, you should try to understand what the patient wants from treatment and begin to focus on the values that in fact are part of the current situation. You might ask, "If a miracle happened, here and now, in your life, how would your life be different?" Most respond, with little or no reflection, that they would be free of pain. If encouraged to imagine how being free of pain (a process outcome) would affect their lives, potentially meaningful treatment outcomes usually begin to appear such as financial, relationship, employment, or leisure outcomes (e.g., "I'll be able to pay my bills;" "My husband will like me again;" "I'll be able to go back to work;" "I'll be able to show my dogs again"). If other process goals come up, such as "I won't be depressed anymore," as with pain encourage them to go further into describing what would be different in their lives without depression. As other outcomes are generated ("I'd go out more—to church on Sundays;" "Maybe I would call an old friend rather than staying home all the time") it may help to list these in two columns (process and treatment outcomes), and show them to the patient for confirmation.

Next, we start to assess their efforts to solve the problem of chronic pain. Most patients can easily list the things they've tried. Often, they will report participation at multidisciplinary pain programs and other culturally supported solutions such as medication use, surgical procedures, injections, physical therapy, massage therapy, and acupuncture. Some patients will indicate they have used various behavioral pain management strategies, such as distraction, application of ice and/or heat, and relaxation/imagery exercises. You should note these and ask the patient to evaluate the workability of these strategies, as demonstrated in the following session transcript.

THERAPIST: So, you said that you were taking medicines to solve the problem of pain?

PATIENT: Yes, I take three medicines for pain now. Dr. Smith just changed one, and I don't know if it's working, but the other two I've been taking for a while.

THERAPIST: Okay. You're taking three medicines. Do you take them as Dr. Smith prescribes them?

PATIENT: Yes, pretty much. I'm not sure they help all that much. Sometimes I take a little more of this one and a little less of this one.

THERAPIST: Okay, you take the medicines, and you are hoping that...?

PATIENT: Well, that the pain will go away.

THERAPIST: And what has happened?

PATIENT: I don't know. I think they help some—dull the pain, but they make me tired and, well, kind of spaced-out and not motivated. My wife says I act like a puppy dog since I increased this one, but maybe that's better than being irritable. I don't know. This one, I know it upsets my stomach, so I have to take another medicine to coat my stomach. I'm really a mess (eyes moisten).

THERAPIST: Okay, you take the medicines, and they dull the pain, make you tired, spaced-out and upset your stomach. Right?

PATIENT: Yes, I guess that's right. It doesn't sound so good, huh?

THERAPIST: I don't know. What are you hoping for when you take the medicines?

PATIENT: That I'll get better, feel like I did before the accident, fix my house up, go to work, be a provider for my family instead of a deadbeat.

THERAPIST: So, you take the medicines hoping that you'll do the things you once did—fix your house, work, provide for your family—and the medicines dull the pain and make you tired and so you don't fix your house or go back to work? Do I have that right?

PATIENT: That's about it, but I don't think I could make it without them. Do you think I should?

THERAPIST: I really don't know. For now, I'm just trying to help you figure out what you're doing and how it's working. If we look closely, maybe we'll be able to see if anything you've tried so far has worked in the sense of really making a difference in your life and changing the problem of pain in a way that makes it less distressing and less of a barrier to doing the things you want to do—like fix your house and go to work. Let's see, I think you said that you went to a pain clinic. How did going to the pain clinic work for you?

PATIENT: That was a waste of time. They thought it was all in my head. They tried to get me to do things that hurt me. I really think it may have made me worse. I actually quit that after a week. I was worse—hurting all over, and I didn't go back to the doctor that sent me to that pain clinic either.

THERAPIST: Okay, a doctor told you to go to a pain clinic and you did. You thought they were making you worse and you quit. How did that work for you?

PATIENT: Well, I'm not sure what you mean. I guess it worked to quit so that they didn't make me damage myself further, but it didn't make my pain go away.

THERAPIST: So, you stopped going to the clinic, and you think that helped you avoid being injured by the program. That did not stop the pain or get you fixing the house or going back to work.

PATIENT: Right, but I felt bad about quitting in a way—I tried not to, but I felt like I had failed again.

THERAPIST: Okay, you went to the program, didn't like it and quit, and felt like a failure. How did that work?

PATIENT: Not so good. I felt ashamed, and I didn't even go to the doctor for awhile—just stayed on the couch until I had to go to get some medicine before I lost my mind.

THERAPIST: So, you tried feeling like a failure and trying not to go the doctor and just laying on the couch. How did that work in solving the problem of pain?

PATIENT: It didn't. I'm here, still in pain.

THERAPIST: So you went to the doctor to get medicine before you lost your mind?

PATIENT: Yes.

THERAPIST: So you took the medicines to avoid loosing your mind. Did they work?

PATIENT: I don't know—I guess, not really.

As you work through the list of change efforts, you can begin to introduce the patient to the concept of observing mental activity. This was done with the above patient:

THERAPIST: "So what else does your mind tell you to do about pain?"

PATIENT: Ignore it—don't be a baby.

THERAPIST: So you belittle yourself for having pain. How does that work?

PATIENT: Not at all—well maybe a little. I don't know. My parents used to criticize me when I got hurt and cried. I think that made me mad. My Dad would say, "Get up. You act like a girl. I'm going to give you something to cry about."

THERAPIST: So you do that—get mad at yourself—to solve the problem of pain?

PATIENT: Yes, I guess I do. Some days, I'm mad at everyone. No one understands what it's like.

THERAPIST: So you get mad. How does getting mad work in terms of solving the problem of pain?

PATIENT: It doesn't. I think getting mad and beating my self up just makes things worse. So, where are you going with this? Am I supposed to have an insight and just get over the pain?

During the process of conducting a "what have you tried, how has it worked, what is it costing you?" analysis, you need to be aware of some potential traps. One is becoming fascinated with the patient's life story, as many chronic pain patients have experienced numerous injuries and traumas. The other is beginning to analyze or evaluate the patient's story at the level of the content of the story. This is very tempting for cognitively trained therapists because of the high level of catastrophic, distorted thinking that is evident. Nevertheless, you need to maintain a focus on assessing the verbal structure of the change agenda and noting the consequences of the strategies that patient has used in the service of eliminating pain.

By getting the patient to name what the desired outcome is and how life would be different if that outcome occurred, the patient's change agenda is exposed naturally. It is usually better not to challenge it at first—it is better to have the patient to walk through that door. Eventually, a name is put on the change agenda: "In order to have a productive, happy life, I must eliminate my pain."

It is worthwhile to ask patients to describe what their mind says should be done ("There's another way—a new way to get rid of pain") and to contrast it with their experience ("Nothing has made for substantial improvement"). You can use the *Man in the Hole Metaphor* (Hayes et al., 1999, pp. 101–104) routinely in early therapy and incorporate common concerns that pain patients often report into it (e.g., finding out what caused them to fall in the hole, self-blame, waiting for the golden steam shovel). Other metaphors often come up in the patient's language that allow the system to be named in a way that is personally relevant. You should empathize with how difficult it is to let go of something that the patient was sure would work, but apparently doesn't. The concept of response-ability can help the patient see can that only they can decide to drop the shovel. No amount of urging, criticism, or advice can do that for them. In some respects, this is the first act of willingness: a choice to stop doing something that doesn't work even while not seeing an alternative.

Often patients with longer histories of pain and disability are fused to their story and fiercely obedient to the control agenda. They can become strident and self righteous with very little prodding and you may find yourself beaten down and ready to agree with or affirm the pain patient's story of victimization. This process may be signaled by private events of your own (e.g., annoyance, boredom, daydreaming, thoughts such as "I am too busy for this"). The way out of stultifying content is to catch the function. For example, instead of arguing with the patient you may simply pause and ask "how does this work for you?"

When the patient can perceive momentarily that their system of controlling pain is unworkable, it is time to bring up the concept of letting go as an alternative to continuing with unworkable pain elimination/avoidance strategies. The *Tug-of-War Metaphor* (Hayes et al., 1999, p. 109) is especially apt, because pain patients can readily perceive their pain as an ugly monster and it gives patients a metaphorical tool for recognizing situations in day-to-day experiences outside of therapy when he or she is tempted to "pick up the rope." Self-monitoring and homework assignments can be used to create awareness of when struggle is present and when letting go is present. We all have opportunities to pick up and drop the rope many times every day.

Control Is the Problem

In this component of ACT we name the chronic pain change agenda and begin to undermine confidence in it. The following session excerpt exemplifies some of the processes involved.

This involves a patient who had worked since childhood to develop control strategies associated with poliomyelitis-related pain. As an adolescent, he had experimented with pain medicines before discovering heroin, which he then used until he lost his young daughter in a motor vehicle accident and began to question the workability of heroin use in his life. He was currently enrolled in a methadone program and was facing physically and psychologically challenging health problems, including Hepatitis C and impending surgery on both feet to correct a problem that prevented walking without extreme pain. He reported being abstinent from heroin for 2 months—his second effort at abstaining. His first occurred several years ago, lasted two-years, and included successful meditation study (which sped up the early ACT sessions). He came to the session in a wheel chair that looked like it needed repair.

THERAPIST: So did you notice anything about times when you picked up the rope or had the urge to?

PATIENT: Actually, I did. I was frustrated at home because I couldn't get into a closet to get something I needed. My wheel chair was too wide. I got mad and stood up and made myself walk. It hurt like hell and the only way I made it was to use an image to distract me from the pain. I came up with it years ago—maybe as a kid.

THERAPIST: Yeah. What was the image?

PATIENT: I imagined that I was being tortured as a prisoner of war. The enemy soldiers were cutting me—making slices on my legs with sharp knives. They were making fun of me, holding their knives up in my face with my blood on them. I kept telling myself that I wouldn't cave in, I wouldn't cry, I wouldn't even flinch.

THERAPIST: Whew! That's quite an image.

PATIENT: It was quite a struggle but you know what... when I got back to my chair—I actually didn't get what I was after—when I got back, I sat down and cried. I felt overwhelmingly sad (patient began to tear)... because I realized that I have done this for years. I have probably damaged my feet so that they can't be fixed, even with this surgery—like I won't be able to walk again.

THERAPIST: That's pretty sad. Can you make room for being sad about that?

PATIENT: I guess I need to.

THERAPIST: We can work on making room. Did you notice anything else while you were sitting there in your chair?

PATIENT: Well, I think I was getting ready to criticize myself—you know, "Stupid, you should have... whatever." But I didn't. I just sat there and I had this image of myself as a young boy. All my brothers and sisters were upset with me because we weren't going somewhere fun—a fair or carnival or something. My Mom had said we couldn't go because it was too much trouble to take me. I felt ashamed, like I didn't want to be there... or here. I just wanted to evaporate. And, then, I started thinking about how to score something. Honest to God, I could taste the heroin on my tongue the moment I thought about it. From that moment, I knew I was going to try to score. It was like that—like a gun that had been discharged but just hadn't hit the target yet.

THERAPIST: What kind of emotions did you experience once you started thinking about using?

PATIENT: I was hurting all over—not just my feet. I was hurting all over. My skin was just crawling, and I was having trouble breathing—really felt out-of-control, and I tried to get a handle on it, but I couldn't.

THERAPIST: So, what did you do when you couldn't get a handle on it?
PATIENT: Well, I told myself to knock it off—that I could get kicked out of the clinic—the methadone clinic.
THERAPIST: So, you threatened yourself, more or less. Did that work?
PATIENT: No. It seemed like the more I tried, the worse I felt and the more I wanted to use.

Most of the typical ACT exercises and metaphors for this phase of treatment can be used with chronic pain populations, and these were used with this patient. Psychoeducation is also relevant: it helps for the patient to understand that the trap of suppression and control is built into human language, and this struggle is not their fault. The following research story (which has been written to apply to Hispanic patients working in an agricultural region), is an example: "A study was done recently. The experimenter divided people into two groups. Participants in each group came into the room for the experiment, one at a time. In group one, the experimenter started by asking, "Do you know about donkeys—4 legs, smaller than horses?" When the participant said yes, the experiment then continued, "Good, now I want you to put this puzzle of an apple orchard together and talk aloud as you do so—talk about anything you like." The experimenter gave the same instructions to the participants in group two, with one exception. After asking the patients to put the puzzle together, he said, "Talk aloud as you work. Talk about anything you want, except donkeys. Don't talk about donkeys. Okay?" You can then ask the patient to guess what happened. Many guess that the group two participants were able to control their language and talked less about donkeys. Others are unsure. You can continue: "What happened was that the ones who were instructed to be unwilling to talk about donkeys—talked less about donkeys for the first five minutes of working on the puzzle, but then their rate of talking about donkeys jumped much higher that the other group."
The following is an excerpt from the same session with the above patient, who did call a dealer to score. However, he had to hang up when his sister came home.

PATIENT: So, I was calling this other place I thought I might make a connection, but my sister came into the trailer. She sat down right by me, so I couldn't talk without her hearing. She just seemed to know something was wrong. She's like that—intuitive, you know. I felt really guilty because she has helped me out a lot—taking me to the clinic and making sure I have food and all. So, I just hung up. But I was really hurting and whacked, you know, and I just started bawling.
THERAPIST: You did? You started crying. How did that work?

PATIENT: I think it worked. My sister asked me if I'd like to talk. I said maybe. She got up and made some tea. She drinks tea. She was very kind, and she listened to me.

THERAPIST: How did that work—crying and talking to your sister?

PATIENT: Well, I didn't use and my sadness passed, so I'd say that worked. Like I told you the first time I met you, I want to have honest relationships with people I love—that's important to me.

THERAPIST: Okay. So that's the kind of thing that gives meaning to your live—maybe dignifies the struggle you have with pain and heroin. Best I can figure, we don't control feelings—pain or sadness—so it's a matter of learning to experience them without having to beat ourselves up or use drugs.

The therapist (PR) went on to discuss *Clean and Dirty Discomfort* with this patient (Hayes et al., 1999, pp. 136). It is not pain per se that is lethal to the conduct of one's life, it is what we do about pain that makes it toxic. In this case, we discussed his clean and dirty emotional responses to the frustration of not being able to get in the closet and the sadness he experienced when making room for his urge to use an illegal drug to escape from this thoughts and feelings. We talked about his learning to have more compassion for himself (like his sister did) and about the context of self where that can happen.

When not focused on gauging and controlling pain, pain patients often experience sadness, as the above client did. His way of expressing his experience suggests that he is moving quickly through this phase of treatment and that he is clearly aware of how frustration with his lack of independence triggers both avoidant behavior and avoidant feelings. In seconds, he'd moved from being unable to reach something in a closet to hopelessness and action planning concerning obtaining a powerful, consciousness-altering substance. His way of talking about his experience suggested that he was ready to move into the next phase of treatment.

Defusion and Self as an Ongoing Process

A somewhat educational approach can be used to speed progress. For example, it helps to note the difference between primary (descriptive) and secondary (evaluative) attributes (i.e., red shirt/ugly shirt; doctor in white coat/good doctor; warm sensation/excruciating sensation). The *Finding A Place to Sit Metaphor* (Hayes et al., 1999, 152–153) can help explain the difference between mental activity (describing and evaluating) and experiencing (sitting). It is also useful for patients to know that naturalistic studies of natural cognition indicate that much of our self-evaluative thinking is negative.

It is best to link interventions like these to patient action and engagement. For example, you might invite patients to speculate on how this aspect of human experiencing might challenge attempts to achieve healthy happy lives through the elimination of negative private experiences. Some patients need specific exercises to help them defuse, while others step back more readily. You need to be very attentive to patient language and to notice when a patient starts to demonstrate defused language spontaneously.

The following excerpt is from the last few minutes of the session described in the previous section. It illustrates how a patient can move quickly into more of an observer stance.

> THERAPIST: So, let's see. You were crying and thinking about using drugs again to avoid feeling what?
>
> PATIENT: To avoid feeling like a deadbeat, a bummer, a cripple that's just in the way, like ouch! I don't like to say this, but it's there in my mind—like a person that shouldn't have been born, a mistake, a freak.
>
> THERAPIST: And when you say that right now, what is it that you are feeling?
>
> PATIENT: I'm sad. I just feel sad. If this makes sense, I almost feel sorry for my mind, but not for me.
>
> THERAPIST: That makes sense to me. It's like you're feeling your sadness, but you are feeling it differently . . . with more acceptance and more compassion.
>
> PATIENT: Yeah, and that works, but I don't know how to hold on to it. I'm scared I'll lose it and get stuck again in struggle. I've got some real nasty patterns of escaping, and I don't want to lose it again.
>
> THERAPIST: And can you make room for feeling scared?
>
> PATIENT: You know, I think scared is harder for me than sad. Sad, I can watch. Scared kind of melts me down.
>
> THERAPIST: Let's watch that melt down together, shall we? Let's look at it. You've got some nasty patterns of escape and you're scared of going back to them? What else is your mind telling you?

During this phase of treatment, while listening to the patient explore the contents of his or her mind you might develop a list of hot thoughts, feelings and/or experiences, write these down and later hand them to the patient one at a time asking, "Is there anything about this that you can't have at the observer level?" For more anxious patients, relaxation and diaphragmatic breathing exercises can be used in conjunction with acceptance strategies. In the BOSE procedure (Robinson, 1996), the patient (1) Breathes in a relaxed way, (2) Observes mental activity, (3) Stimulates mental and emotional activity (by drawing a hot thought from a bowl of hot thoughts written on small slips of paper), and (4) Embraces his or her private experience. Defusion exercises such as *Passengers on the Bus* (Hayes et al., 1999, 157–158) or "Milk, milk, milk" (Hayes et al., 1999, 154–156) are useful in this phase but they should be modified to fit pain per se (e.g., you may start with "Milk, milk, milk" but should move to "Pain, pain, pain." See Masuda et al., in press for the empirical results of such modifications).

Many chronic pain patients have a strong pattern of reason-giving, and it is more difficult to undermine the pervasive impact of this kind of literal thought. It is important to help these patients notice their reasons and to learn to use them when they work and to perceive them as mental clatter when they don't work. The following is an excerpt from a session midway through treatment from a patient who had developed musculoskeletal pain and against medical advice withdrew from all normal activities on the belief that her providers had failed to detect and treat an underlying condition. Her well-established social network rallied around her, and she became progressively more disabled.

THERAPIST: So you planned to go for a walk with your neighbor this morning, but you didn't.

PATIENT: Yes, I felt tight and my legs ached, and I thought I might not be able to make it around the pond with her. It's a half mile.

THERAPIST: So, you didn't go because you thought you might not make it around the pond and your legs ached. Any other reason?

PATIENT: No, I don't think so.

THERAPIST: Can you think of any reason somebody else might give for not going for a walk?

PATIENT: I don't know. Maybe if they're tired . . . or maybe they don't want to be with the person they planned to walk with.

THERAPIST: Okay. Were those reasons for you?

PATIENT: No.

THERAPIST: Do you think they're valid reasons?

PATIENT: I guess so.

THERAPIST: Can you think of any reasons that are not good reasons for going for a walk?

PATIENT: Not good reasons? Mmmm . . . I guess being lazy isn't a good reason.

THERAPIST: Could you be lazy and go for a walk?

PATIENT: I guess.

THERAPIST: And could you be tired and go for a walk?

PATIENT: I guess so. What's your point?

THERAPIST: Well, it's like our minds are really good at coming up with reasons—some we like and think are good and others we evaluate as bad. Maybe reasons don't really cause us to do things or not do things, but sometimes we get fooled into thinking that they do...ever think that reasons seem more potent than they actually are—in terms explaining why we do things?

The Take Your Mind for a Walk exercise (Hayes et al., 1999, pp. 162–163) can be adapted to help patients explore reason giving by asking the patient to require that the mind generate one or more reasons for all of *its* activities. This usually brings a little lightness to the process of observing the endless reason-giving that is often present in the lives of patients troubled by chronic pain.

Self as Context

In this phase of treatment, the goal is to help the chronic pain patient see that there is a place in which pain with all of its negative baggage can be experienced in a non-toxic way. This is accomplished primarily through the use of standard ACT metaphors and experiential exercises (e.g., *Observer Exercise* and the *Chessboard Metaphor*, Hayes et al., 1999, pp. 190–196). Often, the patient exhibits a greater sense of humor and lightness in regards to himself or herself during this phase of treatment. Patients who have a history of traumatic injury related to pain onset seem often to benefit from the *Observer Exercise*, and it can be combined with the *Tin Can Monster Exercise* for more concentrated work (Hayes et al., 1999, pp. 171–174). As the client acquires a more solid place to stand, willingness is often employed spontaneously in day to day experiences outside of the treatment context.

Valuing

Values support coordinated and directed actions over long time frames. They are more abstract and global than concrete goals, and, unlike goals, they cannot be permanently achieved. Value-driven behavior change is more likely to be sustained over time than goal-driven behavior change.

Chronic pain patients often struggle with discussing values for several reasons. One is that these discussions tend to prompt strong emotional responses, including both sadness and distress. Chronic pain patients are experiencing huge discrepancies between what they care about and how they are living every day. Further, they are often confused about the difference between values and feelings. Many believe that their private experiences such as pain or depression make it impossible live in a valued way. The *Argyle Socks Exercise* (Hayes et al., 1999, pp. 211–212) can be helpful because it provides a non-threatening introduction to the idea that feelings are not obstacles to values; that one can have feelings inconsistent with a value and continue to behave in ways that are consistent with the value.

Standard ACT exercises can be used to experience the difference between choice and judgment. Choice, decision and responsibility are important in values work, particularly with pain patients who undeniably have many good reasons for their actions. The very essence of chronic pain patients is the justification of actions (or lack thereof) by pointing to pain. Buried in this lexicon is the crippling and unworkable assumption: "A person can't just go out and make something of their life when pain is present. Pain is the anti-thesis of what a healthy life is supposed to look like."

In the end, the pain patient is going to have to make a choice between falling on the sword of their "control, eliminate and justify" model of coping or to engage in something entirely different. Choosing another option in the name of closely held life values is the conduit for this shift.

Values work is usually done in a brief way early in treatment and then in depth later in treatment. Values work goes quickly with patients who are new to chronic pain and more slowly with those who are more entrenched. The following transcript is from a fourth appointment with a chronic pain patient who sustained a disabling leg injury in an orchard accident. All of his previous employment experiences were agricultural.

THERAPIST: So, in an ideal world you would be working and able to provide for your family. What type of work would you like to do?

PATIENT: I want to do something physical. I cannot work in the fields now. I want to do something well, something that makes the world better.

THERAPIST: So, you want to make money working inside, using your body, and making the world a better place. You will be providing for your family.

PATIENT: Yes. I would like to speak more English so that I can work in a clinic like this.

THERAPIST: It is nice to speak Spanish and English. If you learn to speak more English, what do you imagine you will do in a clinic like this?

PATIENT: I could clean here and make it nice for the doctors. I am a hard worker.

THERAPIST: Okay. Good. Now, tell me about the relationships you would have with your employer and co-workers.

PATIENT: I would come to work on time and do the jobs I am told to do. I would have a pleasant face, and I would not complain.

THERAPIST: What would you do when you had more pain at work?

PATIENT: I would notice it. I would put it in the bowl of soup that is my mind and keep working.

THERAPIST: And what else?

PATIENT: I would try to do something different—rest, slow down or work in a different way.

THERAPIST: What do you think could stop you from working at this kind of job?

PATIENT: I don't know. I guess thinking that I could not do the job, that the pain was too much, that the doctors had failed to make me strong enough—all that.

THERAPIST: If you had those thoughts, could you choose to put them in the bowl, accept them and continue working?

PATIENT: I don't know. That is the choice I want.

As we complete the values assessment and begin to set goals, we identify skill-deficits (e.g., assertion, language, job training, problem solving, etc.) to address in the final phase of ACT.

Building Patterns of Committed Action

In this phase of treatment, you work concretely with the chronic pain patient to support willingness to have pain experiences, to accept them for what they are, and to make behavioral changes necessary to create a more meaningful life. Invariably, moving in a valued life direction is going to bring up a lot of old triggers. Not only does this type of action stimulate unwanted thoughts, feelings, and sensations, it also directly threatens the integrity of the patient's story.

Many of the standard ACT exercises are very useful in this stage (Eye Contact, Joe the Bum Metaphor, the Jump Metaphor, Swamp Metaphor). The FEAR (Fusion with thoughts, Evaluation of experience, Avoidance of your experiences, Reason giving for your behavior) and ACT (Accept your reactions and be present, Choose a valued direction, Take action) algorithms help patients continue in behavior change efforts. Behavioral skill training is used, in a standard fashion, to fit the clinical need. You should also encourage patients to involve loved ones at the conclusion of treatment, and, together, summarize treatment for members of the support system (e.g., teach them the FEAR and ACT algorithms).

Group and Classroom Application

All of the metaphors and exercises used in individual treatment are useful in group treatment (see Chapter 14). Group members can partner with each other in exercises and more written handouts can be used.

Individual homework can still be assigned and followed up at the next meeting. Groups offer an advantage over individual treatment for chronic pain patients who are socially isolated and who have been disabled for longer time periods. Also, the psychology of isolation that is so pervasive in chronic pain leads such patients to believe that their pain is worse than anyone else and consequently, no one else will ever understand how hard their pain is to deal with. Coming into a room full of chronic pain patients with the same belief can be a real wake up call for some patients.

CLINICAL CONSIDERATIONS

Chronic pain patients encounter numerous obstacles to participation in psychological treatment of any kind. Typically, they present to medical settings, where behavioral health providers are often absent. Medical providers who respond to their suffering are often influenced by alternative theories of pain, by corporate mandates to alleviate pain, and by enthusiastic drug representatives encouraging them to prescribe opiates. During their first few years of care-seeking, chronic pain patients' beliefs about pain control strategies may be strengthened by interactions with medical providers and by experience of short-term benefit in response to the numerous procedures and medication treatments they typically receive. All too often, patients enter psychological treatment after years rather than months of suffering and disability. Many bounce around the health care system, propelled for the most part by failure to respond to treatment and the frustration of providers who prefer to treat patients with other kinds of problems that are more responsive to medical interventions. When fortunate enough to be referred to an effective multidisciplinary pain treatment program, many patients encounter long wait lists, lack of insurance coverage, and a lack of coordination of care among various medical providers. These barriers need to be addressed by changes in the health care system. Then, dissemination of ACT treatments can become feasible for a large group of patients.

At the level of the individual chronic pain patient, there are a number of common obstacles to successful treatment. The first is the failure to measure outcomes. Chronic pain patients benefit a great deal from the concrete feedback supported by regular assessment of outcomes. Additionally, you need to make adjustments quickly in treating chronic pain patients because of their low threshold for failure and tendency to discount the importance of mental factors in the first place.

A second obstacle is failure to develop a collaborative relationship. For all of their challenging interpersonal features, chronic pain patients are actually quite dependency focused and the highly egalitarian quality of the

ACT treatment relationship can be confusing. As therapists, we don't tell such patients what the "right" way to cope is. That is left up to the patient to choose, based upon contact with their direct experience. Additionally, chronic pain patients may fail to follow through with homework activities and may present with considerable irritability. You thus need to pay very close attention to relationship development throughout the course of treatment. Questions that reflect on the how the therapeutic relationship is working include: Were your concerns addressed today? Did you feel understood? Are you disappointed about anything that happened or didn't happen today? Patient responses to these types of questions can provide you with important information that will allow you to detect and resolve any relationship issues that arise over the course of treatment.

A third obstacle is that of patient motivation for treatment. Several chronic pain research groups have made an effort to develop approaches to grouping patients in an effort to match patients and treatments to optimize clinical and cost outcomes. These include using the Pain Stages of Change Questionnaire (PSOCQ) (Kerns, et al., 1997) to classify patients into readiness categories of pre-contemplation, contemplation, action, or maintenance. While this approach has shown some promise in identifying patients at risk of prematurely dropping out of a pain self-management program (Kerns & Rosenberg, 2000), and while predicting drop outs may be important to researchers, the practitioner needs a clinical solution to prevent drop outs. As of this writing, the technology for that is just not there.

Many patients are so demoralized by the results of their health and mental health care that they have little positive expectation for treatment. They may see ACT therapists as useful in assisting with obtaining time loss or disability benefits, rather than as a true treatment resource. This may be addressed in several ways. First, disability determination services need to be handled by other professionals. Your role must be to provide help with making changes to improve quality of life. Information can be provided however about the resources available for services related to financial compensation. It is worthwhile to point out that research shows that most patients who settle financial matters related to a chronic pain syndrome continue to struggle with a lowered quality of life. ACT is a set of methods that may help the patient obtain a high quality of life, whether pain continues or not and whether the patient is compensated for suffering or not.

A final obstacle in ACT treatment is that of the patient's hearing that the therapist is seeing pain as "all in their mind." This should be placed upfront by saying that all pain is real and that it occurs in the body and mind. Most chronic pain patients need to have this affirmed on a regular basis, while they learn skills needed for greater self-acceptance. At heart, many pain patients believe their chronic difficulties with pain somehow prove that they are broken and different from other people in the world. Validating the reality of pain experience and the world view it can create is my version of the ACT philosophy, "You can only start from where you are, not where you'd like to be".

Another potential clinical issue is that chronic pain patients often have inadequate social support resources, and this needs to be addressed as soon as possible. It can be helpful to ask the patient to identify a cheerleader for their ACT work. When this is not possible, their primary care provider may be willing to play this role and to support the patient by seeing them briefly (5–10 minutes) on a regular basis (every 1–2 weeks) during ACT treatment. Family members, while well intentioned, may actually under-mine patient success in ACT treatment. It can be helpful for the patient to bring a spouse or caregiver to sessions for that reason. In such sessions an overview of ACT can be provided and concrete suggestions made concern-ing their support of the patient. The goal is to get natural supports in the patient's environment activated in a way that does not reinforce chronic pain behavior but instead promotes the core ACT messages of letting go of futile struggle, focusing on acceptance rather elimination, and using value based actions to build a healthy life with pain in the picture.

ACT with Pediatric Chronic Pain

There are a few dominant differences in ACT work with pediatric pain. Children's level of verbal abstraction is lower (based upon their age) and their pain experience is more direct. The layers and layers of evaluative thinking and chronic pain "mentality" that is characteristic of adults is absent. Children usually rely heavily upon overt behavioral avoidance (not going to PE classes, laying down at home, restricting social activities) as the primary strategy for controlling or eliminating pain. Over time, the focus on pain elimination or control results in a very constricted behavior pattern and the child loses contact with valued activities in life. The child will report a general unhappiness with life and may present with the symptoms of emotional disorders (i.e., sadness, anger loss of interest in activities, withdrawal from friends, falling grades). However, as with adult patients, the child attributes all of this to the chronic pain condition and believes that pain elimination is the only way to correct the unhappiness. The lower level of verbal abilities of children does not necessarily pose a major problem in conducting ACT, but you need to use a creative and more flexible way of communicating with the child (see Chapter 10).

The second dominant difference in ACT work with pediatric pain is that parents have a great deal of control over children's lives and will often intentionally or unintentionally reinforce avoidance behaviors because of their unwillingness to see their child in pain. Parents carry many of the beliefs about pain and pain control that are seen in adult populations with chronic pain (i.e., the goal of treatment is to find the cause of pain and eliminate it, a person can't be expected to function while pain is present). This makes ACT work with pediatric pain a little more complicated because there are often actually 2 or 3 clients in the room at any one time (i.e., the pain patient, Mom, and Dad).

CLINICAL INTERVENTIONS

Because both the child and parents come into treatment with a somatic focus on pain (i.e., there must be something medically wrong and the goal is to find what it is), it is vital that all members of the ACT team share the same philosophies in the following areas: the genesis of pain and disability, the final goals of ACT treatment, and the ACT interventions that are most likely to succeed with each patient. Treatment teams will frequently encounter situations where both the medical and behavioral health staff will have to agree to decline parental demands for further medical assessments or additional pharmacological strategies. This type of close collaboration is essential when new symptoms emerge or when the family has come across another possible "cure."

Control Is the Problem

When conducting the initial assessment with the child and family members, the goal is to establish an understanding of what activities or pursuits are being avoided, what the presumed causes of this avoidance are, and what the costs have been in terms of the child's life. This is similar to the "What have you tried? How has it worked? What has it cost you?" approach described earlier, but it is done in a more superficial way to start with and then revisited after values and goals work has been done. It is vital that both child and parents (or other adults acting as "coaches") understand that we are working with a general pattern of avoidance that is more or less established and reinforced within the child's family, social and school contexts. This, in itself, is a form of defusion. With children it helps to make these ideas more concrete. For example, you might draw a "cake" with pieces labelled "pain," "worry," "sadness," "disappointment," "no friends," and so on. Unpleasant reactions to some of the pieces can themselves be pieces, such as "don't want it." To make the general pattern more of a focus it helps to label the whole cake: the child and parents may agree to use the term "unpleasantness" to talk about the pain experience, emotional responses to pain, behavioral avoidance and so forth. The goal is to have the parents and child widen the definition of pain from a simple perceptual experience that has a definite medical cause, to an integrated pattern of perceptions, thoughts, emotions and behaviors that are in the service of not having pain.

Valuing and Building Patterns of Committed Action

Children, especially the very young, have a difficult time conceptualizing values in the abstract sense. You should try to be very concrete, perhaps asking about things they would like to do that would be "fun" or "cool." For the child with chronic pain, physical activities are commonly the most concrete and obvious goals that come to mind, because most of the behavioral avoidance has been the area of physical activities. So, for example, the child might pick the goals of "biking to school" or "attending a dance class." Empowerment is an essential part of this process, particularly with children. When they experience success with a concrete goal, it helps their general outlook on pain and the role it can (or can't) play in their life. Additional value-based goals are often generated following success with the simpler ones.

For some patients, it is particularly difficult to plan for and think about the future (i.e. discuss values and future dreams). In this case, you might ask something like: "What would your life be like if a fairy one day sat on your bed when you woke up in the morning, promising that the pain was gone and it won't come back." Often, this will elicit a lot of potential valued actions that the child is currently avoiding in the attempt to control pain.

Defusing Barriers

A modification of the *Monsters on the Bus Metaphor* can be used to make defusion more concrete. In this version the "pain monster" wants the child to "go left" (towards no pain) by lose out on a lot of fun and cool things that are on the right. Once the children get it you can ask questions like "who decided today—you or the pain monster?" This is a way of defusing from control-based thinking, and promotes the idea that each day is a choice.

Creative hopelessness work tends to occur after we have clarified the child's values and goals. More concrete processes help. For example, a visual metaphor such as that presented in Figure 13.1 can be used, drawn

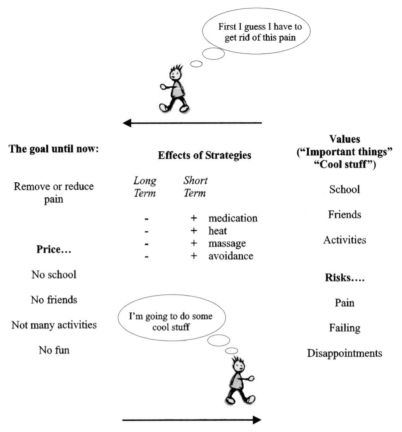

Figure 13.1. An example of how to help children notice the difference between moving toward their values and trying to first get rid of pain.

on a flip chart or erasable blackboard. Together we talk through the valuable or cool things the child holds as important (e.g., seeing friends), and we mark all those that include pain or risk of pain. Then, we look at what the child has thought they needed to do with pain in order to do these things, which almost always reverts to the goal of not having or greatly reducing pain (the left facing arrow in Figure 1). We then list what has been done to achieve this (medicine, medical tests and treatments, behavioral avoidance, etc). After validating the child's efforts in these areas (which have often been considerable) we look at the short and long term results of efforts. Almost always the short term effects are positive, while the long term effects are neutral or negative. We validate their continuation of efforts, as people often continue to do things with short term positive effects. At the same time, we point to the long term effects and ask if something new is needed. Then, we examine valued actions are examined and consider which will produce physical pain or the risk of pain. Normally, the child will conclude that it is not, under the present circumstances, possible to achieve both "no pain" and "important and cool stuff" at the same time. Based on this we can go on discussing the choice that needs to be made— in which direction to go. Are you going to go in the direction the pain monster wants you to go in, or the direction you want to go in? This helps the parents and child cement their understanding of what the central issue is and allows everyone on the treatment team to communicate using the same style of ACT consistent language.

Direct Contextual Interventions

Children are highly dependent on the social systems they live within. The contextualistic philosophy underpinning ACT suggests that the familial, social and educational milieu that surrounds the child should be mobilized. Parents suffer when seeing their child in pain. Moreover, in a number of situations, children are not expected to be independent or take full responsibility for their actions. Parents are acculturated to step in and protect their child and this nurturing role is positively reinforced by the society (being a good parent, being there for your child). Parents are just as fused with beliefs about pain and emotional responses to pain as the child. Thus, you should try to incorporate parents (or other significant adults) in treatment, especially for younger children.

One way to work with parents is to ask them to learn to coach their son or daughter. You should emphasize that it is not easy being a parent in general and the difficulty level increases substantially when a son or daughter has a lot of pain. Most parents want to do the "right thing" in response to this, but the right thing (help eliminate the pain) at first blush may be the wrong thing later on. From an ACT perspective, the main barrier that parents have to move through is fusion with various thoughts and feelings that are naturally elicited when a son or daughter is in constant pain. Coaching a son or daughter who is in pain elicits fear and a variety of negative and provocative thoughts: uncertainty about whether this non-medical approach will work, doubts about whether their coaching is their best choice or whether they are bad parents for not allowing things that would ease the pain/distress for a little while (staying home from school, using a wheelchair). This unpleasantness and the experiential avoidance it generates can be targeted using a variety of ACT acceptance and defusion interventions for the parents themselves (see Chapter 10). By doing this, we can help the parents increase their psychological and behavioral flexibility in the presence of pain. This also allows parents to empathize more with their child's situation, while at the same time supporting valued life outcomes.

The main emphasis in parental coaching is to encourage building the child's independence from pain related behaviors (i.e., always needing parental assistance doing a physical chore, using a wheelchair, lack of physical activities at or after school, staying home from school). By stepping back and allowing the child to be exposed to pain as pain, while at the same time coaching the child to do "fun" and "cool" things, ACT breeds a kind of psychological freedom.

It can be helpful to teach children to elicit support from those systems that promote valued outcomes rather than supporting chronic pain. For example, you might ask, "How do you want your parents to support you?" This will generate a variety of ideas and discussions about the pros and cons of "recruiting" a parent (or a friend) to support asking Mom or Dad to "support me when I need to do things I'm scared of or that might hurt." The same thing can be done with friends.

Another social system that frequently needs to be enlisted to support the child's growth is the school. Whether or not to intervene with the school can be a delicate question. Usually, if there are school related consequences of the chronic pain (e.g., the child is getting a low grade in P.E. because of pain-related refusals), it makes sense to get involved. The main objective is to get the school counsellor, parents and child to agree upon actions that are in alignment with the child's stated values and goals. This might involve identifying a counsellor or teacher to serve as an informal ACT coach that the child can turn to for support. By insolving these natural supports, we are directly altering the contextual features of the child's environment and this is likely to have an effect on his or her subsequent success in responding to pain, not with behavioral avoidance, but instead with valued action.

Conclusion

There is a saying in the chronic pain field: "I never met a chronic pain patient that didn't start out as an acute pain patient." This tells us something very important. Our biomedical concepts about injury and pain lead to a management model that may at times actually breed chronic pain syndrome. As a health care system, we are simply failing at the task of giving patients with pain complaints an operable framework for dealing with pain. Instead of the philosophy of "feel goodism" that is running rampant in our culture, maybe we should incorporate ACT messages at the point of initial contact with the medical system (see Chapter 12). There is always a pain incident that starts the process, and that is the teachable moment for patients. For example, a patient who struggles with musculo-skeletal pain for several weeks after a motor vehicle accident may be empowered early on to accept pain experiences, use behavioral approach strategies to manage pain to some degree, and to maintain a clear commitment to continuing to function in valued areas of living.

Chapter 14

ACT in Group Format

ROBYN D. WALSER AND JACQUELINE PISTORELLO

The ACT materials and issues in this book have been discussed both in the context of individual therapy and group interventions, but no specific focus has been given to the special considerations that arise when ACT is delivered in a group format. There are many reasons to believe that delivering ACT in a group format may actually enhance its effectiveness in certain ways and there is a developing clinical literature to support this assumption. Nevertheless, adapting ACT for group work requires attention to a variety of issues. For several years, the authors have been involved in the development and application of ACT groups with a variety of clinical complaints and patient populations. The goals of this chapter are to:

- Summarize past and current efforts focused on adapting ACT to groups,
- Identify advantages of delivering ACT in a group format,
- Highlight issues to consider prior to starting an ACT group,
- Discuss ACT-specific processes within the group format,
- Address the issue of obtaining informed consent, and finally,
- Describe how each of the core areas of ACT is adapted for group work.

PREVIOUS STUDIES OF ACT ADAPTED TO THE GROUP FORMAT

There are currently several published studies specifically evaluating ACT in group format (e.g., Bond & Bunce, 2000; Hayes, Bissett, Kohlenberg, Roget, Niccolls, Pistorello, Fisher, & Masuda, in press; Zettle, 2003; Zettle & Rains, 1989) and several additional studies are currently underway, or completed and under review. The range of problems treated by ACT in groups is impressive. These studies or ongoing projects have targeted substance abuse (Bissett, 2002; Hayes, Wilson, Bissett, Gifford, Piasecki, Batten, Byrd, & Gregg, in press), smoking cessation (Gifford, Kohlenberg, Hayes, Antonuccio, Piasecki, Rasmussen-Hall, & Palm, in press), stress (Bond & Bunce, 2000; Huxter, 2003), anxiety (Block, 2002; Karekla, 2003; Zettle, 2003), depression (Folke & Parling, 2004; Zettle & Raines, 1989), trauma (Follette & Pistorello, 1991; Orsillo & Block, 2003; Walser, Westrup, Loew, Gregg & Rogers, 2002; Walser, Westrup, Rogers, Gregg & Loew, 2003), coping with medical illnesses (Gregg, 2004; Páez, Luciano, Gutiérrez, Montesinos, & Gómez, 2003), risk of academic failure (Wilson, 2003), general college adjustment issues (Pistorello & Leonard, 2003), chronic pain (Ederyd, 2003), counselor stigma, prejudice, and burnout (Hayes et al., in press), and parental coping with the problems of disabled children (Blackledge, 2004). ACT groups have been used with children and adolescents (Murrell & Wilson, 2003; Lundgren, Mansson, & Dahl, 2003), and in combination with individual therapy (e.g., Bissett, 2002; Gifford, 2003). Group treatments have ranged from single sessions of several hours' duration (e.g., Blackledge, 2004; Hayes et al., 2003), to multiple sessions spread over several weeks (e.g., Zettle & Raines, 1989). In general these approaches have been effective, sometimes more so than empirically supported alternatives (e.g., Bond & Bunce, 2000). There is consistent evidence that ACT groups produce their effects through processes predicted by an ACT model (e.g., Bond & Bunce, 2000; Gifford et al., in press; Hayes et al., in press; Zettle & Raines, 1989).

ADVANTAGES OF APPLYING ACT IN A GROUP FORMAT

There are a number of advantages of applying ACT in the group setting. First, ACT lends itself well to interactive process, especially experiential exercises, metaphors and debriefing discussions. Although each client will be on their own individual journey in group, one of the more useful events in group is listening to the experience of other clients following an exercise. Reactions can converge or diverge, offering an opportunity for group members to receive support and validation, as well as alternative viewpoints, from their peers. For example, in one ACT intervention clients are asked to imagine talking to themselves as a child. Clients are encouraged to have that child ask of him or herself now, what that child needed or wanted. This exercise may be emotionally difficult for some clients and group process may help facilitate a positive experience for those who are struggling. In a recent group, one client was unable to "give the child what she needed," in this case safety from recurrent childhood sexual abuse, but she heard another survivor who reassured her own child that she would always have herself to count on and that she would turn out "okay" in the long run. Later, the first client noted that hearing this account provided her with ways of "standing with her child."

Second, group participants can help with the delivery of ACT material. Some concepts in ACT may be difficult to grasp. Different clients will understand the information in different ways. Often hearing how others understood the material can clarify the issue for the individual, particularly when the group contains members with different levels of insight. Sometimes the metaphors or images suggested spontaneously by other group members work better than does the original intervention put forth by the therapist. If interpretations emerging from group processes are ACT consistent, this interactive process can allow ACT therapists to adopt a language that fits the particular group or subpopulation.

Third, it is easier to recognize when someone else is "hooked" rather than oneself. Group work thus provides a forum for receiving feedback that is more "objective". A metaphor commonly used in ACT is that of honing one's "tuning fork"—that is, being able to detect when a psychological context of acceptance, defusion, and valued action has been established and when it has not. This can be a difficult task for group members, as they grapple with their largely automatic patterns of experiential avoidance. When these behaviors occur in group, greater self-awareness of unworkable patterns of behavior is a frequent outcome.

Fourth, the group provides a fertile ground for very powerful interventions. To see others engage in willingness exercises and express their thoughts regarding the exercises can both encourage and move clients. Since many fears and negative thoughts are socially focused, the group setting can both stimulate negative content and create a social context for acceptance and defusion. It also provides a social context for making public commitments to one's values (an ACT process of known value, see Hayes, Rosenfarb, Wulfert, Munt, Zettle, & Korn, 1985).

Fifth, clients have the opportunity to be present with peers that are "showing up", practicing willingness, and this in turn functions as a form of modeling and exposure. In an ACT group, the client gets to be present to emotional experience in a fairly undefended fashion. Within this context, clients can realize that emotional content in the presence of others is just that, content, and not something that is "dangerous" or "life threatening." Doing something different, such as being vulnerable in the presence of others, can feel literally like jumping off a cliff with no rope. However, the client learns experientially that "death" does not occur and that they can take a risk and be present. The group context can be quite helpful in nudging individuals towards taking such a leap of faith, both by observing others and by being emotionally supported by others.

CONSIDERATIONS PRIOR TO STARTING AN ACT GROUP

There are many factors that go into starting an ACT group including picking the group facilitators, determining the length, structure and frequency of group meetings, determining how and when to integrate individual therapy sessions as well as deciding upon the composition of the group itself. In this section we will examine each of these issues in some detail.

Facilitators: Quantity and Quality

Anyone facilitating an ACT group should first attend one or more intensive ACT training workshops, and have some experience delivering ACT in an individual therapy format. It is important to experience first hand the full range of issues relevant to ACT, from creative hopelessness to values, and to be able to bring those core processes to bear on the moment. The vulnerability one experiences during such trainings may help group facilitators "get present" with the emotions, thoughts, and evaluations that a group member might also experience.

Although an experienced ACT therapist could certainly conduct a group alone, a 2-member team might help track ACT relevant group processes more effectively. Additionally, two ACT therapists can keep the group moving in an ACT consistent direction when small errors are made.

Facilitators: Informed Consent

There is an issue of informed consent for facilitators as well as clients, particularly if one of the facilitators is a trainee or is an experienced therapist who is relatively unfamiliar with ACT. These groups can be almost as evocative for facilitators as they are for group members. We have found a dramatic difference in the level of "emotional stirrings" experienced by facilitators who were running coping skills groups versus ACT groups. With ACT, the facilitators as well as clients are asked to "sit" with a number of difficult emotions. Not "rescuing" clients from emotional pain can be very uncomfortable for the facilitators. Thus, facilitators must be aware of what they are likely to experience before agreeing to participate.

Intensive Workshop or Weekly Therapy

Although ACT is often conducted in the individual therapy format, the preferred model for training ACT therapists is an intensive group workshop followed by extensive clinical supervision in a group format (Strosahl, Hayes, Bergan, & Romano, 1998). ACT training workshops typically involve an intense, personally-relevant, experiential group format (usually about 25 hours of actual training). This format can have a powerful impact on participants and the question arises: If this seems to work for clinicians, why not for clients? Some practitioners have attempted to adapt ACT in groups to a workshop format. We are unaware of any work that has delivered a full workshop protocol to clients, but shorter day-long versions have been used (Blackledge, 2004; Gregg, 2004; Hayes et al., 2003). The findings of these preliminary studies have been positive and undoubtedly more work exploring this model will be done.

The clinician deciding whether to do a workshop or weekly format should consider logistical and ethical/legal factors. The first aspect to consider is treatment compliance. If clients can be attracted to a day-long workshop, they are likely to complete the entire treatment. However, if ACT groups extend across weeks, drop outs will undoubtedly occur, either due to logistical issues and/or to emotional avoidance that is triggered by group therapy content. There may be ethical and legal concerns, depending on the treatment context, in conducting an intensive workshop with clients, such as the potential that people might "fall apart" and feel unable to contain their emotions. In these litigious times, practitioners may be concerned about conducting a treatment that falls outside of the "customary and usual" weekly meetings, and thereby possibly rendering themselves vulnerable to lawsuits. Careful screening of potential participants, extensive informed consent processes, and systemic support from colleagues might be appropriate preventative measures.

Group Only versus Group Plus Individual

ACT groups have been conducted both alone and in combination with individual psychotherapy (typically individual ACT). Given unlimited resources, one might hypothesize that the latter would be preferable due to its higher treatment dosage, but this remains an empirical question. There are no studies evaluating the value of adding group to individual ACT treatment, or vice-versa. Unlike some other contemporary behavioral treatments (e.g, DBT, Linehan, 1993), ACT does not compartmentalize the material to be presented in individual and group formats. However, some ACT exercises lend themselves better to group and some combined protocols have used a group model to deliver specific ACT content (e.g., Gifford et al., in press).

If group and individual are conducted concurrently, it is worthwhile to have partial, but not complete, overlap in material covered in the two formats. Some exercises or issues might be saved strictly for group, so that clients sense that each format has a unique role to play. At the same time, maintaining continuity between group and individual treatment content will help reinforce some of the ACT moves that are more difficult to grasp. Some questions to consider when making the decision to add group to individual therapy include: Is there likely to be a benefit from greater treatment dosage? Are resources limited? Is the target population likely to benefit by the addition of a group (e.g., clients feel stigmatized, different, or isolated)? Do you find yourself running out of time in individual sessions with clients? Is there adequate client flow to support running a group program?

Combining Group and Individual Therapy: Sequence and Separation

Clients often have reservations about attending a group at the outset of therapy. In such instances, establishing a therapeutic alliance while exposing the client to ACT concepts in individual therapy might be helpful. For individuals with pervasive experiential avoidance, the prospect of a group, particularly one of high intensity, might seem overwhelming. Experience with ACT in the individual therapy model may assuage the client's fears about entering a group. We have been very successful in providing ACT in individual therapy first, and then placing clients in a group, where the material is more thoroughly covered (Pistorello & Leonard, 2003).

ACT groups can also be used as an entry point into individual therapy. This model seems particularly well suited for brief ACT groups or workshops, or for group ACT interventions that have a somewhat more restricted focus (e.g., dealing with self-stigma; dealing with the barriers to therapeutic engagement). Indeed, focused ACT groups of this kind could easily be combined with individual treatment from other models.

Group Composition

In conducting general therapy groups, facilitators often express strong preferences as to the group composition, such as not including clients with personality disorders or creating a homogeneous group in terms of presenting problems. In general, individuals exhibiting pervasive and costly experiential avoidance and cognitive fusion, particularly those in close contact with their pain, are excellent candidates for ACT group work. We typically do not make a distinction based upon the client's diagnoses because ACT is more concerned with addressing the universal processes that lead to human suffering.

Individuals who appear to have few internal resources to cope with the emotional aftermath of significant personal disclosures might well be coached into proceeding cautiously with disclosures in group. Cautions of that kind have to be delivered with skill: You don't want the client to hear the message that they are "broken" or "incapable" in some way. For some clients, significant emotional disclosure in the initial stages of therapy may be overwhelming. Thus, we think it is helpful to coach clients in how best to engage group processes that fit their immediate coping resources.

Group Structure and Format

ACT is adaptable to a wide variety of clinician preferences, clients and treatment contexts. However, it also follows a particular outline with each content area building on the next. Clinicians do not necessarily have to follow the format as it is laid out in the ACT book. It makes sense to be flexible. In research, most ACT groups have been closed groups; that is, individuals are not allowed to start at different times, and the group is structured for a specific number of sessions. Depending on the context (e.g., inpatient units), or if individuals have previous exposure to ACT, open enrollment groups might be an option. We are currently working out the logistics of an open enrollment group and we are hopeful about its success.

One of the challenges in open groups becomes getting the essential ACT material into each session while satisfying the needs of both oldest and newest group members. For example, if "control is the problem" was covered in the previous session, it might be difficult for a new member to quickly grasp the idea of "experiential acceptance." Generally, including elements of several ACT processes in each group, and cycling the method and focus over sequential sessions might do this, but no research is yet available to provide firm guidance on this issue. It is necessary to decide prior to starting an ACT group whether or not the group will be closed and whether or not a manual will be followed. It is strongly recommended that you the therapist put together an outline of the topics to be covered at each session, while being flexible enough to realize that the timing of a group intervention can be just as important as its delivery.

Another aspect of the group structure is its length. We have commonly run ACT groups in both ninety-minute and three-hour formats (with one break). Interestingly, none of our clients have complained that group sessions were too long—generally at the end of treatment they have reported that group length "was just right."

While ACT groups can be flexible, it is important not to create a group model that ignores one or more of the core processes that define ACT (i.e., acceptance, defusion, contact with the present moment, self as context, values, and building patterns of committed action). All components of the ACT model seem appropriate for group application and all should be considered in the group process unless a good rationale for cutting a component is determined.

Conducting ACT Groups

Setting the Stage: Informed Consent

Committing to the Process and Showing Up to Every Group

We have found in our group work, especially in closed groups, that a missed session can create problems. The individual may feel as if the group has moved on in significant ways in his or her absence. This can be particularly pronounced when a powerful experiential exercise was conducted and the group felt especially connected to the material and issues at hand. Although having other group members recap what happened last session is an option, this verbal report, often resorted to in other forms of group therapy, does not fit well with the ACT focus on experientially driven behavior change. As in most therapies, the client should be referred out if unable to attend sessions consistently. This absence threshold seems to be reached earlier in ACT than in other groups. Therefore, getting the client to commit to attending every session seems like the best solution. We recommend that this commitment to group occur first in an individual group intake with both facilitators, where the content and form of the group are explained to the client. This commitment will later be brought up with the entire group during the first session. During the individual intake, the client must understand that this group will be highly experiential, that discomfort is likely to occur, and that commitment to sticking with the group process is imperative.

We have relied on a couple of strategies to increase commitment. One strategy is to explain that the ACT group builds sequentially and is more demanding in this sense and that the client should only commit if ready for such a challenge. Another involves using a "devil's advocate" commitment strategy (Linehan, 1993a) where you invite the client to argue for why he or she should participate in such a challenging process. This is best used as a gentle strategy, and facilitators should not forcibly argue against group participation.

Rescuing Limits

Sometimes clients, or facilitators, will have a strong impulse to rescue someone in the group who appears to be struggling or "getting worse" by social standards—even though the distress may be the result of contacting experientially avoided material. Generally, rescuing is unadvisable and thus, during the informed consent process, it is wise to inform the client that discomfort, experienced by either self or others, is quite likely. The restriction on rescuing and reassurance should be explained: the group will create an open, accepting, and safe space for all its members. Rescuing someone in distress can accidentally send the message that other clients in the group are too damaged to feel what they feel.

Talking About How Things Get Worse Before They Get Better

It often seems worthwhile to tell prospective group members that they may feel worse before they feel better and that others might have the same experience. ACT can be an evocative approach, and if avoidance is abandoned, what was previously avoided will generally be experienced.

Not Knowing Everything Right Up Front—This is a Story That Builds

Some clients may feel some distress when all of the stages of therapy are not explicitly delineated up front. We have had clients ask, "Are you toying with us?" because not all parts of the ACT model are presented in the initial sessions and because certain ACT strategies include undermining well-established control strategies (e.g. therapist saying, "If you think you've got it, that's not it."). These reactions tend to surface during creative hopelessness interventions, although they may emerge at other stages as well. For example, when first covering control is the problem, some clients will remark, "How can I possibly stand feeling this way?" In individual work, these missing links may be easier to address, but in group, such doubts may not be voiced publicly. Therefore, asking the group to be willing to participate as the foundation of the therapy is laid, even when they don't know what exactly the house will look like when finished, can prevent them from tuning out or buying into the thought that they are being "toyed with." Clients should be warned that on occasion they might be asked to sit with some confusion during group, particularly in the beginning.

Doing Experiential Exercises in Group

The therapist will need to ask the clients to be willing to participate in activities that are both challenging and sometimes unusual—not fitting the "normal" definition of therapy. However, remind the clients that the exercises are designed to help. Depending on the client's history and current presentation (e.g., trauma history), you may also note that the exercises are not dangerous and that, although they involve closing one's eyes, this is *not* hypnosis. Ask the clients to respect the process of experiential exercises for both themselves and others.

Getting Group Members "On Board"

Discussing personal struggles in a group can be very difficult and frightening. This is no different than in other groups, but ACT does to some extent require a different type of participation. Clients have been informed that they will be participating in a highly experiential therapy, and this can increase group members' anxiety levels. During the first session, encourage clients to *intend for this to work* as individuals and as a group. Facilitators should also express their intentions and concerns, modeling the same openness that is being asked of clients.

Letting Group Members Be Where They Are

It is important to let each client know that the ACT group provides the opportunity for each member to go on an individual journey while in the company of fellow travelers. Therefore, it is important to respect that each group member is in a different place with respect to their personal problems, with some being more willing to "lean in" than others. We generally ask individuals in the first session to notice if they are overly focused on evaluating other group members, and if so, to gently ask this question: "What is this in the service of for me?" As defusion exercises are introduced in treatment, social comparisons of this kind can also be addressed using ACT defusion interventions (e.g., "if you find yourself thinking comparative thoughts about others, thank your mind for that thought").

Group Dynamics and Process from an ACT Perspective

The process of ACT group work is focused on undermining aspects of the socio-verbal community that promote experiential avoidance and cognitive fusion. This factor is particularly important in conducting an

ACT group, because the group context itself is a social community that exerts fairly predictable influences on its members.

Assumptions about Process

There are several operating assumptions in conducting ACT groups. First, all events are grist for the ACT mill. Any emotional reaction that shows up for a client is "okay", and intense ones may often be harnessed for powerful group work. Events that present themselves as barriers (e.g., a client wants to get up and leave) are usually exactly what needed to occur, and can be accepted, defused from, experienced, and so on as part of the process. It is thus important for group facilitators to be well versed in the ACT philosophy and approach in order to quickly conceptualize and respond to group events from an ACT-consistent perspective. Second, the focus should largely be here-and-now not there-and-then (e.g., "What is showing up now?" "Would you be willing to sit with that right now?"). Third, the focus is on experiencing events as an ongoing process, not "talking about" them. In order to make these discriminations, the ACT facilitators need to develop a "tuning fork" for direct, defused and accepting contact with public or private experiences. The goal is to contact events "as they are, not as what they say they are"—in other words, the goal is to contact experience as it is experienced, without adding or subtracting from that contact.

Group Check-Ins

Many traditional group sessions begin with a "check-in" activity, in which each client reviews his or her week; thus, clients with prior group experience may enter the group with the expectation that there will be a check-in. In ACT groups, it is best to dispense with this process, as it can set the stage for lengthy "there-and-then" conversations that might derail the group focus on direct experience and ACT work. This is particularly problematic if the therapy is time limited. As a rule, most "check-ins" devolve into "I feel better" or "I don't feel better." Both of these moves are a problem from an ACT perspective. The point of ACT is to *feel* better not to feel *better*. That can only happen in the moment: not when talking about times in the past or future.

Process versus Content

In most ACT groups, facilitators have to pay close attention to group process, but the content of ACT interventions is still important. The process versus content issue is particularly relevant to two areas in ACT groups: 1) balancing the actual content of clients' verbal reports with the function of such reports, and 2) balancing the delivery of ACT material with promoting clients' in-session experience.

With respect to the first issue, facilitators need to address the function, rather than the form, of client material. For example, a group member with a history of inability to form close interpersonal relationships reported at the end of a highly intimate dyadic exercise (see "eyes on" exercise below) that she did not understand the purpose of the exercise. "What does this exercise do?" she asked in a seemingly calm and polite manner. Her manner made this "move" difficult to detect, as there was no immediate sense of anger or accusation, just a calm question. Instead of responding to the content here (e.g., "Well, the purpose is to . . ."), the facilitator moved in closer and with compassion and gentleness asked the person to notice what was showing up right then and there for her. The facilitator had sensed that a discussion about the exercise would probably function to support her avoidance of the emotional discomfort caused by the exercise. The client replied that she was still feeling confused about the purpose of the exercise. Then, the facilitator entreated her to look further (e.g., "see if you can dig deeper—what else is there?")—at that moment she broke into tears and said that she had a sense of sheer panic when she experienced being close to someone. Later, other group members told her that her calm, cool, and collected persona actually created a wedge between her and them, as they felt unable to relate to her constant "togetherness."

This kind of process can be very powerful, not only for the individual but for others witnessing it. Yet, it is sometimes difficult to see the emotional avoidance or cognitive fusion at work in the social milieu of a group, where the rules of conduct often favor such processes. This is one reason for having two facilitators, as we all run the risk of getting "caught" at the content level.

The second issue involves balancing didactic content and in the moment experience. Because ACT actually includes a didactic component, it might be easy to fall into a purely psycho-educational model where the facilitators provide "lectures" about ACT principles. Although not harmful per se, it is a threat to effective ACT work if the facilitators become so focused on discussing the principles of ACT, or structured exercises, that present moment experience is neglected. In general, you should avoid the temptation to be overly didactic, or as we say, "a sage on the stage." Overdone, this approach can confuse group members, create less empowerment and distance between you and the group members. The group needs to "experience" ACT, not to "understand" or "believe" it, and that requires a commitment to staying in the present moment as the therapist.

Responding at a process level does not mean "processing." Sometimes, you may choose not to "process" a particular concern or complaint, because doing so might function as a form of experiential avoidance. When hearing feedback from a client about an experiential exercise, it is not out of order to just nod and gently smile or simply thank the client. Such neutral responses can create a space in the present moment for the client to "show up" to the immediate experience. You don't have to dispense any pearls of wisdom to make this experience something bigger than it is. Allowing clients to sit with whatever they are experiencing rather than focusing on therapists' response to it is a constant challenge in ACT groups. Knowing when to sit still and when to intervene is a key factor in conducting an ACT group.

Recognizing Experiential Avoidance in Group Interactions

In group, a number of socially supported behaviors can lead to messages of "don't feel what you are feeling." For instance, it can be difficult to let an individual cry in group. Many a group member will want to offer a Kleenex, give a hug, or chime in with reassurance or words of wisdom. The overall message in each of these actions is dominantly one of avoidance: Stop feeling what you feel, so that I don't have to feel what I feel. This is why limitations on rescuing and reassurance are so important. Letting someone cry without handing him a Kleenex (the person can ask for a Kleenex if it is needed) is an honorable way to let the individual be present with pain without first demanding that the person do something different. The therapist may not even need to address the crying (though often it would be addressed). The issue is one of function. Encouraging a client to stay in the psychological present—inviting "this experience"—can be empowering. Done properly this is not a cold stance. It is the opposite. It is a stance of kindness, acceptance and love that honors the difficulty of being human.

Experiential avoidance may show up in other group interactions as well. Working hard to get group members to "get it," can actually result in the opposite of what an ACT therapist might intend. For instance, it is not unusual for group members to use "understanding" or "figuring it out" in the service of their existing control strategies. One client stated something like this in an ACT group: "If I can truly understand this avoidance thing, then I will be able to control my life and not be anxious." You need to look for similar forms of emotional control that will be far less obvious. Confusion is a common example because it presents itself as a need for understanding, not as an emotion itself. Allowing the client to feel confused while the group moves on can be difficult, but it may be the very thing that is needed. Letting the client feel confusion and accepting it fully can be liberating for the client.

When the Therapist Is Feeling Stuck

If the therapist and/or group seem to be stuck, remember to look at the process. What could be happening from an ACT perspective? Explore the issues described above, including too much focus on content versus process, one-upmanship, and/or ongoing experiential avoidance by either clients or facilitators, to name a few. When conducting ACT, you should first and foremost look at your own behavior: Is there something we are missing here? Bring a "beginner's mind" to this question.

Level of Participation

There is a generally accepted notion that in order for therapy to work, one must be an active participant. This applies to ACT as well, but a client's silence is not necessarily a sign of nonparticipation since much of the process occurs intrapersonally as well as interpersonally. In fact, forcing the client to participate may undermine the goal of allowing the client to be in the present moment. ACT is an empowering treatment, allowing each person in the group to actively "choose" the stance he or she is willing to take. Level of overt participation is a matter of client choice.

Clinical judgment is paramount in these circumstances, and there are times when you need to prod a client to respond. However, it is not always necessary for a client to be in the room "with their mouths," as long as he is there with his "experiential feet," so to speak. This is an advantage of group over individual, as it creates more room for such inner journeys.

A few strategies might be helpful in encouraging higher levels of participation in group. For example, during values clarification, facilitators may instruct clients to report on how they are living out their values *in the group milieu*. Questions such as "If you were to hide out, how would you do it here?" might also be helpful during the first couple of sessions. One strategy, borrowed from Eastern traditions, might be to ring a bell periodically in group and to have people rate themselves, silently, on one or both of these questions ("How am I living out my values right here and now?" "How much am I hiding?"). Having these questions written on a board in the group room might be helpful.

Interpersonal Conflict in Group and the ACT Approach

Interpersonal conflicts in the group provide an opportunity to model defusion, acceptance, getting present, valuing and committed action. The behavior demonstrated in the group is most likely the behavior that gets the individual in trouble outside of group. There is nothing unique about this idea, but ACT provides a number of different solutions to the issue. Instead of trying to "work things out" between two clients, you might ask each individual to get present with the immediate process. As facilitator, you should consider what the client might be trying to avoid or what fears might be showing up for this person. Some key questions to ask the clients involved in such situations include: "What is showing up for you right now, any emotions, thoughts, evaluations, or urges?" "Is there something about this situation that seems very familiar to you, as if you've been here before?" "How else does this interfere with your life?" "What has this kind of interaction gained or lost you in the past?"

The Therapists' Role/Participation in Group

Much of what has been written elsewhere in this book about the ACT therapeutic relationship and the role of the therapist applies to ACT delivered in group format. That is, the therapists must have compassion for the clients' struggle, treat clients with dignity and respect, and be willing to "show up" in group as another human being. Many therapists assume the role of "helper" or "the knowing one." Although this might be the case at a content level in terms of the information the therapist can provide, it is not true at the experiential level. Being willing in sessions is one of the more powerful tools in ACT, but particularly so in ACT groups. It provides modeling, decreases separateness, gives "permission", and helps clients develop their own "tuning fork" for what is real experientially. However, the group context makes "being present" harder than in individual therapy (e.g., more people are relying on you, a colleague might be evaluating you), and, as such, even more growth enhancing. Running ACT groups and workshops is a powerful experience for facilitators, as well as clients.

There are two characteristics of ACT group therapists that seem worth discussing: Being irreverent and being bold. In ACT groups, the use of humor, "straight shooting" ("so now what?"), sarcasm (e.g. "here we go again?"), can all have an impact that is favorable if done appropriately. The irreverence should point to the *system*, not the individual, as the problem. Mocking the system can be playful, but not disrespectful of the person. Irreverence done well in a group can help all group members to laugh lightly at a system that doesn't need to be taken so seriously in the first place. A little self-deprecating humor on the part of ACT group facilitators tends to be helpful in this regard. In general, using "we" as the pronoun instead of "you" corroborates the fact that "we are all in the same boat." A word of caution: if irreverence does not come naturally to a clinician, it is best avoided, until he or she can find his or her own "irreverent voice."

In a group setting, irreverence that comes across as mockery can be very destructive.

There is some degree of risk taking involved in conducting ACT properly. You as the facilitator need to be bold: to say what it is that group members may be reluctant to say; to do creative things that fit the moment; to risk failure or embarrassment. This is not an invitation to be reckless, but rather an invitation to be open to the possibilities of the moment. It may be that the thing you are not saying is the thing the client needs to hear. It may be that the idea you have of a new issue or exercise is occurring for exactly the right reasons.

This quality of boldness can be interrupted in at least two ways. First, the therapist may "buy" thoughts about being right or wrong in the delivery of the therapy and thus stop being bold. In addition to interrupting the flow of process, you might feel intimidated, and when unwilling to experience this feeling, work hard to sound smart or to deliver the therapy "correctly." The cost is you lose those moment-by-moment risks that could be taken in the service of helping your clients. For example, ACT group facilitators may become so committed to following the protocol, in order to get it "right" or to avoid negative evaluation by a colleague, that they miss opportunities to get connected with clients.

Second, you as the facilitator may buy the thought that your clients "can't handle" what is there to be said. In this case, you take a "kid glove" approach and treat group members as if they are fragile. One client in an ACT group had been feisty, oppositional, and emotionally distant throughout the first several sessions. Finally, the therapist decided to take a risk and asked the client 'what was happening to him in the room, what was he trying to avoid by the aggression and persistence in stating how difficult his problems were compared to the others'? The client initially backed down and tried to get the group to focus on other members, and, the room became more comfortable. If making the room comfortable (e.g., "managing" the client) had been the goal, as it often is in other forms of group therapy, one could have stopped here. However, to be helpful to this client, the therapist needed to go further. She got up and crossed the room, sat next to the client and pursued the issue. With continued "in the moment" questioning, the group learned that the client was confused about ACT principles and was afraid he would be seen as a failure by other group members if he admitted it. The therapists were able to show how his avoidance of confusion actually caused more confusion by distancing him from the very people who could help him understand. The client came back the next session stating that this event had been the most powerful experience he had had in therapy. This type of outcome is not unusual: often it is the bold moves by ACT group facilitators that lead to this type of impact.

CLINICAL INTERVENTIONS: CORE ACT AREAS AND APPLICATION
OF TECHNIQUES IN GROUP

Beginning and Ending Each Group

Starting and ending each group with a meditation/mindfulness can further the goal of promoting deliteralization and acceptance. Many of the defusion techniques in ACT involve mindfulness. Table 14.1 provides a short list of mindfulness exercises with which to begin or end a group. There are numerous mindfulness exercises, and the therapists should be thoughtful yet creative in applying these techniques.

First Session

Some of the usual conventions may apply in the first ACT group session, such as review of rules and introduction of members. Some of the rules that apply to ACT groups include: confidentiality; respecting each individual and allowing each person to be where he or she is without rescuing; intending for this to work; making room for discomfort and other aversive emotions such as confusion; not leaving the room if upset; if at all possible, not missing sessions or coming in late or leaving early. Most

Table 14.1. Examples of Exercises to Begin and End ACT Group Sessions

- Observer Exercise: notice physical sensations, thoughts, feelings, and roles. (Hayes et al., 1999, p. 192)
- Toy soldiers on a parade: imagining each toy soldier carrying a sign, where each private experience is acknowledged. (Hayes et al., 1999, p. 159)
- Leaves on a stream: notice each private experience as a leaf going down a stream. (Hayes et al., 1999, p. 159, same as "soldiers in a parade")
- Noticing your breath: in and out, temperature, continuity, gap between in and out breath. (Thich Nhat Hahn)
- Welcome anxiety, my old friend (Thich Nhat Hahn). On the in-breath, say silently to yourself " Welcome anxiety." On the out-breath, say silently to yourself "My old friend." Repeat this silently 10 or so times. Anxiety may be substituted with any other aversive private experience: sadness, confusion, pain.
- Mindfulness of sounds: focusing on sounds one can hear.
- Mindfulness of touch: bring in objects of different textures and forms, ask clients to close their eyes and have their hands out, and then place one object in each person's hands. Ask them to focus on the sensation of touch: texture, temperature, form.
- Physicalizing: Ask clients to concentrate on a private event they are struggling with, give it shape, size, form, color, and texture. (Hayes et al., 1999, p. 170).
- Expanding the Bubble of Awareness. Ask clients to imagine themselves, then the building, then the area, then the city, then the state, then the country, and then the world.

of the issues addressed during the initial individual intake for prospective group participants should be revisited during the first session (e.g., Informed Consent).

A useful exercise for a first session is having people write on an index card answers to the following questions: 1) What do you really want in life? 2) What are the internal barriers to getting there? 3) What are the barriers that you are willing to discuss in this group? 4) What are some of the barriers that you would never be willing to discuss? Participants are instructed to write these answers down for their eyes only, to use code for answers to #4 if they are concerned about others' reading it, and to carry the card with them for a while. It is recommended that clients keep this card somewhere safe, where they can review it later. The facilitators will ask clients to revisit these questions during the last session(s). Although they are never asked to share the actual information written down, some may choose to do so. This exercise can be very powerful for clients, with some individuals at the end of group noting that even their #4 answers were shared in group, although at first they were certain they never would be.

Applying Core ACT Processes for Groups

We will now discuss the presentation of ACT core concepts in a group setting. For the most part, the content of ACT materials presented in group will follow that discussed in this and other books (e.g., Hayes, Strosahl & Wilson, 1999), and will not be repeated here. For present purposes, we will note where the presentation of material may differ in a group format, and some potential examples and issues pertinent to each of the core areas. Exercises specific to group settings, either developed by the authors or borrowed from ACT workshop trainings provided to clinicians, will be discussed in more detail. For clarity of presentation, the following discussion assumes a closed, time-limited group format, though clinical experience shows the core processes can be adapted to an open format.

Creative Hopelessness

Creative hopelessness can work very well in the group setting. We often have clients in the group generate a list of all that they have done to try to get rid of negatively evaluated emotional experience. The different strategies can be written on a flip chart or board. Sometimes, depending on how savvy the group members are, the facilitators may have to help the group generate the list. Questions like "Do you know of anyone who drinks when they are stressed?" or "Does anyone here pick a fight with one person when upset with someone else?" may get the group going. If the group is composed of individuals who have had multiple treatments and interventions, one can also ask the number of different therapists, number of different medications, number of other groups, and the number of years of struggle. In the group setting, large numbers can usually be generated. Clients can review their own, as well as others', unsuccessful efforts to control undesired private events. The compilation of all these strategies, written on the board for all to see, tends to generate a powerful sense of creative hopelessness, without as much self-blame and judgment, because the pervasiveness, as well as the ultimate futility, of control strategies becomes apparent.

Values Clarification

The advantage of doing values clarification earlier in a group setting is that this element of ACT is more interactive than creative hopelessness and this may help with the development of group cohesiveness. There are multiple ways of presenting this material and we will discuss our two favorite options, one is didactic and the other experiential. While the didactic approach may be well-suited for beginning sessions, we only recommend the experiential approach for later group stages or if group members are ACT veterans already.

After providing a general introduction to values assessment (e.g., explaining difference between values and goals), the didactic approach involves breaking the group into teams or dyads, distributing the values assessment homework sheets, and asking each person to pick one area and write down their valued direction, current success, and barriers to living out the value in that area. Then, each group member is asked to share this information with the other person(s) in the group, who are to stay "present" and listen without judgment. The selection of one values area is a time management issue: having every group member share one area can easily consume an hour or more of group. Consequently, the remainder of the values assessment exercise is assigned as between session homework. The completed exercise is discussed in more accelerated form during the following group session. In very brief group interventions, sharing the values clarification in this way may not be possible and may simply be assigned as homework for one's private clarification. Actually, the latter strategy worked well in one instance where group consisted of only five 3-hour sessions (Pistorello & Leonard, 2003).

A more experiential alternative, often undertaken in ACT training workshops, is to bypass the writing down of values and completion of forms. This approach, better suited for later sessions, involves having members break into subgroups and sit closely, gather one's thoughts until ready to stand up and declare one's values in one or more domains. The instructions call for the other individual(s) in the subgroup to remain absolutely present to this person's declaration of values. Standing up, the individual declaring his values is asked to do so without defense or rationale, just a statement of what he would like his life to be about. If the other group members(s) feel that the person was unable to achieve any aspect of this assignment, they have the option of asking the person to declare values again, until the person is able to "be present". Facilitators should make sure that this "corrective feedback" is being delivered appropriately and with gentleness by other clients. If the ACT group is small, this exercise can be done as a whole group exercise.

Some of the same barriers to values clarification in individual work may show up in group. The social context may make it even harder for people to tease out what they really value versus what is socially desirable. The more experiential value declaration exercise outlined above can help one tackle this barrier, as other participants in the smaller group may be able to "call" someone relying on social standards without making contact with what comes up.

Control as the Problem

Control as the problem in the group setting can often have a playful quality and can provide group members with some hope about where they are headed. One may need to remind the clients that being able to see the problem is not the answer to avoiding emotional experience. Clients may try to solve the problem of emotional control, but in these early stages are likely to be turning this problem, once again, into an unworkable solution— stop trying to control so that I don't have to feel what I feel. This can be couched as another effort to dig oneself out of a hole.

One exercise involves bringing in Chinese handcuffs, straw tubes that are inexpensive and readily available in bulk on the internet. Prior to distributing the handcuffs, you the facilitator can ask clients who are familiar with these gadgets not to say anything to others in group until they have had a chance to play with them. The personal experience element is crucial if this exercise is to be helpful, and therefore, we generally ask group members not to look at others but rather just focus on their own experience for a few minutes. The instructions include asking clients to get their fingers "nice and stuck" and then try to get their fingers unstuck without breaking the handcuff. After a few minutes, help group members debrief the exercise. During the discussion, some of the questions to ask include: "When your fingers were stuck, what did you feel like doing right away?" "What did you notice about how this worked for you?" " When, if at all, did you try something different?" "What feelings, thoughts, action urges, or evaluations showed up for you during this exercise?" "Were some of these emotions and thoughts familiar to you?" Sometimes, it may happen that someone pulls so hard that it breaks the handcuff and he or she may say "Well, I got out of it, didn't I?" At this point, the facilitators may point out the cost to doing so.

If there are group members that have been demanding "understanding and answers", this might be a good opportunity to have them notice the importance of direct experience and the corresponding futility of verbal analysis. You might ask: "What do you think the impact of this exercise would have had on you if we, without distributing the cuffs, had said at the outset: OK. Now, we are going to give you some handcuffs, you are going to try to pull your fingers out when stuck, but this will only get you further stuck. So, you must push in to get your finger out." Some clients in the group may really "get" this and be able to help others in group. One group member noted at the end of group that she had left her Chinese handcuff visibly displayed in her home as a reminder that sometimes "leaning in" or doing the unlikely thing can be the effective thing to do.

Defusion

Some cognitive defusion strategies seem to be particularly amenable to group interventions—mindfulness and establishing language conventions are two such instances. First, conducting mindfulness exercises at the beginning and end of each group provides valuable practice opportunities for group members. In meditation, the importance of a sangha, or a group to support the practice, is often emphasized among experts (e.g., Chodron), as a facilitative element for continued practice. The same can be said about ACT groups: sharing experiences of mindfulness exercises may allow participants to let go of self-judgments while promoting persistence in developing the skills. Second, the language conventions discussed in individual ACT can be much more readily, and consistently, reinforced in a group format. The facilitators can create a community environment that relies on the more cumbersome, but potentially useful, statements such as "I'm having the thought that I'm a failure" instead of saying "I'm a failure" to highlight the difference between one's thoughts and their content. The impact of establishing a language convention in a community composed of more than just one client and a therapist can be powerful. It is not unusual for people to start catching each other speaking from a "fused" point of view or articulating an evaluation as if it were a description. You should actively enlist group members to follow the ACT language conventions and to help each other out.

Another defusion intervention focuses on helping group members notice the cost of buying thoughts. Prior to orienting clients to the exercise, distribute badges and heavy felt pens to everyone in the group. Then ask clients to come up with a negative self-referential evaluation that they avoided sharing with others, but that they would be willing to wear on a badge today for all to see. Sharing an example or two may be necessary at this point: "For example, some people may notice that they go the extra mile to be pleasant and nice to everyone because deep down they are afraid that they are actually 'bad' or 'selfish.' In this case, the person would write either 'bad' or 'selfish' on the badge." It is important to limit to one or two words only. Some examples from previous groups include the following: "evil," "needy," "boring," "lazy," "hypocrite," and "dumb," to name a few. After group members write the word(s) in big letters, they put on the badge and keep the badge on for the remainder of the session. Group members are instructed to look at each other's badges but refrain from discussing their own or others in any way. It is particularly helpful if clients can interact socially, such as during a break, when wearing these badges. This playful exercise has a surprising impact: most group members report that these avoided self-evaluations rapidly lose their power to generate negative affect or stimulate behavioral avoidance. At the end of a recent ACT training workshop, participants actually went to a restaurant wearing the badges, much to the surprise of the waiters!

Another defusion exercise appropriate for groups is the "cross-cutting categories", originally developed for dealing with stigma (Hayes et al, 2003). Connecting with other humans in a "present moment" way is undermined by verbal evaluation. We are quick to categorize and evaluate people we do not know (e.g., bald, fat, intelligent, poor, outgoing) and this precludes seeing the human being, rather than the evaluation. A similar process tends to occur within a therapy group. The cross-cutting exercise consists of asking a volunteer group member to answer a few intimate questions. The group is asked to remember (silently, to themselves) what they thought when this group member was first introduced. Evaluations and interpretations are especially important. The facilitator then proceeds to ask several personal questions (asking permission each time), such as "Would you be willing to share with us when was the last time you cried?" or "Would you be willing to share something that you worry most about in your family?" The participant is asked to keep answers very short and not to explain them. The group is asked to watch what happens in their own minds. The questions need to tap into many domains, one after another. After a number of such questions are asked and answered something very tangible happens. When the group is asked what is happening inside them, they can often state what it is: a human being has shown up.

Self as Context

We have found that some of the self as context interventions (e.g., observer exercise, leaves on a stream) can actually be presented, or repeated, at the beginning or ending of each group session. The exercises can be modified to fit the context of the group setting. For example, if group members have experienced the observer exercise, you can modify it to have clients notice the role that they are about to take (e.g., group client) and the role they are leaving as they enter the group (e.g., worker, student). Similarly, the exercise can be reversed at the end of group, to help clients transition from their role as clients to their outside lives.

Another self as context intervention is to have group members physically enact the bus metaphor with one client as the driver and 3–4 others as "passengers" on the bus. To conduct this exercise, a large space must be available so that this group of people can move freely around. The group member playing the driver goes ahead and the passengers follow. The rule is that passengers cannot touch the driver, but they can get close, shake their finger, or yell. The driver is told to drive the bus where he or she wants it to go. The clients playing the passengers are given written instructions on how to behave. Prior to group, facilitators select a number of "passengers" to put on the bus and write out each role down on an index card. For example, there might be the "anxiety" passenger that keeps predicting the worst, encouraging the client to turn left (when she might want to try right), and generally acting fearfully. Other potential passengers might be: anger (e.g., shaking finger with intensity at driver), critical parent (e.g., "You are not driving well"), guilt (e.g., "You're being selfish"), shame (e.g., "I'm a bad person"), or even self-praise (e.g., "I am a great driver"). Have the group act this out for a few minutes and then share the experience of the exercise from the driver, passengers, and observers' points of view.

Another exercise involves having the client write thoughts on a card or on a sticky note. The therapist can ask a client for a thought that they struggle with, such as "I shouldn't be angry". The therapist then writes that thought on an index card and has the client tape it somewhere on their body where it can be easily read. The therapist then asks, "What shows up next?" It might look like, "I am bad for being angry." That too is taped to the client's body. The therapist continues this process until the client has 15–20 thoughts taped to him or her. You can also do this with positively evaluated thoughts, adding to the 15–20, so that they now have 35 or so cards taped to themselves. Either do this for each member of the group, depending on size, or have the other clients participate in the same fashion until all are "wearing their thoughts." Then have the clients get up and move around, take a walk. Have them notice that they can carry these thoughts and continue "on their life path." There is a self there that holds the thoughts, and is not the thoughts.

On occasion, a therapist may encounter a client who has no sense of self, even after completing these and the exercises in the ACT book. These clients may have learned throughout their lives that they "do not exist." These might be clients who were sexually abused as children or who are dominated in controlling, abusive relationships. The sense of self in these cases can be damaged or lost; they live to serve others and find it difficult to locate a personal sense of self beyond content. Here, the therapist can take time with the client to have them notice very simple things about themselves. The therapist can ask questions like, "Who is the person saying that they have no self?" "Who am I sharing this experience with right now in the room, can you locate that person?" "Who is hearing this question?" From here the therapist can slowly help the client begin to build a sense of himself or herself as a person who is currently experiencing and present.

Willingness and Acceptance

One willingness/acceptance exercise that is useful in ACT groups or workshops is to highlight the difference between pain versus trauma using an interactive didactic visual approach. Using a blackboard or equivalent, draw an inner circle and write "PAIN" in the middle, while explaining that pain is inevitable in life, that no matter how "good" or "skillful" we are, something painful will happen: people we love will die, we will not get a promotion, a relationship will end, we will get a bad grade, someone might betray our trust, and so forth. Explain that there is no way that pain can be completely avoided; yet, "what is it that we almost immediately try to do when we experience pain?" Someone will inevitably volunteer that the instinctive human response is to "push it away." Then, ask people to volunteer some of the ways that we push pain aside, and while doing so, draw a bigger circle around the inner one, and write what people are saying between the two circles. Some of the strategies people will volunteer could include drinking, working long hours, withdrawing from others, picking a fight, gambling, cutting, attempting suicide, and so on. Then note that the circle can keep getting bigger: we feel pain, then we drink, then we miss class, then we blame ourselves for missing classes. With each layer, draw another circle, then explain that the inner circle of pain is just that. Then, write "TRAUMA" in the outer circles, noting that by not accepting pain, we often create trauma. Often, group members refer to the inner and outer circles in subsequent sessions. In fact, it might be a thread to pick up in later sessions, by asking clients who are discussing ongoing struggles: "Where do you think you are right now—inner or outer circle?"

Most of the aversive private experiences we attempt to control or avoid frequently get traced back to fears of interpersonal rejection. The ACT group is a rich medium for exposure and transformation of stimulus functions of such private events. Some exercises targeting increased willingness and acceptance may in particular contribute significantly to therapeutic movement.

An example is the "eyes-on" exercise. In this exercise, individuals sit across from each other in dyads, knees-to-chair. They are asked to look each other in the eye, without talking or communicating, while noticing what comes up and letting each reaction be. Laughter, restlessness, avoidance of eye contact, and staring the person "down" are some of the initial defensive responses to this exercise. The facilitator generally orients the participants to various dimensions of responding in a sentence or two to be followed by periods of silence (e.g., "Just notice that these are human eyes you are looking at." "See if you can let go of any chatter you have about the other person and allow yourself to be with that person"). This process continues for 3–5 minutes. After the exercise, allow group members to share their experiences with their partner and then open it up for the group to process. You should avoid putting forth interpretations or intellectualized renditions of group members' commentaries. It can be tempting to get involved in this way because it is not unusual for members to "explain" themselves to the other person or to the group or perhaps ask for reassurance that they are okay (e.g., "I was afraid that I was staring too much"). This is usually not the time to call people on these subtle avoidance moves—just listen.

Being emotionally present with another human being, while silently looking at their eyes, can be quite powerful. When encouraged to let each of defensive and fused behaviors go, individuals inevitably reach deeper layers, having to do with self and other evaluations first, then fear and vulnerability, and lastly, a place of quiet appreciation for the common humanity shared by two people. In one of our groups, this exercise was unanimously nominated as the most beneficial therapy experience (Pistorello & Leonard, 2003). Although "eyes on" is conducted in individual ACT therapy, various concerns sometimes keep therapists from carrying it out there. Groups afford the opportunity for this intimate exercise to occur without concerns that the client will feel that the therapist is being inappropriate.

Commitment

Building patterns of committed action is the linchpin of ACT and the group context can be quite helpful in fostering the motivation to carry out one's commitment. As was mentioned earlier, commitments made in public are more likely to be followed. A commitment exercise commonly used in groups is known colloquially as the "Big Look." This exercise has the most impact when used in the last group session.

The Big Look consists of having all group members sit in chairs facing the front of the room, where, one by one, each person is asked to come up to the front, perhaps 6 feet away from the first row, and spend a minute or two looking into each client's eyes while letting go of defenses and "being present" with everyone else. This occurs silently, except for the active verbal encouragement of the facilitator (quite similar to the "eyes on" exercise). Then, when the facilitator releases the person to do so, they are asked to stay in contact with the group and to state what they intend to carry forward from here. More specific instructions might be to ask the client to state what it is that they will stand for or be about in their lives. You as the facilitator need to make sure the process does not devolve into a story or act, and you need to make sure that all group members stay fully present to the human being sharing material with them.

You may occasionally encounter a client who refuses to stand and commit in front of the group. There may be several reasons behind this action including feeling emotionally overwhelmed, avoidant, scared, etc. The therapist can move on to another group member and let the client know that they will return to them in a bit, or ask the client to carry whatever is going on with them up to the front of the room, reminding them that whatever it is, it is not what it says it is. Gentle compassion on your part is needed, as this tends to be a very powerful exercise. If the client still refuses, don't make a big deal of it and move on. The client will know at this point that the problem is fusion with negative content and you might want to talk with the client briefly after the exercise.

CONCLUSION

ACT in the group context is an exciting intervention. Not only can all the same interventions delivered individually be applied in group, but a whole new set of rich exercises become possible in a group context. Sharing the psychological space that ACT opens up with a group of fellow human beings truly brings the core of the work home. We have much to learn about this work and how it can best be done, but it seems clear that group interventions will continue to be a important component of the range of interventions available to ACT therapists.

References

Abramowitz, J. S. (1997). Effectiveness of psychological and pharmacological treatments for obsessive-compulsive disorder: A quantitative review. *Journal of Consulting and Clinical Psychology, 65*, 503–515.

Addis, M. E., & Carpenter, K. M. (1999). Why, why, why?: Reason-giving and rumination as predictors of response to activation and insight-oriented treatment rationales. *Journal of Clinical Psychology, 55*, 881–894.

Addis, M. E., & Jacobson, N. S. (1996). Reasons for depression and the process and outcome of cognitive-behavioral psychotherapies. *Journal of Consulting and Clinical Psychology, 64*, 1417–1424.

Alcoholics Anonymous (1976). *Alcoholics Anonymous*. New York: AA World Services.

Alcoholics Anonymous (1953). *Twelve steps and twelve traditions*. New York: AA World Services.

Allgulander, C. (1994). Suicide and mortality patterns in anxiety neurosis and depressive neurosis. *Archives of General Psychiatry, 51*, 708–712.

American Psychiatric Association (1980). *Diagnostic and statistical manual of mental disorders* (3th ed.). Washington, DC: Author.

American Psychiatric Association (1994). *Diagnostic and statistical manual of mental disorders* (4th ed.). Washington, DC: Author.

Amir, M., Kaplan, Z., Efroni, R., Levine, Y., Benjamin, J., & Kotler, M. (1997). Coping styles in post-traumatic stress disorder (PTSD) patients. *Personality and Individual Differences, 23(3)*, 399–405.

Antony, M. M., & Barlow, D. H. (Eds.) (2002). *Handbook of assessment and treatment planning for psychological disorders*. New York: Guilford Press.

Antony, M. M., Roth, D., Swinson, R. P., Huta, V., & Devins, G. M. (1998). Illness intrusiveness in individuals with panic disorder, obsessive compulsive disorder, or social phobia. *Journal of Nervous and Mental Disease, 186*, 311–315.

Armeli, S., Tennen, H., Todd, M., Carney, M. A., Mohr, C., Affleck, G., & Hromi, A. (2003). A daily process examination of the stress-response dampening effects of alcohol consumption. *Psychology of Addictive Behaviors, 17(4)*, 266–276.

Bach, P. & Hayes, S. C. (2002). The use of Acceptance and Commitment Therapy to prevent the rehospitalization of psychotic patients: A randomized controlled trial. *Journal of Consulting and Clinical Psychology, 70*, 1129–1139.

Bargh, J. A. & Chartrand, T. L. (1999). The unbearable automaticity of being, *American Psychologist, 54*, 462–479.

Barkham, M., & Shapiro, D. A. (1990). Brief psychotherapeutic interventions for job-related distress: A pilot study of prescriptive and exploratory therapy. *Counselling Psychology Review, 3(2)*, 133–147.

Barlow, D. H. (2002). *Anxiety and its disorders: The nature and treatment of anxiety and panic.* (2nd ed.). New York: Guilford Press.

Barlow, D. H., & Craske, M. G. (2000). *Mastery of your anxiety and panic (MAP-3): Client workbook for anxiety and panic.* (3rd ed.). San Antonio, TX: Graywind/Psychological Corp.

Barlow, D. H., Gorman, J. M., Shear, M. K., & Woods, S. W. (2000). Cognitive-behavioral therapy, imipramine, or their combination for panic disorder: A randomized controlled trial. *Journal of the American Medical Association, 283*, 2529–2536.

Barsky, A. J., Coeytaux, R. R., Sarnie, M. K., & Cleary, P. D. (1993). Hypochondriacal patients' beliefs about good health. *American Journal of Psychiatry, 150 (7)*, 1085–1089.

Beck, A. T. (1967). *Depression: Clinical, experimental and theoretical aspects.* New York: Harper & Row.

Beck, A. T. (1987). Cognitive models of depression. *Journal of Cognitive Psychotherapy: An International Quarterly, 1*, 5–37.

Beck, A. T. (1993). Cognitive therapy: Past, present, and future. *Journal of Consulting and Clinical Psychology, 61*, 194–198.

Beck, A. T., Brown, G., Berchick, R. J., Stewart, B. J., & Steer, R. A. (1990). Relationship between hopelessness and ultimate suicide: A replication with psychiatric outpatients. *American Journal of Psychiatry, 147*, 190–195.

Beck, A. T., Freeman, A., & Davis, D. (2004). *Cognitive therapy of personality disorders.* New York: Guilford Press.

Beck, A. T., Rush, A. J., Shaw, B. F., & Emery, G. (1977). *Cognitive therapy of depression.* New York: Guilford.

Beck, A. T., Steer, R. A., & Brown, G. K. (1996). *Beck Depression Inventory—Second Edition Manual.* San Antonio: The Psychological Corporation.

Beck, A. T., Steer, R. A., Kovacs, M., & Garrison, B. (1985). Hopelessness and eventual suicide: A 10-year prospective study of patients hospitalized with suicide ideation. *American Journal of Psychiatry, 142*, 559–563.

Beck, A. T., Ward, C. H., Mendelson, M., Mock, J. E., & Erbaugh, J. K. (1961). An inventory for measuring depression. *Archives of General Psychiatry, 4*, 561–571.

Bentall, R. P., & Kinderman, P. (1999). Self-regulation, affect, and psychosis: the role of social cognition in paranoia and mania. In T. Daglish & M. J. Power (Eds.), *Science and practice of cognitive behavior therapy* (pp. 353–381). Chinchester, England: Wiley.

Bentall, R. P. (2001). Social cognition and delusional beliefs. In P. W. Corrigan & D. L. Penn (Eds.), *Social cognition and schizophrenia* (pp. 123–148). Washington, D. C.: American Psychological Association.

Bernstein, D. A., Borkovec, T. D., & Hazlett-Stevens, H. (2000). *New directions in progressive relaxation training: A guidebook for helping professionals.* Westport, CT: Praeger.

Bieling, P. J. & Kuyken, W. (2003). Is cognitive case formulation science or science fiction? *Clinical Psychology: Science & Practice, 10*, 52–69.

Biglan, A. (1989). A contextual approach to the clinical treatment of parental distress. In G. H. S. Singer & L. K. Irvin (Eds.), *Support for caregiving families: Enabling positive adaptation to disability* (pp. 299–311). Baltimore, MD: Brookes.

Biglan, A., & Hayes, S. C. (1996). Should the behavioral sciences become more pragmatic? The case for functional contextualism in research on human behavior. *Applied and Preventive Psychology: Current Scientific Perspectives, 5*, 47–57.

Bissett, R. T. (2002). Processes of change: Acceptance versus 12-step in polysubstance-abusing methadone clients. *Dissertation Abstracts International, 63* (02), 1014B.

Blackledge, J. T. (2004). *Using Acceptance and Commitment Therapy in the treatment of parents of autistic children.* Unpublished doctoral dissertation, University of Nevada, Reno.

Block, J. A. (2002). *Acceptance or change of private experiences: A comparative analysis in college students with public speaking anxiety.* Unpublished doctoral dissertation, University at Albany, State University of New York.

Block, J. A., & Wulfert, E. (2002, May). Acceptance or change of private experiences: A comparative analysis in college students with a fear of public speaking. In R. D. Zettle (Chair), *Recent outcome research on Acceptance and Commitment Therapy (ACT) with anxiety disorders.* Symposium conducted at the 28th Annual Meeting of the Association for Behavior Analysis, Toronto, Ontario.

Boeschen, L. E., Koss, M. P., Figuerdo, A. J., & Coan, J. A. (2001). Experiential avoidance and Posttraumatic Stress Disorder: A cognitive mediational model of rape recovery. *Journal of Aggression, Maltreatment, & Trauma, 4,* 211–245.

Bond, F. W. & Hayes, S. C. (2002). ACT at work. In F.W. Bond & W. Dryden (Eds.), *Handbook of brief cognitive behaviour therapy* (pp. 117–140). Chichester: Wiley.

Bond, F. W. & Bunce, D. (2000). Outcomes and mediators of change in emotion-focused and problem-focused worksite stress management interventions. *Journal of Occupational Health Psychology, 5(1),* 156–163.

Bond, F. W., & Bunce, D. (2001). Job control mediates change in a work reorganization intervention for stress reduction. *Journal of Occupational Health Psychology, 6,* 290–302.

Bond, F. W. & Bunce, D. (2003). The role of acceptance and job control in mental health, job satisfaction, and work performance. *Journal of Applied Psychology, 88,* 1057–1067.

Borkovec, T. D. (2002). Life in the future versus life in the present. *Clinical Psychology: Science and Practice, 9,* 76–80.

Borkovec, T. D., Alcaine, O., & Behar, E. (2004). Avoidance theory of worry and generalized anxiety disorder. In R. G. Heimberg, C. L. Turk, & D. S. Mennin (Eds.), *Generalized anxiety disorder: Advances in research and practice* (pp. 77–108). New York: Guilford.

Borkovec, T. D., Hazlett-Stevens, H., & Diaz, M. L. (1999). The role of positive beliefs about worry in generalized anxiety disorder and its treatment. *Clinical Psychology and Psychotherapy, 6,* 126–138.

Borkovec, T. D., & Roemer, L. (1995). Perceived function of worry among generalized anxiety disorder subjects: Distraction from more emotionally distressing topics? *Journal of Behavior Therapy and Experimental Psychiatry, 26,* 25–30.

Borkovec, T. D., & Ruscio, A. M. (2001). Psychotherapy for generalized anxiety disorder. *Journal of Clinical Psychiatry, 62,* 37–45.

Bornstein, P. H., Hamilton, S. B., & Bornstein, M. T. (1986). Self-monitoring procedures. In A. R. Ciminero, K. S. Calhoun, & H. E. Adams (Eds.), *Handbook of behavioral assessment* (2nd ed., pp. 176–222). New York: Wiley.

Bosma, H., Marmot, M. G., Hemingway, H., Nicholson, A. C., Brunner, E., & Stansfeld, S. A. (1997). Low job control and risk of coronary heart disease in the Whitehall II (prospective cohort) study. *British Medical Journal, 314,* 558–564.

Branstetter, A., Wilson, K. G., & Mutch, D. G. (August 2003). *ACT and the treatment of psychological distress among cancer patients.* Paper given at the World Conference on ACT, RFT, and the New Behavioral Psychology, Linköping, Sweden.

Breslau, N., Davis, G. C., Andreski, P., & Peterson, E. (1991). Traumatic events and posttraumatic stress disorder in an urban population of young adults. *Archives of General Psychiatry, 48,* 216–222.

Brier, A., Schreiber, J. L., Dyer, J., & Pickar, D. (1991). National Institute of Mental Health longitudinal study of chronic schizophrenia: Prognosis and predictors of outcome. *Archives of General Psychiatry, 48,* 239–246.

Brown, T. A., Campbell, L. A., Lehman, C. L., Grisham, J. R., & Mancill, R. B. (2001). Current and lifetime comorbidity of the DSM-IV anxiety and mood disorders in a large clinical sample. *Journal of Abnormal Psychology, 110,* 49–58.

Burns, D. D. (1980). *Feeling good: The new mood therapy.* New York: William Morrow.

Burns, D. D. & Spangler, D. L. (2001). Do changes in dysfunctional attitudes mediate changes in depression and anxiety in cognitive behavioral therapy? *Behavior Therapy, 32,* 337–369.

Carrascoso, F. J. L. (2000). Acceptance and commitment therapy (ACT) in panic disorder with agoraphobia: A case study. *Psychology in Spain, 4,* 120–128.

Carroll, K. M., Rounsaville, B. J., Nich, C., & Gordon, L. T. (1994). One-year follow-up of psychotherapy and pharmacotherapy for cocaine dependence: Delayed emergence of psychotherapy effects. *Archives of General Psychiatry, 51(12),* 989–997.

Chambless, D. L., Sanderson, W. C., Shoham, V., Johnson, S. B., Pope, K. S., Crits- Christoph, P., Baker, M., Johnson, B., Woody, S. R., Sue, S., Beutler, L., Williams, D. A., & McCurry, S. (1996). An update on empirically validated therapies. *The Clinical Psychologist, 49,* 5–18.

Chiles, J. & Strosahl, K. (1995). *The suicidal patient: Principles of assessment, treatment & case management.* Washington D.C.: American Psychiatric Press.

Chiles, J. & Strosahl, K. (in press). *Handbook for the clinical assessment and treatment of the suicidal patient.* Washington D.C.: American Psychiatric Press.

Cioffi, D., & Holloway, J. (1993). Delayed costs of suppressed pain. *Journal of Personality and Social Psychology, 64,* 274–282.

Clement S. (1995). Diabetes self management education. *Diabetes Care, 18,* 1204–1214.

Cockburn, J., Thomas, R. J., McLaughlin, S. J. & Reading, D. (1995). Acceptance of screening for colorectal cancer by flexible sigmoidoscopy. *Journal of Medical Screening, 2* (2), 79–83.

Cohn, L. G., & Hope, D. A. (2001). Treatment of social phobia: A treatments-by-dimensions review. In S. G. Hofmann & P. M. DiBartolo (Eds.), *From social anxiety to social phobia: Multiple perspectives* (pp. 354–378). Boston: Allyn & Bacon.

Corrigan, P. W. (2001). Getting ahead of the data: A threat to some behavior therapies. *The Behavior Therapist, 24,* 189–193.

Corrigan, P. W., & Penn, D. L. (2001). Introduction: Framing models of social cognition and schizophrenia. Social cognition and social functioning in schizophrenia. In P. W. Corrigan & D. L. Penn (Eds.), *Social cognition and schizophrenia* (pp. 3–40). Washington, D. C.: American Psychological Association.

Corrigan, P. W., Reinke, R. R., Landsberger, S. A., Charate, A., & Toombs, G. A. (2002). The effects of atypical antipsychotic medications on psychosocial outcomes. *Schizophrenia Research, 63,* 97–101.

Couttreax, J., Note, I., Yao, S. N., Lafont, S., Note, B., Mollard, E., Bouvard, M., Sauteraud, A., Bourgeois, M., & Dartigues, J. F. (2001). A controlled trial of cognitive therapy versus intensive behavior therapy in obsessive compulsive disorder. *Psychotherapy and Psychosomatics, 70.*

Cox, T., Griffiths, A., Barlowe, C., Randall, R., Thomson, L., Rial-Gonzalez, E. (2000). *Organisational interventions for work stress: A risk management approach.* Norwich UK: Health and Safety Executive/Her Majesty's Stationary Office.

Craske, M. G. & Sipsas, A. (1992). Animal phobias versus claustrophobias: Exteroceptive versus interoceptive cues. *Behaviour Research and Therapy, 30,* 569–581.

Curtis, G. C., Magee, W. J., Eaton, W. W., Wittchen, H. U., & Kessler, R. C. (1998). Specific fears and phobias: Epidemiology and classification. *British Journal of Psychiatry, 173,* 212–217.

Dahl, J. (1992). *Epilepsy: A behavior medicine approach to assessment and treatment in children.* Göttingen, Sweden: Hogrefe & Huber.

Dahl, J., Brorson, L. O., & Melin, L. (1992). Effects of a broad-spectrum behavioral medicine treatment program on children with refractory epileptic seizures: An 8 year follow-up. *Epilepsia, 33,* 98–102.

Dahl, J., Wilson, K. G. & Nilsson, A. (in press). Acceptance and Commitment Therapy and the treatment of persons at risk for long-term disability resulting from stress and pain symptoms: A preliminary randomized trial. *Behavior Therapy.*

Davis, J. M., Schaffer, C. B., Killian, G. A, Kinard, C., & Chan, C. (1980). Important issues in the drug treatment of schizophrenia. *Schizophrenia Bulletin, 6,* 70–87.

De Ridder, D. & Schreurs, Karlein (2001). Developing interventions for chronically ill patients: Is coping a helpful concept? *Clinical Psychology Review, 21(2),* 205–240.

Dimitriou, E. C., Lavrentiadis, G., & Dimitriou, C. E. (1993). Obsessive-compulsive disorder and alcohol abuse. *European Journal of Psychiatry, 7,* 244–248.

Dobson, K. S. & Khatri, N. (2000). Cognitive therapy: Looking backward, looking forward. *Journal of Clinical Psychology, 56,* 907–923.

Dohrenwend, B. P. & Dohrenwend, B. S. (1981). Socioenvironmental factors, stress, and psychopathology. *American Journal of Community Psychology, 9,* 128–164.

Eccleston, C., Morley, S., Williams, A., Yorke, L., & Mastroyannopoulou, K. (2002). Systematic review of randomised controlled trials of psychological therapy for chronic pain in children and adolescents, with a subset meta-analysis of pain relief. *Pain, 99(1–2),* 157.

Edelman, R. J. (1987). *The psychology of embarrassment.* Chichester, England: Wiley.

Ederyd, B. (August 2003). *What works in a valued direction: A pragmatic clinical perspective.* Paper presented at the World Conference on ACT, RFT, and the New Behavioral Psychology. Linkoping, Sweden.

Edwards, L. C. & Pearce, S. A. (1994). Word completion in chronic pain: Evidence for schematic representation of pain? *Journal of Abnormal Psychology, 103,* 379–382.

Ehlers, A. (1993). Somatic symptoms and panic attacks: A retrospective study of learning experiences. *Behaviour Research and Therapy, 31,* 269–278.

Eifert, G. H. & Heffner, M. (2003). The effects of acceptance versus control contexts on avoidance of panic-related symptoms. *Journal of Behavior Therapy and Experimental Psychiatry, 34,* 293–312.

Feldner, M. T., Zvolensky, M. J., Eifert, G. H., & Spira, A. P. (2003). Emotional avoidance: An experimental test of individual differences and response suppression using biological challenge. *Behaviour Research and Therapy, 41,* 403–411.

Flaxman, P. E. & Bond, F. W. (under review). Comparing the process and outcome of change- and acceptance-oriented worksite stress management interventions.

Foa, E. B., & Kozak, M. J. (1986). Emotional processing of fear: Exposure to corrective information. *Psychological Bulletin, 99,* 20–35.

Foa, E. B., & Kozak, M. J. (1995). DSM-IV field trial: Obsessive-compulsive disorder. *American Journal of Psychiatry, 152,* 90–96.

Folke F., & Parling, T. (2004). *Acceptance and Commitment Therapy in group format for individuals who are unemployed and on sick leave suffering from depression: A randomized controlled trial.* Unpublished thesis, University of Uppsala, Uppsala, Sweden.

Follette, V. M. (1994). Survivors of Child Sexual Abuse: Treatment using a contextual analysis. In S. C. Hayes, N. S. Jacobson, V. M. Follette, & M. J. Dougher (Eds.), *Acceptance and change: Content and context in psychotherapy* (pp. 255–268). Reno, NV: Context Press.

Follette, V. M., & Pistorello, J. (1995). Couples therapy. In C. Classen & I. D. Yalom (Ed.), *Treating women molested in childhood* (pp. 129–161). San Francisco: Jossey-Bass.

Follette, V., & Pistorello, J. (July 1991). *Group treatment for women sexually abused as children.* Paper presented at the annual meeting of the Society for Psychotherapy Research, Lyons, France.

Fontana, A. & Rosenheck, R. (1993). A causal model of the etiology of war-related PTSD. *Journal of Traumatic Stress, 6*, 475–500.

Forsyth, J. P., Parker, J., & Finlay, C. G. (2003). Anxiety sensitivity, controllability, and experiential avoidance and their relation to drug of choice and addiction severity in a residential sample of substance abusing veterans. *Addictive Behaviors, 28*, 851–870.

Fordyce, W. E. (1976). *Behavioral methods for chronic pain and illness.* St. Louis, MO: Mosby.

Garcia, J. M., & Perez, M. (2001). ACT as a treatment for psychotic symptoms: the case of auditory hallucinations. *Analisis y Modificacion, 27*, 455–472.

Garret, J. T. & Garrett, M. (1996). *Medicine of the Cherokee*, Santa Fe, NM: Bear & Company.

Gaudiano, B. and Herbert, J. (2004). *ACT for psychosis.* Unpublished manuscript. Drexel University.

Gifford, E. V., Kohlenberg, B. S., Hayes, S. C., Antonuccio, D. O., Piasecki, M. M., Rasmussen-Hall, M. L., & Palm, K. M. (in press). Applying a functional acceptance based model to smoking cessation: An initial trial of Acceptance and Commitment Therapy. *Behavior Therapy.*

Gorman, J. M. (1996). *The new psychiatry.* New York: St. Martin's Press.

Gould, R. A., Buckminster, S., Pollack, M. H., Otto, M. W., & Yap, L. (1997). Cognitive behavioral and pharmacological treatment for social phobia: A meta-analysis. *Clinical Psychology: Science and Practice, 4*, 291–306.

Gould, R. A., Otto, M. W., & Pollack, M. H. (1995). A meta-analysis of treatment outcome for panic disorder. *Clinical Psychology Review, 15*, 819–844.

Gratz, K. L., & Roemer, L. (2004). Multidimensional assessment of emotion regulation and dysregulation: Development, factor structure, and initial validation of the Difficulties in Emotion Regulation Scale. *Journal of Psychopathology and Behavioral Assessment, 26*, 41–54.

Greco, L. A. (2002). *Creating a context of acceptance in child clinical and pediatric settings.* Paper presented at the annual meeting of the Association for the Advancement of Behavior Therapy. Reno, NV.

Greco, L. A., & Eifert, G.H. (2004; in press). Treating parent-adolescent conflict: Is acceptance the missing link for an integrative family therapy? *Cognitive and Behavioral Practice, 11.*

Greer, S. (1991). Psychological response to cancer and survival. *Psychological Medicine, 21*, 43–49.

Gregg, J. (2004). *Development of an acceptance-based treatment for the self-management of diabetes.* Unpublished doctoral dissertation, University of Nevada, Reno.

Grove, W. M., & Andreasen, N. C. (1992). Concept, diagnosis and classification. In E. S. Paykel (Ed.), *Handbook of affective disorders* (2nd ed., pp. 25–41). New York: Guilford.

Guthrie, R., & Bryant, R. (2000). Attempting suppression of traumatic memories over extended periods of time in acute stress disorder. *Behaviour Research and Therapy, 38*, 899–907.

Gutiérrez, O., Luciano, C., Rodríguez, M., & Fink, B. C. (in press). Comparison between an acceptance-based and a cognitive-control-based protocol for coping with pain. *Behavior Therapy.*

Haddock, G., Tarrier, N., Spaulding, W., Yusupoff, L., Kinney, C., & McCarthy, E. (1998). Individual Cognitive-Behaviour Therapy in the treatment of hallucinations and delusions. *Clinical Psychology Review, 18*, 821–838.

Harmon. T. M., Nelson, R. O., & Hayes, S. C. (1980). The differential effects of self-monitoring mood versus activity in depressed patients. *Journal of Consulting and Clinical Psychology, 48*, 30–38.

Hawton, K. (1992). Suicide and attempted suicide. In E. S. Paykel (Ed.), *Handbook of affective disorder* (2nd ed., pp. 635–650). New York: Guilford.

Hayes, S. C. (1984). Making sense of spirituality. *Behaviorism, 12*, 99–110.

Hayes, S. C. (1987). A contextual approach to therapeutic change. In N. Jacobson (Ed.), *Psychotherapists in clinical practice: Cognitive and behavioral perspectives* (pp. 327–387). New York: Guilford.

Hayes, S. C. (1992). Verbal relations, time, and suicide. In S. C. Hayes & L. J. Hayes (Eds.), *Understanding verbal relations* (pp. 109–118). Reno, NV: Context Press.

Hayes, S. C. (1993). Analytic goals and the varieties of scientific contextualism. In S. C. Hayes, L. J. Hayes, H. W. Reese, & T. R. Sarbin (Eds.), *The varieties of scientific contextualism* (pp. 11–27). Reno, NV: Context Press.

Hayes, S. C. (1994). Content, context, and the types of psychological acceptance. In S. C. Hayes, N. S. Jacobson, V. M. Follette, & M. J. Dougher (Eds.), *Acceptance and change: Content and context in psychotherapy* (pp. 255–268). Reno: Context Press.

Hayes, S. C. (Ed.). (1989). *Rule-governed behavior: Cognition, contingencies, and instructional control.* New York: Plenum.

Hayes, S. C. (in press). Acceptance and Commitment Therapy, Relational Frame Theory, and the third wave of behavior therapy. *Behavior Therapy.*

Hayes, S. C., Barnes-Holmes, D., & Roche, B. (Eds.). (2001). *Relational Frame Theory: A Post-Skinnerian account of human language and cognition.* New York: Plenum.

Hayes, S. C., Bissett, R., Korn, Z., Zettle, R. D., Rosenfarb, I., Cooper, L., & Grundt, A. (1999). The impact of acceptance versus control rationales on pain tolerance. *The Psychological Record, 49*, 33–47.

Hayes, S. C., Bissett, R., Roget, N., Padilla, M., Kohlenberg, B. S., Fisher, G., Masuda, A., Pistorello, J., Rye, A. K., Berry, K. & Niccolls, R. (in press). The impact of acceptance and commitment training and multicultural training on the stigmatizing attitudes and professional burnout of substance abuse counselors. *Behavior Therapy.*

Hayes, S. C. & Brownstein, A. J. (1986). Mentalism, behavior-behavior relations and a behavior analytic view of the purposes of science. *The Behavior Analyst, 1*, 175–190.

Hayes, S. C., Follette, V. M., & Linehan, M. M. (in press). *Mindfulness, acceptance, and relationship: Expanding the cognitive behavioral tradition.* New York: Guilford Press.

Hayes, S. C. & Hayes, L. J. (1989). The verbal action of the listener as a basis for rule- governance. In S. C. Hayes (Ed.), *Rule-governed behavior: Cognition, contingencies, and instructional control* (pp. 153–190). New York: Plenum.

Hayes, S. C., Hayes, L. J., & Reese, H. W. (1988). Finding the philosophical core: A review of Stephen C. Popper's World Hypotheses. *Journal of Experimental Analysis of Behavior, 50*, 97–111.

Hayes, S. C., Masuda, A., Bissett, R., Luoma, J. & Guerrero, L. F. (in press). DBT, FAP, and ACT: How empirically oriented are the new behavior therapy technologies? *Behavior Therapy.*

Hayes, S. C., Rosenfarb, I., Wulfert, E., Munt, E., Zettle, R. D., & Korn, Z. (1985). Self-reinforcement effects: An artifact of social standard setting? *Journal of Applied Behavior Analysis, 18*, 201–214.

Hayes, S. C., Strosahl, K. D., & Wilson, K. G. (1999). *Acceptance and Commitment Therapy: An experiential approach to behavior change.* New York: Guilford Press.

Hayes, S. C., Strosahl, K. D., Wilson, K. G., Bissett, R. T., Pistorello, J., Toarmino, D., Polusny, M., A., Dykstra, T. A., Batten, S. V., Bergan, J., Stewart, S. H., Zvolensky, M. J., Eifert, G. H., Bond, F. W., Forsyth J. P., Karekla, M., & McCurry, S. M. (in press). Measuring experiential avoidance: A preliminary test of a working model. *The Psychological Record.*

Hayes, S. C., & Wilson, K. G. (1994). Acceptance and commitment therapy: Altering the verbal support for experiential avoidance. *The Behavior Analyst, 17*, 289–303.

Hayes, S. C., Wilson, K. G., Gifford, E. V., Bissett, R., Piasecki, M., Batten, S. V., Byrd, M., & Gregg, J. (in press). A randomized controlled trial of twelve-step facilitation and Acceptance and Commitment Therapy with polysubstance abusing methadone maintained opiate addicts. *Behavior Therapy.*

Hayes, S. C., Wilson, K. G., Gifford, E. V., Follette, V. M., & Strosahl, K. (1996). Emotional avoidance and behavioral disorders: A functional dimensional approach to diagnosis and treatment. *Journal of Consulting and Clinical Psychology, 64,* 1152–1168.

Hayward, C., Killen, J. D., Kraemer, H. C., & Taylor, C. B. (2000). Predictors of panic attacks in adolescents. *Journal of the American Academy of Child and Adolescent Psychiatry, 39(2),* 1–8.

Health and Safety Executive. (2003). *Work related stress.* Retrieved August 4, 2003, from http://www.hse.gov.uk/stress/test.htm.

Heffner, M., Sperry, J., Eifert, G. H. & Detweiler, M. (2002). Acceptance and Commitment Therapy in the treatment of an adolescent female with anorexia nervosa: A case example. *Cognitive and Behavioral Practice, 9,* 232–236.

Heimberg, R. G. (1991). *A manual for conducting Cognitive-Behavioral Group Therapy for social phobia (2nd ed).* Unpublished manuscript, State University of New York at Albany, Center for Stress and Snxiety Disorders, Albany, NY.

Heimberg, R. G., Liebowitz, M. R., Hope, D. A., Schneier, F. R., Holt, C. S., Welkowitz, L. A., Juster, H. R., Campeas, R., Bruch, M. A., Cloitre, M., Fallon, B., & Klein, D. F. (1998). Cognitive behavioral group therapy vs. phenelzine therapy for social phobia: 12–week outcome. *Archives of General Psychiatry, 55,* 1133–1141.

Hirschfield, R. M. (1996). Placebo response in the treatment of panic disorder. *Bulletin of the Menninger Clinic, 60(2),* A76–A86.

Holden, E. W., Deichmann, M. M., & Levy, J. D. (1999). Empirically supported treatments in pediatric psychology: recurrent pediatric headache. *Journal of Pediatric Psychology, 24(2),* 91–109.

Hollon, S. D., & Kendall, P. C. (1980). Cognitive self-statements in depression: Development of an automatic thoughts questionnaire. *Cognitive Therapy and Research, 4,* 383–395.

Horowitz, M. J. (1986). *Stress response syndromes* (2nd ed.). Northvale, New Jersey: Nathan Aronson.

Horowitz, M. J., & Becker, S. S. (1971). The compulsion to repeat trauma: Experimental study of intrusive thinking after stress. *Journal of Nervous & Mental Disease, 153,* 32–40.

Howard, K., Kopta, S., Krause, R. & Orlinsky, D. (1986). The dose effect relationship in psychotherapy. *American Psychologist, 41,* 159–164.

Howard, K. I. (1992). The psychotherapeutic service delivery system. *Psychotherapy Research, 2 (3),* 164–180.

Huerta, F. R., Gomez, S. M., Molina, A. M. M., & Luciano, M. C. S. (1998). Generalized anxiety: A case study. *Analisis y Modificacion de Conducta, 24,* 751–766.

Huxter, M. (2003). *Using mindfulness, concentration and wisdom to manage stress, depression and anxiety: A course workbook.* Unpublished manuscript.

Ilardi, S. S. & Craighead, W. E. (1999). Rapid early response, cognitive modification, and nonspecific factors in cognitive behavior therapy for depression: A reply to Tang, & DeRubeis. *Clinical Psychology: Science & Practice, 6,* 295–299.

Jacobson, N. S., Dobson, K. S., Truax, P. A., Addis, M. E., Koerner, K., Gollan, J. K., Gortner, E., & Prince, S. E. (1996). A component analysis of cognitive-behavioral treatment of depression. *Journal of Consulting and Clinical Psychology, 64,* 295–304.

Jacobson, P. B., & Butler, R. W. (1996). Relation of cognitive coping and catastrophizing to acute pain and analgesic use following breast cancer surgery. *Journal of Behavioral Medicine, 19,* 17–29.

Janicke, D. M., & Finnev, J. W. (1999). Empirically supported treatments in pediatric psychology: recurrent abdominal pain. *Journal of Pediatric Psychology, 24 (2),* 115–127.

Jensen, M. P., Nielson, W. R., Romano, J. M., Hill, M. L., & Turner, J. A. (2000). Further evaluation of the Pain Stages of Change Questionnaire: Is the transtheoretical model of change useful for patients with chronic pain? *Pain, 86 (3)*, 255–264.

Jex, S. M. (1998). *Stress and job performance*. London: Sage.

Kabat-Zinn, J. (1994). *Wherever you go, there you are: Mindfulness meditation in everyday life*. New York: Hyperion.

Kabat-Zinn, J. (1990). *Full catastrophe living: Using the wisdom of your body and mind to face stress, pain and illness*. New York: Delacorte.

Karekla, M. (2003). *Panic control group treatment compared to an acceptance enhanced version of PCT for individuals suffering from panic disorder*. Unpublished manuscript.

Karekla, M., Forsyth, J. P., & Kelly, M. M. (in press). Emotional avoidance and panicogenic responding to a biological challenge procedure. *Behavior Therapy*.

Kashdan, T. B., & Herbert, J. D. (2001). Social anxiety disorder in children and adolescents: Current status and future directions. *Clinical Child and Family Psychology Review, 4*, 37–61.

Kashikar-Zuck, S., Graham, T. B., Huenefeld, M. D., & Powers, S. W. (2000). A review of biobehavioral research in juvenile primary Fibromyalgia syndrome. *Arthritis Care and Research, 13*(6), 388–397.

Kerns, R. D., Rosenberg, R., Jamison, R. N., Caudill, M. A., & Haythornthwaite, J. (1997). Readiness to adopt a self-management approach to chronic pain: The Pain Stages of Change Questionnaire (PSOCQ). *Pain, 72*, 227–234.

Kessler, R. C., Sonnega, A., Bromet, E., Hughes, M., & Nelson, C.B. (1995). Posttraumatic stress disorder in the National Comorbidity Survey. *Archives of General Psychiatry, 52*, 1048–1060.

King, D. W., King, L. A., Foy, D. W. & Gudanowski, J. (1996). Prewar factors in combat-related posttraumatic stress disorder: Structural equation modeling with a national sample of female and male Vietnam veterans. *Journal of Consulting & Clinical Psychology, 64*, 520–531.

Kirmayer, L. J. & Robbins, J. M. (1996). Patients who somatize in primary care: A longitudinal study of cognitive and social characteristics. *Psychological Medicine, 26*(5), 937–951.

Kirsch, I., Moore, T. J., Scoboria, A., & Nicholls, S. S. (2002). The emperor's new drugs: An analysis of antidepressant medication data submitted to the U.S. Food and Drug Administration. *Prevention & Treatment, 5*, pp. np

Kivimaki, M., Leino-Arjas, P., Luukkonen, R., Riihimaki, H., Vahtera, J., & Kirjonen, J. (2003). Work stress and risk of cardiovascular mortality. *British Medical Journal, 325*, 857–60.

Kuipers, E. (2000). Psychological treatments for psychosis: evidence based but unavailable? *Psychiatric Rehabilitation Skills, 4*, 249–258.

Kurtz, E. (1979). *Not God: A history of Alcoholics Anonymous*. Minneapolis, MN: Hazelden Information Education.

Kushner, M. G., Abrams, K., & Borchardt, C. (2000). The relationship between anxiety disorders and alcohol use disorders: A review of major perspectives and findings. *Clinical Psychology Review, 20*(2), 149–171.

Lazarus, R. S. & Folkman, S. (1984). *Stress, appraisal and coping*. New York: Springer.

Leary, M. R. (1983). A brief version of the Fear of Negative Evaluation Scale. *Personality and Social Psychology Bulletin, 9*, 371–375.

Leary, M. R., Knight, P. D., & Johnson, K. A. (1987). Social anxiety and dyadic conversation: A verbal response analysis. *Journal of Social and Clinical Psychology, 5*, 34–50.

Leon, A. C., Portera, L., & Weissman, M. M. (1995). The social costs of anxiety disorders. *British Journal of Psychiatry, 166 (Suppl. 27)*, 19–22.

Levitt, J. T., Brown, T. A., Orsillo, S. M., & Barlow, D. H. (in press). The effects of acceptance versus suppression of emotion on subjective and psychophysiological response to carbon dioxide challenge in patients with panic disorder. *Behavior Therapy*.

Linehan, M. M. (1993). *Skills training manual for treating Borderline Personality Disorder*. New York: Guilford.

Linehan, M. M. (1993). *Cognitive-behavioral treatment of borderline personality disorder*. New York: Guilford.

Linehan, M. M., Armstrong, H. E., Suarez, A., Allmon, D., & Heard, H. L. (1991). A Cognitive-behavioral treatment of chronically parasuicidal borderline patients. *Archives of General Psychiatry, 48*, 1060–1064.

Lipkens, G., Hayes, S. C., & Hayes, L. J. (1993). Longitudinal study of derived stimulus relations in an infant. *Journal of Experimental Child Psychology, 56*, 201–239.

Litz, B. T., Orsillo, S. M., Kaloupek, D. G., & Weathers, F. (2000). Emotional processing in posttraumatic stress disorder. *Journal of Abnormal Psychology, 109*, 26–39.

Litz, B. T., Orsillo, S. M., & Wagner, A. W. (2001). A preliminary investigation of the role of strategic withholding of emotions in PTSD. *Journal of Traumatic Stress, 14*, 149–156.

Livesley, W. (Ed.). (2001). *Handbook of personality disorders: Theory, research and treatment*. New York: Guilford Press.

Livesley, W. & Jackson, D. (1986). The internal consistency and factor structure of behaviors judged to be associated with personality disorder. *American Journal of Psychiatry, 143*, 1473–1474.

Lobban, F., Haddock, G., Kinderman, P., & Wells, A. (2002). The role of metacognitive beliefs in auditory hallucinations. *Personality and Individual Differences, 32*, 1351–1363.

Luciano, C. & Cabello, F. (2001). Bereavement and Acceptance and Commitment Therapy (ACT). *Análisis y Modificación de Conducta, 27*, 113, 399–424.

Luciano, C., & Gutierrez, O. M. (2001). Anxiety and Acceptance and Commitment Therapy (ACT). *Análisis y Modificación de Conducta, 27*, 373–398.

Luciano, C., Visdómine, J. C., Gutiérrez, O., & Montesinos, F. (2001). ACT (Acceptance and Commitment Therapy) and chronic pain. *Análisis y Modificación de Conducta, 27*, 473–502.

Lundgren, T., Mansson, J., & Dahl, J. (2003). *ACT applied in an intensive camp setting to a group of adolescent females with self-destructive behaviors*. Unpublished manuscript.

March, J. S. & Muelle, K. (1998). *OCD in Children and Adolescents: A Cognitive-Behavioral Treatment Manual*. New York: Guilford.

Maris, R. W., Berman, A. L., Maltsberger, J. T., & Yufit, R. I. (1992). *Assessment and prediction of suicide*. New York: Guilford.

Marlatt, G. A. (1994). Addiction, mindfulness, and acceptance. In S. C. Hayes, N. S. Jacobson, V. M. Follette, & M. J. Dougher (Eds.), *Acceptance and change: Content and context in psychotherapy* (pp. 175–197). Reno, NV: Context Press.

Marlatt, G. A., & Gordon, J. R. (Eds.). (1985). *Relapse prevention: Maintenance strategies in the treatment of addictive behaviors*. New York: Brunner/Mazel.

Marlatt, G. A., & Witkiewitz, K. (2002). Harm reduction approaches to alcohol use: Health promotion, prevention, and treatment. *Addictive Behaviors, 27*, 867–886.

Marx, B. P. & Sloan, D. M. (in press). The role of emotion in the psychological functioning of adult survivors of childhood sexual abuse. *Behavior Therapy*.

Massion, A., Warshaw, M., & Keller, M. (1993). Quality of life and psychiatric morbidity in panic disorder versus generalized anxiety disorder. *American Journal of Psychiatry, 150*, 600–607.

Masuda, A., Hayes, S. C., Sackett, C. F., & Twohig, M. P. (in press). Cognitive defusion and self-relevant negative thoughts: Examining the impact of a ninety year old technique. *Behaviour Research and Therapy*.

Maher, B. A. (1988). Anomolous experience and delusional thinking: The logic of explanations, in T. F. Oltmanns & B. A. Maher (Eds.) *Delusional beliefs*. New York: Wiley.

McCracken, L. M. & Eccleston, C. (2003). Coping or acceptance: What to do about chronic pain. *Pain, 105*, 197–204.

McCracken, L. M. (1998). Learning to live with the pain: Acceptance of pain predicts adjustment in persons with chronic pain. *Pain, 74*, 21–27.

McCracken, L. M. , Vowles, K. E., & Eccleston, C. (2004). Acceptance of chronic pain: Component analysis and a revised assessment method. *Pain, 107*, 159–166.

McLean, P. D., Whittal, M. L., Thordason, D. S., & Taylor, S., Soechting, I., Taylor, S., Soechting, I., Koch, W. J., Paterson, R., & Anderson, K. W. (2001). Cognitive versus behavioral therapy in the group treatment of obsessive compulsive disorder. *Journal of Consulting and Clinical Psychology, 69*, 205–214.

Mennin, D. S., Heimberg, R. G., Turk, C. L., & Fresco, D. M. (2002). Applying an emotion regulation framework to integrative approaches to generalized anxiety disorder. *Clinical Psychology: Science and Practice, 9*, 85–90.

Meyers, R. J., Miller, W. R., & Edwards, G. (Eds.). (2001). *A community reinforcement approach to addiction treatment.* New York: Cambridge University Press.

Miller, W. R. (1996). Motivational interviewing: Research, practice, and puzzles. *Addictive Behaviors, 21*(6), 835–842.

Miller, L. J., O'Connor, E., & DiPasquale, T. (1993). Patients' attitudes toward hallucinations. *American Journal of Psychiatry, 150*, 584–588.

Miller, W. R., & Rollnick, S. (Eds.) (1991). *Motivational interviewing: Preparing people to change addictive behavior.* New York: Guilford.

Miller, W. R., & Rollnick, S. (2002). *Motivational Interviewing: Preparing people for change* (2nd ed.). New York: Guilford Press.

Miner, C. R., Rosenthal, R. N., Hellerstein, D. J., & Muenz, L. R. (1997). Prediction of compliance with outpatient referral in patients with schizophrenia and psychoactive substance use disorders. *Archives of General Psychiatry, 54*, 706–712.

Montesinos, F. (2003). ACT, sexual desire orientation and erectile dysfunction. A case study. *Analisis y Modificación de Conducta, 29*, 291–320.

Montesinos, F., Hernández, B., & Luciano, C. (2001). Application of Acceptance and Commitment Therapy (ACT) in cancer patients. *Análisis y Modificación de Conducta, 27*, 503–524.

Morley, S., Eccleston, C., & Williams, A. (1999). Systematic review and meta-analysis of randomized controlled trials of cognitive behaviour therapy and behaviour therapy for chronic pain in adults, excluding headache. *Pain, 80*(1–2), 1–13.

Mueser, K. T., Bennett, M., & Kushner, M. G. (1995). Epidemiology of substance use disorders among persons with chronic mental illnesses. In A. F. Lehman & L. Dixson (Eds.), *Double jeopardy: Chronic mental illness and substance abuse in persons with severe mental illness* (pp. 9–25). New York: Harwood.

Murrel, A. & Wilson, K. (2003). *Use of ACT groups with adolescents and children.* Unpublished manuscript.

Myers, J. K., Weissman, M. M., Tischler, G. L., Holzer, C. E., Leaf, P. J., Orvaschel, H. A., et al. (1994). Six-month prevalence of psychiatric disorders in three communities: 1980–1982. *Archives of General Psychiatry, 41*, 959–967.

Narayan, K. M., Gregg, E. W., Engelgau, M. M., Moore, B., Thompson, T. J., Williamson, D. F., et al. (2000). Translation research for chronic disease: the case of diabetes. *Diabetes Care, 23*, 1794–1798.

Narrow, W. E., Rae, D. S., Robins, L. N., & Regier, D. A. (2002). Revised prevalence based estimates of mental disorders in the United States: Using a clinical significance criterion to reconcile 2 surveys' estimates. *Archives of General Psychiatry, 59*(2), 115–123.

Nicholas, M. K., Wilson, P. H. & Goyen, J. (1991). Operant-behavioral and cognitive-behavioral treatment for chronic low back pain. *Behaviour Research and Therapy, 29*, 235–238.

Norris, F. H. (1992). Epidemiology of trauma: Frequency and impact of different potentially traumatic events on different demographic events. *Journal of Consulting and Clinical Psychology, 60*, 409–418.

Norton, P. J., & Hope, D. A. (2001). Kernels of truth or distorted perceptions: Self and observer ratings of social anxiety and performance. *Behavior Therapy, 32*, 765–786.

Orsillo, S. M. & Block, J. L. (2003). *Commitment to valued action groups in the treatment of trauma.* Unpublished manuscript.

Orsillo, S. M., Roemer, L., Block Lerner, J., & Tull, M. T. (in press). Acceptance, mindfulness, and cognitive-behavioral therapy: Comparisons, contracts and applications to anxiety. In Hayes, S. C., Linehan, M. M., & Follette, V. C. (Eds.), *Mindfulness, and acceptance.* New York: Guilford.

Öst, L.-G. (1989). One-session treatment for specific phobias. *Behaviour Research and Therapy, 27*, 1–7.

Paez, M., Luciano, C., Gutiérrez, O., Montesinos, F. & Gómez, I. (August 2003). *Impact of breast cancer in the patient's life. Acceptance versus control-focused based protocols.* Paper given at the World Conference on ACT, RFT, and the New Behavioral Psychology, Linköping, Sweden.

Parkerson, G. (1996). *User's Guide for the Duke Health Profile (Duke).* Manual available from author at Dept. of Community and Family Medicine, Box 3886, Duke University Medical Center, Durham, North Carolina, 27710.

Patterson, M. L., & Ritts, V. (1997). Social and communicative anxiety: A review and meta-analysis. In B.R. Burleson (Ed.), *Communication Yearbook 20.* Thousand Oaks, CA: Sage.

Paul, P. H., Marx, B. P., & Orsillo, S. M. (1999). Acceptance-based psychotherapy in the treatment of an adjudicated exhibitionist: A case example. *Behavior Therapy, 30*, 149–162.

Penn, D. L., Combs, D., & Mohamed, S. (2001). Social cognition and social functioning in schizophrenia. In P. W. Corrigan & D. L. Penn (Eds.), *Social cognition and schizophrenia* (pp. 97–122). Washington, D. C.: American Psychological Association.

Pennebaker, J. W., Kiecolt, G., Glaser, J. K., & Glaser, R. (1988). Confronting traumatic experience and immunocompetence: A reply to Neale, Cox, Valdimarsdottir, and Stone. *Journal of Consulting and Clinical Psychology, 56*, 638–639.

Pepper, S. C. (1942). *World hypotheses: A study in evidence.* Berkeley: University of California Press.

Pistorello, J. & Leonard, L. (August 2003). *Acceptance and Commitment Therapy applied to a counseling center setting: Data and lessons learned.* Paper presented at the World Conference on ACT, RFT, and the New Behavioral Psychology. Linkoping, Sweden.

Pistorello, J., Follette, V. M., & Hayes, S. C. (2000). Long-term correlates of childhood sexual abuse: A behavior analytic perspective. In M. J. Dougher (Ed.), *Clinical behavior analysis* (pp. 75–98). Reno, NV: Context Press.

Pollock, L. & Williams, M. (2001). Effective problem solving in suicide attempters depends upon specific autobiographical recall. *Suicide and Life Threatening Behavior, 31*, 386–396.

Pollack, M. H., Penava, S. A., Bolton, E., Worthington, J. J. III, Allen, G. L., Farach, F. J., & Otto, M. W. (2002). A novel cognitive-behavioral approach for treatment-resistant drug dependence. *Journal of Substance Abuse Treatment, 23*, 335–342.

Polusny, M. A., & Follette, V. M. (1995). Long-term correlates of child sexual abuse: Theory and review of the empirical literature. *Applied and Preventive Psychology, 4*, 143–166.

Polusny, M. A., Rosenthal, M. Z., Aban, I., & Follette, V. M. (2002). *Experiential avoidance as a mediator of the effects of adolescent sexual victimization on adult psychological distress and alcohol use.* Manuscript submitted for publication.

Pratt, C. W., Gill, K. J., Barrett, N. M., & Roberts, M. M. (1999). *Psychiatric rehabilitation*. San Diego, CA: Academic Press.

Puder, R. S. (1988). Age analysis of cognitive-behavioral group therapy for chronic pain outpatients. *Psychology and Aging, 3*, 204–207.

Purdon, C. (1999). Thought suppression and psychopathology. *Behaviour Research and Therapy, 37*, 1029–1054.

Quick, J. C. & Tetrick, L. E. (2002). *Handbook of occupational health psychology*. Washington, DC: American Psychological Association.

Rachman, S. J. (1997). A cognitive theory of obsession. *Behaviour Research and Therapy, 35*, 793–802.

Rapee, R. M., Craske, M. G., & Barlow, D. H. (1995). Assessment instrument for panic disorder that includes fear of sensation-producing activities: The Albany Panic and Phobia Questionnaire. *Anxiety, 1*, 114–122.

Resnick, H. S., Kilpatrick, D. G., Dansky, B. S., Saunders, B. E., & Best, C.L. (1993). Prevalence of civilian trauma and posttraumatic stress disorder in a representative national sample of women. *Journal of Consulting and Clinical Psychology, 61*, 984–991.

Richardson, A., Adner, N., & Nordstrom, G. (2001). Persons with insulin-dependent diabetes mellitus: acceptance and coping ability. *Journal of Advanced Nursing, 33*, 758–63.

Robinson, P. (1996a). *Living life well: New strategies for hard times*. Reno: Context Press.

Robinson, P. (1996b). *Treating depression in primary care*. Reno: Context Press.

Robinson, P. & Brockey, A. (2000). Conducting research on chronic pain in a managed care setting: A trail guide. In S. D. Lande & R. J. Kulich (Eds.), *Managed care and pain* (pp. 87–104). Glenview, IL: American Pain Society.

Robinson, M. E., Riley, J. L., Myers, C. D., Sadler, I. J., Kvaal, S. A., Geisser, M. E., & Keefe, F. J. (1997). The Coping Strategies Questionnaire: A large sample, item level factor analysis. *Clinical Journal of Pain, 13*, 43–49.

Robinson, P., Del Vento, A., & Wischman, C. (1998). Integrated treatment of the frail elderly: The group care clinic. In Blount, S. (Ed.), *Integrated Care: The Future of Medical and Mental Health Collaboration*, New York: Norton.

Robinson, P. & Hayes, S. C. (1997). Acceptance and commitment: A model for integration. In N. A. Cummings, J. L. Cummings, et al. (Eds), *Behavioral health in primary care: A guide for clinical integration* (pp. 177–203). Madison, CT: Psychosocial Press.

Roemer, L., & Borkovec, T. D. (1993). Worry: Unwanted cognitive experience that controls unwanted somatic experience. In D. M. Wegner & J. Pennebaker (Eds.), *Handbook of mental control*. Englewood Cliffs, NJ: Prentice Hall.

Roemer, L., Litz, B. T., Orsillo, S. M., & Wagner, A. W. (2001). A preliminary investigation of the role of strategic withholding of emotions in PTSD. *Journal of Traumatic Stress, 14*, 149–156.

Roemer, L. & Orsillo, S. M. (2002). Expanding our conceptualization of and treatment for generalized anxiety disorder: Integrating mindfulness/acceptance-based approaches with existing cognitive-behavioral models. *Clinical Psychology: Science and Practice, 9*, 54–68.

Rogers, E. S., Anthony, W. A., Toole, J., & Brown, M. A. (1991). Vocational outcomes following psychosocial rehabilitation: A longitudinal study of three programs. *Vocational Rehabilitation, 1*, 21–29.

Rosenberg, S. D. & Tucker, G. J. (1979). Verbal behavior and schizophrenia: The semantic dimension. *Archives of General Psychiatry, 36*, 1331–1337.

Rüsch, N, & Corrigan, P. W. (2002). Motivational Interviewing to improve insight and treatment adherence in schizophrenia. *Psychiatric Rehabilitation Journal, 26*, 23–32.

Sanderson, W. C., DiNardo, P. A., Rapee, R. M., & Barlow, D. H. (1990). Syndrome comorbidity in patients diagnosed with a DSM-III-R anxiety disorder. *Journal of Abnormal Psychology, 99*, 308–312.

Schlenker, B. R. (1987). Threats to identity: Self-identification and social stress. In C. R. Synder & C. Ford (Eds.), *Coping with negative life events: Clinical and social psychology perspectives.* New York: Plenum Press.

Segal, Z. V., Williams, J. M. G., & Teasdale, J. D. (2002). *Mindfulness-based cognitive therapy for depression: A new approach to preventing relapse.* New York: Guilford.

Sensky, T., MacLeod, A. K., & Rigby, M. F. (1996). Causal attributions about common somatic sensations among frequent general practice attenders. *Psychological Medicine, 26(3),* 641–646.

Shafran, R., Thordarson, D., & Rachman, S. (1996). Thought action fusion in obsessive compulsive disorder. *Journal of Anxiety Disorders, 5,* 379–391.

Shalev, A. Y., Peri, T., Canetti, L., & Schreiber, S. (1996). Predictors of PTSD in injured trauma survivors: A prospective study. *American Journal of Psychiatry, 153,* 219–225.

Shipherd, J. C., & Beck, J. G. (1999). The effects of suppressing trauma-related thoughts on women with rape-related post-traumatic stress disorder. *Behaviour Research and Therapy, 37,* 99–112.

Singer, G. H., Irvine, A. B., & Irvin, L. K. (1989). Expanding the focus of behavioral parent training. In G. S. L. Irvin (Ed.), *Support for caregiving families* (pp. 85–102). Baltimore: Brookes.

Slade, P. D. (1972). The effects of systematic desensitization on auditory hallucinations. *Behaviour Research and Therapy, 10,* 85–91.

Smyth, J. M., Stone, A. A., Hurewitz, A., & Kaell, A. (1999). Effects of writing about stressful experiences on symptom reduction in patients with asthma or rheumatoid arthritis: A randomized trial. *Journal of the American Medical Association, 281,*1304–1309.

Solyom, L., DiNicola, V. F., Sookman, D., & Luchins, D. (1985). Is there an obsessive psychosis?: Aetiological and prognostic factors of an atypical form of obsessive-compulsive neurosis. *Canadian Journal of Psychiatry, 19,* 69–78.

Steil, R., & Ehlers, A. (2000). Dysfunctional meaning of posttraumatic intrusions in chronic PTSD. *Behaviour Research and Therapy, 38,* 537–558.

Steketee, G., & Frost, R. O. (1998). Obsessive-compulsive disorder. In A.S. Bellack & M. Hersen (Eds.), *Comprehensive clinical psychology: Vol 6. Adults: Clinical formulation and treatment.* Oxford: Pergamon.

Strosahl, K. (1991). Treatment of the personality disordered patient. In C. Austad & W. Berman (Eds.), *Psychotherapy in managed health care: The optimal use of time and resources* (pp. 185–201). Washington DC: American Psychological Association.

Strosahl, K. (2001). The integration of primary care and behavioral health: Type II changes in the era of managed care. In N. A. Cummings, & W. O'Donohue et al. (Eds.), *Integrated behavioral healthcare: Positioning mental health practice with medical/surgical practice* (pp. 45–69). San Diego: Academic Press.

Strosahl, K. D., Hayes, S. C., Bergan, J., & Romano, P. (1998). Assessing the field effectiveness of Acceptance and Commitment Therapy: An example of the manipulated training research method. *Behavior Therapy, 29,* 35–64.

Strosahl, K. & Linehan, M. (1983). Basic issues in behavioral assessment. In A. Ciminero, K. Calhoun & H. Adams (Eds.), *Handbook of behavioral assessment* (2nd Edition) (pp. 12–60). New York: Wiley.

Sullivan, M. J. L., Thorn, B. E., Haythornthwaite, J., Keefe, F., Martin, M., Bradley, L., & Lefebvre, J. C. (2001). Theoretical perspectives on the relation between catastrophizing and pain. *Clinical Journal of Pain, 17,* 52–64.

Sullivan, M. J. L., Bishop, S. R., & Pivik, J. (1995). The Pain Catastrophizing Scale: Development and validation. *Psychological Assessment, 7,* 524–532.

Sullivan, M. J. L., Stanish, W., Waite, H., Sullivan, M. E., & Tripp, D. (1998). Catastrophizing, pain, and disability following soft tissue injuries. *Pain, 77,* 253–260.

Tanouye, E. (2001, June 13). Mental illness: A rising workplace cost. *The Wall Street Journal*, pp. B1, B6.

Taylor, S., & Cox, B. J. (1998). An expanded Anxiety Sensitivity Index: Evidence for a hierarchic structure in a clinical sample. *Journal of Anxiety Disorders, 12*, 463–483.

Teasdale, J. D., Moore, R. G., Hayhurst, H., Pope, M., Williams, S., Segal & Z. V. (2002). Metacognitive awareness and prevention of relapse in depression: Empirical evidence. *Journal of Consulting and Clinical Psychology, 70*, 275– 287.

Terry, D. J. & Jimmieson, N. L. (1999). Work control and employee well-being: A decade review. In C. L. Cooper & I. T. Robertson (Eds.), *International review of industrial and organizational psychology*. Chichester: John Wiley & Sons.

Thompson, R. J., Gil, K. M., Abrams, M. R. & Phillips, G. (1992). Stress, coping and psychological adjustment of adults with sickle cell disease. *Journal of Consulting and Clinical Psychology, 60*, 433–440.

Thorn, B. E. & Boothby, J. L. (2002). Targeted treatment of catastrophizing for the management of chronic pain. *Cognitive and Behavioral Practice, 9*, 127–138.

Tien, A.Y. (1991). Distributions of hallucinations in the population. *Social Psychiatry and Psychiatric Epidemiology, 26*, 287–292.

Turk, D. C., & Okifuji, A. (2002). Psychological factors in chronic pain: Evolution and revolution. *Journal of Consulting and Clinical Psychology, 70*, 678–690.

Turk, D. C., Meichenbaum, D. & Genest, M. (1983). *Pain and behavioral medicine: A cognitive-behavioral perspective*. New York: Guilford Press.

Turk, D. D., & Okifuji, A. (1996). Perception of traumatic onset, compensation status, and physical findings: Impact on pain severity, emotional distress, and disability in chronic pain patients. *Journal of Behavioral Medicine, 19*, 435–453.

Turkington, D., & Siddle, R. (2000). Improving understanding and coping in people with schizophrenia. *Psychiatric Rehabilitation Skills, 4*, 300–320.

Turner, J. A. & Clancy, S. (1988). Comparison of operant behavioral and cognitive-behavioral group treatment for chronic low back pain. *Journal of Consulting and Clinical Psychology, 56*, 261–266.

Turner, J. A., Clancy, J. A., McQuade, K. J. & Cardenas, D. D. (1990). Effectiveness of behavioral therapy for chronic low back pain: A component analysis. *Journal of Consulting and Clinical Psychology, 58*, 573–579.

Turner, J. A., Jensen, M. P. & Romano, J. M. (2000). Do beliefs, coping, and catastrophizing independently predict functioning in patients with chronic pain? *Pain, 85*, 115–125.

Twohig, M. & Woods, D. (in press). A preliminary investigation of acceptance and commitment therapy and habit reversal as a treatment for trichotillomania. *Behavior Therapy*.

Ulmer, J. F. (1997). An exploratory study of pain, coping, and depressed mood following burn injury. *Journal of Pain and Symptom Management, 13*, 148–157.

U.S. Department of Health and Human Services, Office of Applied Studies. (2003). *Results from the 2002 National Survey on Drug Use and Health: National Findings*. Washington D.C.: U.S. Government Printing Office.

van Balkom, A. J. L. M., van Oppen, P., Vermeulen, A. W. A., van Dyck, R., Nauta, M. C. E., & Vorst, H. C. M. (1994). A meta-analysis on the treatment of obsessive-compulsive disorder: A comparison of antidepressants, behavior and cognitive therapy. *Clinical Psychology Review, 14*, 359–381.

Walser, R. D. & Hayes, S. C. (1998). Acceptance and trauma survivors: Applied issues and problems. In V. M. Follette, J. I. Ruzek, & F. R. Abueg (Eds.), *Cognitive-behavioral therapies for trauma* (pp. 256–277). New York: Guilford Press.

Walser, R. D., Loew, D., Westrup, D., Gregg, J., & Rogers, D. (November 2002). *Acceptance and Commitment Therapy: Theory and treatment of complex PTSD*. Paper presented at the meeting of the International Society of Traumatic Stress Studies. Baltimore, MD.

Walser, R. D., Westrup, D., Rogers, D., Gregg, J., & Loew, D. (November 2003). *Acceptance and Commitment Therapy for PTSD.* Paper presented at the meeting of the International Society of Traumatic Stress Studies. Chicago.

Warshaw, M. G., Dolan, R. T., & Keller, M. B. (2000). Suicidal behavior in patients with current or past panic disorder: Five years of prospective data from the Harvard/Brown Anxiety Research Program. *American Journal of Psychiatry, 157,* 1876–1878.

Watkins, E. & Teasdale, J. (2001). Rumination and over general memory in depression: Effects on self focus and analytical thinking. *Journal of Abnormal Psychology, 110,* 353–357.

Wearden, A. J., Morriss, R. K., Mullis, R., Strickland, P. L., Pearson, D. J., Appleby, L., Campbell, I. T., & Morris, J. A. (1998). Randomised, double-blind, placebo-controlled treatment of fluoxetine and graded exercise for chronic fatigue syndrome. *British Journal of Psychiatry, 172(6),* 485–490.

Wegner, D. M., & Zanakos, S. (1994). Chronic thought suppression. *Journal of Personality, 62,* 615–640.

Wegner, D. M., Schneider, D. J., Carter, S. R., & White, T. L. (1987). Paradoxical effects of thought suppression. *Journal of Personality and Social Psychology, 53,* 5–13.

Weissman, A., & Beck, A. T. (November, 1978). *Development and validation of the Dysfunctional Attitude Scale.* Paper presented at the annual meeting of the Association for Advancement of Behavior Therapy. Chicago, IL.

Weissman, M. M., Bland, R. C., Canino, G. J., Faravelli, C., Greenwald, S., Hwu, H. G. et al. (1996). Cross-national epidemiology of major depression and bipolar disorder. *Journal of the American Medical Association, 276,* 293–299.

Wells, A. (1995). Meta-cognition and worry: A cognitive model of generalized anxiety disorder. *Behavioural and Cognitive Psychotherapy, 23,* 301–320.

Wells, A., & Davies, M. (1994). The Thought Control Questionnaire: A measure of individual differences in the control of unwanted thoughts. *Behaviour Research and Therapy, 32,* 899–913.

Widiger, T. (2001). Official classification systems. In W. Lively (Ed.), *Handbook of personality disorders: Theory, research and treatment* (pp. 60–83). New York: Guilford Press.

Widiger, T., Trull, T., Hurt, S., Clarkin, J. & Frances, A. (1987). A multi-dimensional scaling of the DSM-III personality disorders. *Archives of General Psychiatry, 44,* 557–563.

Wicksell, R. K., Dahl, J., Magnusson, B. & Olsson, G.L. (under review). ACT within a behavior medicine approach – effective in rehabilitation of children and adolescents with chronic pain? – A case study.

Williams, J. E. (1976). Self-monitoring of paranoid behavior. *Behavior Therapy, 7,* 562.

Williams, K. E., Chambless, D. L., & Ahrens, A. (1997). Are emotions frightening? An extension of the fear of fear construct. *Behaviour Research and Therapy, 35,* 239–248.

Wilson, K. G. (2003). *ACT with college students at risk for academic failure.* Unpublished manuscript.

Wilson, K. G. (2002). *A working Manual for The Valued-Living Questionnaire (version 11–13–02).* Available from the author.

Wilson, K. G. & Groom, J. M. (2002). *The Valued Living Questionnaire.* Unpublished manuscript. Available from the first author at Department of Psychology, University of Mississippi, University, MS.

Wilson, K. G., & Hayes, S. C. (1996). Resurgence of derived stimulus relations. *Journal of the Experimental Analysis of Behavior, 66,* 267–281.

Wilson, K. G., Hayes, S. C., & Byrd, M. R. (2000). Exploring compatibilities between Acceptance and Commitment Therapy and 12-step treatment for substance abuse. *Journal of Rational-Emotive Behavior Therapy, 18(4),* 209–234.

Wilson, K. G. & Murrell, A. R. (in press). Values work in Acceptance and Commitment Therapy: Setting a course for behavioral treatment. In S. C. Hayes, V. M. Follette, & M. M. Linehan (Eds.), *Mindfulness and acceptance: Expanding the cognitive behavioral tradition.* New York: Guilford Press.

Young, J., Klosko, J. & Weishaar, M. (2003). *Schema therapy: A practitioner's guide.* New York: Guilford.

Zaldívar, F. & Hernández, M. (2001). Acceptance and Commitment Therapy (ACT): Application to experiential avoidance with agoraphobic form. *Análisis y Modificación de Conducta, 27,* 425–454.

Zettle, R. D. (2003). Acceptance and commitment therapy (ACT) versus systematic desensitization in treatment of mathematics anxiety. *Psychological Record, 53,* 197–215.

Zettle, R. D., & Hayes, S. C. (1986). Dysfunctional control by client verbal behavior: The context of reason-giving. *The Analysis of Verbal Behavior, 4,* 30–38.

Zettle, R. D., & Hayes, S. C. (1987). Component and process analysis of cognitive therapy. *Psychological Reports, 64,* 939–953.

Zettle, R. D., & Hayes, S. C. (2002). Brief ACT treatment of depression. In F. W. Bond & W. Dryden (Eds.), *Handbook of brief cognitive behaviour therapy* (pp. 35–54). Chichester: Wiley.

Zettle, R. D., & Rains, J. C. (1989). Group cognitive and contextual therapies in treatment of depression. *Journal of Clinical Psychology, 45,* 438–445.

Index